THE COMPLETE ENNEAGRAM

THE COMPLETE ENNEAGRAM

27 Paths to Greater Self-Knowledge

Beatrice Chestnut, PhD

SHE WRITES PRESS

Published 2013
Printed in the United States of America
ISBN: 978-1-938314-54-4
Library of Congress Control Number: 2013912436

For information, address:
She Writes Press
1563 Solano Ave #546
Berkeley, CA 94707

This book is dedicated to David and Charlotte, in the hope that they will grow up in a more conscious world.

You need not, and in fact cannot, teach an acorn to grow into an oak tree; but when given a chance, its intrinsic potentialities will develop. Similarly, the human individual, given a chance, tends to develop his particular human potentialities....In short, he will grow, substantially undiverted, toward self-realization.

But, like any other living organism, the human individuum needs favorable conditions for his growth "from acorn into oak tree;" he needs an atmosphere of warmth to give him both a feeling of inner security and the inner freedom enabling him to have his own feelings and thoughts and to express himself. He needs the good will of others, not only to help him in his many needs, but to guide and encourage him to become a mature and fulfilled individual. He also needs healthy friction with the wishes and wills of others. If he can thus grow with others, in love and in friction, he will also grow in accordance with his real self.

—Karen Horney, MD, in
Neurosis and Human Growth:
The Struggle Toward Self-Realization

CONTENTS

Introduction:

Self-Awareness and the Enneagram

The faculty of voluntarily bringing back a wandering attention, over and over again, is the very root of judgment, character, and will. No one is compos sui [master of himself] if he have it not. An education which should improve this faculty would be the education par excellence.

—William James, *Principles of Psychology*

Between stimulus and response, there is a space. In the space there is the power to choose our response. In our response lies our growth and our freedom.

—Victor Frankl

MANY PEOPLE TODAY SEEK ANSWERS to such questions as "Why do I do the things I do?" or "How can I have more fulfilling relationships?" or "How can I achieve better results in my work and live a more satisfying life?"

When we want or need to make some sort of positive change in our lives, we understandably look for a path to greater self-understanding that's both easy-to-use in everyday life and effective in helping with life's many challenges.

Being able to change your behavior is central to any personal growth effort, and at the same time it's incredibly difficult, given the power of our unconscious habits. In order to change behavior to achieve personal growth, we must develop one capacity: We must develop the ability to create the mental and emotional space inside ourselves to observe and understand what we are doing and think about why we do it. From this starting point of being able to see our thoughts and feelings in action instead of just being absorbed by them, we can begin to see more clearly where and how we are stuck in a habit and how we can make the conscious choice to do something different. If we have the mental room to reflect on the nuts and bolts of our habitual functioning, we open the door to greater self-understanding.

In this book, I hope to achieve two goals. First, to show how ancient wisdom teachings illuminate the idea that self-knowledge—which I define as the capacity to observe, think about, and own your thoughts, feelings, and actions—is the key to real growth and the ability to live a happier, more balanced life. And second, to provide a map and a set of instructions—your owner's manual for your own self—that will show you how to expand your self-knowledge so you can start or deepen your study of your self in a way that leads to positive change.

You can create a seismic shift in your life through increasing your self-knowledge, and this book will help you examine the unconscious and automatic thoughts, feelings, and actions that make up most of what you do every day. It will teach you ways to make these moments more conscious and purposeful. From ancient times through today, this practice is the foundation for leading a life that is more creative, flexible, whole, effective, authentic, and content.

The Common Truth of the Human Condition: We Are Asleep

EACH OF US IS UNIQUE and endowed with great potential, but *we exist in a kind of waking sleep* because of our early childhood programming.

The good news is, much of what we need to know about how to achieve greater peace, freedom, and self-knowledge has been around for hundreds or maybe thousands of years, encoded in ancient teachings, philosophy, myths, and symbols. However, it can be difficult for modern people to access these timeless truths about what it means to be human and how we can transform ourselves to manifest our highest possibilities. The purpose of this book, therefore, is to introduce, explain, and translate central aspects of a profound wisdom tradition that has been around for centuries, but has only been rediscovered in the last fifty years or so.

This ancient teaching begins with the idea that in order for us to grow and change—to develop our ability to make more conscious choices—we first need to know how we truly operate in the present. To become all that we can be, we must start where we are and know exactly where and who we are. One of our deepest unconscious patterns is the false belief that we already know ourselves well enough to understand why we think, feel, and act the way we do. I will argue that, in fact, we don't; and that thinking we do know who we are is part of the problem.

In order to know ourselves and evolve in positive ways, we first need to see that we essentially operate in a kind of "waking sleep." Without conscious effort, we function to a large degree mechanically, according to habitual patterns, as we go about our everyday lives. Our "sleep" is the unexamined belief we all have that we live lives of relatively unlimited freedom, when the opposite is true: We respond in predictable, repetitive ways according to the dictates of our early programming, much like uniquely specialized machines. And like machines, we have no power to grow out of this pre-programmed condition as long as we have no conscious understanding of how our existence is limited by our programming. We don't always understand what we don't understand and we are limited to the degree that we don't recognize our limitations.

This idea that the human condition naturally places us in this state of unconscious, automatic behavior can be found in both Western psychological theory and Eastern spiritual traditions. Indeed, we can see evidence of our own "waking sleep" in the ways in which we repeat the same comfortable habits day after day, and how we regularly tune out and go "on autopilot." When we go into a room and forget why we went there, or when we are reading a book and realize we did not really take in the content of the last page, or when we feel ourselves engaging in conversation while our minds are simultaneously "drifting," or when something significant happens and we can't really feel our emotions in response to it—all of these are telltale signs that our habits are running the show. Perhaps it's more accurate to say that our habits *are* the show. Our work, therefore, is to learn to pay attention more consistently to what is actually happening in our lives.

In psychological terms, this "dimming of consciousness" expresses the fact that as a basic survival mechanism, the human psyche automatically "goes to sleep to," or dissociates from painful experiences as a way of surviving or staying safe in the world. While we humans are remarkable creatures, we have some basic limitations. It is impossible to be aware of everything that is going on all the time and advantageous to learn ways of thinking and acting that help minimize pain and danger, or increase feelings of comfort and safety. But while it may be good for our survival and our comfort to avoid an awareness of our own pain and fear—especially early on in life—if we don't examine the ways we do this as we get older, we fall asleep to who we are and all that we might be.

How does this habit of falling asleep to ourselves get started? How and why do we come to be this way? Human babies have the longest period of dependency of all mammals, so human children possess inborn, wired-in defense mechanisms that protect them from being too overwhelmed or harmed by psychological or emotional threats. Over time, early and necessary (and sometimes life-saving) defensive maneuvers and coping strategies evolve into "patterns" of thinking, feeling, and behaving. These patterns come to operate like "organizing principles," or beliefs about how the world works and how we must act in order to survive or thrive. These patterned coping strategies turn into invisible and automatic "habits" that influence where your attention goes and what adaptive strategies you employ to interact in the world.

For instance, a child who feels constant pressure to "be good" may develop coping strategies that help her to be "perfect," thereby avoiding criticism or punishment. Another child with a different set of outside influences and inner factors may protect himself from threats by developing a strategy of hiding his vulnerability, finding ways to exert control, and seeming to be fearless. Each of us automatically adopts specific strategies for defending ourselves against threats, and these strategies work together to make up the organizing principles of our personalities.

The behavior patterns we develop to meet early threats eventually devolve into habits of mind that trigger automatically—even when the original threats are long gone and we are not confronting anything even remotely like them in the present. Our psyches develop this desensitized "waking sleep" to protect us from early emotional pain, but we end up staying asleep to what's going on in our lives as we move into adulthood. This misalignment between our ingrained habits and our yearning to live authentically and spontaneously becomes a source for all kinds of suffering, dissatisfaction, and unhappiness. The early coping strategies we don't need anymore become unseen prisons that constrain how we think, feel, and act in ways that feel so familiar and integral that we forget we have the capacity to choose other options. In this way, we go to sleep to ourselves while thinking we are still awake. We lose our freedom to engage creatively and consciously in the world without even knowing we've lost it.

Many spiritual traditions attempt to explain our dissociation, or to practice ways to stay conscious to ourselves, but I believe that we only have to look to our own lives to see how we fall into old unconscious patterns that can make us unhappy. Here is an example of this from my own experience: When I was growing up, I focused a lot on relationships—on making other people happy as a way of helping me feel safe. My strategy for avoiding the pain of other people's criticisms or rejections was to be charming and pleasant. I would "make people like me" by being likable and pleasing so that I didn't have to suffer from the bad feelings connected to disapproval and separation. Without being conscious of it, this led to me going to sleep to my own feelings, needs, and desires, because if I asserted my own feelings and needs, I might come into conflict with someone who didn't want to deal with my anger or sadness, or couldn't meet my needs. Over time, I lost touch with what I was feeling moment to moment. My roommate in graduate school once observed that I never got angry. I was surprised by this at first, but then I realized it was true. To serve my main life strategy of getting along with others and avoiding any kind of problem in relationships, I had lost touch with the natural flow of my emotions and the ability to know what I needed and wanted. And, for a long time, I didn't even know this was happening.

The self-protective habits I acquired early on in life caused problems for me later because these habits represent self-limiting strategies based on an overly narrow perspective of my capacity to manage life's many situations. Each in our own way, we unavoidably get stuck in an early response pattern that served us in our first environment, but has since become the source of our day-to-day unconsciousness. However, if we can notice, pay attention to, and study these habitual response patterns, we can do the liberating "self-work" of understanding them, working against them, and letting them go. Sometimes, just seeing a habit and understanding why it developed can be enough to free yourself from its grip. In other cases, with more stubborn or deeply ingrained patterns, you may need to work with yourself in specific ways over time to fully overcome and reverse the automatic nature of your programming. Either way, the first steps are to understand that we all fall asleep and to notice how you go to sleep to yourself.

Another Common Truth of the Human Condition: We Can Wake Up

Fortunately, the basic truth that we are stuck in our unconscious patterns goes hand in hand with another core truth about the human condition: This "waking sleep" is also the starting point for the crucial process of waking up. The ability to wake up is not only possible, but also an inherent part of being human. We fall asleep as we come into this world and acquire a personality, but the potential for conscious growth and transformation is part of our makeup. In fact, many ancient wisdom traditions say that this task of waking up to become aware of who we are represents the purpose of human life on earth.

So if your automatic patterns of feeling, thinking, and behaving put you to sleep to your own life, how do you wake up? We can become more conscious (and wake up) by learning how to observe and study ourselves more objectively.

This process gradually deepens self-knowledge by building our conscious understanding of who we really are and what is really going on. But while the capacity to wake up is part of our nature, doing the work it takes to awaken requires consistent effort. If we get lazy, we are in danger of falling asleep again.

The self-observation that can free you from your own brand of "waking sleep" begins with the conscious experience of perceiving your own unconsciousness. The practice of looking for your own automatic patterns of thinking, feeling, and acting builds a more objective interior capacity for self-awareness separate from these patterns. Over time, this effort engenders an ability to recognize when you have gone on automatic, or when your "program" is running. (As my cousin, Chris Fasano, used to say, you start to "catch on to your own game.") This self-observation creates a separation between your patterns and your consciousness so that you can watch automatic thoughts, feelings, and actions unfold without "being one" with them or judging them (or yourself) as good or bad. You need this separation to have the mental space to detach from these habits of mind—to let them go and make other choices more consciously.

The first step for anyone who wants to wake up and evolve out of mechanical habits is to start to observe those habits. Usually, we are so accustomed to doing what we do that we don't question any of it. So the entry point is to catch yourself snoozing, to slow down and make an active effort to observe yourself consciously and see what you are doing with more distance or objectivity. And to do this, you need to learn how to pay attention to what you are paying attention to (and not paying attention to).

Both psychological method and spiritual teachings point to simple forms of meditation practice as the best way to develop and expand the capacity to self-reflect and exercise conscious intention. Most of all, meditation helps to build up your ability to notice and consciously stabilize or shift your "focus of attention." Self-reflection and self-inquiry—asking yourself, "What am I paying attention to and why?"—allow you to answer deeper questions about the "what, why, and how" of your thoughts, feelings, and actions, instead of just taking them all for granted.

Another way ancient tradition expresses this basic form of meditative practice as the practical key to success in nearly every domain is through the concept of "concentration," or the "faculty of fixing maximum attention on a minimum of space." When we can develop some ability to still the automatic thoughts of the mind through concentration, we start to build a "zone of silence" within ourselves that we can draw upon in everyday life to support our self-observational efforts.

The practice of self-observation consists of putting your attention on your thoughts, feelings, and actions in the present moment and bringing your focus back over and over again from wherever it inevitably wanders. Studying your own thinking, feeling, or doing in the present moment without judgment becomes your chosen "object of attention," rather than allowing your mind to continue being preoccupied with its usual reactive, habitual patterns. This mindfulness activity is an exercise in becoming more conscious to what is going on inside you and remembering to be more purposeful in tuning in to yourself more often. As with repetition in physical exercise, the "attentional muscle" strengthens through a consistent effort to notice where your attention goes and then shift it back to a focus you have chosen consciously.

This attentional-muscle-strengthening process also allows you to develop and actively employ an "inner witness." The cultivation of an internal "witnessing consciousness" is a key ingredient in both meditation practices and many forms of psychotherapy. And, paradoxically, it's both incredibly simple and extremely difficult to do. The basic practice of exercising your attentional muscle is easy in that it involves a straightforward activity that you can do anytime and anywhere. However, it can be challenging to sustain the consistent effort it takes to actually do it. "Self-remembering"—remembering to pay conscious attention to yourself—never becomes habitual, so it takes practice to develop the capacity to actually pay attention, notice when you aren't paying attention, shift attention, and, in doing that over and over again, effectively self-observe and become more "awake."

Happily, we are living at a moment in history in which people from different fields of study are all beginning to see this basic act of self-awareness as the vital ingredient in personal development. From psychotherapy to spirituality to philosophy to brain science to leadership training and business development, people working on the question of "What promotes human growth and well-being?" in varied areas are focusing on these same elements as the factors that stimulate positive change, effectiveness, health, and fulfillment. What has previously been the exclusive territory of spiritual directors and psychotherapists has entered the mainstream of thinking about what it means to be human and how we can develop our innate human capacities to achieve greater freedom and happiness. And it all begins with the simple idea of developing the ability to pay attention, and in doing so, generating a clearer understanding of what is going on inside you.

The Enneagram as a Map for Developing Self-Awareness

THE AGE-OLD INJUNCTION, "Know Thyself," inscribed on the Temple of Apollo at Delphi in ancient Greece, was based on profound philosophical teachings that recognized that the key to knowledge of the natural world and human possibilities within it begins with studying our individual "selves," as well as our physical environment. This cornerstone wisdom of Western culture saw the study of the human being from the inside (each of us working to understand our own inner territory) as a necessary project that went hand in hand with the scientific study of the outside world.

In the last century, a few individuals have rediscovered a powerful long-lost teaching that conveys a clear vision of how we humans function. This teaching was encoded in something called *The Enneagram*, which basically means "a drawing of nine." The Enneagram symbol is a nine-pointed star inscribed in a circle that provides a framework for, among other things, a personality type system of twenty-seven distinct character "archetypes." In recent years people all over the world have recognized this ancient wisdom as something genuine, amazing, and life changing.

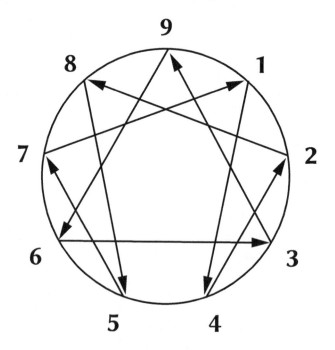

On the surface, the Enneagram is a personality type system of nine inter-connected personality archetypes or types. Each of those nine types is connected to four others arrayed around a symbolic diagram. The Enneagram symbol has ancient and mysterious origins; it represents an elegant model of some of the fundamental laws of the universe expressed in mathematical terms that reflect patterns discernible in the natural world, including in the human ego or personality.

Archetypes are models or prototypes that help us discern and make sense of universal patterns. According to Carl Jung, archetypes are "typical modes of apprehension"—or "patterns of psychic perception and understanding common to all human beings."[1] Jung took this concept of the archetype from the ancient Greeks, who viewed the world in terms of "archetypal principles," reflecting a vision of the cosmos as "an ordered expression of certain primordial essences or transcendent first principles" and archetypes as "clarifying universals in the chaos of human life."[2] More recently, author Carolyn Myss defines "our own personal archetypes" as "the psychic lenses through which we view ourselves and the world around us."[3]

The basic core of the teaching associated with the Enneagram reflects the very same messages communicated by the world's oldest mystical, psycho-spiritual, and philosophical traditions: the ability to observe and reflect upon your experience through the development of an "inner witness" allows you to acquire greater self-knowledge, which creates the possibility of attaining a higher state of consciousness. The Enneagram not only provides a great deal of help in the process of increasing self-awareness—by showing the "inner witness" what to pay attention to—but also provides a method for how we can change and grow based on that vision.

As we begin to "study" ourselves, it helps to have some sort of guidance. We think, feel, and do so many things every day—how can we even begin to make sense of it all? This is where the Enneagram comes in. As an ancient and universal model of human development and transformation, the Enneagram offers an accurate and objective view of the archetypal patterns that structure the human personality. As such, it provides a much-needed map for those of us who seek to understand ourselves on a deeper level.

The Enneagram describes three "centers of intelligence," nine personality "types," and twenty-seven "subtypes" that provide an amazingly accurate picture of personality in terms of the patterns associated with the way we function. The main idea is that your personality—all of what you think, feel, and do—is made up of patterns. Even when you try to pay attention more carefully to what is going on inside you, these patterns can be hard to detect because you have been doing what you do for so long that the "patterning" in what you do has become invisible to you, in the same way a fish doesn't "notice" the water he's swimming in. The Enneagram helps you see these personality patterns in yourself.

How does this process work? And how does it lead to positive change? It turns out that the many coping strategies we use to get along in life can be grouped into a finite number of categories, or personality types. By providing detailed descriptions of the typical thoughts, emotions, and behaviors that make up nine basic personality types (and the three subtypes of each of those nine types), the Enneagram highlights how these habitual patterns get enacted so you can start to see them for yourself.

The Enneagram's personality descriptions thus provide a map of twenty-seven specific sets of themes and patterns. Once you find yourself in one of these types by matching what you observe yourself doing to one of the Enneagram personalities, you gain access to a large amount of information that can help you recognize and understand the patterns in your thoughts, emotions, and actions.

Central to the effectiveness of the Enneagram as a growth tool is the fact that it is not a static model. We are complex and transformable beings, and as a dynamic map of change, the Enneagram reveals how we develop habits and also how we can free ourselves over time from restrictive habitual patterns we don't even realize we are limited by. Beginning to understand your own personality type allows you to better notice your personality patterns as they are happening—to "catch yourself in the act" more often—and release yourself from being trapped by choosing not to remain unconscious to those patterns.

One psychotherapy client I worked with, a lawyer in his late forties whom I'll call Max, came in suffering from a great deal of anxiety, which caused him to continually doubt himself. This constant self-doubt stopped him from moving forward in his life. He was unable to separate from his wife, even though it was clear to him that the relationship wasn't working and he needed to end it. He tortured himself internally by endlessly questioning every move he wanted to make. His talent for analysis that made him a successful lawyer also contributed to his tendency to imagine negative scenarios he might get stuck in. His belief in his own essential "badness" caused him to imagine that others were judging him and condemning him. Through the course of our therapy together, I recognized that he was a "Self-Preservation Six," someone who experiences an ongoing sense of fear and uncertainty, and who engages in a pattern of circular thinking characterized by questioning and doubt. Even though he was a kind, well-intentioned, intelligent person, he was so paralyzed by his habit of imagining fearful scenarios that he was unable to act in decisive ways in support of his own well-being.

By using the Enneagram to guide our understanding of Max's dilemma, we were able to zero in on and deal with his most important inner conflicts: 1) his false belief that he was bad and so would be condemned and rejected by others despite evidence to the contrary; 2) his sense that if he acted on his own behalf in a decisive way, bad things would happen; and 3) his mental habits that kept him trapped in fear and anxiety—he had confidence in his analytical mind, but he doubted everything and was therefore unable to feel safe in the world. By using the Enneagram map, we were able to first define and then understand Max's key issues and afterward provide ways for him to work through them. As a Self-Preservation Six his central issue was that he had not developed a strong sense of inner authority (because his father threatened and abused him and didn't protect or support him); therefore, he had become stuck in and ruled by a defensive strategy run amok. In trying to think his way to certainty and safety using his strong analytical mind, he got caught in an endless loop of fear and questioning and was unable to find a way to feel safe and powerful. He was able to address his heightened anxiety and move forward in his life as he learned to see his thinking patterns from a larger perspective and engage specific practices that worked against these tendencies.

Perhaps because of its deep symbolic meaning and its ancient heritage, the Enneagram system captures the complexity of human habits; the personalities communicated through it are helpful portrayals of twenty-seven distinct sets of patterns of thinking, feeling, and behaving. According to the wisdom tradition associated with the model, personality is seen as a "false self," necessary up to a point to interact safely in the world, but also the means by which we lose touch with our "true self"—which gets buried in the background as our "false self" comes to the forefront to deal with life.

According to the Enneagram, while the false self or personality is the "problem," in that we get so identified with it and mistakenly think it is all of who we are, it is also the vehicle for getting back to the true self. As we learn to see through the automatic functioning of the false self or conditioned personality, we can learn to let it drop or we can work with it more consciously so that we become less fixated on a narrow perspective and become more creative and flexible. As such, the Enneagram contains a vision and a path for breaking out of old habits and realizing your true potential.

Conclusion

IN ARTICULATING THE POWER of the Enneagram, this book builds most directly on the work of two authors and teachers, Oscar Ichazo and Claudio Naranjo. Oscar Ichazo developed the Enneagram in Chile in the 1960s as part of a larger program of human transformation. Claudio Naranjo, a psychiatrist with a broad range of knowledge and experience in psychological and spiritual approaches to human development, learned the model from Ichazo in 1970 and translated the Enneagram's types into Western psychological language. Naranjo refined and expanded the descriptions of the types as he taught the material over the next decades, starting in Berkeley in the 1970s. It was from Naranjo's original group of students that the Enneagram leaked out and spread around the world. While many different authors have now published excellent books on the Enneagram, this book focuses mainly on Naranjo's descriptions of the types, the subtypes, and the nature of the path of conscious development and the work it entails.

In its exploration of why the Enneagram is such a powerful tool for self-knowledge, however, this book builds upon a foundation that is even deeper and broader than the significant, pioneering contributions of Ichazo and Naranjo. It comes out of an ancient wisdom tradition that provides a vision of our larger human purpose and a map for realizing it, as well as my own studies in the fields of psychology and personal development. In particular, I have drawn on my training as a psychotherapist, my own personal "self-work," and the many lessons I learned from my most direct Enneagram teachers, Helen Palmer and David Daniels. While I will cite the sources of the ideas I present throughout this book, it is important to say at the outset that these two individuals have shaped how I think about these topics to a degree that can be hard to quantify. Their teachings provide the foundation of my understanding of this important work.

Most of all, I hope to translate a profound wisdom tradition and highlight the timeless truths it reveals, while integrating the valuable information it has to offer with modern insights into what helps us grow and create positive change. By bringing out the incredibly deep and powerful truths that have been lost to us for centuries, I hope to inspire you to prioritize your own development as the key to success in everything you might do in life. And while this "work on self" challenges us to stretch ourselves beyond our comfort zones and confront things we'd rather stay asleep to, it is also a great adventure of the kind immortalized in epic poems and classic myths that can liberate our energies to live our lives in more peaceful, alive, authentic, and meaningful ways. My hope is that this book describes a vision and a method that advances the goal of greater self-awareness and clarifies the path to achieving it in a way that inspires you forward on your own journey of personal evolution.

CHAPTER 1:

The Enneagram as a Framework for Understanding the Multidimensional Nature of Personality

To be human is to become visible
while carrying what is hidden as a gift to others.
To remember the other world in this world
is to live in your true inheritance.

You are not a troubled guest on this earth,
you are not an accident amidst other accidents
you were invited from another and greater night
than the one from which you have just emerged.

Now, looking through the slanting light of the morning window
toward the mountain presence of everything that can be
what urgency calls you to your one love?
What shape waits in the seed of you
to grow and spread its branches
against a future sky?

—David Whyte, from his poem,
"What to Remember When Waking"

THE TERM "PERSONALITY" generally refers to the part of your character that develops to interface with the outside world. Our personalities are shaped through the intersection of our innate qualities and our early experiences with parents, caregivers, family, and friends, as well as other influences in our physical, social, and cultural environments.

What is Personality?

MOST OF US THINK OF OUR PERSONALITY as "who we are." We equate the idea of personality—the "you" who the people in your life would say they know—with our sense of identity. But according to the Enneagram, you are more than just your personality—the personality that you and others associate with your "self" is only part of who you are. As in Western psychology, the Enneagram views the personality as a "false self" that develops to allow your (vulnerable and young) "true self" to adapt, fit in, and survive among other humans. This perspective holds that personality is a "defensive" or a "compensatory" self whose coping strategies developed to help us fulfill our needs and reduce our anxieties.

Personality as Ego and Shadow: What You See and Don't See in Yourself

Just as light illuminating an object also casts an area of darkness, said Carl Jung, the conscious brightness in how you see yourself creates a "Shadow" aspect of personality that goes unseen, like a blind spot.[1] Attributes you think of as "bad"—feelings of anger, jealousy, hatred, and inferiority—get relegated to your shadow and become unconscious. (People who tend to focus on their negative characteristics, conversely, may hide some of their typically "positive" feelings or qualities in their Shadow.) The Shadow represents everything we refuse to acknowledge about ourselves that nonetheless impacts the way we behave. Being blind to parts of ourselves means that there is often a difference between the person we think we are—or the person we would like to see ourselves as—and who we really are as we walk through the world.

We each repress our Shadow aspects because they make us feel uncomfortable or bad about ourselves; but making these qualities unconscious gives them the power to create unintended problems in our lives and relationships when they influence us in ways we don't see. Developing our "true" self requires us to know, accept, and integrate all parts of our selves, including our Shadow elements. The Enneagram can help us do that.

The Enneagram's 360-Degree View

The Enneagram describes personality types in terms of conscious patterns of thinking, feeling, and behaving along with their repressed Shadow aspects. As a result, it is an excellent tool for doing the hardest part of consciousness work: realizing, owning, and accepting your blind spots.

I attended the first meeting of what would later become the International

Enneagram Association at Stanford University in Palo Alto, California, in 1994. At this gathering of Enneagram enthusiasts from all over the world, Franciscan priest and author Richard Rohr gave an amazing talk in which he likened the mystic symbol of the Enneagram to the archetypal "Wheel of Fortune," which epitomizes life as having inevitable ups and downs. He observed that Western culture is oriented to the "ascent"—the upside of things—and therefore has a harder time with the "descent" part of life's wheel. Because the Enneagram gives us a way to see our dark sides without judgment, Rohr said, the Enneagram is an invaluable tool for helping us accept and manage the descent.

Rohr eloquently expressed a profound truth. Our human (egoic) tendency is to want to feel good (and to avoid feeling bad) about ourselves. But without a way of recognizing, accepting, and addressing all of who we are, including the Shadow side and difficult parts of our experience, our personal growth stops and we remain asleep to our potential. The Enneagram reveals the truth of what we might see as the "good" and the "bad" parts of our habitual programming, allowing us to compassionately address the disowned and "fixated" (stuck) parts of our personalities and to embrace ourselves as we truly are.

The Enneagram Personality Map

The Enneagram helps us identify specific patterns of personality and their accompanying Shadows by describing the habits and traits of twenty-seven "false selves" in a systematic way. It considers personality according to its predominant "center of intelligence:" body/physical, heart/emotional, or head/intellectual. Each of these three centers is then further divided into three personality types, for a total of nine types.

Grouped according to their centers, the personality types and the connecting lines between them draw the figure of the ancient mystical symbol that is the Enneagram diagram. Beyond the three centers and the nine types is a third level of depth that divides each of the nine Enneagram types into three distinct sub-personalities, or "subtypes," based on the relative emphasis of *three basic instincts*. The resulting twenty-seven subtypes are unique personality types based on how each of the nine types are shaped by the three most central instinctual drives that we all share: Self-Preservation, Social Interaction, and Sexual (or One-to-One) Bonding.

The Three Centers

The wisdom tradition behind the Enneagram holds that humans are "three-brained beings"—that we function through three different "centers of intelligence." These centers represent the three modes of perception, processing, and expression: moving or sensing (kinesthetically), feeling, and thinking. Each center's function has its advantages and its disadvantages—its positive uses and its misuses—ways it helps us interpret and interact with the world around us, and ways it can steer us off course.

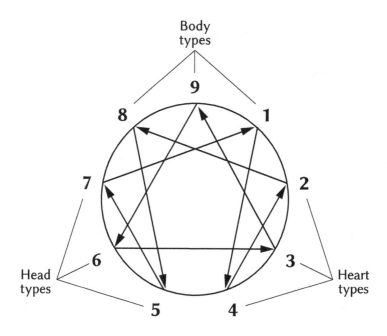

The *"body" center* includes the *"motor" center* (Points 8, 9, and 1), which takes an active part in all physical movement, and the *"instinctive center,"* which corresponds to our instinctual functions. When thought initiates movements within you, your motor center is activated. An impulse from the motor, or gut, center can be a solid guide to right action, but misuse of the motor center can also lead to impulsive behavior or inertia.

The *"heart" center* or *"emotional" center* (Points 2, 3, and 4) regulates the feeling function: the experience and expression of emotions. It allows you to feel your emotions and connect to others through empathy; but overuse (or misuse) can lead to oversensitivity, insensitivity, or emotional manipulation.

The "head" center or *"intellectual" center* (Points 5, 6, and 7) regulates the thinking function: the experience and expression of thoughts, beliefs, and other cognitive activity. While essential for dispassionate analysis and reasoning, this form of intelligence can paralyze you if you get caught up in overanalyzing a situation.

The Nine Personality Archetypes

THE POWER OF THE ENNEAGRAM MAP lies in its highly accurate articulation of the automatic patterns associated with the personalities it describes. Each type has a habitual "focus of attention"—its most prominent patterns of thinking, feeling, and behaving—as well as a central motivating "passion" or "chief feature."

The Passions

Each Enneagram personality type is associated with one of nine "passions," which point to the central emotional-motivational issue for each type. The passions are emotional (and often unconscious) drivers based on an implicit view about what you need to survive and how you can get it. Because the passions are motivated by a sense of lack, they create a basic dilemma or trap around which the personality is organized while striving to meet a basic need that never gets fulfilled.

Understanding the role of the passions is crucial to grasping the Enneagram, because they motivate action out of a hunger for something and yet obstruct us from finding real fulfillment through getting what we need to satisfy that hunger. This is because we only obtain what we really need when we transcend the limited purview of the personality. Only in becoming conscious of our motivations, can we get out of this cycle that leads nowhere.[2]

Body Center Types

Type Nine
Focus of Attention: Nines focus attention on others, on what is going on in the environment, and on avoiding conflict and achieving harmony. Nines typically tune into what other people want, but do not have a clear sense of their own agendas.

Patterns of Thinking and Feeling: Nines focus on getting along with others without "rocking the boat" and creating conflict. They're emotionally steady and do not feel many highs or lows. Though they are anger types, Nines usually don't feel their anger very often—they (unconsciously) dissociate from it as a way to avoid conflict or separation from others—so it tends to leak out in repressed forms, such as stubbornness or passive-aggressive behavior, or escape in big bursts every once in a while.

Behavior Patterns: Nines like to "go with the flow," and they automatically accommodate the agendas of others as a way of unconsciously avoiding expressing (or even registering) any preferences that could lead to conflict, though they may passively resist later when hints of latent desires surface. They dislike feeling controlled, but like structure and clear lines of authority. They make good mediators because they have an easy ability to see all sides of an issue and naturally find the common ground in conflicting points of view.

Passion—Laziness: Laziness refers to an inaction of the psyche, a refusal to see, a resistance to change, and an aversion to effort, especially with regard to being aware of their own inner feelings, sensations, and desires. Rather than reluctance to take action, this passion is more about inattention to self and inertia of the will when it comes to tuning in to what is going on internally.

Type Eight

Focus of Attention: Eights naturally focus their attention on power and control—who has it and who doesn't, and how it's wielded. They think in terms of the big picture and (mostly) dislike dealing with details. They see the world as being divided into "the strong" and "the weak," and they identify with "the strong" to avoid feeling weak.

Patterns of Thinking and Feeling: Emotionally, Eights usually have easy access to anger and (unconsciously) avoid registering vulnerable feelings. They typically appear fearless and can be intimidating to others, often without meaning to be. They like to be in control, engage in black and white thinking, think they know what's best or true, and do not like to be told what to do.

Behavior Patterns: Eights have a lot of energy, can accomplish big things, can confront others when necessary, and will protect people they care about. They can be workaholics, taking on more and more without acknowledging their physical limits, and refuse to experience vulnerable feelings that might slow them down. They can sometimes overwork themselves, even to the point of physical illness.

Passion—Lust. Lust is a passion for excess and intensity in all manner of stimulation. It is a drive to fill up an inner emptiness through physical gratification. Lust in Enneagram terms is "a passion for excess or an excessive passionateness to which sexual gratification is only one possible source of gratification."[3]

Type One
Focus of Attention: Like the "superego" function of Freud's model, Ones focus on noticing error (in the form of deviations from an internally generated ideal), discerning right and wrong, and displaying a reliance on rules and structure.

Patterns of Thinking and Feeling: Emotionally, Ones often feel resentment and irritation or anger that is restrained. The communication of aggression is in conflict with their belief that expressing anger is bad, so anger and other instinctual impulses are typically held back and then leak out as resentment, annoyance, criticism, and self-righteousness. Ones believe that there is a "right way" to do things and that we should all try to be more perfect.

Behavior Patterns: Ones can be perceived as being rigid and highly structured in their behavior, relying on ritual and repetitive forms of doing. Typically, they follow the rules and are reliable, ethical, and hardworking.

Passion—Anger: As an emotional passion, anger appears in its repressed form for Ones as resentment that seeks resolution in pursuing perfection and virtue. Ones display hostility toward the imperfect way things are and try to force things to conform to their ideal of how things should be.

Heart Center Types

Type Three
Focus of Attention: Threes focus attention on tasks and goals to create an image of success in the eyes of others. Threes identify with their work, believing they are what they do, and lose touch with who they really are.

Patterns of Thinking and Feeling: For a Three, thinking centers on "doing"—on accomplishing tasks and goals. Though a heart type, Threes (unconsciously) avoid their feelings because getting caught up in emotion prevents them from getting things done. When they slow down enough for emotions to surface, they may feel a sense of sadness or anxiety related to being recognized for what they do and not for who they are. Threes tend to express impatient anger if someone or something gets between them and their goal.

Behavior Patterns: Threes tend to be fast-paced workaholics. They find it very difficult to slow down and just "be." They can be extremely productive and effective because of their laser-like focus on getting things done and reaching their goals.

Passion—Vanity: Vanity is a passionate concern for one's image or for "living for the eyes of others."[4] Vanity motivates Threes to present a false image to others—to shape-shift into whatever image is the right or most successful image for the context.

Type Two

Focus of Attention: Twos focus on relationships, gaining approval, and seducing others through helpfulness as a strategic way to get their disowned needs met. Twos actively "read" the people around them and align with (what they perceive to be) their moods and preferences in order to maximize the potential for positive connection.

Patterns of Thinking and Feeling: Emotionally, Twos fear rejection and so they frequently repress their feelings in an effort to please others. When their emotions can no longer be repressed, they may display anger, sadness, anxiety, or hurt. Because of these contradictory impulses, Twos may feel emotionally conflicted. Twos also express happy feelings as a way of appearing likable to others.

Behavior Patterns: Twos tend to be upbeat, energetic, and friendly, though sometimes this can mask (and be an overcompensation for) repressed needs and a tendency toward depression. They are driven and hardworking, especially in the service of others or a project they feel passionately about, but they can also be hedonistic and self-indulgent. Twos may also play the role of martyr, sacrificing their own needs and desires to win over others, but then suffering for it.

Passion—Pride: In the language of the Enneagram, pride functions as a need for self-inflation and gets expressed as a false generosity in the service of seduction and self-elevation. Pride also fuels a pattern of self-idealization and grandiosity, followed by a reactive devaluation and self-criticism.

Type Four

Focus of Attention: Fours focus attention on their own feelings, the feelings of others, and interpersonal connection and disconnection. They feel a sense of deficiency about their own worth, so they seek idealized experiences of qualities they perceive as outside themselves.

Patterns of Thinking and Feeling: Fours value authentic expressions of a wide range of emotion. Their thought patterns center on what is missing in a given situation and on longing for whatever they perceive as ideal and somehow unavailable. They appreciate meaningful interactions rooted in real feelings and have a keen aesthetic sensibility based on the translation of emotional experience into artistic expression, but they tend to overidentify with feelings and dwell in melancholy (or anger).

Behavior Patterns: Fours can be reserved and withdrawn, or energetic and active, or both. They are emotionally intuitive, empathic, and intense. While specific behavior patterns vary according to subtype, Fours generally aren't afraid of conflict, will work tirelessly when they feel passionately connected to something, and can see what's missing and speak to it.

Passion—Envy: Envy manifests as a painful sense of lack and a craving toward that which is felt lacking. For Fours, Envy grows out of an early sense of loss that leads to a perception that something good is outside the Four's experience—and that this something is necessary but missing because of an inner deficiency.

Head Center Types

Type Six

Focus of Attention: Sixes focus on thinking about what might go wrong and strategizing and preparing for it. A response to an early experience of danger, Sixes have an adaptive strategy that centers on detecting threats and coping with fear.

Patterns of Thinking and Feeling: It's hard to talk about one kind of Six, be-cause the three Six subtypes are so distinct. This can be traced to the three commonly understood ways of dealing with fear: fight, flight, or freeze. Ana-lytical and strategic in their thinking, Sixes think in terms of how to manage uncertainty to feel safe. They think things through thoroughly, even to the point of getting paralyzed by overanalysis. Aside from fear, they tend to have less access to other feelings, though they can be the most feeling of the Head Types.

Behavior Patterns: Sixes are watchful and alert in different ways, and share a common orientation to authority. They have a strong desire for a good author-ity, but can be suspicious of and rebellious against real-life authorities. Sixes are thoughtful and loyal to those whom they trust. They can be hard work-ers, intent on control and achievement, or they can have a hard time getting things done, getting caught up in procrastination, indecision, and fear of suc-cess. Their constant awareness of what might go wrong makes them excellent problem-solvers.

Passion—Fear: Fear is an unpleasant emotional and physiological response to recognized sources of danger; it usually goes hand in hand with anxiety, which can be more or less conscious, depending on the subtype. Anxiety includes apprehension, tension, or uneasiness related to the anticipation of danger, the source of which is unknown or unrecognized and may originate inside one's own mind.

Type Five
Focus of Attention: Fives believe knowledge is power, so they like to observe what's going on around them without getting too involved, especially emo-tionally. They focus on accumulating information about subjects that interest them and managing their time and energy, which they perceive as scarce, by avoiding entanglements with others.

Patterns of Thinking and Feeling: Fives live in their heads and habitually detach from their emotions. They are sensitive to emotional demands being placed on them. They typically have a narrow range of feeling and almost never show their emotions in public.

Behavior Patterns: Fives are reserved and introverted, need a lot of time alone, and avoid interactions with people who (they fear) might deplete them. They are very analytical and objective, and they tend to spend a lot of time pursuing their intellectual interests.

Passion—Avarice: Avarice is a holding back and holding in—the hoarding of time, space, and resources out of fear of impending impoverishment. It's not so much greediness as retentiveness, a "drive to hold on to what [they] already have rather than [a] drive to acquire more."[5]

Type Seven

Focus of Attention: Sevens avoid unpleasant feelings by focusing on what feels pleasant and by keeping the mood upbeat to the point of reframing negatives into positives. A fear of being trapped in discomfort fuels quick thinking, creative problem-solving, and a focus on positive future possibilities.

Patterns of Thinking and Feeling: Sevens have quick, synthesizing minds, with which they find links between the commonalities in different subjects, making rapid mental associations. Emotionally, Sevens like feeling happy or joyful emotions and dislike feeling fear, anxiety, sadness, boredom, pain, or discomfort. Their attitude is, "Why feel pain if you can feel happy instead?"

Behavior Patterns: Sevens are energetic, fast-paced, innovative, and active. They usually have many interests and activities, which they pursue with enthusiasm. Sevens like planning for fun and maintaining many options, so they can keep their mood up and shift to the most pleasant option if one plan becomes undesirable or untenable.

Passion—Gluttony: While we commonly think of gluttony in connection with food and eating too much, in the language of the Enneagram, gluttony is a passion for pleasure and a desire for more—an excessive indulgence in consuming whatever brings pleasure.

The Twenty-Seven Subtypes[6]

SUBTYPES EXIST WITHIN EACH of the nine types, broken down into three distinct versions according to how the *passion* of each type combines with one of three *instinctual biases* or *goals* that all social creatures share, directed either toward *Self-Preservation, Social Interaction,* or *Sexual (or One-to-One) Bonding.*

When the passion and the dominant instinctual drive come together, they create an even more specific focus of attention, reflecting a particular insatiable need that drives behavior. These subtypes thus reflect three different "subsets" of the patterns of the nine types that provide even more specificity in describing the human personality.

Our Animal Drives: The Three Instinctual Goals

Self-Preservation: The Self-Preservation instinct focuses attention on and shapes behavior around issues related to survival and material security. It generally directs energy toward safety and security concerns, including having enough resources, avoiding danger, and maintaining a basic sense of structure and well-being. Beyond these basic concerns, the self-preservation instinct may place emphasis on other areas of security in terms of whatever that means for a person of a specific type (once it mixes with one of the nine passions).

Social Interaction: The Social instinct focuses attention on and shapes behavior around issues related to belonging, recognition, and relationships in social groups. It drives us to "get along with the herd"—our family, the community, and the groups we belong to. This instinct also relates to how much power or standing one has relative to the other members of "the group" in terms of whatever that might mean for a person of a specific type.

Sexual Bonding: The Sexual instinct focuses attention on and shapes behavior around issues related to the quality and status of relationships with specific individuals. Sometimes referred to as the "One-to-One" instinct, it generally directs energy toward the achievement and maintenance of sexual connections, interpersonal attraction, and bonding. This instinct seeks a sense of well-being through one-to-one connections with people in terms of whatever that means for a person of a specific type.

All three of these instincts operate in all of us, but usually only one is dominant in each individual—and when the powerful biological drive of that dominant instinct is put in service of the "passion," it fuels a more specific expression of the personality, resulting in a more nuanced character (a subtype) of the main personality type.

The Countertypes

For each of the nine types, there is a "countertype" subtype. In every case, with each of the nine points of the Enneagram, there are two subtypes that go with the flow of the energy of the passion and there is one that is upside-down: one that doesn't look like the others and goes against the main energetic direction of the passion. This "counter-passional" type is called the "countertype" of the three subtypes. For example, the "counter-phobic" Sexual Six is the most well known of the countertypes. It's a Six who's unafraid. The passion of the Six is Fear, but the Sexual subtype goes against fear by being strong and intimidating as a way of coping with fear.[7]

The Subtypes in Brief

The brief descriptions of the subtype personalities that follow provide an overview of this third level of the Enneagram's structure and highlight two important aspects of subtype: the movement from center to passion to instinct that defines each personality, and the "countertype" of each of the type's group of three subtypes. We will explore each of these personalities in greater depth in the proceeding chapters.

Body Center Subtypes

Nines

Self-Preservation Nine: "Appetite"

Instead of feeling an ongoing connection to their feelings, desires, and power, Self-Preservation Nines focus on merging with physical comforts and routine activities, such as eating, sleeping, reading, or doing crossword puzzles. SP Nines are practical, concrete people who focus on everyday things rather than abstractions.

Social Nine: "Participation" (countertype)

Social Nines fuse with groups. They act out laziness when connecting with their own inner life by working hard to be a part of the different groups in their lives. Fun-loving, sociable, and congenial characters, Social Nines can be workaholics, prioritizing the group's needs above their own. This high level of activity makes them the countertype of the three Nine subtypes.

Sexual Nine: "Fusion"

Sexual Nines express the passion of laziness by merging with the important people in their lives. Sexual Nines unconsciously take on the attitudes, opinions, and feelings of others, because it can feel too hard to stand on their own. These Nines tend to be kind, gentle, shy characters who are not very assertive.

Eights

Self-Preservation Eight: "Satisfaction"

Self-Preservation Eights express the passion of lust through a focus on getting what they need for survival. SP Eights have a strong desire for the timely satisfaction of material needs and an intolerance for frustration. SP Eights know how to survive in difficult situations and feel omnipotent when it comes to getting what they need. They are the least expressive and the most armed of the three Eight subtypes.

Social Eight: "Solidarity" (countertype)

Social Eights express lust and aggression in the service of others. A social antisocial person, this is the countertype of the Eights, a helpful Eight who appears less aggressive and more loyal than the other two Eight subtypes. The name "Solidarity" emphasizes their tendency to offer help when people need protection.

Sexual Eight: "Possession"

Sexual Eights express lust through rebellion and the need to possess everyone's attention. Sexual Eights are intense, charismatic characters who want to have control and influence. Instead of seeking material security, they try to get power over things and people. The name "Possession" refers to an energetic takeover of the whole scene—a need to feel powerful through dominating the whole environment.

Ones

Self-Preservation One: "Worry"

Self-Preservation Ones are the true perfectionists of the three Ones. They express the passion of anger through working hard to make themselves and the things they do more perfect. In this subtype, anger is the most repressed emotion; the defense mechanism of reaction formation transforms the heat of anger into warmth, resulting in a friendly and benevolent character.

Social One: "Non-adaptability"

Social Ones (unconsciously) consider themselves to be perfect; they express anger through focusing on being the perfect model of "the right way" to be. They have a teacher mentality that reflects an unconscious need for superiority. In the Social One, anger is half-hidden—there's a transformation of the heat of anger into cold. This is a cooler, intellectual personality type in which the main theme is control.

Sexual One: "Zeal" (countertype)

Sexual Ones focus on perfecting others; they are more reformers than perfectionists. The only One who is explicitly angry, they act out anger through their intense desire to improve others and get what they want. They feel entitled in the way a reformer or a zealot can feel entitled: they believe they have a right to change society and get what they want because they have a higher understanding of the truth and the reasons behind "the right way to be." The countertype of the Ones, they are more impulsive and outwardly angry—they go against the "counter-instinctive" tendency of the One to repress anger and impulses.

Heart Center Subtypes

Threes

Self-Preservation Three: "Security" (countertype)

The Self-Preservation Three has a sense of vanity for having no vanity. This Three also wants to be admired by others, but avoids openly seeking recognition. Not just satisfied with looking good, the SP Three strives to *be* good. They are determined to be a good person—to match the perfect model of how a person should be. Being the perfect model of quality implies virtue, and virtue implies a lack of vanity. SP Threes seek a sense of security through being good, working hard, and being effective and productive.

Social Three: "Prestige"

Social Threes focus on achievement in the service of looking good and getting the job done. They act out vanity through their desire to be seen and have influence with people. They enjoy being on stage in the spotlight. Social Threes know how to climb the social ladder and achieve success. These are the most competitive and most aggressive of the Threes. They have a driving need to look good and possess a corporate or sales mentality.

Sexual Three: "Charisma"

Sexual Threes focus on achievement in terms of personal attractiveness and supporting others. In this Three, vanity is not denied (as in the SP Three) nor embraced (as in the Social Three), but is somewhere in between: it's employed in the service of creating an attractive image and promoting important others. These Threes have a harder time talking about themselves and often put the focus on others they want to promote. They put a lot of energy into pleasing others and they have a family/team mentality.

Twos

Self-Preservation Two: "Privilege" (countertype)

Self-Preservation Twos "seduce" like a child in the presence of grown-ups as a way of (unconsciously) inducing others to take care of them. Everyone likes children, and the SP Two adopts a youthful stance as a way of getting special treatment well beyond childhood. As the countertype, it's less easy to see pride in this Two because they are more fearful of and ambivalent about connecting with others. The title "Privilege" reflects this Two's desire to be loved and prioritized just for being who they are, not for what they give to others. Related to the youthful stance, these Twos are playful, irresponsible, and charming.

Social Two: "Ambition"

The Social Two is a seducer of environments and groups—a powerful, leader type whose pride manifests as a sense of satisfaction in the conquest of an audience. This is a more adult Two in whom pride is the most obvious; the Social Two cultivates an image of being an influential, supercompetent person worthy of admiration. The name "Ambition" reflects this person's desire to "be on top," and as a result of this lofty position, receive advantages and benefits. This Two "gives to get" the most and always has a strategic angle when expressing generosity.

Sexual Two: "Seduction/Aggression"

One-to-One Twos seduce specific individuals as a way of getting needs met and feeding their pride. Similar to the "femme fatale" archetype (and male equivalent) this Two employs the methods of classical seduction to attract a partner who will meet all their needs and give them whatever they want. The name "Aggressive-Seductive" suggests a character who is appealing, but who also wants to wield some power. Energetically like a force of nature, this is a person who becomes irresistible, who inspires great passions and positive feelings as a way to meet needs in life.

Fours

Self-Preservation Four: "Tenacity" (countertype)

The Self-Preservation Four is long-suffering. As the countertype of the Fours, SP Fours are stoic in the face of their inner pain and they don't share it with others as much as the other two Fours. This is a person who learns to tolerate pain and to do without as a way of earning love. Instead of dwelling in envy, SP Fours act out their envy by working hard to get what others have and they lack. More masochistic than melodramatic, these Fours demand a lot of themselves, have a strong need to endure, and have a passion for effort.

Social Four: "Shame"

The Social Four suffers more, feels more shame, and is more sensitive than the other two Fours. Envy fuels a focus on shame and suffering as they employ a strategy of seducing others into meeting their needs through an intensification of pain and suffering. They experience a sense of comfort in feeling melancholy. Envy also manifests in lamenting too much, taking on the victim role, and focusing on a sense of their own inferiority. Social Fours don't compete with others as much as they compare themselves to others and find themselves lacking.

Sexual Four: "Competition"

Sexual Fours make others suffer as an unconscious way of trying to rid themselves of painful feelings of deficiency. In denying their suffering and being more shameless than shameful, they express their needs more and can be demanding of others. In seeking to be the best, they express envy in its manifestation as competition. They express "an envy that wants," unconsciously turning their pain at inner lack into feelings of anger about not getting what they need from others.

Head Center Subtypes

Sixes

Self-Preservation Six: "Warmth"

Self-Preservation Sixes express the passion of fear through a need for protection, for friendship, and for banding together with others. In seeking protective alliances, SP Sixes endeavor to be warm, friendly, and trustworthy, which is why they bear the name "Warmth." This most "phobic" of the Sixes has difficulty expressing anger, feels uncertain, and engages in a lot of self-doubt.

For SP Sixes, fear manifests as insecurity, and they focus on relationships as a way of feeling safer in the world.

Social Six: "Duty"

Social Sixes express fear through a need to deal with anxiety by relying on abstract reason or ideologies as a frame of reference. Obeying authority through knowing what the rules are helps them to feel safe in the world. Unlike the SP Six, this Six has more certainty and can be "too sure" of things as a way of dealing with the anxiety of uncertainty. Social Sixes focus on precision and efficiency. They adhere to whatever the guidelines are as form of having a protective authority.

Sexual Six: "Strength/Beauty" (countertype)

Sexual Sixes express fear by going against fear—by becoming strong and intimidating. Trusting themselves more than others, these Sixes have the inner programming that when you are afraid, the best defense is a good offense. They take on a powerful stance, both in what they do and how they look, as a way of holding the enemy at a distance. Their anxiety is allayed through skill and readiness in the face of an attack.

Fives

Self-Preservation Five: "Castle"

The Self-Preservation Five expresses avarice through a focus on boundaries—a need to be "encastled" in a sanctuary where they feel protected from intrusion and have control over their boundaries. SP Fives have a passion for being able to hide behind walls and know that they have everything they need to survive within those walls. They are the least expressive of the three Fives and they try to limit their needs and wants so that they can avoid being dependent on others.

Social Five: "Totem"

The Social Five expresses avarice through a need for "super-ideals," relating to others with common interests through knowledge and shared values (rather than emotional connection). In this Five, avarice is connected to knowledge. Needs for people and for the sustenance that relationships provide get channeled into a thirst for information. "Totem" refers to a passion for high ideals, the need to idealize experts and seek knowledge connected to whatever ultimate values this Five adheres to. Social Fives engage in a search for the ultimate meaning to avoid experiencing life as meaningless.

Sexual Five: "Confidence" (countertype)
Sexual Fives express avarice through a search for ideal exemplars of absolute love. This is a Five with a romantic streak. The name reflects their need to find a partner who fulfills an ideal of trust. The most emotionally sensitive of the Fives, they suffer more, resemble Type Four more, and have more overt desires. They have a vibrant inner life that may be expressed through artistic creation but are still cut off from others in many ways.

Sevens
Self-Preservation Seven: "Keepers of the Castle"
The Self-Preservation Seven expresses gluttony through making alliances and creating opportunities for gaining an advantage. Pragmatic and self-interested, these Sevens find safety through networking and being alert to opportunities that support their survival. The name "Keepers of the Castle" refers to their way of establishing a partisan network of allies through which they create safety and satisfy their needs. Cheerful and amiable, they have a love of pleasure and tend to get what they want.

Social Seven: "Sacrifice" (countertype)
As the countertype, Social Sevens go against gluttony through conscientious efforts to be of service to others. Conscious of wanting to avoid exploiting others, they have a need to be good and pure and to sacrifice their own needs in supporting the needs of others. They have a passion for being seen as good for the sacrifice of their own desires. They express an ascetic ideal and make a virtue of getting by on little. They express idealism and enthusiasm as a way of making themselves feel active and valued in the world.

Sexual Seven: "Suggestibility"
Sexual Sevens express gluttony through a need to imagine something better than ordinary reality. Gluttons for things of a higher world, they are idealistic dreamers with a passion for living in their imaginations. Sexual Sevens look at things with the optimism of someone who is in love; they see the world through rose-colored glasses. "Suggestibility" refers to being somewhat naive and easy to hypnotize. Light-hearted and enthusiastic, they focus on exciting possibilities and pleasurable fantasies, and they believe they can do everything.

Charting Your Personal Growth Path

A QUESTION THAT USUALLY ARISES after people identify their Enneagram type is "Now what?" Once you know your type and subtype, what do you do with that information to create positive change? This is the most powerful aspect of the Enneagram: it's a model of transformation that indicates a path for growth.

By first remembering to observe the things we do; then inquiring more deeply into why and how we do the things we do; and eventually actively working against our old habits and toward our higher aspects, we initiate an ongoing learning process focused on knowing ourselves better to the point where we can make more conscious choices more regularly.

The first step along this journey of inner growth is about *self-observation as the path to dis-identifying from your personality*. Self-observation is about creating space. When you can observe your personality's patterns in action, you make room inside yourself to see what you think, feel, and do from more of a distance, with more objectivity. This allows you to witness your key habitual patterns as they are happening. In these sections I will highlight specific patterns for each type to observe in themselves.

The second step along this growth path is to look more deeply into what you are doing through *self-inquiry and self-reflection*. Self-inquiry is about understanding both the root causes and the consequences of the patterns you observe. I help you to start this process by identifying what I see as each type's "key issues" and offering ideas about "what to do" to address those issues.

The third task connected with this model is *self-development*. Self-development involves actively working to achieve change. Through observing and understanding your personality's key patterns, you have the power to overcome your defensive habits and do things differently. Having awareness about your central patterns, their sources, and their consequences makes it possible to make new choices because you are no longer caught up in unconscious, automatic actions and reactions.

In this last section of each of the archetype chapters, I offer type-based guidance in terms of two distinct "Enneagramatic paths" of transformation: 1) the *Inner Flow* of the change process following the arrow lines within the diagram, and 2) the vertical "Vice to Virtue" path of development: understanding your "Vice" (the unconscious operation of the passion) so that you can work toward embodying your higher "Virtue" (the antidote for the passion).

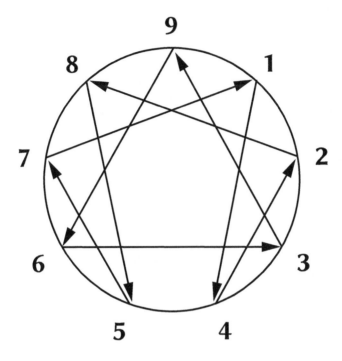

To make the Inner Flow a clearer outline for self-work, I offer my own theory of how to use this map. [8] In short, I believe the Enneagram's arrow lines point in the direction of each type's specific path of psychological and spiritual growth and away from important characteristics and experiences we had to repress in childhood (but periodically return to for a sense of security). These connection points indicated by the Enneagram diagram help us see how we can aim to embody the higher aspects of these two specific points to further our inner journey: *the point ahead of our core point* represents key challenges we need to master to become more whole and *the point behind our core type* along the arrow lines represents issues from the past that we need to reintegrate such that we can reclaim what we disowned in childhood to ground and support our forward movement along the path indicated by the arrows.

By seeing the point ahead of our core point along the arrow lines as not only a "stress" or "defensive" point that we get driven to in distress, but a key opportunity for growth through meeting the specific challenges represented by that point, I highlight the ways we can expand our capacities through consciously seeking to manifest the high side qualities of what I call our "growth-(through)-stress" or "stress-growth" point. By seeing what has been called the "security" or "heart" point (the point behind our core point along the arrow lines that I am calling the "child-heart" point) as a point that represents parts of ourselves we had to leave behind in childhood (but occasionally return to in times of stress or security as a resource) I suggest ways in which we can more consciously re-own these aspects to support our growth. In these ways, I seek to clarify this Inner Flow map in the "self-development" sections, and suggest how each type can take advantage of these avenues of growth.

Lastly, I will highlight the "Vice to Virtue" path that takes us from living under the sway of the *passion* (or vice) of the personality toward manifesting a greater realization of the higher *virtue* for each type, which functions as an "antidote" to the emotional passion. I will also provide suggestions for each subtype's more specific tasks on this Vice to Virtue journey toward the true self.

Conclusion

My hope is that by understanding the nature and function of your personality and the steps required to expand beyond it, you can envision and enact a path of conscious self-liberation. If we can see the personality not as all of who we are but as a necessary survival mechanism, we can rise above this "lower self" and embody our higher capacities. If we have the courage to be honest with ourselves about the things we know we do, the things we avoid knowing we do, and the adaptive strategies that ultimately limit us, we can begin to take part in what author Cynthia Bourgeault calls "the dance of self-manifestation" that is the "cosmic task entrusted to us as human beings."[9] If we can recognize the Shadow cast by our personality, consciously bear the suffering we normally defend against, and accept all of who we are, we can open up endless possibilities for ourselves. The next chapter tells more of the story of the wisdom tradition behind the Enneagram and how it communicates this profound map of personal evolution.

CHAPTER 2

The Enneagram as a Universal Symbol of an Ancient Teaching:
The Perennial Wisdom View of the Human Purpose

Wisdom is an ancient tradition, not limited to one particular religious expression but at the headwaters of all the great sacred paths. From time immemorial there have been Wisdom schools, places where men and women have been raised to a higher level of understanding...Wisdom has flowed like a great underground stream from these schools, providing guidance and nurturance, as well as occasional sharp course corrections, to the flow of human history.

—Cynthia Bourgeault, *The Wisdom Way of Knowing*

MANY WHO WRITE ABOUT THE STATE of humanity today point out that at this moment in history, we suffer from a crisis of meaning. We strive to get more money or more status or more inner peace, but the things that are supposed to make us happy often leave us feeling empty. For all our affluence, we find it hard to connect to deeper experiences of truth that can help us know, love, and accept ourselves and others and understand our role in the human collective and the universe.

The wisdom teaching behind the Enneagram conveys a powerful vision and highly effective path for human growth because it comes out of a universal understanding of human purpose and possibility. This body of knowledge can be found in the root teachings of all the world's major spiritual traditions, as well as in many ancient philosophical teachings, and it communicates a view and process of human transformation that religious studies scholar Huston Smith has described as the "forgotten truth" of "human unanimity." It begins with the injunction to "Know Thyself," and it provides a map that can direct us in this crucial project.

Smith argues that this perennial wisdom provides a "pattern" or "model of reality" that we need today to orient ourselves in the world and gain a sense of confidence about who we are. The Enneagram provides a visible geometric model of the unity of the common messages underlying the world's religions and the wisdom tradition they represent. Smith looks to the same tradition I am highlighting here and finds "a viable pattern for our time."[1]

In this chapter I sketch out elements of this ancient wisdom as it is communicated through the structure and symbolic meaning of the Enneagram, so that we can use it as a pattern for orienting ourselves in the world. When I refer to the "ancient wisdom behind the Enneagram," I am specifically talking about the perennial philosophy as Aldous Huxley defines it: a metaphysical philosophy and a practical psychology that "finds something in the soul similar to, even identical with, divine Reality"[2] and points the way to manifesting our potential.

Though we have lost touch with it in recent times, this perennial wisdom has been repeated over and over for centuries. The Enneagram is just one of the forms in which it has been encoded for future generations. By exploring the meaning of this knowledge—both as it is symbolized in the Enneagram and in its other forms—we can use it in everyday life to reduce our anxieties and increase our sense of meaning and purpose.

The Perennial Wisdom Teaching Expressed by the Enneagram

FOR EACH OF US, the path of personal transformation starts with the effort to *know ourselves*: the call to see beyond the limited patterns and closed perspectives we have relied on for so long. Author Cynthia Bourgeault presents an instructive parable in her book *The Wisdom Way of Knowing* that captures the essence of what this ancient knowledge tradition says to us about us:

Once upon a time, in a not-so-far-away land, there was a kingdom of acorns, nestled at the foot of a grand old oak tree. Since the citizens of this kingdom were modern, fully Westernized acorns, they went about their business with purposeful energy; and since they were midlife, baby-boomer acorns, they engaged in a lot of self-help courses. There were seminars called "Getting All You Can out of Your Shell." There were woundedness and recovery groups for acorns who had been bruised in their original fall from the tree. There were spas for oiling and polishing those shells and various acornopathic therapies to enhance longevity and well-being.

One day in the midst of this kingdom there suddenly appeared a knotty little stranger, apparently dropped "out of the blue" by a passing bird. He was capless and dirty, making an immediate negative impression on his fellow acorns. And crouched beneath the oak tree, he stammered out a wild tale. Pointing upward at the tree, he said, "We...are...that!"

Delusional thinking, obviously, the other acorns concluded, but one of them continued to engage him in conversation: "So tell us, how would we become that tree?" "Well," he said, pointing downward, "it has something to do with going into the ground ...and cracking open the shell."

"Insane," they responded. "Totally morbid! Why, then we wouldn't be acorns anymore."[3]

This "acornology" story spells out our human situation according to the wisdom tradition behind the Enneagram specifically and the perennial philosophy generally. Before we do the conscious work of self-development, we are the seeds of what we may become. To transform from our "acorn-self" into our "oak tree–Self," we must traverse our underground territory—allow our defenses to crack open and break down—and consciously integrate our disowned feelings, blind spots, and Shadow traits so that we can shake off the limiting outer shell of our personality and grow into all that we are meant to be. Nature brings us part of the way, but to fully manifest our potential, we need to make conscious efforts to grow—and the Enneagram can guide us in this transformation.

Knowledge is a function of being, so to make the improvements in our world that we so desperately need to make, we must advance our capacity for consciousness. The perennial philosophy's vision of human "being" and its methods for achieving transformation contain a few basic elements, which I summarize here in terms of the larger vision of our human purpose and the way to enact that purpose.

The Vision: The Wisdom View of Humanity and the Universe
The cosmic perspective of this ancient wisdom sees each human as possessing a "divine spark," an inherent capacity for manifesting a higher state of being that is interconnected with the rest of the living universe. It sees human life, nature, and the universe as being ordered by the same laws, principles, and patterns. By seeing and understanding those patterns, we can achieve more

wholeness within ourselves and find a greater sense of unity and harmony with the natural world.

As we grow up, we become identified with a "personal ego," which represents both a false (acorn) self that is necessary for survival and a vehicle for the self-work required to realize the fullness of the larger (oak tree) Self we may become. The perennial wisdom tradition teaches us, however, that we can create a useful separation between our false self and the rest of our consciousness through a concerted effort to know and experience our depths. Through this space between the pure awareness of our inner witness and the habits of the false self, we may effectively "dis-identify" with our personality's programming and make room for more conscious choices, which are both directed by and supportive of our higher (oak tree) Self.

Aldous Huxley expresses this vision in his description of the perennial philosophy, beginning with the idea "That art thou," a Sanskrit phrase central to Hindu thought. "That are thou" is what the roughed-up acorn was telling the other acorns: they aren't just acorns; they are potential oak trees. The idea that there is a part of us that *is* "That"—the "That" being something we might call "divine source" or the Tao or the Absolute Principle of existence—leads to another core idea of this ancient philosophy: that our human purpose is for each of us to discover this higher Self for ourselves, to find out (and become) "Who we really are."

The Way: The Wisdom View of the Process of Human Transformation Mapped by the Enneagram

The wisdom way to greater freedom, peace, and wholeness starts with an active effort to know yourself. And, according to this tradition, the path to self-knowledge necessarily involves discipline and hard work, so you have to want to do it—you must have the motivation to sustain you through the process.

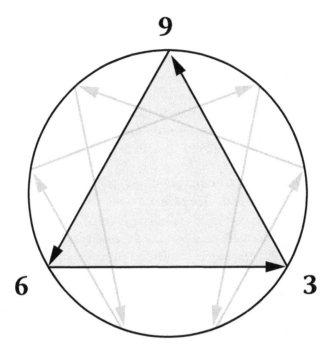

The wisdom path involves three basic steps that can be mapped on the inner diagram of the Enneagram. The first step, symbolized by a core transformational theme connected to Type Three, is *dis-identification from the Personality through self-observation*; the second phase, represented by Type Six, is *surrendering to the fear and emotional suffering associated with loosening ego defenses* (so that you can put down your defenses and integrate your Shadow); and the third step, symbolized by Type Nine, is *actively working toward transcendence and union* (so you can rise above the limited view of the Personality and merge with a greater sense of wholeness and peace).[4]

1. Dis-identification from the Personality through self-observation (the Three point).

In this phase of self-work, meditative practice helps you to still your mind so that you can more easily create the inner "space" in which to watch yourself, thereby creating a separation between your witnessing consciousness and the habits and patterns you observe. Eventually, as you get better and better at making this kind of reflective space inside yourself, you will loosen the hold your old habits and patterns have on you such that you will have the ability to make different choices.

Dis-identifying from the false self's habitual focus on the desires, passions, and fixations of our Personality requires us to develop *humility* because the Personality wants to stay in charge. But like a machine or someone who is asleep, your Personality is limited in its ability to act in the world and can only grow to a point. When you can see this, you can initiate an effective program of personal development. When you can challenge the Personality's control, you begin the process of building up a conscious center of gravity within you that is the nucleus of your higher or "greater" or essential Self.

2. Surrendering to the fear and emotional suffering associated with loosening ego defenses (the Six point).

When you engage in a process of conscious growth and start to dis-identify with (or challenge the dominance of) your Personality and its defenses, fear inevitably arises. This next step in the wisdom path of transformation entails a willingness to feel this fear rather than falling back into the usual patterns of your Personality (which are kept in place by fear). Allowing yourself to experience the emotional territory underneath your defenses in a conscious way enables you to integrate your Shadow (your disowned and warded-off feelings) and move forward in your evolution.

While we often don't like to admit it, some level of conscious suffering is necessarily connected to growth. Truly knowing yourself and transcending the conditioned Personality means integrating the parts of yourself that you don't like or don't want to see. Like the acorn in the parable, growth toward your higher Self requires a kind of breaking open so that the shell of the Personality can be shed and the deeper truth of who you are can emerge. Fear is an understandable part of becoming less defended and more open, and it can take many forms—including a resistance to change. This fear needs to be respected, but it must also be surrendered to, consciously faced, and worked through so that it doesn't thwart your ability to grow.

By allowing yourself to recognize your unconscious patterns and feel the emotions your Personality has helped you avoid, you release the considerable energy you have been (unconsciously) expending to keep your defenses in place. But this means experiencing the feelings you have created buffers against. This is why this wisdom tradition teaches that the path of growth is hard work and requires much effort and humility. But if you have the fortitude to feel and discover the meaning behind the deeper truths and feelings your defenses have been keeping you from, you open up to the possibility of a whole new way of being.

3. *Actively working toward transcendence and union (the Nine point).*

When you can maintain an ongoing practice of self-observation, self-study, and self-development, you can gradually attain the greater freedom, connectedness, balance, wholeness, and creativity that come with living from your higher "Self." This higher Self represents a more conscious, integrated state of being that is available to all of us when we do the work of dis-identifying with the Personality and facing our fear and our pain. We can experience this higher state of being when we are able to dis-identify with the Personality and merge with something larger than ourselves through meditative practice and conscious self-work. As suggested by the main themes of the "high side" of the Nine point, this opens us up to an experience of a greater sense of union with our true Self, with others, and the natural world.

Although our defenses protect us from pain, they also fend off positive experiences, like receiving love and experiencing true union with others. As we loosen the defensive grip of the Personality, we become more receptive to a deeper experience of love and connection, and we develop a greater ability to call on the strategies and strengths of all nature's archetypes instead of just being preoccupied with one way of doing things.

In the chapters that follow, I will explain how the vision and technology associated with this ancient wisdom tradition come alive in the Enneagram. As we will discover, the Enneagram symbolizes this wisdom path through both its message and its mathematical-geometric structure, which expresses universal laws of nature that show how this ancient vision can be enacted, and reveal the methods for achieving it.

The Enneagram as Universal Symbol:
The Ancient Wisdom Expressed through the
Language of Mathematics and Sacred Geometry

According to ancient wisdom traditions, the cosmic vision of human transformation and the technology for getting there are communicated to us through universal laws conveyed in the language of archetypes and mathematics. For ancient philosophers in contact with older forms of wisdom, arithmetic and geometry expressed archetypal principles that represented clues to a deeper understanding of the universe. Far from being just "servants of commerce," numbers and mathematical principles were studied in terms of the meaningful recurring patterns they revealed in nature.

Pythagoras and Plato believed numbers and shapes symbolized divine principles; for them mathematics was central not only to calculation, but also to the "deep cosmic canon of [the] design" of nature.[5] In ancient Greece, math was studied as the foundation of all other fields of knowledge, from philosophy to art to psychology, because these early philosophers saw symbolic mathematics as providing a "map of our own inner psychological and sacred spiritual structure."[6] The symbolic power of the Enneagram comes out of this ancient tradition that views geometry as sacred—as revealing an archetypal patterning or order that structures the growth processes of living things, whether it be the petals of a flower, the unfurling of a fern, the dimensions of a sea shell, or the development of the human psyche.[7]

The Symbolic Meaning of the Enneagram

The word "Enneagram" means "drawing of nine," and the Enneagram symbol is a nine-pointed star inscribed in a circle. Though its exact origins remain unknown, the symbol is thought to be thousands of years old. It is made up of three symbolic forms: the circle (symbolizing "the law of one" or "unity"), the inner triangle (symbolizing "the Law of Three" or "trinity"), and the "hexad" (symbolizing "the Law of Seven," or the steps in a process as manifest in the octave of the musical scale). The symbol is thus structured, fundamentally, by the combination of the Law of Three and the Law of Seven inscribed in a circle or unified whole. The circle symbolizes eternity, the Law of Three represents creation, and the Law of Seven suggests cyclic, ordered functioning. Together these symbols communicate the idea that we live in a universe that is perpetually developing and that there is an essential unity behind the multiplicity of forms evolving in the natural world.

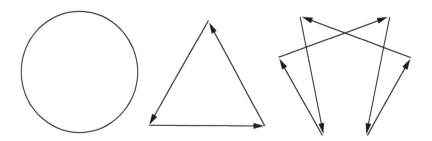

The deep significance and power of the Enneagram symbol is reflected in its expression of naturally occurring patterns in the universe. According to G. I. Gurdjieff, one of the main sources of information about the Enneagram, "for the man who is able to make use of it, the enneagram makes books and libraries totally unnecessary." Gurdjieff told his students: *"Everything* can be included and read in the Enneagram. A man may be quite alone in the desert and he can trace the Enneagram in the sand and in it read the eternal laws of the universe."[8] He describes the Enneagram as one of many symbols designed by ancient spiritual masters to communicate "objective knowledge" of humankind and the universe over time and generations.

We often think of modern society as being on the leading edge of human knowledge, and in many ways it is; but Gurdjieff claimed that we have lost touch with information about the nature of the universe that was known long ago. The people who possessed this knowledge looked for ways to transmit it in forms that would be comprehensible to future generations—in stories, parables, and diagrams like the Enneagram, which could be communicated without alteration from one school to another, from one era to another.[9]

The Circle and the Law of One

For ancient mathematical philosophers, unity was "a philosophic concept and a mystic experience expressible mathematically" in the geometric shape of the circle.[10] The circle that encloses the Enneagram diagram, then, represents unity, wholeness, and the natural order of the universe. The idea that "all is one," or that there is an underlying unity to all things, even when we can't perceive it, is conveyed by the fact that when any number is multiplied or divided by one (unity), it remains itself: "Unity always preserves the identity of all it encounters."[11] The Law of One as represented by the circle was a metaphor for the cosmic creation process beginning from a dimensionless center (the point or source) and expanding out equally in all directions.

In addition to symbolizing unity and the cyclical nature of process, the idea of *one* as expressed through the circle also communicates something about enclosure—the boundaries around a specific process or realm. The circle of the Enneagram, then, can be seen as enclosing the developmental process of an individual human being. What is inside the circle connotes the finite nature of the Personality, and all that lies outside the circle is "the infinite" that lies beyond the comprehension of the conditioned Personality.[12]

The Inner Triangle and the Law of Three

The triad is the form of the completion of all things.
—From *The Theology of Arithmetic*

The Enneagram's "inner triangle" represents the Law of Three. The Law of Three states that *three forces*—an active force, a passive force, and a neutralizing (or reconciling) force—must enter into every kind of creation. A mundane example is that of a sailboat: the boat is the passive force, the wind is the active force, and the sail is the neutralizing or reconciling force. Physicists call this trinity of forces "action, reaction, and resultant."[13]

Gurdjieff said that every phenomenon is the manifestation of three forces—that one or two forces alone cannot produce anything. When we see that something is stuck in the same place and not coming to fruition or completion, this is often because a third force is lacking. Until we transcend our ego-based viewpoint, however, we usually don't have the perceptual ability to see the third force at work.

We can begin to see the Law of Three at work in psychological growth if we look at what is needed for an individual to achieve some sort of change. Normally, when we have a hard time changing something—stopping smoking, resolving a conflict, losing weight, changing a relationship dynamic—it is because we are reacting to what is happening in a habitual, mechanical way. However, if we can bring a "third force" in, something besides action and reaction plays a role, and we can make a shift. As Michael Schneider points out, "opposites are balanced by a third, mediating element that reconciles a conflict, healing the split of polarity and transforming separate parts into a complete and successful whole."[14] A properly chosen third factor synthesizes opposites, creating a relationship that unifies them.

Just as the circle is the geometric figure that represents "one," the triangle is the geometrical representation of the Law of Three. The universal significance of the Law of Three can be seen in the many "trinities" at the center of the world's major spiritual teachings. There are many examples of threefold gods in ancient mythologies and existing religions. The Hindus have Brahma the Creator, Vishnu the Preserver, and Shiva the Destroyer; in Christianity, the "Trinity" is the three "persons" of God: the Father, the Son, and the Holy Spirit and all that they represent. The Buddha taught that we get trapped in the endless cycles of life and death by creating karma based on the three poisons: *ignorance* or delusion, *craving*, and *aversion*. These parallel the three core points of the enneagram – with unconsciousness or ignorance being the key theme represented by the Nine point, aversion being the underlying move of the Six point, and craving or desire being associated with the Three point. We find many forms of "threefoldness" in the world as well: the stages of life of birth, life, and death; the three dimensions of space (length, width, and height) and time (past, present, and future); and the three primary colors.[15]

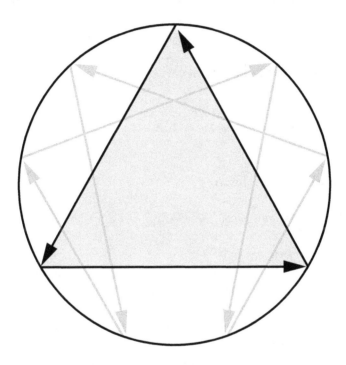

The Enneagram system too has many significant expressions of "three-foldness." There are three "brains" or centers of intelligence[16] marked by the three points of the Enneagram's inner triangle; there are three types associated with each of the three centers; and there are three subtypes of each of the nine types. The twenty-seven personalities give us the whole "psychological Enneagram," expressed mathematically by "three threes" or three cubed: 3 x 3 x 3. In addition, there are three main types we can consciously use in specific ways to bring about change in ourselves: our core type and the two types connected to our core type by the "inner flow" arrow lines of the Enneagram diagram.

The inner triangle of the psychological Enneagram symbolizes the three aspects necessary to bring anything into being: an advancing force, a resisting force, and a reconciling force that mediates between and brings the first two together. The Three point represents the proactive force (Threes focus on actively "doing"). The Six point represents the resistant force or "antithesis" (Sixes tend to resist through questioning, doubting, and testing). The Nine point is the reconciling force (a key Type Nine characteristic is the tendency to bring different ideas together to create harmony and reach a consensus).[17]

The Hexad and the Law of Seven

> *Those who are free of the passions*
> *Observe the signs of the making.*
> *Those who see its signs*
> *Yield to its rhythm.*
> *Those who crave the passions*
> *Are blinded to the signs,*
> *And see not the cause but only its effects.*
>
> *So begins all knowing.*
> 　　　　　—From Chapter 1, *"Origins,"* of the *Tao Te Ching*
> 　　　　　by Lao Tzu (translated by David Burke)

While the Law of Three symbolizes how something new comes into being, the Law of Seven reveals the way things happen in terms of a process or a sequence of steps. The wisdom tradition behind the Enneagram indicates that there is a "law of order" distinct from the "law of creation"—that creation is ordered in a certain way. The Law of Three represents something created purposely or intentionally, while the Law of Seven describes a cyclical process of transformation.

Ancient mathematicians considered the number seven to be symbolic of transformation.[18] The Law of Seven can be seen at work in the ancient Greek philosophers' belief that the only constant in the universe is change. Heraclitus famously said that all things are subject to an endless process of becoming: no one can step twice into the same river.[19]

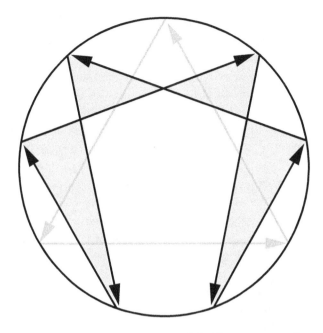

The movement along the arrow lines of the Enneagram indicates specific steps in a cycle of transformation. This flow of the cycle of transformation, symbolized by the lines of the "hexad" piece of the symbol, charts a process of change that can be likened to the organic unfolding of natural processes as expressed in the idea of "The Way" or *the Tao* as described in the *Tao Te Ching*, the main text of Taoism. Personality, then, as represented by the Enneagram, can be seen as a form of getting stuck or "fixated" at one point along this natural path of change—a defensive mechanism through which we protect ourselves, but also resist the natural flow or rhythm of life.

The Significance of Nine

Nine represents the boundary between the mundane and the transcendental infinite.
> —Michael S. Schneider, *A Beginner's Guide to Constructing the Universe: The Mathematical Archetypes of Nature, Art, and Science*

The Enneagram's circle of nine points can be seen as a boundary between the finite or the mundane nature of human life (as experienced by the Personality) and the infinite that lies beyond human consciousness—the larger reality of the universe that is beyond human comprehension when we are fixated in the Personality's limited viewpoint. Nine is the final number in the base-10 system that has a specific identity. As such, it symbolizes the highest achievement in a specific endeavor: the utmost boundary.

The ancient Greeks called nine "the horizon." For them it also represented that which encloses or binds the essential elements of any event into a whole. A. G. E. Blake explains that in the Enneagram diagram, "the apex point 9 is unique" because "it represents the beginning and end of the cycle…that which gives the form of the whole. It is the source of the purpose that has to be realized."[20]

We can find many correlations between the Enneagram's nine types and certain elements of ancient wisdom that are found in different forms of classic texts.

According to the Kabbalah, for example, the essence of the unknowable divine is portrayed in a diagram called the "Tree of Life." This Tree has ten *Sefirot*, or numbers that represent divine principles, nine of which correspond directly to the nine Enneagram archetypes. (The tenth, *Keter*, is placed above the Enneagram diagram, as it reflects the Messiah's soul and so doesn't relate to the human Personality.)[21]

Homer's epic poem, *The Odyssey*, is structured in terms of the nine different "lands" Odysseus visits during his quest to get home after the Trojan War. Each of these nine lands presents obstacles that Odysseus must overcome if he is to continue on his journey homeward. This archetypal journey of homecoming is a metaphor for the inner journey of personal growth toward "home" or the true self. Amazingly, the characteristics of the nine lands, and the characters who populate them, parallel exactly the issues and traits of the nine personalities described by the Enneagram—and Odysseus visits them *in the same order* as they appear counterclockwise around the Enneagram. In this work and in Homer's *The Iliad*, a person's main identifying characteristic is usually what leads to their undoing. This exactly mirrors what we will see in the Enneagram's personality types: each personality's greatest "strength" can also be its fatal flaw or most significant obstacle.

Similarly, we find versions of the Enneagram's nine passions in the "sins" or unconscious patterns that prevent humans from reaching Heaven in Dante's epic poem, *The Divine Comedy*. The threefold structure of Dante's *Inferno, Purgatory,* and *Paradise,* and the nine levels in the different sections of the moral geography of the underworld he constructs, also highlight some of the same themes mapped by the Enneagram: dis-identification *(Inferno),* purification through conscious suffering *(Purgatory),* and transcendence *(Paradise).*

The Inferno describes the lessons the main character, Dante the Pilgrim, learns about the different kinds of "sins," the unconscious drives of the passions described by the Enneagram. Dante poetically portrays the nature of the passions and their consequences in the "underworld"—the "unconscious" or the Shadow. This classic of Western literature thus explores the human personality starting with its deepest Shadow aspects. In the type chapters that follow, examples from the *Inferno* help illustrate the character and effect of the passions at the core of the nine types when we don't make conscious efforts to become aware of them. These punishments for our unchecked unconscious drives are exacted in the "underworld" of our unconsciousness, when we fail to do the work entailed in facing our Shadow sides.

The Modern Rediscovery of the Ancient Wisdom Encoded in the Enneagram

WHEN I FIRST ENCOUNTERED THE ENNEAGRAM in 1990, I was amazed at the specificity and precision with which it described me to myself. Like many people who become interested in the system and fascinated by its accuracy, I wanted to know where it came from. Learning about the symbol's origins has given me a deeper personal understanding of the insights it offers.

One of the modern sources of information about the diagram and a student of Gurdjieff's, J. G. Bennett, says that this "cosmic secret of perpetual self-renewal" was discovered more than four thousand years ago in Mesopotamia by a brotherhood of wise men and then passed down from generation to generation.[22]

The rediscovery of the Enneagram in the last century came about through the work of three key individuals: G. I. Gurdjieff, Oscar Ichazo, and Claudio Naranjo. All three presented Enneagram-related ideas to small groups of students in the context of psychological and spiritual growth work: Gurdjieff in Russia and Europe beginning in the early 1900s; Oscar Ichazo starting in Chile in the 1960s; and Naranjo in Berkeley, California, after studying briefly with Ichazo in 1970.

Who were these people and what did they say about the Enneagram and the knowledge behind it? By briefly exploring the distinct teachings of these three key sources, we get a better sense of the nature of the lineage of the ancient wisdom it expresses.

G. I. Gurdjieff

Gurdjieff presented the Enneagram symbol and a practical teaching of self-work called "The Work" or "The Fourth Way" to students in Russia and Europe beginning in the early 1900s. He communicated a system of "hidden" knowledge he said came from many sources, but primarily from esoteric Christianity. However, Gurdjieff did not connect the Enneagram symbol to psychological types, other than to discuss the three types of individuals connected to the three centers of intelligence.

Gurdjieff was born in Russian Armenia around 1866. His father was a Greek bard and Gurdjieff himself suggested his father had participated in some way with "an oral tradition stretching back to mankind's past."[23] When he was still a young man he traveled extensively in the Middle East, Asia, Egypt, and North Africa, making contact with many diverse secret societies and hermetic organizations—religious, philosophical, occult, political, and mystic—that were largely inaccessible to the ordinary person.[24] He eventually began teaching in Russia in 1914.

A controversial figure to this day, part of Gurdjieff's teaching method was to obfuscate through his presentation of himself as a way of challenging people's usual thinking. He purposefully triggered his students' habitual Personality reactions to demonstrate the ways in which they were fixated in mechanical, automatic functioning.

Gurdjieff's teachings portrayed humankind as living in a kind of waking sleep. His "Fourth Way" approach held out the possibility of finding a path out of mechanical functioning through self-knowledge:

> It is possible to stop being a machine, but for that it is necessary first of all *to know the machine*. A machine, a real machine, does not know itself and cannot know itself. When a machine knows itself it is then no longer a machine, at least, not such a machine as it was before. It already begins to be *responsible* for its actions.[25]

Gurdjieff continually stressed the fact that this "work on self" requires strenuous effort because the mechanical state of the Personality makes falling back asleep a continual and likely possibility. He taught that the Personality consists of different ways we buffer ourselves against the reality of our lives, helping us maintain a kind of illusion about what we can actually "do" in the world. Through active self-observation and intentional "self-remembering," he said, we could eventually evolve beyond the mechanical state associated with our Personality.

Gurdjieff also said that each person has a "chief feature," also called the "passion," which is central to the operation of the Personality. Likening it to "an axle around which the 'false personality' revolves,"[26] Gurdjieff said that every person's work consists of "struggling against this chief fault." That people have different chief features explains why there can't be one general set of rules for human growth: "What is useful for one is harmful for another. One man talks too much; he must learn to keep silent. Another man is silent when he ought to talk and he must learn to talk."[27]

Oscar Ichazo

The Enneagram of psychological types as it is widely known and used today comes to us from the work of Oscar Ichazo. Originally from Bolivia, Oscar Ichazo first taught his program of psychological and spiritual development in Chile in the 1950s and '60s. As part of his original work developing a method of personal transformation, he taught the core ideas of what we now know as the "Enneagram of personality" under the name "Protoanalysis," a process that was designed to bring about human transformation according to methods based on science, reason, and rationality.

While Ichazo does not cite many specific sources for his model, other than to say that he developed it himself, he references Aristotle and neo-Platonism as sources and is thought to have been influenced by his studies in the near and far East, especially in Afghanistan. He has said that the knowledge behind his Arica School came to him "from many sources" he encountered in his specific quest.

Ichazo explains that Protoanalysis "is based on the questions: *What is humankind?; What is the Supreme Good of humanity?;* and *What is the Truth that gives meaning and value to human life?*"[28] He describes his work as scientific in that it does not ask the participant to have faith in anything, but instead studies, measures, and analyzes the psyche. In 1978, when asked by an interviewer to explain what Arica was, he said:

> Arica provides a new theory about the psyche; it provides a new method of scientific comprehension. And because Arica has this theory about the psyche, it has also evolved a method for making the psyche fulfilled and clear in the sense of being able to develop its potential to its fullest, if that is possible. That's the aim of Arica—by having the complete and entire knowledge of our psyche, to enable ourselves to handle our problems faster, easier, and clearer.[29]

Today, forty years after the founding of Ichazo's school, his teaching represents a thoroughly articulated view of the human psyche and its possible transcendence.

Ichazo's "Enneagram of Fixations" (as opposed to the many other "Enneagrams" he uses in the Arica work) describes groupings of psychological traits that have resulted from some early injury to the psyche and a corresponding compensation of some kind. In his original system, Ichazo directed his students to work with their "Fixations," which he defined as the points where "our psyche has been wrongly predisposed," or focused, based on a lack (or unmet need or trauma) that completely colors and defines a personality type.[30] According to the Arica teaching, each individual has a core type or "fixation" in each of the three centers of intelligence. Thus, they describe the personality in terms of a "Trifix" or a triad of types—one in each center—according to a specific formula in which they determine which point one is fixated upon in each center. (For example, my Trifix is 2-7-1.)

Like Gurdjieff, Ichazo describes the fixated behavior associated with the Personality, or ego, as mechanical: "The ego-conditioned behavior has the appearance of being completely mechanical, or the work of an automaton whose behavior is dramatically obvious and repetitive."[31]

Claudio Naranjo

Claudio Naranjo, a Chilean-born, American-trained psychiatrist, learned the Enneagram model from Oscar Ichazo when he traveled to Arica, Chile in 1970. After this trip, Naranjo created a group oriented toward psychological and spiritual development (called SAT, or Seekers After Truth, an allusion to Gurdjieff's work) in Berkeley, California. Naranjo asked the members of this group to keep the Enneagram confidential, but it leaked out and eventually made its way into the mass market when the first books describing the Enneagram personality types were published in the late 1980s. [32]

In many ways, Naranjo was the ideal person to recognize the meaning of the Enneagram and bring it to a wider audience. He was a key figure within the human potential movement in the United States in the 1970s, and he had worked with Fritz Perls, the founder of Gestalt therapy, a form of existential psychotherapy that emphasized awareness of the present moment and the physical body as the key to change. By the time he studied the Enneagram of Fixations with Ichazo, Naranjo had already developed a deep knowledge of a wide range of theories and practices associated with personal growth, including psychoanalytic psychology, existential therapies, Karen Horney's personality theory, Gurdjieff's Fourth Way work, Sufism, and Buddhist meditation. So, he not only recognized the Enneagram's usefulness as a catalyst for growth, he also developed it further, using his own intuitive understanding to communicate it through the lens of existing psychological and spiritual approaches to self-development.

Naranjo saw the value of Ichazo's work and integrated it with his own broad view of human development, weaving together an even more refined description of the personalities based on Ichazo's original "Protoanalytic" (Enneagram) process. Like Ichazo, he didn't teach the Enneagram as a stand-alone tool, but rather as one piece of a more expansive program of self-work designed to help people understand their patterns and habits and work to transcend them.

Through his writings, Naranjo communicates the Enneagram as an overarching theory related to and able to integrate and make sense of many different theoretical trends in Western psychology and Eastern spiritual practices. This book is based on Naranjo's interpretation of the Enneagram personality types and subtypes. Although he credits Ichazo as the source of this model, most of the Enneagram content in the many books that have been published internationally are based most directly on Naranjo's work.

Conclusion:
Where We Are and Where We Wish to Be

The same basic ideas of the wisdom tradition encoded in the Enneagram can be found throughout human history in diverse forms. From philosophic traditions that explore eternal questions of human existence to Eastern spiritual texts that define the relationship of humanity to the "ground of being," and from epic poetry that portrays our estrangement from ourselves as the starting point of a journey of homecoming to the insights of Western psychology, renderings of this knowledge echo throughout recorded history.

The Enneagram represents a model of wholeness: each of the points of the Enneagram not only describes individual personalities but also characterizes certain archetypal elements that are universal. Each point also expresses a range of possibilities—a vertical dimension that indicates an archetype's higher aspect of expression when its fixated aspects can be loosened and transcended, and a lower side that describes a more unconscious, automatic, "fixated" level of functioning.

Growth, then, as revealed by the perennial philosophy and the Enneagram map, is a process of observing ourselves, suffering through our fears and disowned Shadow aspects, and working to manifest our higher potentials. In the following chapters, which describe each of the Enneagram's archetypes and their respective journeys of homecoming, I trace the development of the Personality, the three different subtype forms it can take, and the path toward liberation. By identifying ourselves within this timeless, sacred framework, we can join in this ancient tradition and contribute to what must be a collective effort to increase the level of human consciousness.

CHAPTER 3

The Point Nine Archetype:
The Type, Subtypes, and Growth Path

The opposite of home is not distance, but forgetfulness.

—Elie Wiesel

Type Nine represents the archetype of the person who seeks to harmonize with the external environment as a way of staying comfortable and peaceful, even though this means a loss of contact with their internal environment. Akin to the meaning behind both "fusion" and "union," this archetype's drive is to maintain a sense of calm and connectedness through merging with the outside and diminished awareness of the inside.

Type Nines are the prototype for that tendency in all of us to tune out our own inner knowing as a way of "going with the flow" and "not rocking the boat." As discussed in the introduction, this is a basic aspect of our human condition: we all experience a lessening of consciousness as an attempt to buffer ourselves from the pains and discomforts of everyday life. We all feel tempted to take the path of least resistance from time to time. The Nine archetype represents the model for wanting to stay comfortable, resist change, and do what's easiest, even if that means not asserting yourself or falling asleep to your own priorities as a way of getting along with others. Nines thus represent the prototype for all the personality types of the universal human tendency to go on automatic and remain asleep to ourselves.

The Nine archetype can be seen at the societal level in cultures that put the collective ahead of the individual, and also in the concept of bureaucracy. The same underlying principles are at work when large institutions become resistant to change through an unconscious maintenance of the status quo, an inability to make creative decisions, and a disconnection from the original animating principles that might drive innovation and evolution.

In the Enneagram framework, Type Nines are adaptable, likable, and easygoing. They specialize in detecting tension and finding ways to mediate and diffuse conflict. Oriented toward inclusion, consensus, and harmony, they excel at understanding and valuing different perspectives and mediating between them to resolve disputes and maintain peace. They are genuinely caring and unselfish, and their specific "superpower" lies in providing steadfast support to others in a way that makes everyone around them feel honored and included.

As with all the archetypal personalities, however, Type Nines' gifts and strengths also represent their "fatal flaw" or "Achilles heel," as they can over-adjust to others and then have a hard time registering their own desires and asserting their own agendas. They get in their own way by focusing too much attention on what others want and deferring excessively to the people around them. By accommodating others and avoiding conflict in order to achieve comfort, they end up becoming deaf to their own inner voice. However, when they can learn to wake up to themselves, access their own internal compass, and initiate action on their own behalf, they can balance their attention to others with an ability to act in support of themselves.

The Type Nine Archetype in Homer's *Odyssey*: The Lotus-Eaters

The Odyssey is a classic story about the importance of "homecoming" as a metaphor for the inner journey that brings us "home" to the true self.[1] As the hero of *The Odyssey*, Odysseus's central goal is to get home. In the symbolic language of *The Odyssey*, home is not only a specific place, but also a state of being in which we embody our true nature and are recognized for who we really are. The true self, as "home," is the "root of all wanting and choosing."[2]

The first place Odysseus and his fleet visit after leaving Troy and sailing homeward at the end of the Trojan War is the land of the Lotus-Eaters. The Lotus-Eaters are an easygoing, friendly tribe who "live on a flowering food" called lotus. They are a pleasant people, but they have no desires at all; they've snuffed them out with their self-deadening herb. They are unable to choose one path of action over another because they have fallen asleep to their guidepost, their "home:" who they really are and what they are supposed to become. They are stuck at a fork in the road, unable to choose a direction.

The Lotus-Eaters offer Odysseus's men lotus, which makes them "forget the way home."[3] Under the influence of the lotus, Odysseus's men want to stay in the Lotus-Eaters's land. Odysseus has to find them and take them back to the ship by force, where he ties them to the rowing benches so they can resume their journey.

Without the knowledge of what it means to be "at home," we don't have much reason to engage in the difficult journey that leads to the real self. The Lotus-Eaters exemplify the Nine archetype of falling asleep to the needs and wants of the true self. Without the desire to manifest the higher possibilities of who you are, you lose focus; you can't locate the motivation to act or the direction in which to go—there's nothing to set your compass by. And without a sense of or a desire for home, it's easy to want to simply stay comfortable in "Lotus Land."

The Type Nine Personality Structure

LOCATED AT THE TOP OF THE ENNEAGRAM, Type Nine belongs to the "body-based" triad, associated with the core emotion of *anger* and a focus of attention related to *order*, *structure*, and *control*. While Eights "overdo" anger and Ones are at odds with their anger, Nines "underdo" anger. While their relationship to anger plays a formative role in shaping their personality, most Nines report not feeling anger very often (though they may erupt on rare occasions).

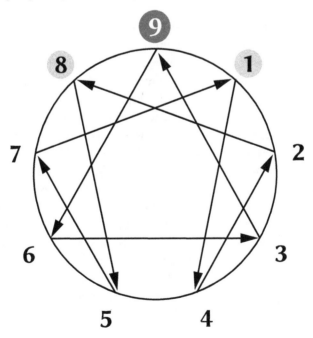

We all have the capacity for angry feelings, but Nines habitually avoid contact with their anger because they focus so much on staying comfortable, and anger can easily bring them into conflict with others. So, even though Nines are anger types, they may not have regular contact with their anger, and it tends to leak out in various forms of passive-aggressive behaviors. Nines' focus on order and control takes the form of liking the support that structure provides and the habit of passively resisting being controlled by others (often despite seeming to go along).

As body-centered types, Nines sense their environment kinesthetically and have a primary connection to "gut knowing." Paradoxically, Nines can be cut off from their gut instincts. The Nine personality is shaped in a fundamental way by the habit of "going to sleep" to the ongoing experience of anger inherent in their body-based center of intelligence.

The body-centered types are also referred to as the "self-forgetting" triad, in that Types Eight, Nine, and One all tend to "forget" themselves through a kind of psychological inertia that occurs with regard to their physical needs. These three types, each for their own reasons, tend to put their needs and wants in the background, ignoring their practical and physical requirements for things like rest and relaxation (Eights), play and pleasure (Ones), and priorities, preferences, and opinions (Nines).

The Early Coping Strategy: Type Nine

Nines often report that they grew up in a family in which their opinions weren't heard, in which others were more forceful in expressing their opinions, or where the best strategy to feeling calm and avoiding upset was to go along with what others wanted. Through this experience of being overlooked or overpowered, a Nine learns to specialize in being someone who is easygoing and accommodating of others, but who, when asked for an opinion, doesn't know what he wants and finds it easier to let others decide.

Nines typically have an unmet need for a satisfying sense of union—a feeling of belonging or connectedness with others who would see and affirm the Nine's individuality. When they were children, Nines may not have received the attention they needed, and their wishes and preferences typically weren't listened to and acted upon. Sometimes the Nine was a middle child or one of many children, or he may have had a parent who was forceful in exerting control. Nines often decided as children to resign themselves to going along with what others want in order to maintain positive connections with others.

Whatever the individual case, Nines tend to give up on asserting their desires and adopt a coping strategy that involves forgetting themselves (and the pain of not getting what they want) and overadjusting to others as a way of finding peace and avoiding conflict. Nines can't tolerate conflict because it seems to them to lead to separation. Relationships are life-sustaining when we are young, and Nines play the role in the family of mediating between people to reduce tension and maintain the sense of connection that feels crucial to their survival.

The Nine coping strategy is thus an overadjustment to others—an unconscious accommodation of what other people want and a "forgetting" of what they want—and their attention goes to harmonizing with those around them rather than asserting themselves. This over-adjustment reflects their experience that any strong feeling or preference on their part may put them in conflict with others; at an unconscious level, their personality is set up to avoid adversarial interactions at all costs. For Nines, the cost of this tendency is their connection to their own inner experience.

Self-denying behaviors and overadjustment are the Nine's ways of creating the merged state they long for with others. They feel pain over being too much on their own too soon in their development; by staying connected to outside support, Nines find the comfort they seek.

Mark, a Self-Preservation Nine, describes his childhood situation and the development of his coping strategy:

He was the youngest of four children. His father was a large, angry, critical man with a deep voice and a perpetual scowl on his face, probably a Sexual One. His mother was a Type Nine who tried to maintain a sense of harmony in the family by taking on his father's agenda and preventing his outbursts of anger. Mark learned early on that there were rules that had to be followed: his father's rules. Self-determination and self-expression were allowed only within the limited constraints of what was acceptable to his father. To breach those boundaries meant being the object of his father's criticism and anger. Mark's siblings—one Type One and two Type Nines—also took on their father's agenda, and were all too happy to correct their youngest brother's behavior, grammar, opinions, and performance. His father's anger disturbed him deeply, and he could sense that it also disturbed his mother. Mark learned early on that preventing his father from getting angry helped him maintain his connection to both parents. The easiest way to do that was to go along with whatever his father wanted.

The Main Type Nine Defense Mechanism: Dissociation

Just as Nines represent the prototype of the universal human tendency to go to sleep to our own inner experience, their main defense mechanism, *dissociation*, is a component of all defense mechanisms as well.

When we are young, the defensive structure of the personality grows up in response to some sort of pain or discomfort that is too much for our young psyches to withstand. There are clear advantages to dissociating when we experience something traumatic or painful: we cut off the pain and the memory of something that is extremely difficult to endure. The problem with this defense, however, is that when we use it habitually in situations in which our survival is not at risk—as a way to buffer ourselves from the minor discomforts of everyday life—we can lose touch with ourselves altogether in a way that prevents us from growing.

Sometimes referred to as "narcotization," the principal way Nines dissociate from psychological pain or discomfort is through a kind of dimming of awareness, through putting themselves to sleep in various ways. Through immersing themselves in one activity or another—reading, eating, watching TV, or doing crossword puzzles—Nines distract themselves as a way of avoiding their own feelings, needs, and wants. Through many different kinds of unconscious maneuvers, including joking around, talking too much, or focusing on inessentials, Nines water down their experience of life, their interactions with others, and their contact with themselves to buffer themselves against the pain of separation, of not being heard, or of not feeling a sense of belonging.

The Type Nine Focus of Attention

Nines focus their attention on others, on what is going on in the environment, on avoiding conflict, and on creating harmony. Nines typically pay attention to what other people want, preferring to go along with the flow of others' desires rather than to state their own preferences. This habit of blending in with their environment allows them to avoid discomfort and create a kind of defensive (often artificial) peace. But when our attention focuses on one aspect of our experience, there is also a sphere of life that we don't pay attention to: while Nines' attention is focused outward on the environment and on other people, they neglect their inner experience.

Based on the coping strategy of harmonizing with what's going on around them, Nines typically pay attention to sensing how people and environments "feel" in terms of energetic tension vs. calm. They take in others' perspectives as their own to avoid disconnection and conflict. As a result, Nines have a natural talent for mediation because they deeply understand others' points of view. They easily focus on the commonalities between opposing arguments and are motivated by their love of peacefulness to help people find compromises based on highlighting the common ground between them.

Having an "other-focused" style of attention, Nines pay a great deal of attention to what the people around them want, think, and feel, and much less attention to what they themselves want, think, and feel. The experience of others is so much in the forefront of their perception that they often report a sense of not knowing what they want. When questioning a Nine about something as everyday as "What do you want for dinner?" a typical reply is, "I don't know, what do you want?"

As a result of the habit of focusing on others and not on themselves, Nines can feel that they are unimportant and not worthy of others' attention. Other people seem far more prominent, to the point that their own agendas fade into the background.

It can be so hard for Nines to attend to and find their own inner direction that at times they can only locate a sense of inner motivation when it is tied to the wishes of others. I was once in a process group in which everyone was trying to help a Nine say what he wanted. In every case, with every effort the group members made to inquire into what he wanted, the answer was always the same: he wanted what we wanted.

Nines' attention often gets pulled away from their immediate priorities by different elements in their environment; they experience difficulty concentrating because they shift their attention from the center of their experience to the periphery.[4] Other people and less essential tasks can seem more worthy of attention than their own priorities. Nines also get distracted in more deliberate ways, "as if driven by a desire not to experience or not to see."[5] It can be stressful for Nines to act on their own behalf—it can inspire anxiety about performance—and so they distract themselves with less important activities as a way of avoiding the pressure of having to act.

The Type Nine Emotional Passion: Laziness

Laziness is the passion of Type Nine. The words sloth, laziness, psychospiritual inertia, acedia, indolence, and ignorance (in the Buddhist sense) all communicate the same thing: a tendency to fall asleep to yourself. Laziness refers to the tendency we all have to go unconscious to our inner experience, to operate in automatic, pre-programmed ways because we don't consciously attend to all of the feelings, beliefs, and experiences that might drive our behavior if we were aware of them. For Nines, "psychological inertia" manifests as a deadening of feeling, an inability to know what they want, an incapacity to contact themselves, and a hesitance to voice strong opinions or assert their will in the world.

In *The Enneagram of Passions and Virtues*, Sandra Maitri defines the Type Nine passion of "laziness" as an "inattention to self," a "self-neglect," a muffling or tamping down of a Nine's inner life.[6] Nines may not seem "lazy" at all in the usual way we think of the term (i.e., a reluctance to do things), though they might; they are primarily lazy about paying attention to themselves.

The earliest word used to define the Nine's passion (within the fourth-century Christian Contemplative tradition) was "acedia." Derived from the Greek word *a-chedia* (no-care), acedia refers to "a laziness of the psyche and of the spirit, rather than a tendency to inaction."[7] In psychological terms, Naranjo explains that acedia "manifests as a loss of interiority, a refusal to see, and a resistance to change."[8] Most importantly, Nines become lazy about attending to their own internal life in a way they don't see, such that they lose a sense of their own being but don't know it.

Naranjo further defines the "psychological inertia" of the Nine personality by characterizing the Nine as someone who lacks fire and passion, someone who suffers from a loss of inwardness and imagination. The passion of psychological laziness also entails a deadening of feelings, which may be apparent, as when someone doesn't communicate much about herself, or hidden, as when the Nine overcompensates by actively conveying a genial or jovial disposition.

The passion of psychological laziness causes Nines to go deaf to their inner voices, which causes an "eclipse" of the inner witness.[9] Under the sway of this passion, Nines unconsciously forget themselves, losing contact with their emotions, their instincts, and their ability to detect and act on their natural animal impulses. Thus, laziness brings with it a sense of "not wanting to see, not wanting to be in touch with one's experience."[10] This directly impacts Nines' ability to become aware of their internal patterns—and since we all need to become aware of our internal patterns in order to build the muscle of self-awareness, Nines may stay locked in their "acorn shell" until they finally learn to make contact with their desire to break it open.

The Type Nine Cognitive Mistake:
"Going Along to Get Along Is the Only Way to Go"

We all get stuck in habitual ways of thinking that influence our beliefs, feelings, and actions; this continues even after the mental models that create our overall perspective aren't accurate anymore. While the passion shapes the personality's emotional motivations, the "cognitive fixation" or "cognitive mistake" preoccupies the personality's thought processes.

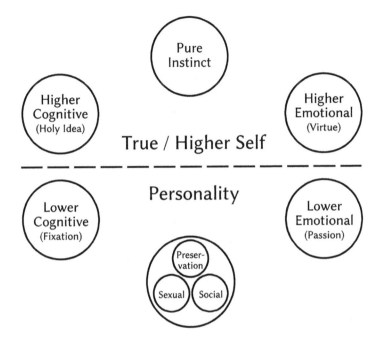

In Nines, the mental fixation (called "Indolence" by Ichazo) that supports the passion of sloth refers to a habit of not actively thinking about or caring to think about your own priorities. Sloth governs Nines' habit of falling asleep to their inner experience. Indolence leads Nines to ignore and neglect themselves. Then they create all manner of guiding thoughts, beliefs, and core ideas related to living out their passion for forgetting themselves.

Psychologist Jerome Wagner contends that because Nines feel neglected early on and lack a sense of belonging, they organize themselves around patterns of thinking connected to an assumption that they aren't important and don't have much to offer.[11] Nines end up neglecting themselves and not listening to their own inner voice as a result of a deep belief in their own unimportance.

According to Wagner, to support the passion of psychological laziness, Nines hold the following core beliefs as organizing psychological principles.[12]

- I don't matter. It's easier that way.
- What I think and feel isn't that important. And that's okay. Other people just feel more strongly about things than I do.
- It's not okay to be angry or upset because that puts you at odds with others.
- It's more important to be nice or peaceful than to be true to myself.

- It's not good to show anger because conflict destroys positive connections with others.
- If I'm not present and accessible to others, I'm safe.
- I don't know what I want, and it's not that important anyway.
- I'm incapable of knowing what I want.
- Knowing what I want and asserting my desires in the world of others takes too much work and will alienate people I need or want to stay connected to.
- It's easier to go along with what other people want than go to the trouble of asserting what I want.

Nines believe that it's always best to avoid open conflict, and so in many situations will think, "Why rock the boat?" They can't see any reason to disrupt things on their account. Given these key beliefs, it seems natural for them to take the path of least resistance and give others what they want so they can stay comfortable and undisturbed.

The Type Nine Trap:
"Staying Comfortable Eventually Creates Discomfort" or "Putting Yourself in a Coma Seems Like a Good Way to Avoid Conflict"

As it does for each type, the cognitive fixation or "mental trance" of Type Nine leads the personality in circles. It presents an inherent "trap" that the limitations of the personality cannot resolve.

Despite Nines' unconscious need to preserve a sense of comfort and calm at all costs, the truth is that avoiding conflict and an awareness of their own desires leads to the creation of the discomfort and disharmony Nines are trying to avoid. The pursuit of comfort inevitably produces discomfort because it requires willfully ignoring some basic truths, like the constructive and unifying potential of conflict and the necessity of expressing your real feelings in order to establish deep connections.

For Nines, the desire to maintain harmony necessitates a deadening of their own consciousness, inner aliveness, and passion, which limits the quality of their engagement with life. And overadapting to others eventually creates a sense of dissatisfaction that can leak out through passive-aggressive behavior and lead to the kind of conflict the adaptation was designed to prevent in the first place.

The Key Type Nine Traits

Over-Adjustment and Merging

The prominent Type Nine habit of adapting themselves to others' agendas represents an "*over*-adjustment" because Nines typically don't just meet others halfway, they lose the ability to access what their positions are and give in to others completely—often without anyone knowing they've done it. While Nines often help others to find compromises, they can tend to proactively erase their own wants and needs to avoid experiencing a scenario of conflicting needs altogether.

Type Nine individuals' tendency to yield excessively to others entails a postponing of the satisfaction of their own desires. This self-denial goes along with the strategy of over-adjustment. As Naranjo explains, "excessive adaptation to the world would be too painful to endure without self-forgetfulness."[13]

Nines "merge" with others, but what does this mean? Merging happens when Nines "take in" the positions, feelings, and desires of another person to the point that they feel like they're their own. They lose the boundaries between themselves and other people. This is especially easy for Nines because they usually don't know what they want and can have a hard time telling the difference between their own agenda and someone else's.

Unconsciously, Nines feel motivated to retain the symbiotic bonds of early childhood, so for them disconnection can feel catastrophic. Nines orient themselves in relation to other people, so losing connections can make them feel lost and adrift. Because of this—often without even being conscious of why they are doing it—Nines do everything they can to maintain a connection with important others, even to the point of going to sleep to their own inner truth.

Resignation

At the heart of the Nine's coping strategy of "going along to get along" is their tendency to resign themselves to not getting what they want. In line with this, they (often unconsciously) give up on the effort to even know what they want.

Nines give up on themselves out of a deep belief that it doesn't pay to assert yourself. As Naranjo says, "it is as if the individual endorsed a strategy of playing dead to stay alive (yet becoming tragically dead-in-life in the name of life)."[14] Their core belief that it's not worth it to stand up for what they want leads to a resignation that undergirds many other Nine traits involving laziness with regard to their own desires. Giving up on what they want makes it much easier to go along with what other people want.

Easygoing Nature/Affability

Although the downside of giving up your desires to go along with the agendas of others is that you become more and more disconnected from yourself, the upside is that people tend to find you likable, pleasant, and easy to be around. And most Nines do fit this description: they don't make many demands on others, they are emotionally steady, and they can be solid sources of support and friendship. Their habit of avoiding conflict and tension motivates them to be easygoing and affable.

Of course, Nines' reputation for being congenial, friendly, and generous comes at a price—namely, a stronger connection to their own anger and opinions. And despite their amiable disposition Nines can be hard to deal with at times, especially when they've been so easygoing that they find themselves doing things they don't want to be doing and so become stubborn or irritable. Overall, though, Nines tend to be laid-back, fun-loving individuals.

Indecision

Nines often struggle with procrastination and indecision. Like Homer's Lotus-Eaters, Nines tend to be disconnected from their internal guidance system, so they can experience extreme difficulty when they need to access their desires to make a decision. While they may have preferences in daily life, it may be hard for them to choose one life path over another, one career over another, or one action over another.

Sometimes, however, Nines can more easily locate their preferences in the negative: while they may not know what they want, they may know what they *don't* want. When this is the case, as the flip side of the tendency to overadapt to others' wishes, they may silently go against what others want.

The Type Nine Shadow

Nines have blind spots related to their passion of laziness and their central strategy of going to sleep to their own depths in order to get along more easily with others. What they really want, their feelings, their opinions, and their sense of their own inner truth can all be Shadow aspects for Nines, who unconsciously avoid finding out what they want as a way of maintaining a sense of comfort, safety, and connectedness with others. It can be hard for Nines to take a firm position, express a preference, or feel strong emotions, because they habitually "forget" themselves to more easily flow with others. When asked what they want, many Nines say they simply don't know.

Nines don't want to experience their anger, so their aggression represents a big blind spot. They also don't want to own anything—strong opinions, desires, and emotions—that might somehow pit them against the important people in their lives, so these may all reside in their Shadow. Nines believe that any kind of tension can lead to separation, so they tend to deny anything inside themselves that might cause an energetic disruption in their personal connections. Much of their inner life, therefore, can be something of a blind spot. Along with this, they can be blind to instances where there is a legitimate need for conflict or an honest discussion.

The presence of anger in the Nine Shadow heightens the possibility that it will leak out in passive-aggressive forms, such as stubbornness, passive resistance, procrastination, and irritability—and they may not see how this happens or how it impacts others. Like the other body-based types, Nines don't like being told what to do; while they will usually say yes to others as a way of avoiding the conflict that might arise if they overtly refuse a request, they can often say yes when they mean no. In this way—by passively resisting what others want them to do—they hold on to a sense of independence and avoid being controlled by the desires of others even while seeming to be adaptive and flexible. They may also be unaware of this whole dynamic.

Nines focus on maintaining a sense of peace and comfort, so the need for change can also be part of their Shadow. This can include avoiding realities like needing to get a job or change careers or leave a relationship—anything that might inspire the need to act or the need for change, as Nines can get stuck in the inertia of wanting to maintain the status quo.

Because Nines dislike attracting attention and can be compulsively unselfish, their positive achievements or desire for recognition may also represent blind spots. Nines usually do not want to get attention, even for the good things they do, so they tend to share the credit with others to avoid the discomfort of drawing the focus to themselves.

The Shadow of the Type Nine Passion:
Sloth in Dante's Underworld

From the perspective of the Enneagram, the shadow of the Type Nine personality has a fitting punishment and an appropriate placement in Dante's underworld. In the symbolic world of *The Inferno*, the Passion of Sloth is "sinful" in that it represents a laziness that causes the individual to waste life day after day, resisting natural energy and initiative. In the Type Nine personality, Sloth can engender a deep, barely perceptible simmering resentment or passive resistance that most often isn't expressed at all. Accordingly, the Pilgrim finds these

Slothful shades punished alongside the Wrathful in the muddy river Styx. But while the actively angry "Wrathful" spirits "constantly tear and mangle each other," the Slothful can be detected under the muddy surface only by the bubbles that indicate their presence:[15]

> beneath the slimy top are sighing souls who make these waters bubble at the surface; your eyes will tell you this—just look around.
>
> Bogged in this slime they say, 'Sluggish we were in the sweet air made happy by the sun, and the smoke of sloth was smoldering in our hearts; now we lie sluggish here in this black muck!' This is the hymn they gurgle in their throats but cannot sing in words that truly sound.

Like their more visibly angry neighbors, the Slothful are embedded in the muddy mire of their Passion symbolized by the "slimy waters" of the swamplike river Styx. But unlike the "Wrathful" Type Ones, Nines' anger is much deeper and more buried, so the Slothful are depicted in Dante's underworld as "sighing souls" who are, like their anger in life, submerged beneath the surface.

The Three Kinds of Nines:
The Type Nine Subtypes

THE PASSION OF TYPE NINE IS LAZINESS (or sloth), defined as a psychological resistance to actively living from your deeper self or your own sense of "being"— an aversion to being aware of your own inner feelings, sensations, and desires.

The three Type Nine subtype personalities all express this passion of psycho-spiritual laziness, but they act it out in three distinct ways depending on which of the three main instinctual drives—self-preservation, social relationship, or sexual bonding—dominates. The passion of laziness thus gets expressed through Nines' strong unconscious need to merge with something or someone else as a way of distracting themselves from their own sense of being—or from the pain of not being connected to their own sense of being.

In this way, all three Type Nine subtypes express a need for fusion, but they fuse or merge with different things as a way of finding the comfort and connectedness they lack within themselves or with others. The Self-Preservation Nine fuses with physical comforts and activities, the Social Nine fuses with groups, and the Sexual Nine fuses with other individuals. Focusing somewhere else, however, allows Nines to continue to avoid connecting more deeply with their own inner sense of being. The three Nines all share a passion for self-deadening, which takes the form of laziness or inactivity or incapacity with regard to their own feelings, needs, and wants.

The Self-Preservation Nine: "Appetite"

The combination of the passion of laziness and the dominant instinct for self-preservation in Nines results in a personality subtype that Naranjo, following Ichazo, calls "Appetite." The deeper motivation of this subtype of Type Nine is finding a sense of comfort in the world through the satisfaction of physical needs. This personality finds satisfaction in activities such as eating, reading, playing games, watching television, sleeping, or even working (if work is a comfortable thing to do).

Whichever form of activity is chosen by a given Self-Preservation Nine, the key is that this Nine expresses his or her need to find protection and well-being by merging with an experience of the satisfaction of concrete needs. In giving their attention over to a favored activity in this way, these Nines simultaneously avoid or "forget" their own being—or the pain of not being connected to their own being—and find a substitute sense of "being" in the comfort of the fulfillment of routine, everyday appetites.

For Self-Preservation Nines, it feels safer to take refuge in physical comfort, or in a routine that structures their experience in concrete and familiar ways, than to have to show up in the world and risk potential conflict or overstimulation. It's easier to erase yourself by losing yourself in comfortable activities than to reveal yourself or open yourself up to whatever unpredictable or complex thing might be happening in the outside world.

The name "Appetite" doesn't refer just to eating, but also to the need to find a sense of well-being through the fulfillment of various physical needs—for food, for comfort, for restfulness, or for something interesting to pay attention to that provides a sense of support or structure or peace. Appetite also refers to concreteness, to the grounding aspect of fulfilling physical and material needs in simple, straightforward, tangible, and enjoyable ways. One Self-Preservation Nine I know focuses her self-care efforts on physical fitness and dieting in specific, routine ways. She belongs to a gym where she exercises with a close-knit community of people who all participate in regular early-morning workouts and support each other by going on periodic diets together based on the clearly articulated structure of a practical nutritional methodology.

Self-Preservation Nines are concrete people, oriented to immediate experience, who don't relate much to abstractions or metaphysical concepts. With these Nines there is less "psychological mindedness" and introspection and more focus on tangible and immediate "things to do." They find experience much easier to deal with than theory. They don't always put their experience into words, however—they don't talk a lot about what is going on inside them in general.

Naranjo describes the meaning behind "Appetite" as a kind of excessive "creature-likeness," characterized by an "I eat therefore I am" or an "I sleep therefore I am" attitude that erases the question of "being" in a larger sense. For these Nines, the ordinary facts of life get in the way of thinking about abstract things, like what might be lacking in their experience. These are people who live life in a more simple, direct way.

More than the other two Type Nine subtypes, these Nines tend to want more time alone. Like the other Nines, Self-Preservation Nines habitually focus their attention on other people and on their environment, but Self-Preservation Nines can actually find it more relaxing and grounding to be by themselves, as it allows them to more fully relax into whatever activity they are engaged with. These individuals also tend to have a distinctive sense of humor characterized by a wry and self-deprecating attitude.

Nines are very loving people, but deep down they usually don't have the sense of being loved—it's as if they have resigned themselves to not actively receiving love for themselves. For the Self-Preservation Nine, the search for comfort in pleasurable activities may reflect a desire for compensation for their deeper sense of abnegation, or a giving up of the need for love, with the fulfillment of other appetites. The jolliness or fun-loving spirit of this type of Nine, though it is a very real, very endearing characteristic of this personality, may be another kind of compensation for an early lack—they substitute fun for love.

Self-Preservation Nines tend to be active and intuitive, and they express a kind of subtle strength. This is the most "Eight-ish" of the three Nine subtypes. Their sense of inertia with regard to taking action places them firmly in the Nine type, so they are unlikely to be mistaken for Eights, but they do have forceful energy, especially in contrast to the Sexual Nine, which is a much less assertive character. Self-Preservation Nines have a stronger presence than the other two Nine subtype personalities, and they can be more irritable and stubborn. It can be very difficult for them to accept that another person is right. This subtype also lives a life of excess more than the other Nines, and while they don't get angry very often, they can express the "fury of a peacemaker" when they get mad at people who cause problems.

Daniel, a Self-Preservation Nine, speaks:

Growing up in the Midwest, people often said that I was "a good eater." I think they meant it as a compliment. But it was true that eating was always a source of pleasure for me. It has also been something that I've indulged in when under a lot of stress. I managed a political campaign when I was in my early twenties and gained twenty-five pounds in a few short months. Today I recognize my relationship to food is a compensation for a lack of feeling loved, and I'm learning how to give that love to myself rather than just eating.

I love sleep, but sometimes it's more of an escape than a physiological need. A Nine friend of mine was telling me about an argument he got into. He said he was so mad he needed to go take a nap. I could totally relate. Routines are comforting, too. For many years I followed the same routine whenever I'd turn on my computer: first check e-mail, then go to a series of five different websites, all in the same order each time, multiple times per day. Often, I'd have many more important things to do, but I needed the comfort fix provided by visiting familiar websites before I could begin working.

Being alone feels relaxing because merging into eating or sleeping or watching TV doesn't take much effort. But I've learned that just staying comfortable doesn't help me with the important task of regaining autonomy and a sense of myself. For that I need to settle in to the harmony of my own being, which takes a lot of work because I have unresolved internal conflicts and my own position isn't immediately clear to me.

Some people have asked me if I might actually be a Type Eight because I seem more embodied than other Nines and I have learned over time to be more assertive. I take that as a compliment! I've intentionally used my Eight wing to support my personal development by practicing expressing myself, experiencing my anger, and taking action.

The Social Nine: "Participation" (Countertype)

Social Nines express the passion of psychological laziness (or sloth) through merging with the group, working hard in support of group interests, and prioritizing the group's needs above their own. Social Nines are congenial characters with a need to feel like they're a part of things—a need that expresses an underlying feeling of being different or not fitting in with the group or community. This person is a light-hearted, sociable, fun-loving character who expresses a driving need to be involved in the group.

The Social Nine's need to participate comes from their deeper feeling of not belonging to the group. This feeling drives the Social Nine to overcompensate by being generous and sacrificing whatever is necessary to meet the needs of the group as a way of earning membership. They have an intense need to feel that they are a part of things, because they don't feel that they are. They feel like they have to do something extra in order to be included in a group, so they work twice as hard to support the group to make sure they belong.

Social Nines have a passion for doing what is necessary to pay the ticket for group admission, for being one with that group—but it takes a lot of effort. Social Nines can be workaholics; they feel a need to work hard and give a lot. But it's not just work—they energetically demonstrate friendliness and sociability; they don't show their pain; they don't burden others; and they don't show people how much energy it takes to devote so much effort to the community. These are people who are generous and unselfish, mindful of the group, and gifted in meeting the needs of others to the point where they sacrifice themselves to satisfy the responsibility others want to put on them.

In contrast to the other two Nine Subtypes, who tend to be more subdued characters, Social Nines are very outgoing and energetic—this is what makes this the counter-type Nine. Social Nines have a special brand of strength because they feel motivated to fight for the needs of the group. Social Nines are extroverted, expressive, and forceful, and so they go against the inertia typical of Type Nine in some ways—but on the inside they still have a sense of laziness about their own needs and wants.

Social Nines make very good leaders—the best kind of leaders, in fact—in the sense that they are good, unselfish people who strive to satisfy the responsibility given them. They can be especially gifted mediators; they naturally want to translate differing opinions so that everyone is heard and conflict in the group is avoided. They put a lot of energy into their work as a leader. They have an ability to bear a lot, sometimes to the extent that they become a "human punching bag." These Nines give of themselves unconditionally as a response to a deeper (sometimes unconscious) fear of abandonment, conflict, separation, and the potential loss of peace and harmony.

Social Nines like to control things, and they like to talk a lot. Because they work so hard for the group, they may have no time left for themselves. They tend to have very full lives—full of everything but themselves.[16] And while Social Nines get their identity and their sense of reality from belonging, they often doubt their own existence, their own sense of self.

The outward expression of this subtype is more happy than sad, but theirs may ultimately be a kind of partial participation: underneath their cheerful exterior, their sense of not belonging persists and creates a kind of sadness that isn't communicated to others. They don't feel their suffering very much—but they don't feel extreme, euphoric highs, either. They are more in the middle emotionally—neither hot nor cold—and they may be somewhat detached from their emotions and sensations.

Social Nines can look like Type Threes because they work very hard and accomplish a lot without showing the stress of it. But they differ from Threes in that they are much more reluctant to be in the spotlight and they don't support the group to create an image or to win admiration from others. They may also be mistaken for Twos because they are active in meeting the needs of others, but they have much less need for approval and appreciation than Twos, and are generally more emotionally steady.

Maya, a Social Nine, speaks:

I was raised as part of a group. Growing up in a large family with five siblings, I often found myself mediating between family members in order to reduce conflict and to promote tolerance, understanding, and consensus. Around controversial dinner table topics, for example, when the conversation got heated, I was often in the middle—translating, explaining, and trying to get each side to see the other's point of view. As a result, I did well leading groups. In high school, for example, I was president of several different societies and clubs. In my early career, I often succeeded in setting up groups that promoted teamwork and cohesiveness, including a volleyball team. Today, I still screen the environment, especially new ones, to know how to best fit in and orient myself quietly to the needs of the whole. When making a decision that will affect an entire group, I like to hear all the different opinions, synthesize them, and then consolidate them in my mind before making a decision. My feelers are always out, reading the milieu around me.

The Sexual Nine: "Fusion"

Sexual Nines unconsciously express a need to be through another—to gain a sense of "being" they don't find inside themselves through fusion with somebody else. They unconsciously use relationships to feed their sense of being because it can feel too challenging or threatening to be on their own; they substitute another person's agenda for their own because it feels more comfortable to stand or be through another. These Nines may not even realize they have made this substitution, however; it often happens at a subconscious level.

Sexual Nines are not connected to their own passion for living (in the good sense of the term "passion"), and so they try to locate it by blending with another person. When they are in close relationships, they may have the sense that there are no boundaries between their experience and that of important others. The merging with the other takes the form of an energetic taking on of feelings, attitudes, beliefs, and even behavior. These Nines feel a sense of loneliness or abandonment that seems like it can only be filled by another person, whether or not they realize it consciously.

The problem inherent in this stance, of course, is that true union—a real relationship between two people—requires that both people stand on their own feet before coming to meet each other. But Sexual Nines may experience difficulty in standing on their own two feet, being grounded in themselves, and living out their own sense of purpose, so they look for it in another person.

Individuals with this subtype can merge with a partner, a parent, a close friend, or any important person as a way of finding a life purpose and avoiding their own experience of the lack of such purpose. They have a sense of uncertainty about their own identity and a lack of structure in their lives, and they look to other people to satisfy their sense of who they are and what they want without realizing that this is happening.

Sexual Nines tend to be very kind, gentle, tender, and sweet. They are the least assertive of the Nines. However, the tenderness they express, like other gestures of caring that come from the personality rather than the real self, can be, to one extent or another, false. More than the other two Nine subtypes, these Nines can have a difficult time locating their own motivation to act in support of their own initiatives. They can even know they want to do something and not be able to do it for a long time, especially if it involves any kind of conflict with others.

Sexual Nines defend against the pain of early separation (and separations in general) by unconsciously denying the existence of boundaries. This is an attempt to avoid being aware of their own deeper sense of isolation, aloneness, and individuality.[17] This Nine may have the sense that "I am when with the other." In maintaining the important connections in their lives, they may be so focused on meeting the needs of others that they betray their own needs. When this occurs, they may engage in passive-aggressive forms of rebellion, such as avoiding someone or ignoring something important in a way that affects the relationship.

Sexual Nines can resemble Type Fours, as they may feel a sense of melancholy and experience and express similar themes and feelings related to relationships. Having their center of gravity in others means they have a special sensitivity to the wishes and moods of the important people in their lives and an acute awareness of the push-pull connection and disconnection dynamics in a relationship. However, while Fours are self-referencing, Sexual Nines are primarily other-referencing, and they may take on the feelings of another as opposed to having more immediate awareness of their own emotional ups and downs, as Fours do.

Sexual Nines may also share central concerns with Type Twos in that they can lack a solid sense of self and then look to their important relationships as a way to find self-definition or a sense of identity. Twos differ from these Nines, however, in that they focus more attention on constructing an image. Twos also usually enjoy being the center of attention, while this is much less comfortable for Sexual Nines.

Cynthia, a Sexual Nine, speaks:

My experience of the Passion of Sloth has felt less like laziness and more like an incapacity: a sense of being unable to go inside and connect with a deeper aspect of myself. In fact, I always had a fear of connecting with my deeper sense of self, or, more accurately, a fear of discovering that there was actually nothing there. My sense of security comes from a feeling of being connected to a special other—first and longest, to my mother, who had no problem telling me who I was or who I should be, what I should think or feel, and who didn't leave much space for me to come to that on my own. It wasn't that she was domineering—it was more that I was so exquisitely attuned to her that the merest flicker of disapproval might threaten the connection I felt to her.

If I ever lost my connection to my mother I felt anxiety related to a sense of not knowing what I wanted or needed. In retrospect, I can recognize that my anxiety reflected a fear that she would abandon me if I wanted or did something she disapproved of. Connection to her, and the protection that merger with her offered, ensured that I wouldn't experience the terrible feeling of being out of harmony. The feelings I had if I was ever not connected to her—anger, rage, or the pain of rejection caused by disobedience—were so awful that I don't remember even allowing myself to be aware of them past the age of three or four.

As I grew older, I learned that I could substitute the connection to my mother with the connection to a best friend or partner. If I were in the company of someone who was willing to make decisions, take the lead, or tell me what to do or how to be, I could relax and go along. I was always anxious about disrupting that connection, and I was typically agreeable and easygoing in order to ensure it, to such an extent that I often couldn't locate my own opinion at all if it differed from that of my special other. I've always said that if you need someone to run your errands with you, I'm your girl. In adolescence, I developed a strong feeling of self-rejection: I didn't feel that I really had a personality and envied those who did. Of course, once I was certain of the merger with my special other, I could also find my sense of rebellion: being told who or how to be would sometimes rub me wrong and I could react in a passive-aggressive way that was out of character with my usually sweet nature. In its worst form this looked like cheating on romantic partners or acting out in ways that were so split off I didn't even recognize myself.

Fortunately, my life circumstances have been such that I was unable to completely lose myself in a merger with a partner. In reaction to a disastrously controlling early relationship, I unconsciously chose men who were so emotionally distant that they didn't take over my soul, even though I thought I wanted them to. This has forced me to develop a strong sense of self and a clear sense of purpose, whereas I think if I'd had a partner I would have remained lost and aimless, still wanting to be directed.

Over the years, I have learned how to be with myself in deeper and deeper ways, and in midlife I actually enjoy being on my own, treasure my meditation practice, and have a wonderful community. I occasionally still long for another to tell me what to do, but typically only regarding small decisions. My sense of who I am, both positive and negative, is clearer than it's ever been, and I trust that my personality indeed exists and is even visible to others. My early experiences have resulted in a finely honed intuition and the ability to empathize with and attune to others quite deeply; to see from multiple perspectives at once, but also to locate my own feelings and opinions and trust that my relationships can withstand differences of opinion. I am aware, however, that even though I have made great strides in independence and my capacity to be alone, there are many things I haven't attempted in life (i.e., travel abroad or buying a home) without a special other by my side to lend me courage.

"The Work" for Type Nine: Charting a Personal Growth Path

ULTIMATELY, AS NINES WORK ON THEMSELVES and become more self-aware, they learn to escape the trap of creating discomfort and disharmony by erasing themselves in an attempt to create peace and harmony. By creating a stronger connection to their own inner world, asserting their needs and wants, and acting more powerfully on their own behalf, they can avoid their tendency to overadjust to others to the point of forgetting themselves completely.

For all of us, waking up to habitual personality patterns involves making ongoing, conscious efforts to observe ourselves, reflect on the meaning and sources of what we observe, and actively work to counter automatic tendencies. For Nines, this process involves observing the way they go to sleep to their own depths in order to get along with others; exploring the ways they seek to stay comfortable and avoid their own feelings and desires; and making active efforts to connect with themselves as much as they endeavor to stay connected to others. It is particularly important for them to learn to access their desires, manifest their own power, and act on their own behalf.

In this section I offer some ideas about what Nines can notice, explore, and aim for in their efforts to grow beyond the constraints of their personality and embody the higher possibilities associated with their type and subtype.

Self-Observation: Dis-Identifying from Your Personality by Watching It in Action

Self-observation is about creating enough internal space to really see—with fresh eyes and adequate distance—what you are thinking, feeling, and doing in your everyday life. As Nines take note of the things they think, feel, and do, they might look out for the following key patterns:

Forgetting yourself to more easily go along with the wishes and wills of others

Observe what happens when you or someone else asks you what you want. If you don't know, note what it's like not to know and how you feel when you look for a preference and can't find one. Tune in to what's going on when you do have a priority and you distract yourself with less important matters. Look out for ways you engage in passive-aggressive behavior and note any clues to what you might be angry or upset about. Observe any activities you engage in that help you go to sleep to yourself.

Avoiding and diffusing conflict as a way of staying comfortable and denying separation

Observe all the ways in which you seek to diffuse tension, mediate conflict, and avoid disharmony. What kinds of things to you do? How do you feel when conflict threatens? Observe what kinds of things make you feel uncomfortable and watch what you do to try to stay comfortable.

Getting stuck in inertia with regard to your own priorities

Observe what happens when you need to act on something and you don't. How are you distracting yourself? What are you avoiding? Note what happens inside you when you have a decision to make. What do you get out of staying on the fence and not deciding? Note what happens when change happens or might happen, and any reactions you have.

Self-Inquiry and Self-Reflection: Gathering More Data to Expand Your Self-Knowledge

As Nines observe these and other related patterns in themselves, the next step on the Enneagram growth path is to *understand* these patterns more. Why do they exist? Where do they come from? What purpose do they serve? How do they get you in trouble when they are intended to help you? Often, seeing the root causes of a habit—why it exists and what it is designed to do—is enough to allow you to break out of the pattern. In other cases, with more entrenched habits, knowing how and why they operate as defenses can be a first step to eventually being able to release them.

Here are some questions that Nines can ask themselves, and some possible answers they can consider, to get more insight into the sources, operation, and consequences of these patterns:

How and why did these patterns develop? How do these habits help Type Nines cope?

Through understanding the sources of their defensive patterns and how they operate as coping strategies, Nines have the opportunity to become more aware of how and why they go to sleep to themselves as a way to avoid uncomfortable or painful experiences. If Nines can tell the story of their early life and look for ways that tuning out their inner experience helped them in specific ways—perhaps to avoid particular feelings or experiences related to separation or not being heard and valued—they can have more compassion for themselves and recognize how their coping strategies operate. These insights into why Nines fell asleep in the first place and how this works as a protection can help them see how these defenses have ensured their psychological survival, but also how they've kept them trapped in their "acorn-self" by cutting them off from the aliveness and creativity of their true (oak tree) Self.

What painful emotions are the Type Nine patterns designed to protect me from?

For all of us, the personality operates to protect us from painful emotions, including what psychological theorist Karen Horney calls our "basic anxiety"—a preoccupation with the emotional stress of not getting basic needs fulfilled. Nines adopt a strategy that allows them to dissociate from painful emotions so that they don't exist anymore. Difficult feelings related to not being supported and recognized, or not feeling connected or included, can conveniently be forgotten. This potentially false sense of comfort comes at a high price, however: the disconnection from your internal life. If Nines can work to discover what feelings they habitually avoid as part of their pattern of overadjusting to others and under-attending to themselves, they can make more conscious decisions about whether they want to remain asleep or wake up to more of who they really are.

Why am I doing this? How do the Type Nine patterns operate in me now?

Through reflecting on how these patterns operate, the three kinds of Nines can begin to have a greater awareness of how their defensive patterns happen in everyday life—and in the present moment. If they can consciously catch themselves in the act of distracting themselves from themselves, or neglecting their internal world of desires and emotions, they can wake up to the deeper motivations that drive them to forget themselves in order to flow with others. It can be eye-opening for Nines to see how they actively *don't* make an effort to get what they want. They may not realize that, as William James famously said, "when you have a choice to make and you don't make it, that is in itself a choice." By understanding when they give up and why, how they have difficulty knowing what they want and why, and how they fail to stand up for themselves and why, they can create the basis for the motivation necessary to reverse these patterns if they choose to.

What are the blind spots of these patterns? What do Type Nines keep themselves from seeing?

To really increase their self-knowledge, it will be important for Nines to remind themselves about what they *don't* see when their personality programming is driving the show. Nines can be compulsively unselfish, so they habitually don't pay attention to their own needs, wants, and priorities—their own agendas. If your own desires aren't on your radar screen, it makes it hard to take care of yourself and get what you want. If you have a blind spot where your anger, passion, and power would normally be, how can you stand up for yourself or make your mark in the world? If you go to sleep to your anger, what happens to it? You may be acting out your anger in passive-aggressive or active-explosive ways that undermine you. In the process of neglecting themselves, Nines fail to own their positive qualities and their ability to impact others more powerfully in positive ways. Focusing on looking for what you don't see may help you get out of the habit of taking yourself for granted and putting others way ahead of yourself.

What are the effects or consequences of these patterns? How do they trap me?

The irony of the Nine strategy is that by trying to stay connected to others by blending with their agendas, they neuter their relationships. By not being more known to yourself, you can't make yourself more known to the people who like and love you. By not knowing and saying what you want, you might not get what you want from the people you are connected to, which limits the quality of those connections and leaves you feeling empty and dissatisfied. By not recognizing your naturally occurring anger, you may be acting it out through passive forms of resistance that don't serve you and infuriate others. By not valuing yourself enough to do the work of building a stronger connection to your inner world, you also invite others devalue you.

Self-Development:
Aiming for a Higher State of Consciousness

For all of us who seek to wake up, the next step in working with type-based knowledge of the personality is to begin to inject more conscious effort into everything we do—to begin to think, feel, and act with more choice and awareness. In this section I provide some ideas for Nines about "what to do" after they've observed their key patterns and done some investigation into their sources, operation, and consequences.

This last section is divided into three parts, each corresponding to one of three distinct growth processes connected with the Enneagram system: 1) "what to do" to actively counter the automatic patterns of your core type described above in the "self-observation" section, 2) how to use the Enneagram's Inner Flow arrow lines as a map of growth, and 3) how to study your passion (or "Vice") and consciously seek to embody its opposite: the antidote, the higher "Virtue" of the type.

The Three Main Type Nine Personality Patterns: "What to Do" to Address Them

Forgetting yourself to more easily go along with the wishes and wills of others

Practice "remembering yourself." One of the first things Gurdjieff tells us all to do when we embark on a course of conscious self-work is to try to "remember ourselves" all the time. This means tuning into yourself, feeling yourself, and being conscious of yourself in the moment. We all need to learn to remember ourselves; but for Nines, who are the prototype personality of the way we fall asleep to ourselves, it is especially important to pay close attention to what you are thinking, feeling, and doing in an ongoing, mindful way. Self-remembering is the antidote for self-forgetting.

Ask yourself what you want (and ask others to ask you too). Make it a practice to ask yourself what you want on a regular basis. At first, it may be discouraging, because you probably won't know some (or much) of the time. But if you continue to ask yourself what you want with the intention of finding out, at some point you will start getting regular answers. I once worked with a couple, one partner of which was a Type Nine. At one point he told his partner that it really helped him when she asked him what he wanted. Encouraging others to ask you what you want energetically invites you to assume that you do know what you want (and you want others to recognize you have preferences), even if you need some time to get in touch with your "internal compass."

Fake it until you make it. If you don't know what you want, try making things up. When I'm working with psychotherapy clients who have a hard time accessing their inner knowledge, I ask them to take a guess or make something up. And guess what? They often make an excellent "guess" that helps them tap into their inner truth. So start believing that, somewhere inside, you know what you want, and just take a stab at it. Over time you will develop a clearer channel to that part of you that does know what you want and need.

Avoiding and diffusing conflict as a way of staying comfortable and denying separation

Reframe conflict as a good thing that brings you closer to people. Lean on your Eight wing and recognize that fighting with people can be a good way to get to know each other, learn to trust one another, and resolve differences in a way that strengthens connections. Learn to enjoy expressing what you think.

Work to get in touch with your anger and be more direct. Maintaining a sense of comfort by avoiding your emotions involves denying or neglecting an important part of who you are. Your anger is connected to your power and your passion for living. Remind yourself that experiencing your anger doesn't mean you have to express it—but if you can tap into it more, you can work on being more direct about what you want and how you feel, which will improve your relationships, not damage them. People appreciate directness. And when you go along to get along and later realize you didn't want to go along at all, surfacing your disagreement at that point can cause more problems than it would have if you were direct at the beginning.

Take baby steps toward conflict by practicing giving and receiving feedback. My Nine friend, Matt, says that for Nines, feedback *is* conflict. So practice giving feedback to people you trust—and let yourself start with something really small and work up from there. Work on owning your power and reminding yourself that you have the strength and the steadiness to handle whatever comes—and that conflict (or feedback) does *not* automatically lead to separation.

Getting stuck in inertia with regard to your own priorities

Remind yourself that staying comfortable leads to discomfort. Maintaining a sense of comfort often involves denying practical realities that will eventually cause major discomfort. Be positive and proactive and coach yourself through change by thinking through to the likely end of what will happen if you stay on the fence and resist the natural flow of evolution in your life. Ask for support from others in brainstorming about what you might want to do as a way of unearthing and examining the possibilities—without letting them tell you what to do. Challenge your avoidance by gently reminding yourself that not choosing is actually a choice, and by thinking about the likely consequences of inaction as well as action. Allow yourself to imagine or fantasize about positive outcomes. Remind yourself that you can have what you want, but you have to act (however slowly) to make it happen.

The Inner Flow for Type Nine: Using the Arrow Lines to Chart Your Growth Path

In Chapter 1, I introduced an Inner Flow model of the arrow lines that define one dimension of the dynamic movement within the Enneagram framework. The connections and flow between each core Type, its "growth-(through)-stress," or "stress-growth" point, and its "child-heart-(security)" point, or "child-heart" point, map one kind of growth path described by the symbol. As a reminder, the arrow lines can be seen to suggest one kind of growth path for each type:

- The direction from the core point along the arrow is the path of development. The "stress-growth" point ahead represents specific challenges the nature of our core point personality places in front of us.
- The direction against the arrow from the core point to the "child-heart" point indicates issues and themes from childhood that must be consciously acknowledged and owned so that we can move forward and not be held back by unfinished business from the past. This "child–heart" point represents qualities of security we have unconsciously repressed, occasionally return to in times of stress or security, and which must be reintroduced consciously in support of moving forward along the arrow lines.

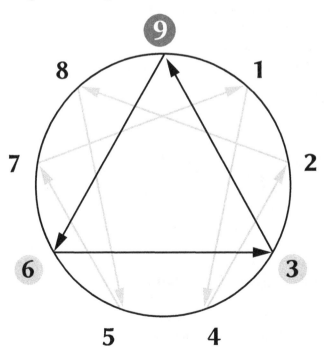

Type Nine Moving Forward to Type Six: Consciously Using the Six "Growth–Stress" Point for Development and Expansion

The Inner Flow growth path for Type Nines brings them into direct contact with the challenges embodied in Type Six: allowing for a clearer perception of fears, anxieties, thoughts, and feelings about what might go wrong as a way to motivate action and mobilize the inner resources of faith and courage. Not surprisingly, Nines can find the anxiety and sense of threat they might feel as they move to Six to be uncomfortable. But these feelings (experienced consciously and managed mindfully) can help move Nines out of inertia and stimulate them to action in support of themselves. This shift may involve a greater sense of urgency about tapping into real desires, as well as genuine capacities for taking action to handle problems and deal with threats to their well-being. As inaction and staying comfortable can, in the extreme, represent real threats to Nines' safety and well-being, moving to Six can help Nines find reasons to act on their own behalf.

The Nine working consciously in this way can make ready use of the tools healthy Type Sixes themselves use: analytical skills and proactive activity in support of self-protection. The Six stance has a basis in intuiting and tuning in to threats to the self and maintaining an alertness to security concerns, which can serve to balance out Nines' focus on staying comfortable and distracting themselves with inessentials. The mental activity of vigilance and critical analysis natural to the Six helps Nines to go into their heads to more purposefully analyze what is going on in their lives and how they may be forgetting themselves in ways that undermine their security. The intuitive ability of Sixes also helps Nines develop more active ways to access what is going on inside them.

Type Nine Moving Back to Type Three: Consciously Using the "Child–Heart" Point to Work through Early Issues and Find Security in Support of Moving Forward

The path of growth for Type Nines calls for them to reclaim their ability to actively "do" to further their own goals. Nines' early impulses to accomplish things and set their own course of action may not have been seen and supported in childhood, which likely motivated the adoption of a survival strategy oriented to going along with others rather than staying focused on their goals and ambitions. Nines may have felt that as children they had to decide between their own needs and wants and those of important others, and so going along with others and muting their own goals may have been something they did to cope.

When there isn't very much awareness around the move to Three, it can occur as an anxious and confused sense of "doing" in response to extreme situations of not having done enough. Navigated consciously, however, a Nine can use "the move to Three" developmentally to reestablish a healthy balance between supporting and attuning to others and doing what it takes to further their own achievements. Nines can focus on the qualities of this "child–security" point to understand what they may have needed to go to sleep to in themselves in the past to get along in the world. "Moving back to Three" can thus be a way of re-engaging with their lost sense of initiative and self-interested action. For this reason, it can be both a move toward a sense of security and a way to embrace and reintegrate something that had to be avoided early on, such that Nines can free themselves up to move forward on their growth path toward the Six Point.

By reincorporating Type Three qualities, Nines can consciously remind themselves that it's okay to want some attention for themselves and that it's important to value themselves and their accomplishments. Instead of quietly avoiding things and resisting others' demands by disappearing, Nines can seek to embody the high side of Three and spark themselves to act in positive ways to reach specific goals by thinking more about how they appear to others. In this way, Nines can use their Three child-security point as a way of reclaiming their inner doer, and balance out their talent for deeply understanding the perspectives of others with a deeper understanding of their own desire for productivity and effectiveness for their own sake.

The Vice to Virtue Conversion:
Accessing Sloth/Laziness and Aiming for Right Action

The developmental path from Vice to Virtue is one of the central contributions of the Enneagram map in highlighting a usable "vertical" path of growth to a higher state of awareness for each type. In the case of Type Nine, the Vice (or passion) of the type is laziness (or sloth), and its opposite, the Virtue, is *right action*. The theory of growth communicated by this "Vice to Virtue conversion" is that the more we can be aware of how our passion functions and can consciously work toward the embodiment of our higher Virtue, the more we can free ourselves from the unconscious habits and fixated patterns of our type and evolve toward our "higher" side or "oak tree–Self."

As Nines become more familiar with their experience of laziness and develop the ability to make it more conscious, they can take their work further by making efforts to focus on enacting their Virtue, the "antidote" to the passion of laziness. In the case of Type Nine, the Virtue of right action represents a state of being that Nines can attain through consciously manifesting their higher capacities.

Right action is a way of being that is awake and engaged and fully present to our natural impulses to know and move toward what we want and need. This higher Virtue encompasses both the ability to actively wake up by witnessing our inner life in an ongoing way and a purposeful focus on our most important desires and priorities. Right action means you can continually remember yourself instead of habitually forgetting yourself, and that you can wake yourself up and get yourself moving when you have fallen asleep. It also means you can more regularly access your own center of gravity and act powerfully and decisively in the world.

Embodying right action as a Nine means you have examined and worked on being more aware of your unconscious tendency to fall asleep to your own depths to the point where you can regularly catch yourself in the act of tuning yourself out and merging with something outside yourself. Achieving right action means you have easy access to your gut, which allows you to come from the seat of your own power and act in conscious ways in the world. We all naturally go up and down along a vertical dimension of this Vice to Virtue continuum—we rise to higher levels of functioning as we work on ourselves, but because it's difficult to stay awake, we also slip back in times of stress. If you are a Nine, consciously aiming to embody right action opens you up to a greater awareness of your self, such that your own natural impulses can spur you to act on your own behalf and in service of a higher good based on your own unique experience. By focusing on right action, Nines can strengthen their conscious ability to manifest their desires in the world as an active contribution to their own happiness and that of others.

When Nines can do the "Vice to Virtue" work of noticing how they tune out the inner voices calling them home in the Homerian sense, they can wake up to their own feelings, instincts, and desires and model for all of us how to strengthen the inner observer in a way that leads us to a more conscious participation in the life of our community.

Specific Work for the Three Type Nine Subtypes on the Path from Vice to Virtue

The path from observing your passion to finding its antidote is not exactly the same for each of the subtypes. The path of conscious self-work has been characterized in terms of "grit, grind, and grace:"[18] the "grit" of our personality habits, the "grind" of our efforts to grow, and the "grace" that comes to us when we strive to be more aware of ourselves, to develop ourselves, and work toward our virtues in positive and healthy ways. According to Naranjo, each subtype has to grind, or exert effort, against something slightly different. This insight is one of the great benefits of understanding the three distinct subtypes of each of the nine types.

Self-Preservation Nines can travel the path from laziness to right action by making conscious contact with their anger more often and being more proactive in thinking through, tapping into, and acting from their own self-interest. Feeling and working with your anger instead of avoiding it can help you connect more thoroughly with your passion and your power; and if you have more awareness of your anger you can connect to an inner sense of strength and fortitude that will help you work to get what you want instead of giving up on it and losing yourself. If you can go for what you want in more direct ways, you can fulfill your deeper desires and bolster your inner sense of being instead of distracting yourself from its absence. Being more directly in touch with your power and passion also allows you to open up more to being loved and having the kind of connections that nurture you instead of the pseudo-connections you normally satisfy yourself with because your "acorn-self" thinks they're all you can get. Instead of the empty calories of your comfortable activities and your enmeshed relationships, allow yourself to feed your appetite for love and presence by accessing your emotions, taking in real love, and making more conscious connections.

Social Nines can travel the path from laziness to right action by getting in touch with any sadness that underlies their upbeat, congenial demeanor and identifying the ways in which their hard work for groups might distract them from their own personal evolution. If you are a Social Nine it will be important for you to slow down and take the risk of sharing more of yourself with others, especially your deeper needs, wants, and feelings. Right action means knowing what's going on in your depths and not being afraid to surface any sadness, anger, or discomfort so that you can allow yourself to be moved by your own personal motives instead of your desire to support others. Stop hiding what is going on inside you as a way of staying comfortable and work to further your own interests as much as you work to further the needs of your family or community. Notice any fear of abandonment, conflict, or loss of peace you may feel, and allow yourself to be with those feelings as a way of loving and supporting yourself. Own the ways in which you *are* part of the group and take in how much people value your hard work and support as a way of actively addressing your deeper needs for belonging.

Sexual Nines can travel the path from laziness to right action by recognizing and acting on their deeper need for separation: making time to be alone more and not always finding a sense of "being" through others. Recognize the ways you may have inadvertently erased yourself to maintain specific relationships and take action to create healthy boundaries with those you are closest to. Notice when you are not "in" yourself. Act to find your own sense of purpose and your own experience of being, and notice how blending with others actually prevents authentic relationships. Fusion mimics real connection, but is in the end only a substitute or a mirage, because it means that you have given yourself up and overadapted to other people. Engage in right action by doing the work it takes to get in touch with your own needs, desires, experiences, and emotions—and, most of all, your own sense of purpose. Make a point of noting ways in which you might differ from important others, and take the risk to voice these differences as a way of affirming who you are as a separate individual. Build relationships from the starting point of your own preferences and aspirations as a way to establish more regular contact with your "true self" and you will create more satisfying relationships in which you can fully be who you are and still feel loved and accepted.

Conclusion

THE NINE POINT REPRESENTS the way we fall asleep to ourselves in order to cope with a world that seems to require us to erase our own sense of being in order to peacefully coexist with others. The Nine path of growth shows us how to transform our inner laziness and the universal tendency to fall asleep to our present experience into the energy and sense of purpose required to wake up to who we are and who we can be. In each of the Type Nine subtypes, we see a specific character who teaches us what is possible when we turn psycho-spiritual inertia into a fully awake ability to further our own evolution through the alchemy of self-observation, self-development, and self-knowledge.

CHAPTER 4

The Point Eight Archetype:
The Type, Subtypes, and Growth Path

True friends stab you in the front.

—Oscar Wilde

TYPE EIGHT REPRESENTS THE ARCHETYPE of the person who denies weakness and vulnerability by taking refuge in fearlessness, power, and strength. This archetype tends to express instinctual drives in a less inhibited way and to push back on whatever might restrict them. A personality with this archetype focuses on asserting control in big ways through an "expansive solution" characterized by domination and intensity. This approach entails identification with a glorified self (rather than a diminished sense of self).[1]

The shades of this archetype exist in similar form in Freud's concepts of the "id" and with his and Jung's ideas about "libido." These concepts seek to describe the energetic force behind the central human instinctual drives—the forceful energy or momentum that moves us to get our animal needs met undeterred. The Type Eight archetype represents a "desire or impulse which is unchecked by any kind of authority." It is "libido [psychic energy] in its natural state" and "the instinctual ground from which our consciousness springs."[2]

Freud saw the id as the part of our psyche that represents "the repository of the instinctual drives, sexual and aggressive."[3] The id operates on the pleasure principle, "demanding satisfaction of drives without delay."[4] The Eight archetype thus conveys the intense drive energy within the dynamic system of the human psyche. The id is the basis of sexual energy in particular, but it is also the desire or charge or energy that motivates all action to get instinctual needs met.

Naranjo points out, however, that while the Eight archetype "would seem a more instinctive manner of being, as in the Freudian conception of an id-centered character," this assumption is not exactly the case, because the Eight personality is "an ego that *sides* with instinct" rather than the expression of instinct itself.[5] "More than id-driven," Naranjo explains, this personality stands against the super-ego; it opposes the part of the psyche that represents the "inner censor" and enforces "the standards and prohibitions of our parents and society."[6]

Pure natural freedom and spontaneity in instinctual movement is a characteristic of the higher Self, but instead the Eight personality expresses an "acorn self" lookalike: an automatic ego reaction opposing any limitations on their instinctual drives. This auto-rebellion against the rules of society or established authority (like those expressed by the Type One archetype) is not free and spontaneous. Naranjo clarifies that this archetype's basis in "counter-repression" and always siding with and defending desires can, in a paradoxical way, make Type Eight rigidly intolerant of constraints. In this way, an excess of libidinal/instinctual drive energy leads Type Eight to excessively crave and drive toward sensate experience. Just as Type One represents the "anti-instinctual" force within the human personality, Type Eight represents the "pro-instinctual" force inside all of us.

In addition to this human drive, the Eight archetype also represents an aspect of the masculine principle, or the *animus*. Just as the Type Two archetype embodies a version of "the inner feminine" principle, the Type Eight archetype communicates the archetypal idea of "the masculine" in women and in men. Naranjo points out that we can see elements of this masculine archetype in Western culture's focus on rationality and taking action, its devaluation of softer emotions, and our prevalent ways of becoming desensitized to violence.[7]

Type Eights are thus the prototype for that tendency in all of us to feel the need to "get big" and take the most direct route to getting what we need by pushing back on internal and external forces that seek to restrain our instinctual impulses. As Enneagram scholar Sandra Maitri puts it, the Eight archetype represents our identification "with the body and with its drives and biological imperatives."[8] Just as the Three archetype represents the way we all take on a personality and the Four archetype highlights the universal presence of the Shadow, the Eight archetype channels the energetic momentum of our animal drives to fulfill our need to thrive and multiply.

The Type Eight personality is lusty, intense, energetic, and powerful. This "under-social" stance motivates rebellion against the restrictive authority of established authorities, rules and conventions. The Type Eight habit of mind motivates them to go up against external power and limitations both as a way of asserting their control and as a way of combating oppression and protecting the weak. This archetype is strong in people who believe in "taking justice into their own hands, rather than delegating to institutions."[9]

The Eight archetype also represents the ways in which we all deny our weakness or smallness and imagine ourselves as powerful enough to do whatever we need to do for ourselves or for others. We all share a tendency to ignore inner and outer constraints when satisfying our needs or defending ourselves becomes urgent enough.

In the Enneagram framework, people with the Type Eight personality are strong, powerful, and fearless. They tend to be very concerned with justice and protective of the oppressed and the needy and can be fair, just, and authoritative. Eights are usually refreshingly direct in their communication and intolerant of "bullshit." They value the truth, and they can confront others and engage in constructive conflict when necessary. Having natural leadership ability, they tend to be honest, straightforward, and effective when it comes to getting things done and making things happen. Eights tend to be fun, generous, and intense, and this combination can make them great friends and exciting companions. They are good "big-picture" thinkers, hard workers, and passionate advocates for the people and causes they care about. They enjoy making order out of chaos and can bring a great deal of energy to bear in accomplishing important tasks in the world, but they may not observe appropriate limits and boundaries. In fact, the Eight "superpower" is superpower.

As with all the archetypal personalities, however, Type Eights' gifts and strengths also reflect their "fatal flaw" or "Achilles heel." Their strength and power often represents overcompensation for not wanting to feel weak or own their vulnerable feelings. Accordingly, Eights may judge themselves or others for having softer feelings or expressing any kind of vulnerability. And because they deny their vulnerability—and don't realize that true strength comes from being able to be vulnerable—they can overdo their forcefulness. Eights often fail to see the negative effects they create by expressing too much power without a balanced recognition of normal human weaknesses. They can be intense and fun-loving, but they may also be overbearing, impatient, and intolerant of frustration. However, when they can balance their personal power and strength with a more conscious awareness of their own weaknesses, vulnerabilities, and impact, they can be courageous (and even heroic) leaders, partners, and friends.

The Type Eight Archetype in Homer's *Odyssey:* The Cyclops

Type Eight characteristics, like autonomy, fearlessness, force, anger, and self-indulgence, could hardly find a more powerful embodiment than the Cyclops. The Cyclops occupy the second land that Odysseus and his comrades visit on their journey home from the Trojan War. The "high and mighty" Cyclops are "lawless brutes" without council or meeting hall. Each of them is "a law unto himself...not a care in the world for any neighbor."[10] The Cyclops "want what they want when they want it, and they take it. They don't suffer shame or guilt or reservations. They're not worried about what others think."[11]

The island these giant creatures inhabit is a land of natural abundance. It yields bumper crops and beautiful flocks of all kinds without tending, as if suffused with powerful natural energy. The Cyclops enjoy this abundance to the fullest—and guard it jealously.

Odysseus and his landing party encounter the Cyclops Polyphemus in his enormous and well-stocked lair. They ask for the mercy Zeus guarantees for any suppliant guest, but the Cyclops lets them know that his kind fears neither gods nor men:

> You must be a fool, stranger, or come from nowhere, telling *me* to fear the gods or avoid their wrath! We Cyclops never blink at Zeus and Zeus's shield of storm and thunder, or any other blessed god—we've got more force by far. I'd never spare you in fear of Zeus's hatred, you or your comrades here, unless I had the urge.[12]

To prove his point, Polyphemus begins eating Odysseus's crewmen one by one.

But Polyphemus knows only his power, not his vulnerability. His appetite and his natural limitations prove to be his undoing. Odysseus gives Polyphemus bowl after bowl of exquisite—and powerful—wine until he falls into a drunken sleep. The Greeks then blind the monster with a fire-hardened spike and escape the lair hidden beneath his lush, wooly sheep. For all his power, the Cyclops can only vent blind anger, casting boulders at the sea in his rage.

The Type Eight character represents the archetype of a lusty, going-for-what-you-want energy—a realization of personal power that supports an antisocial stance capable of breaking rules and rebelling against authority. This same personal power is also naturally self-indulgent and excessive. The Cyclops episode in *The Odyssey* shows how unrestrained appetite and anger can lead to a power—and a downfall—that is larger than life.

The Type Eight Personality Structure

EIGHTS BELONG TO THE BODY-BASED TRIAD, which is associated with the core emotion of anger and themes of power and control. These three types at the top of the Enneagram also habitually "forget themselves," especially with regard to their needs and vulnerabilities. Each of the three personalities in this triad, located around the core point of Type Nine, is shaped—at a basic level—by its relationship to anger and control. Nines underplay anger, exerting power passively through a quiet resistance to being controlled. Ones are in conflict with their anger: they think it's bad to be angry, so they repress it until it expresses as resentment. Ones exert control through adherence to rules, structure, and doing thing the "right" way. Eights, meanwhile, have easy access to angry energy, and they often overdo their anger. They often move impulsively to express their anger before giving themselves time to think. Regarding control, Eights deny their vulnerability and overcompensate by exerting power in direct ways to control what's happening.

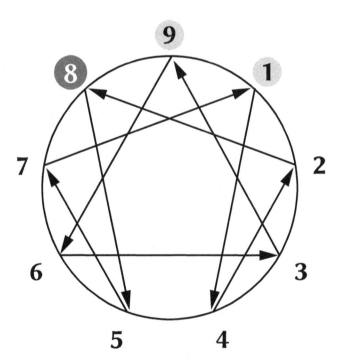

Eights naturally focus their attention on power and control: who has it and who doesn't, and how it's wielded. Other people usually perceive them as having a "big energy" and possessing a great deal of personal power and strength. It often surprises Eights when they get the feedback that others experience them as intimidating, as they usually don't intend to be scary. But their very presence communicates power and strength, so others often project a threatening sense onto them.

Eights also naturally have a lot of energy, and they tend to think in terms of the big picture or larger vision. Type Eight individuals like to move things forward in straightforward ways. They dislike having to pay attention to details or consider what other people want them to do. They are most comfortable when they are in control. They believe that the world is divided into "the strong" and "the weak," and given that choice, they identify with "the strong."

The Early Coping Strategy: Type Eight

Many Eights report having grown up in combative or conflict-heavy environments in which they had to grow up fast to survive. Most were unable to maintain a sense of childlike innocence because they were either deprived or not sufficiently protected as children—often in the face of some sort of violence or neglect. In many cases, the Eight was the youngest, smallest child in a big family. From the perspective of the Eight child, survival depended on denying the fact of being small. Taking on a persona that was bigger and more powerful helped them to deal with a world that did not provide needed love, care, or protection.

Type Eight individuals were thus typically forced to become forceful early on—to leave childhood behind prematurely and become tough in order to protect themselves and sometimes others. To get their needs met, many Eights had to take matters into their own hands and exert control over their environment at an early age. As Naranjo notes, "it is my impression that violence in the home [of an Eight] is more frequent than in the life histories of other characters, and in such cases it is easy to understand the development of insensitivity, toughening up, and cynicism."[13]

In circumstances like these, the Eight child develops a coping strategy based on being strong and taking control in whatever way it is possible to do so. The Eight coping strategy thus centers on the child's need to defensively deny their vulnerability and develop a belief in their invulnerability. As adults, Eights attempt to compensate for their helplessness in the face of the perceived injustices of their childhood by taking justice into their own hands and expressing power in the name of justice.[14]

The Eight personality's approach leads to an ability to automatically become "big" when they are presented with challenges, according to the idea that "the best defense is a good offense." This "bigness" leads to a personality style characterized by a large and impactful energetic presence (Eights often seem larger than they physically are), a big appetite for everything (food, drink, pleasure, sex), and excessive behavior (eating and drinking too much, staying out too late, working too hard).

Because Eights have an early need to feel powerful and so learn to deny their vulnerability, they often feel they can make their own rules and ignore limitations that others place on them. They tend to see reality in their own terms, unconsciously bending their perception of facts and confusing objective reality with their own personal sense of what's true. This stance goes along with having a strong will and a tendency to view themselves as the most powerful person around—they make the automatic assumption that the way they see things is the only way things can be seen.

With a coping style that relies on getting big and powerful to come up against people or difficult conditions, Eights can sometimes be perceived by others as bossy or controlling, though they often just consider themselves direct and honest. Through the development of their specific survival strategy, Eights become skilled at getting what they need and want and also at fighting injustice and protecting those they feel need their support. They pursue their aims through force, intimidation, or aggression. More so than other personalities, Eights are willing to confront or fight with others if they need to.

Eights' strategy of reducing awareness of their own vulnerability allows them to feel very powerful and even invincible. As "self-forgetting" types, they tend to minimize their own physical needs and natural human limitations. Doing so supports their stance of being able to take on a lot—to work very hard and bear the burden of many responsibilities—even when this is detrimental to their health and well-being.

As Naranjo points out, however, "the reverse side of the necessity for mastery is [the Eight's] dread of anything connoting helplessness; this is the most poignant dread he has."[15] This personality draws on power and the will to dominate others as key components in their "offense as defense" approach to life. There is also, as psychologist Karen Horney suggests, an intense need for "vindictive triumph," especially when they feel they've been wronged by someone. Ichazo called this personality "Ego-Venge" to reflect the feelings of vengefulness an Eight can feel as a result of the early need to be able to fight back. Naranjo cites a potent combination of "powerful impulses and insufficient checks" as the force behind the Eight's need for vengeance—but certainly also a lack of contact with inner weakness (and perhaps the vague memory of it) also plays a role.

Amelia, a Type Eight, describes her childhood situation and the development of her coping strategy:

My parents were powerful and charismatic. My father (a Type Seven) considered all "societal rules" irrelevant. He did whatever he wanted and considered himself God. My mother (a Type Four) was drawn to high society living, yet very bitter about my father's sometimes atrocious behaviour. This resulted in many years of very cruel verbal altercations between my parents at home, but never in public.

As they were always traveling, my older brother and I were frequently left with the nanny. My brother was considered the "heir" by my parents and our nanny worshiped him. Although she definitely took care of my very basic needs, I was considered "extra" work and was removed from the house so she could spend more time with my brother. For an example, as a baby, I was placed in a pram and pushed to the end of the garden and left for many hours—and often forgotten. When we were very young children, my brother became a bully and I became his punching bag. I used to do all his chores around the house rather than be painfully beaten, and I was called his "secret servant" by the adults. So from very early on, this situation in which my parents were either absent or constantly fighting and a brother who was favored and allowed to behave badly led me to believe that life was unfair and that I needed to be strong if I was going to survive. My vulnerability and innocence were not attended to or nurtured but on some level I must have understood this as when sent to boarding school at seven years old, I immediately started protecting and looking after those younger and more vulnerable than I.

Even now, as I remember this, I can feel it physically in my body: my jaw is clenching at the thought of the injustice of it and I am infused energetically with a kind of battle armour. It's as if even now, in this moment, I am reacting to the unfairness. I can also observe how I am writing my story in such a direct way. There is little space—then or even now—for my heart to be open to innocence and vulnerability, as I still want to protect the truth of the sweet, tender, and very sensitive child that I was—and in some ways still am. However today, I have a deeper and more appreciative understanding of why that little girl inside of me chose what she considered necessary at that very young age—to be tough and strong!

The Main Type Eight Defense Mechanism: Denial

The main psychological defense mechanism used by Eights is *denial*, especially when it comes to the need to appear strong and hide vulnerability. In order to give themselves a feeling that they can take on any challenge, Eights habitually deny any vulnerabilities they might have. After all, it can be difficult or even impossible to be strong and win the fight if you are preoccupied with your weak points or vulnerabilities. If you can totally deny that you have any weaknesses, you can experience yourself as invulnerable—and having confidence that you can't be hurt is a good feeling to have in trying to win a battle, dominate a situation, or survive difficult circumstances.

Psychologist Nancy McWilliams defines denial by explaining that one way young children handle unpleasant experiences is "to refuse to accept that they are happening."[16] In this way, inconvenient or painful truths can simply be denied and made false. Denial can be understood by anyone who has experienced a catastrophe of some kind, like the death of a loved one. The first reaction a person usually has upon hearing this kind of extreme bad news is "it can't have happened" or "it didn't happen."

Another common defense mechanism associated with Type Eight is *omnipotent control*. Omnipotent control occurs early on in a child's life when a child "makes things happen" by evoking her mother's responsiveness. When the child is hungry, she cries, and the mother brings her food. When she is scared, the mother comes to protect her. At this early point, the child's merger with the mother gives her the sense that she controls the world. Later in life, we can sometimes imagine that things can be made to be the way we want them to be through a combination of denial and confident self-assertion. Thus, Eights sometimes believe they can change the way things are simply by exerting control over them, defensively imagining that they can direct the course of events in whatever way they wish without being subject to the limitations imposed by reality.

The Type Eight Focus of Attention

The coping strategy of denying vulnerability and getting big and strong to deal with conflict and meet needs leads to a focus on power, control, and injustice. Most Eights are adept at coming into a new situation and assessing very quickly who has the power and who doesn't.

Perceiving these differences in power makes Eights highly attuned to situations in which people are being unjustly persecuted or those they care about are in need of protection. (This is especially true of Social Eights, which will be discussed further below.) Eights have a focus on protecting, in part, as a projection of their own denied vulnerability onto someone they feel protective and supportive toward. In this way, they can feel moved to action in response to their own unconscious needs for care without experiencing the pain of feeling vulnerable.

Eights want and need a lot of stimulation, so they can also pay a lot of attention to meeting their needs for pleasure and other forms of satisfaction. They can be intolerant of frustration, so they scan their environment for sources of fulfillment: interesting people, fun things to do, good things to eat and drink, and challenging situations to master. The passion of Type Eight is lust, which implies a strong drive for satisfaction of physical needs. This drive focuses Eights' attention on the fulfillment of their appetites.

Eights like to impose their authority and overcome resistance to their influence and strength. They are naturally drawn to people and situations that could well involve confrontation in order to right injustices, protect others, flush out bad actors, or wrest power from unjust authorities.

Finally, Eights tend to see the world in terms of a grand vision or a broad perspective of what is possible. Their big view of things matches their big energy and their larger-than-life sense of their own power and authority. Eights easily see the big picture and naturally want to create order out of disorder. They generally feel confident about both their vision of the way things are and their ability to make important things happen.

The Type Eight Emotional Passion: Lust

The passion of the Type Eight is *lust*. Naranjo defines lust as "a passion for excess, a passion that seeks intensity, not only through sex, but in all manner of stimulation: activity, anxiety, spices, high speed, the pleasure of loud music, and so on."[17] While lust is often associated mostly with sex, as Naranjo indicates, an Eight's lust is not limited to the realm of sex; rather, it suggests a hunger for many kinds of sensual stimulation and physical fulfillments. Eights have what is at times an insatiable desire for the satisfaction of their desires—and an unapologetic attitude toward the quest for pleasure.

The emotional passion of each Enneagram type constitutes a central focus or drive, and for Eights this often looks like a no-holds-barred approach to life and an intense pursuit of all kinds of pleasures: physical contact, good food, the breaking of taboos, material comforts, and the fruits of hard work. Sometimes this passion for excess attracts them to opportunities in which they can exert their strength and feel their power. Lust leads Eights to look for challenges to overcome and pleasures to enjoy. And lust can often cause Eights to overdo the things they do—to go to extremes. As Naranjo explains,

"Instead of being inhibited, instead of standing in the way of their desires… they side with their desires, they defend them."[18] Instead of repressing their impulses, they purposefully become an enemy of the inner repressor.

As Naranjo points out, the passion of lust, and the traits that signal it— like intensity, contactfulness, and a love of physical indulgences—are "intimately bound" to the core of the Type Eight personality structure and the sensory-motor physicality that undergirds lust. People who have both a primary connection to the body as the basis of their personality, and a central life strategy based on expressing and feeling their physical power, also naturally prioritize the lustful search for physical and sensual fulfillment. As Maitri explains, "perhaps the most complete way of understanding the meaning of lust as it is used in the map of the Enneagram is as an orientation excessively tipped toward the physical."[19]

Eights' lustful predisposition thus contributes to character traits such as "hedonism, the propensity to boredom when not sufficiently stimulated, the craving for excitement, impatience, and impulsiveness."[20] Lust drives Eights toward hedonism almost as the prize in the fight for the right to pleasure and satisfaction or the reward for many struggles of will and power. Thus, lust should be seen less as simply an overriding need for (especially physical) pleasures, and more as a passion for intensity and the right to be excessive.

The Type Eight Cognitive Mistake: "I'm as Strong and Invincible as I Think I Am" or "It's True Because I Said It"

We all get stuck in habitual ways of thinking that influence our beliefs, feelings, and actions, and these patterns continue even after the mental models that create our overall perspective aren't accurate anymore.[21] While the passion shapes the personality's emotional motivations, the "cognitive fixation" or mental "trance" preoccupies the personality's thought processes.

The core issue for Eights is control. The passion of lust and the mental outlook that supports it grow out of an early experience of being hurt by authorities who misused their power. In this situation, Eights' adaptive response is to overcompensate by becoming more powerful than everyone else as a way of assuring they will never be dominated again—and this means needing to have thoughts and assumptions that support their belief in their own strength and abilities.

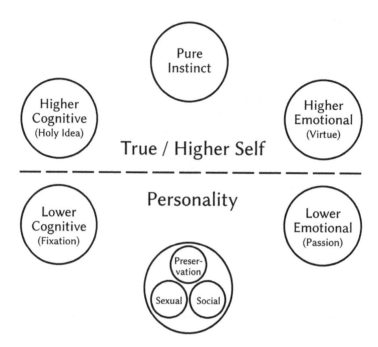

The core beliefs and mental patterns of thinking associated with the Eight mental stance (or "trance")—their need to see themselves as strong and in charge (and not weak)—often involve thoughts that reinforce their self-confidence and invincibility. This same fixation intellectually minimizes the importance of vulnerability and tenderness. Of course Eights want and need affection like everyone else, but they are willing to hold beliefs that reinforce their toughness and power and devalue or work against an acknowledgment of their need for the support of others.

Because their mindset is based on control, justice, and avoiding weakness, Eights may hold some or all of the following key beliefs and mental organizing principles:

- In a tough world, you need to be strong to survive.
- It's bad to be weak or vulnerable. Weak people are not worthy of respect.
- I am stronger and more powerful than other people.
- I can do whatever I want.
- No one can tell me what to do.
- Other people do not have the power to limit me in what I want and what I do.

- I'm not subject to the constraints others might want to put on me.
- I have the power to make things happen and do what I want.
- If some is good, more is better.
- Sometimes you need to break the rules—or make your own rules—to do what needs to be done.
- I work hard and play hard.
- It's not bad to be bad.
- Powerful people tend to take advantage of weaker individuals. I protect the people I care about.
- While I don't necessarily "like" conflict, I can confront others when I need to move forward, get what I want, protect someone, or combat an injustice.

These common Eight beliefs and recurring thoughts support a personality with a powerful, confident, and authoritative self-presentation. Eights develop their sense of their own authority and their independence from external authorities. When they adhere strongly to this mental stance—when they are "in the trance" of their type—it may be much harder for them to observe themselves, see a larger view of things, and "come home" to the deeper, more tender feelings that point the way to their true self.

The Type Eight Trap:
"Avoiding Vulnerability Leaves You Vulnerable"

As it does distinctly for each type, the cognitive fixation for Type Eight leads the personality in circles. It presents an inherent "trap" that the limitations of the personality cannot resolve.

The basic internal conflict for Eights is that while they are fundamentally motivated to deny their vulnerability and exercise control in the world, they may end up creating situations in which they make themselves more vulnerable by not taking their natural human limitations into account. Thus, if they neglect their own physical needs by working too hard and playing too much, they can become physically ill. If they strive to exercise power and control over specific situations, they may end up not being in control through a failure to see the value of diplomacy. Eights' neglect or denial of their own vulnerabilities does not prevent those vulnerabilities from having an influence. If we do not have some consciousness about our own weak points, they tend to impact situations as a direct result of being left unattended.

In the (usually unconscious) quest to avoid feeling helpless at all costs, Eights may go overboard, invoking hostility or misunderstandings by bringing too much power to bear. When Eights deny their own sensitivity, they are more likely to be insensitive to others, which invites others to react insensitively and creates a cycle of aggression.

So, while Eights seek to exert influence in the world through the exercise of their strength and determination, they can end up hurting their cause by overdoing it and inadvertently marshalling forces against themselves. A lack of empathy with the softer emotional side of life wards off deeper connections with others. The Eights' power can result in a negative cycle in which they cannot obtain the nurturing love they really need.

The Key Type Eight Traits

Anger and the Willingness to Confront

Of the three "anger types" at the top of the Enneagram, Eights, in contrast to Nines and Ones, usually have less resistance to confronting people, identifying their anger, and expressing aggressive feelings. Except for possibly the Sexual Four and the Sexual Six, Eights have more access to anger than any other type. They often describe anger as an experience of a strong energy. They are also among the types who are least intimidated by other people's anger. Eights can sometimes be stereotyped as "liking" conflict. However, most Eights will say that they don't necessarily "like" conflict, but can and will engage in it if necessary.

Paradoxically, because Eights can do anger and conflict, this willingness often means they don't have to. Eights are body types with a strong connection to their physical power center. They convey an aura of solidity and strength, which can often mean they don't have to get angry—they can hold their ground, get their way, or make themselves understood without having to express aggression. Eights' relative ease with communicating anger can make them seem fearless, which is true in the sense they are not primarily motivated by fear and habitually denying vulnerable feelings. This fearlessness makes Eights seem powerful and strong—even when they aren't saying anything at all.

When Eights do confront people, it is often in an effort (conscious or unconscious) to discover their true motives. Through conflict, Eights learn what others are made of, what their true intentions are, and how they will wield their power. Again contrary to common stereotypes, Eights don't necessarily "like" anger or conflicts, but they can move more easily into this space than other types and may even use conflict as a way to get closer to other people. Once an Eight has a conflict with you, depending on the outcome, it might mean they'll trust you more. And some Eights will say they can enjoy a good fight.

When Eights do communicate anger, they usually get over it quickly. The energy of anger is gone as soon at it's expressed, as if it's been discharged. Especially in contrast to other types, like Twos or Ones or Nines, after Eights express anger, they usually don't feel regretful or guilty. It simply happened, and now it's over.

Rebelliousness

In describing some of the main characteristics of Type Eight, Naranjo explains that "lust itself implies an element of rebellion in its assertive opposition to the inhibition of pleasure, rebellion stands out as a trait on its own, more prominent in ennea-type VIII than in any other character."[22]

The prototype of the revolutionary activist, Type Eights rebel in the sense that they don't easily acknowledge an authority above themselves. Their natural stance against the rules and conventions set down by authorities inevitably has a flavor of rebellion. As Naranjo explains: "It is in virtue of such blunt invalidation of authority that 'badness' automatically becomes the way to be."[23] And while Eights may get perceived as "bad" to the extent that they don't follow the rules and aren't afraid to go up against the conventional (hierarchical) way of doing things, Eights may or may not see themselves as openly or severely rebellious. They may simply take the position that they are not going to submit to the authority that others might want to have over them. Rather, they see themselves as their own authority and make or break rules as they see fit.

In psychological terms, as Naranjo points out, a generalized attitude of "rebellion against authority can usually be traced back to a rebellion in the face of the father,"[24] who is the archetypal carrier of authority in the family. Many Type Eight individuals have histories in which they learned not to expect anything good from their fathers, so they "implicitly come to regard parental power as illegitimate."[25] When you view the power of the most obvious authority as illegitimate, it is an easy step to assert your own authority as the highest or only authority.

Punitiveness/Revenge

Naranjo cites Ichazo as saying that Eights focus on revenge[26], but he clarifies this by explaining that Eights are not vindictive in an overt way. He states that an Eight individual more commonly "retaliates angrily at the moment and gets quickly over his irritation" and may experience a desire to "get even" as an immediate reaction.[27] In addition to this, Naranjo asserts that vengefulness in the Eight character is more of a deep-seated, long-term trait that motivates them to "take justice into their own hands" in response to the pain or impotence they may have felt as children.

When Eights get hurt by others they may not allow themselves to fully register the pain of that hurt; feeling pain might mean experiencing their vulnerability, which Eights automatically avoid. So, instead of feeling hurt, they may unconsciously act out their feelings by focusing on getting even for being hurt. By putting their focus and energy toward somehow getting revenge, Eights redirect their painful feelings into a show of strength or power—feelings that they are much more comfortable experiencing.

The tendency to want to take revenge on others who have hurt them is also connected to the Eight's central concern with justice. Eights often want to right wrongs committed by others, and their focus on justice and fairness can inspire vengeful feelings toward those they perceive as hurting or exploiting people they want to protect.

Dominance

Eights can dominate situations easily, whether they actively decide to or not. Through their coping strategy of automatically becoming strong and powerful, Eights typically hold a lot of power just by being there. Naturally assertive and ready to show aggression when necessary, they can energetically dominate others even without consciously meaning to.

While Eights like to be in control, they don't always assert their ability to control a situation that already has an acknowledged leader. If there is a vacuum of leadership, however, they are ready (if not compelled) to fill the void. Eights' tendency to dominate represents a compensatory maneuver designed to avoid finding themselves in a weak or undefended position. If you are geared toward avoiding vulnerable feelings, being ready and able to exert power and push back on someone who might inspire those feelings works well as a strategy.

Interestingly, because Eights exude strength, sometimes people around Eights will cede control to them, as many people are happy to have someone else bear the responsibility of taking charge. Alternatively, others may at times feel overpowered by Eights' natural strength and resent them for being pushy, bossy, or overbearing.

Insensitivity

Eights can be perceived as insensitive. This characteristic understandably grows out of their tendency to minimize the presence of softer, more vulnerable emotions like fear, hurt, and weakness. Eights unconsciously distance themselves from these feelings, and, as a result, usually have a default mode that represents a tougher, unsentimental stance. If you are an Eight, being ready to go on the offense and push back at someone who threatens you means you have to lessen contact with vulnerable feelings. This can lead to a defensive emotional posture that others can describe as "insensitive," "callous," "intimidating," or "ruthless."

Autonomy

Eights value their independence and autonomy. Even more prominently, as Naranjo points out, Eights idealize their autonomy. Not wanting to be seen as weak or to find themselves in a vulnerable position, Eights disavow their dependency on others. This renunciation can lead to an independent presentation as well as an avoidance of emotions and experiences that could make them feel their need for other people.

Putting yourself in a position to have to depend on other people sounds like a terrible idea to someone who likes to be in control, doesn't like to be told what to do, and isn't very susceptible to the vulnerabilities associated with dependent relationships. Eights convey invincibility; passive dependency is something that many Eights consider anathema.

Sensory-Motor Dominance

Naranjo calls Eights the most "sensory-motor" of personalities. This means that Eights are firmly rooted in the physical, in the "here and now" sphere of the senses, and in a kinesthetic, body-based way of functioning. Oriented primarily toward the present, they concentrate on what is concrete and what is stimulating *right now*.

The prominence of sensory-motor experience also means that Eights engage in action more than thinking and feeling. Their primary movement is to take action. In line with this tendency toward action and self-assertion, Eights often don't slow down long enough to ponder what they are doing before they do it. Naranjo describes this as a "lusty clutching at the present and an excited impatience toward memory, abstractions, anticipations, as well as a desensitization to the subtlety of aesthetic and spiritual experience."[28] What is most real and compelling to Eights is what stimulates the physical senses in a tangible and immediate way.

Eights can tend to act without thinking things through, and, like the Cyclops, can display an overreliance on taking action. Eights' adherence to the familiar pattern of bold and forceful action sometimes can lead them to miscalculate and overreach in situations where a more nuanced approach would be better.

The Type Eight Shadow

Each type's Shadow reveals the blind spots of the character—what they tend to remain asleep to as part of their survival strategy and resulting focus of attention.

People with Type Eight personalities tend to ignore or minimize any data revealing their own weaknesses and vulnerabilities. This coping strategy works well early on in response to an environment in which they are threatened by powerful people who hurt or neglect them; however, when they reach adulthood, the shadow side of this defense can present many problems. As humans, we all have vulnerabilities, but Eights learn to hide theirs—even from themselves—to build a life based on being strong, resilient, and invincible. As a result, Eights can be completely unaware of some of their own weaknesses, vulnerabilities, sensitivities, and challenges.

Eights are naturally protective of beings they care about and feel responsible for. When Eights call upon their own power in seeking to protect those they perceive as having less power, they often project their own vulnerability onto others. By perceiving vulnerability and weakness as attributes that *others* have, as experiences that are distant from and external to them, Eights can separate themselves from their own vulnerable feelings and yet still act to address weakness. This pattern can reflect Eights' genuine qualities of generosity and courage, but it can also be a way for them to remain unconscious of their own vulnerable side.

While Eights are strong characters, they often don't see or know the impact of their strength; the actual nature of the influence they exert on others may be a blind spot for them. They can intimidate others without meaning to, and they can bring much more than the optimal force to bear on situations. While Eights can be very direct and straightforward in a positive way, they can sometimes be blunt to the point of being hurtful or insensitive when they don't see how much bite may be behind their directness.

Eights can work incredibly hard, but, because they go to sleep to their own vulnerabilities and limitations, they can work themselves to the point of exhaustion and may not know to stop until they become physically ill or injured.

The energy of lust motivates Eights to indulge in fun and pleasurable activities, often to excess, and because their natural human vulnerabilities reside in their Shadow, they may be totally unaware of healthy limits. And while some of this lusty pleasure-seeking can represent a wonderful zest for living and capacity for enjoyment, Eights may party excessively without seeing how their pursuit of pleasure may be overcompensation for an avoidance of their pain or other vulnerable emotions. Not wanting to feel weak or to be seen as weak, they may deny their natural vulnerable feelings through an unconscious flight into excessive eating, drinking, or socializing, which can create problems with their health and in their relationships.

Eights may also have blind spots around how they interpret reality in specific situations or in general. They tend to deny important aspects of what might be true or real when those things don't fit in with the way they want to see things. This narrow perspective can be another aspect of bringing too much power to bear—they can equate their own personal truth with the objective truth and not see the difference.[29] They can believe they are right about everything, or that their opinions are correct interpretations of what is happening, even if they aren't necessarily seeing all of the data completely or accurately. This impulse makes it hard for them to see when they are wrong or mistaken and to apologize.

Eights can get bored if life is not stimulating enough and may push for conflict, intensity, or excess in order to avoid whatever feelings might lie behind their experience of "boredom." When Eights complain about being bored, it often reflects an unconscious avoidance of deeper feelings. Fun and excitement provide an escape from feeling empty, anxious, confused, sad, or powerless, all of which may be emotional blind spots for Eights. The automatic search for intensity, stimulation, and fun keeps those difficult emotional experiences out of their awareness. Eights' passion is lust, and this means they have big appetites—for fun, stimulating experiences, and even work—but their impulsiveness and excessive indulgences can hide the vulnerability, weakness, and darker emotions that they unconsciously deny and relegate to their Shadow.

The Shadow of the Type Eight Passion:
Lust in Dante's Underworld

The passion of lust, like gluttony, "makes reason slave to appetite."[30] In the case of the Type Eight personality, this Shadow passion is a wanton indulgence in many desires, but especially sensual ones. Accordingly, the Inferno casts the Lustful as spirits trapped helplessly in a shifting black wind they are powerless to control:

> *The infernal storm, eternal in its rage, sweeps and drives the spirits with its blast: it whirls them, lashing them with punishment. When they are swept back past their place of judgment, then come the shrieks, laments and anguished cries; there they blaspheme God's almighty power.*[31]

The Lustful have plenty of excuses for giving in to their desire. The Pilgrim is so moved by one seductive love story told by one of the Lustful that he swoons. The Passion of Lust within the Type Eight shadow is thus portrayed in Dante's underworld as a stubborn unwillingness for impulses to be restrained by any boundaries on satisfaction. In addition, the Lustful in the underworld are deep in denial and completely unrepentant. Emblematic of the shadow side of the Type Eight personality, the only regret the Lustful have is being punished at all.

The Three Kinds of Eights:
The Type Eight Subtypes

THE THREE SUBTYPES OF TYPE EIGHT express the passion of lust in three distinct ways. Self-Preservation Eights directly and powerfully pursue the things they need in order to survive. Social Eights have a need to protect others and go up against those who commit injustices. Sexual Eights are passionate and charismatic characters who go against social conventions in a provocative way.

The Self-Preservation Eight stands out as the most defended, or the most "armed," of the Eights. Geared toward getting whatever is necessary to meet their needs, Self-Preservation Eights use their power to find the shortest path between their desires and the satisfaction of their desires. The Social Eight is a mellower, less aggressive Eight, who uses power to protect other people and promote social causes. The Sexual Eight is the most rebellious Eight, using their power to go up against authority and attract people through charismatic shows of intensity.

The Self-Preservation Eight: "Satisfaction"

The Self-Preservation Eight expresses lust through a strong need to obtain what they need for survival. The title given to this type is "Satisfaction." This person has a strong desire for the satisfaction of material needs and an intolerance of frustration, and they have a hard time being patient when it comes to not getting immediate satisfaction of their needs and desires. This intolerance creates a kind of ruthlessness in these Eights about going after what they want and finding ways to get around people who might stand in their way.

Self-Preservation Eights feel compelled to go after what they need very directly without talking about it much—they know how to get things done without a lot of fuss or explanations. These people are the least expressive of the three Eight subtypes: they don't talk much and they don't reveal much. This is a no-nonsense person who doesn't bother with pretenses. Self-Preservation Eights are preoccupied with getting things—and getting away with things.

The driving need of Self-Preservation Eights can be described as an exaggerated ability to take care of themselves and find ways to meet their needs. In their focus on fulfilling their needs, they demonstrate a kind of exaggerated selfishness. They feel omnipotent in being able to satisfy and meet any need, and they disqualify any feeling, person, idea, or institution that opposes their desires. They will go against whatever.

These Eights are characters who know how to survive in the most difficult situations and how to get what they want from other people. Naranjo sometimes refers to Self-Preservation Eights by the name "Survival," because they excel at generating the material support they need to survive and satisfy their desires.

Self-Preservation Eights know how to do business—according to Naranjo, they know how to barter and bargain and get the upper hand over anybody. Because they are strong, powerful, direct, and productive, they may generate dependency in others who come to rely on their control and protection.

The Self-Preservation Eight is the most "armed" and protected of all of the Eights—this is a more Five-ish Eight. They tend to possess a quiet strength; they are survivors who communicate strength without feeling the need to explain themselves. For them—at times, at least—kindness and good intentions don't exist. In their need to be strong to meet their needs, they may devalue the world of feelings. And they may not be aware of the damage they cause to others.

These Eights may seek revenge without knowing why. In this way Self-Preservation Eights differ from the Social Eight or the Sexual Eight personality, both of which usually have a specific reason for acting in vengeful ways. This subtype appears more aggressive than the Social Eight (especially in men) and less openly provocative and charismatic than the Sexual Eight.

The Self-Preservation Eight can be confused with the Sexual One because they express a similar energy related to feeling an urgent need to "get what's theirs." But Naranjo points out that the contrast between the two types lies in the fact that the Self-Preservation Eight is fundamentally under-social, meaning they don't mind going against social norms or breaking the rules, while the Sexual One is over- or hyper-social. Even though Sexual Ones are zealous in going after what they want, they still observe social norms, whereas Self-Preservation Eights care less about social conventions and will make their own rules to satisfy their cravings.

Janet, a Self-Preservation Eight, speaks:

I have always felt a very strong sense of personal responsibility for myself. I couldn't and didn't want to rely on anyone else to ensure I got what I needed from life. In order to do this I have been focused over the years on financial independence and earning my own living—my work, my career, was everything. When my first marriage ended this became my primary objective for nearly a decade, to the detriment of any long-term personal relationship. It's not that I had ambitions to be fabulously wealthy—it was more about ensuring that my financial health was strong so that I felt secure and able to have control over choices about things like buying a new car, getting a new house, or where to go on holiday. I wasn't a miser, and I didn't hoard money. But I did spend money in a sensible and responsible manner. I got a financial advisor many years ago who has helped me with pension planning, good mortgage deals, and investments.

I was married for the second time—to a man eleven years my junior—and for nearly twenty years I was the breadwinner and still retained the "power" when it came to money. This dynamic has gradually changed over the years, and yet I find I am still the one who focuses on our financial affairs. When I feel stressed, this is where I find my anxiety and worry plays itself out—imagining us destitute, homeless, and helpless, which would never happen due to my prudent planning over the years.

The Social Eight: "Solidarity" (Countertype)

The Social Eight is the countertype of the three Eight subtypes. Social Eights represent a contradiction: the Eight archetype rebels against social norms, but the Social Eight is also oriented toward protection and loyalty. They express lust and aggression in the service of life and other people.

This person is "social antisocial." In contrast to Self-Preservation Eights, Social Eights are more loyal, more overtly friendly, and less aggressive. They are helpful Eights—people who are nurturing, protective, and concerned with the injustices that happen to people—yet they also display an antisocial aspect with regard to the rules of society.

Naranjo explains that, symbolically, this character represents the child who became tough (or violent) in protecting his mother against his father. This is someone who bands together with the mother and goes against the patriarchal power and all that is associated with it: violence out of solidarity. Archetypally, this character represents the child who has given up on getting love from the father and allied with the mother against him.

Social Eights are very sensitive to detecting situations in which people are being persecuted or exploited by others that hold more power. When they detect this kind of thing, they tend to act to protect those who are less powerful. Karl Marx, the champion of worker solidarity and outspoken critic of capitalism, may have been a Social Eight.

Overall, this Eight appears more mellow and outgoing and less quick to anger than the other Eights. They tend to rebel in less obvious ways. They are very active, and they may lose themselves through constantly being in action. They may display a disproportionate lust for projects or for collecting things.

Socially, Social Eights like the power a group offers, and they may have difficulty engaging in more "individualized" relationships. In extreme cases, this Eight can tend toward megalomania. In close relationships, they may display a lack of commitment to the partner that hides an unconscious fear of abandonment.

In becoming a protector at too young an age, these Eights typically lose consciousness of their own needs for love and care. While people with this Eight subtype develop a strong ability to care for and protect others, they unconsciously give up their own need for love and replace it with a compensatory movement toward power and pleasure. It's generally hard for an Eight to make their love needs conscious, and while they can seem softer or calmer than the other Eights, Social Eights also have a blind spot where their own needs for love and protection are concerned.

This Eight often doesn't look like an Eight. Ichazo called this subtype

"Friendship," but Naranjo uses the descriptor "complicity" or "solidarity" to distinguish the everyday, positive meaning of the word "friendship" from what he calls the "ego game" of the Social Eights' unconscious personality pattern. According to Naranjo, this individual's main drive is for something like loyalty. The Social Eight subtype is the most intellectual of the three, but these Eights also rebel against the dominant (patriarchal) culture. This rebellion necessarily involves a mixture of authority and intellect because the dominant authority in patriarchal societies tends to promote the intellectual control of impulses and excess. While the Sexual Eight is the most overtly anti-intellectual of the three Eight subtypes, the Social Eight goes up against the power of authority out of a desire to protect the oppressed and, unconsciously, a personal need for the nurturance associated with maternal care.

Male Social Eights can look like Type Nines, and female Social Eights may resemble Type Twos. However, these Eights can be distinguished from Nines and Twos because they act in more direct, powerful ways, engage more readily in conflict, and express more power and control in seeking to protect and support other people.

Annie, a Social Eight, speaks:

I am always doing something for other people and thinking that as soon as this current activity is finished then I'll turn to what I want to do just for me. When I first encountered the Enneagram I thought I was a Two because I didn't identify with the anger or the need to dominate. I was phobic of anger and unaware of my own underlying aggression. I wasn't aware of how controlling my efforts to help felt to others, and I would be hurt when people pushed back and complained.

I frequently get pulled into the leadership role in groups and then get whacked for thinking I know what's best to accomplish the task or project. In high school, to avoid this kind of pain, I started saying, "I'm not a leader. Don't look at me to get this done." It didn't work. When I see something that needs doing, especially if it benefits others, I step in and get it done.

I have always been seen as friendly and yet have not had "best" friends that I was vulnerable with until late in life. It is hard to admit that I need help or concern or comfort. While I care about people and do a lot for them, I am realizing that I don't allow myself to have them matter that much to me. I have often left relationships without a look back. Until recently, I have not been the one who maintains friendships. I both yearn for the closeness friendship provides and feel scared of it—partly because I then feel obligated to take care of the other person no matter what.

I have been frequently hurt and puzzled by other people's reactions to me, and I work consciously to avoid being experienced as "too much" or intrusive. When others experience me this way, I often feel misunderstood. Because of this dynamic, I feel like I have to monitor my energy and impact so others can be comfortable. But I like the amount of energy and drive and decisiveness I naturally have. It is easy for me to start in a certain direction without too much planning and then make a course correction if needed. I have always been physically active, participating in both team and individual sports.

Fortunately, I was guided toward becoming a psychotherapist. In that role I have had a lot of practice with leaning back to hear the other's experience, mirroring their truth back to them, and offering help with an open hand. I feel my openheartedness, but it's more difficult to receive the love and gratitude others have for me. Most importantly, I've learned to trust that each person has their own wisdom and ability to live their life well.

The Sexual Eight: "Possession"

Sexual Eights have a strong antisocial tendency. People with this subtype are provocative people who express lust through open rebellion—through declaring in word and deed that their values differ from the norm. Along with being the most rebellious of the Eight subtypes, the Sexual Eight is, interestingly, also the most emotional.

This outspoken, rebellious Eight likes to be seen as bad – or at least they don't mind it -- and they tend not to feel any guilt over the rebellious things they do. It's almost a matter of pride for Sexual Eights to go against the stream of convention or to disrespect rules and laws.

In childhood, many of these Eights experienced disrespect and a lack of affection and attention from one or both parents, so they decided (consciously or unconsciously) not to recognize maternal or paternal authority. This first rebellion against authority became the template for their strong rebellious tendencies.

The name given to the Sexual Eight is "Possession," which refers to a kind of charismatic taking over (or dominance) of the whole environment—an energetic capture of people's attention. These Eights display the idea of "Possession" in that they can take over a whole scene energetically, becoming the center of things. Sexual Eights like to feel their power by possessing everyone's attention. They express the idea that "the world begins to run when they arrive."[32]

Sexual Eights express a need for dominance and power over others. They don't want to lose control of anything or anyone, and they want to influence people with their words. Everything—whether it is a person or a material thing—is an object to possess. These Eights don't seek material security; rather, they seek to get power over people, things, and situations.

In getting and maintaining this power, Sexual Eights can be fascinating and charismatic. Their power comes through a kind of seductiveness and intensity that differentiates them stylistically from the other two Eight subtypes. As Naranjo explains, these Eights have more colors in their feathers; they are more magnetic and more outspoken. They have great powers of seduction.

These Eights look voraciously for love, sex, and excessive pleasure in life. They seek adventures, risks, challenges, and the thrill of an adrenaline rush. In line with their passionate forward movement into action, they may be particularly intolerant of weakness, dependence, and slow people.

As the most emotional of the Eights, the Sexual subtype displays a great deal of passion that may at times get expressed through emotions that may seem surprising to others and atypical for the other Eights. In these very passionate, emotional Eights, there's often a detachment of the intellect—while Sexual Eights may be very intelligent, they express action and passion more than contemplation in the things they do.

These Eights feel things deeply. This capacity can benefit a good relationship, but it can be a problem when a relationship isn't going well. In romantic settings, Sexual Eights may encourage their partners to become very dependent on them or to treat them as the energetic center of their lives. They demand loyalty, but may not be faithful in return. (England's King Henry VIII may serve as an example.) And they tend to have possessive relationships not only with lovers, but also with friends, objects, places, and situations.

This subtype can usually be readily recognized as Eights and is as not likely to be confused with other types. They may look like Sexual Fours in that both types can be angry, emotional, and demanding, but Sexual Eights distinguish themselves in their deeply confident (or overconfident) manner in contrast with the Sexual Fours' sense of inner deficiency.

Kathy, a Sexual Eight, speaks:

As a Sexual Eight, I like to have a small group of trusted and trusting people around me. When my circle becomes too large, I become uncomfortable and withdraw. I like to be all things to the people in my inner circle, and when that circle becomes unmanageable, it makes me a little "crazy." Others can definitely feel it when I start to pull away. Those who are closest to me definitely notice when I am overcome by people who "need" too much.

On the other hand, I seem to "take care" of those around me. My sexual instinct can make this look like I am dominating or controlling the people around me. Although I am usually very conscious of my power over others, it is often difficult for others to resist the temptation to indulge me. I am absolutely charismatic and can convincingly bring others toward me without appearing to want adulation. People tend to think of me as a "guru," and for the most part I lead and others follow without question. I have been told that my power is like a narcotic to others. And it happens without my having an awareness that it's happening.

My sexual instinct also makes me one of those rare people who can cross others' usual boundaries without making them uncomfortable. I genuinely care about others and that translates into others feeling protected and safe in my presence. Someone close to me made this observation and it resonates with me: "People in your presence find themselves hanging onto your every word...looking to you for approval...seeming submissive and overcome with awe. There is the sense that you are continually looking for an equal—someone who will provide that for you."

I have been told that I exude sexuality. I am overtly sexual; I speak openly and frankly about sex. Perhaps it is partly for shock value, but it is never meant to be offensive. It is an honest and beautiful part of me and it also communicates my vulnerability. I have been told that one cannot be in a room with me without feeling my sexual presence or life force. I think it is part of what makes me so appealing. The charisma is hard to resist.

Naranjo was correct about Sexual Eights. Our colors are more vivid. As a Sexual Eight, my colors shine brightly, except for those times when my energy is zapped by my need to be both protector and protected. I feel an intense passion and zest for life. My energy is bountiful and bold. My powers of seduction can be consuming. Because I need what I give, I am not afraid to be vulnerable. I believe it is precisely this trait that makes me a gifted leader and teacher.

"The Work" for Type Eight: Charting a Personal Growth Path

ULTIMATELY, AS EIGHTS WORK ON THEMSELVES and become more self-aware, they learn to escape the trap of limiting themselves through opposing limits on themselves by developing a clearer awareness of their softer side, tempering action with more thinking and feeling, and learning to moderate their impulses and impact.

For all of us, waking up to habitual personality patterns involves making ongoing, conscious efforts to observe ourselves. As we reflect on the meaning and sources of what we observe, we are actively working to counter automatic tendencies. For Eights, this process involves observing the ways in which they express their power and avoid feeling weak and dependent; exploring how they deny the deeper truth of early and ongoing hurts and overcompensate through being strong; and making active efforts to balance their forcefulness and autonomy with a greater awareness of their emotional depths and relational capacities. It is particularly important for Eights to develop a more direct relationship with their vulnerability and to have the strength to be seen as weak.

In this section I offer some ideas about what Eights can notice, explore, and aim for in their efforts to grow beyond the constraints of their personality and embody the higher possibilities associated with their type and subtype.

Self-Observation: Dis-Identifying from Your Personality by Watching It in Action

Self-observation aims to create enough internal space to really watch—with fresh eyes and adequate distance—what you are thinking, feeling, and doing in your everyday life. As Eights take note of the things they think, feel, and do, they might look out for the following key patterns:

Rebelling against outside authority and denying (internal and external) limitations

Observe your tendency to view yourself as above all forms of authority. Recognize what in you motivates this tendency. Note how you don't accept conventional limits and how you invalidate the voice of conventional authority. Notice what forms this opposition takes, what beliefs you hold that support this view, and what kinds of things you do when you act from a superior sense of yourself as the ultimate authority. Notice any thoughts and beliefs you have about yourself that might be overly grandiose—ways you think of yourself as superior to others that you habitually don't ever question or doubt. Allow yourself to notice if denying your vulnerability fuels this tendency to be grandiose. (Are you repressing your "smallness," and so experiencing an unconscious drive to be "big?") Observe when you are rebellious and what happens when you rebel. Look out for any instances in which your inability to accept limits—whether imposed from the outside or denied on the inside—might actually hurt or undermine you. Try to be aware of the consequences caused by your reluctance to moderate yourself or accept constraint.

Focusing on and acting from power and strength as overcompensation for denied powerlessness and weakness

Observe the ways in which you take refuge in power and strength and how doing so might be a way of avoiding or overcompensating for not wanting to experience deeper feelings of powerlessness, weakness, or impotence. Notice when you are feeling angry and when you feel an impulse to act on it. What kinds of things make you angry and why? Notice what kinds of things you do to assert yourself and express your power in the world. Note when you think in ways that support acting powerfully without considering other options or potential vulnerabilities the situation presents. In general, note how you exert power as a way to avoid feeling any kind of vulnerability. Observe your impulse to confront things and press forward as a way of trying to obtain satisfaction at any price. If it feels difficult to moderate your expressions of aggression, think about why. Notice what role impulsiveness plays in your life and any tendencies you have to avoid thinking through certain actions before you take them.

Avoiding and denying vulnerable feelings and dependence on others

Observe how difficult it is for you recognize and own your more vulnerable emotions. Notice if you judge yourself as being weak if you allow yourself to have a wider range of feelings, and observe the effects of that kind of self-judgment. Note the other kinds of thoughts you have about your softer feelings and how you might rationalize staying away from any kind of emotional experience you label as "weakness." Observe how you manage to maintain a position of power and autonomy in your relationships. Notice when your thinking supports the correctness of your view of things without considering potential ways you might be incorrect or potential vulnerabilities in your perspective. Notice any thoughts that operate to hide your vulnerabilities from yourself. In particular, note any tendency you have to be excessively harsh on yourself (or others) if an awareness of your vulnerability arises. What kinds of things do you do to keep from being aware of your softer feelings?

Self-Inquiry and Self-Reflection: Gathering More Data to Expand Your Self-Knowledge

As Eights observe these and other related patterns in themselves, the next step on the Enneagram growth path is to *understand* these patterns more. Why do they exist? Where do they come from? What purpose do they serve? How do they get you in trouble when they were originally intended to help you? Often, seeing the root causes of a habit—why it exists and what it is designed to do—is enough to allow you to break out of the pattern. In other cases, with more entrenched habits, knowing how and why they operate as defenses can be a first step to eventually being able to release them.

Here are some questions that Eights can ask themselves, and some possible answers they can consider to get more insight into the sources, operation, and consequences of these patterns of personality:

How and why did these patterns develop? How do these habits help Type Eights cope?

Through understanding the sources of their defensive patterns and how those patterns operate as coping strategies, Eights have the opportunity to become more aware of how and why they turn away from their human frailty and toward different forms of expressing power in the world. By examining how they defy and deny as a reaction against being vulnerable, Eights can gain insight into why they employ these defensive strategies. If Eights can honestly tell the story of their early life, they can better understand the ways that being strong instead of weak helped them to survive or feel a sense of well-being. They can have more compassion for themselves in light of the ways they may have needed to silence their own "inner child." If they can reflect on how "coming on strong"[33] was their way of coping in a world that punished weakness, they can get a clearer sense of the ways their "offense as defense" life strategy still operates as a protection.

What painful emotions are the Type Eight patterns designed to protect me from?

For all of us, the personality operates to protect us from painful emotions, including what psychological theorist Karen Horney calls our "basic anxiety"—a preoccupation with the emotional stress of not getting basic needs fulfilled. Eights adopt a strategy that allows them to deny the existence of painful emotions related to being small and vulnerable. They find safety in strength and a sense of invulnerability, so they unconsciously repress fear and other vulnerable emotions. The ways adult Eights habitually act in the world can be seen as forms of compensation for a potentially traumatic experience of helplessness in the face of perceived injustices or actual mistreatment in childhood: "just as they were hurt then, they set out to hurt others now. Just as they felt impotent then, they decided (implicitly, and at a very early age), to avoid weakness at all costs."[34]

The patterns that make up the Type Eight personality are thus a means of denying, avoiding, and defending against a re-experiencing of painful feelings that arose early on. Having a good offense and easy access to aggression allows Eights to shrug aside feeling helpless, fearful, sad, inadequate, and a variety of other painful emotions they felt being small in a world that didn't support their natural sensitivity and vulnerability.

Why am I doing this? How do the Type Eight patterns operate in me now?

Through reflecting on how their key patterns operate, each of the three Eight subtypes can grow their awareness of how these defensive patterns emerge in everyday life—and in the present moment. Self-observing Eights can catch themselves avoiding their softer, more vulnerable needs and emotions or relating to the outside world with a compensatory stance of forcefulness, intimidation, and independence. Insight into their early patterns helps Eights wake up to the deeper motivations that drive their coping strategy of being tough, active, and strong. It can be eye-opening (and transformative) for Eights to see how they habitually and thoroughly avoid being aware of a deep (and precious) part of who they are. By seeing how denial of vulnerability actually makes them less alive, less available for love and relationships, and less whole, Eights can direct some of their motivation toward accepting and reclaiming the softer and sadder feelings that express a beautiful part of the true Self.

What are the blind spots of these patterns? What do Type Eights keep themselves from seeing?

To really increase their self-knowledge, it will be important for Eights to remind themselves about what they *don't* see when their personality programming is driving the show. Eights taking pleasure in their sense of power may not see how, in the name of finding safety through strength, their forceful stance avoids a whole range of emotions and relational needs. Eights can benefit greatly from the realization that being in touch with vulnerable feelings, sensitivity, and needs for love and care is an essential part of having deep relationships. This quality makes it easier for people to care for you and get close to you. To the extent that you actively keep yourself from seeing and feeling your own pain, sadness, loneliness, and inadequacy, you may thwart your ability to empathize with other people when they are having these feelings. The inability to tap into your own depths makes it very difficult to be fully available for relationships. Total invulnerability closes you off from your own capacity to love, to be loved, and to grow. The freedom you feel in acting in powerful ways may keep you from seeing how that focus on power repeats the pattern of neglect that first caused you to have to get big and deny your child-self. Try focusing instead on "looking for what you don't see" to break the habit of neglecting your softer side. By looking for the benefits of opening to vulnerability, Eights will get more of the nurturing they deny themselves in exchange for their defenses.

What are the effects or consequences of these patterns? How do they trap me?

The irony of the Eight strategy is that staying safe through being less sensitive closes off the best avenue for deeper connections with others. The best and healthiest relationships develop when people can feel safe sharing their deepest vulnerabilities. But if you don't even acknowledge your sensitive side and your softer emotions, how can you allow for the stimulation, pleasure, and intensity of human contact that we all crave? It can be tragic for pleasure-loving Eights to unconsciously cut themselves off from life's best source of fun and adventure—a full and complete experience of human intimacy and connection. The deep satisfaction that only healthy human love can provide can be difficult or impossible to achieve without an awareness of your whole, vulnerable, undefended Self. If you're not well known to yourself in this way, you can't make yourself well known to the people who like and love you.

Self-Development:
Aiming for a Higher State of Consciousness

For all of us who seek to wake up, the next step in working with personality type-based knowledge is to begin to inject more conscious effort into everything we do—to think, feel, and act with more choice and awareness. In this section I provide some ideas for Eights about "what to do" after they've observed their key patterns and done some investigation into their sources, operation, and consequences.

This last section is divided into three parts, each corresponding to one of three distinct growth processes connected within the Enneagram system: 1) "what to do" to actively counter the automatic patterns of your core type described above in the "self-observation" section, 2) how to use the Enneagram's Inner Flow arrow lines as a map of growth, and 3) how to study your passion (or "Vice") and consciously seek to embody its opposite, the antidote, the higher "Virtue" of the type.

The Three Main Type Personality Patterns:
"What to Do" to Address Them

Rebelling against, opposing, and denying outside authority and (internal and external) limitations

See how rebellion against limits may lead to self-limitation. When Eights can begin to see how their refusal to accept limits on their freedom actually limits them, they can consider taking the risk to be less defended and more deeply available in the world. Contrary to what they might think, growing into their "higher" side or "oak tree–Self" actually requires them to have more understanding and acceptance of the little, soft acorn kernel that needed to hide in such a very hard shell to survive.

Eights often don't show up in "self-help" contexts, perhaps because they don't want to submit to an authoritative source of learning outside themselves. And this reluctance is understandable, given that Eights' tendency toward rebellion often comes out of an early experience with authority figures failing them. But in placing themselves above external sources of learning, care, and "holding," Eights can potentially end up alone or lonely, even if they don't always allow themselves to fully realize the pain of it. Eights can therefore benefit from finding ways to accept guidance, protection, and care from others, and to relax the need to push back on help from the outside, even if it feels at first like control.

Broaden your view of who has authority over the truth. (Or, How do you know you're not wrong?) Eights can tend to fall into "it's true because I say it's true" ways of thinking. When you are so accustomed to (defensively) seeing yourself in the power position, it may be hard to concede the reality that you aren't the authority on everything. By believing so much in their position as "Top Dog," Eights sometimes trick themselves into believing everything they think. And because Eights look so authoritative (and believe they are speaking the objective truth), they can make others believe them too. So, in the end, this Eight habit of focusing on the(ir) truth can obscure what is actually true.

As Sandra Maitri points out, when your sense of self is primarily grounded in the physical, your sense of reality can be more skewed than you realize: "when the physical is the only dimension of reality that we are perceiving, we may believe that we are seeing things as they are, but in fact we are seeing through a distorted lens."[35] Even in science, "the most revered of modern disciplines," Maitri comments, being "objective—seeing things as they are—means only giving credence to what can be perceived and measured using our physical senses."[36] And scientific reliance on the physical as the only source of truth persists even though scientific findings have also shown that the expectation of the observer can affect the results. In much the same way, Eights can adhere firmly to their own sense of truth and its basis in their personality, even though this ego stance (by definition) is a limited view of "the truth" seen differently from other, equally legitimate perspectives.

For this reason, it's important for Eights to make sure they question their own authority once in a while and not just rebel against external sources of power and knowledge simply out of habit. Eights can grow by learning to accept or allow for others' disagreement and not just believe that they have a monopoly on what's objectively true. If you allow yourself to check and see if you might be wrong once in a while, you can actually deepen your self-confidence and practice opening up to the experience of admitting a mistake.

Learn about limits. At its extreme, having no limits can itself be very limiting. If you push yourself to work harder and harder without observing your normal human limitations, you can make yourself sick or hurt yourself. If you eat too much or drink too much or play too much you can cause real damage to yourself or others. Eights sometimes risk endangering their health, their freedom, their relationships, and their well-being by resisting moderation and reasonable constraints. If Eights can become more conscious of why they have needed to be powerful and rebellious to cope, they can begin to accept not always having to be so strong. This practice helps them to break free of the limiting protections of their "acorn shell" personality by developing a healthy relationship to limitation instead.

Focusing on and acting from power and strength as overcompensation for denied powerlessness and weakness

Consult your head and your heart more before taking action. Being conscious and wise about the actions we take often requires considering different forms of data. Eights habitually tend to move into action without thinking or feeling things through. When Eights see themselves moving quickly or impulsively into action, they can benefit from experimenting with slowing down, analyzing the situation more, and consulting their emotions for additional information.

Use your aggression as a clue to underlying feelings. One of the advantages of being an Eight is that you have easier access to your anger and aggression than many other personalities. This connection to anger generates power and advantage, but it also often serves to hide the more vulnerable feelings that motivated the anger in the first place. We all get angry when we are hurt. Looking for what's underneath this anger can help Eights get in touch with feelings of pain and helplessness. When Eights have a clear sense of the vulnerable feelings that might be motivating their anger, they are even more powerful and constructive leaders. Eights can benefit enormously by making it a practice to search for, recognize, and allow themselves to experience any vulnerable feelings their anger may keep them from noticing. Doing so gives them a deeper understanding of themselves and more information with which to deal with the hurt that caused their anger in the first place.

Reframe vulnerability and weakness as expressions of great strength. Like Eights, most people in Western culture see power and strength as "good" and weakness and vulnerable feelings like helplessness, powerlessness, and fear as "bad." But this value judgment is a product of the personality archetype of our culture—it's not objectively true. Feelings are just valid; they aren't "right or wrong" or "good or bad." Eights get out of balance by relating to the world through "strong" feelings and ways of behaving while repressing or avoiding "weak" ways of feeling and behaving. They don't access all of who they are, and they stop themselves from growing into all they might become. It is therefore very important for Eights to try to recognize the truth of the counterintuitive idea that *it takes a great deal of strength to allow yourself to be truly vulnerable.*

Avoiding and denying the existence of vulnerable feelings and dependence on others

Catch yourself in the act of avoiding vulnerability and dependence. Eights habitually and automatically deny their vulnerability and dependence on others. Often, it can seem to Eights that these important aspects of themselves just don't exist. But as Eights become aware of themselves and develop a greater consciousness of their personality patterns, they have the opportunity to show real inner toughness by integrating their vulnerability rather than avoiding it through displays of strength. Eights that see how they deny their vulnerability and dependence, and work to incorporate a deeper experience of their more tender feelings bring their whole selves to interactions and relationships. They become truly powerful and can grow to champion that truth in a more profound and spiritually mature way.

Regularly inquire into your emotional depths and allow yourself to experience more of your feelings. I've heard Eights say that they wake up angry. They can tend to dwell on the angry side of the emotional spectrum: impatience, irritation, frustration, and rage. Eights also have greater access to more upbeat feelings, like excitement, than some other types, as they don't indulge in as much negative or limiting self-talk. But in focusing on the feelings they do tend to feel, they unconsciously avoid—and so never or rarely feel—more vulnerable feelings like pain, sadness, disappointment, confusion, fear, and loss. The Eight becomes more armed than other personalities because his coping strategy revolves around disowning vulnerability to become big and powerful.

Eights expand their capacity for growth, relationship, and aliveness in the present when they consciously choose to experience their emotional depths. For this reason, it can help Eights to regularly ask themselves about what they might be feeling that they are not aware of. With support from others in this delicate process, Eights can learn to relax their defenses against feeling all their feelings and practice opening up to letting in more love and compassion.

Make needs for love more conscious. Most Eights have trouble making their needs for love conscious. In the case of the Eight personality, the main factor in defending against giving and receiving real love is giving up on love. Early on, Eights may have had the sense that love was not available to them and so it was a better idea to go for power and pleasure than to seek the comforts that love can provide. Eights often come to believe that it's foolish or weak to expect to be loved, so they cut themselves off from that part of their psyche that really needs it. But all people are moved by love (every personality is a different form of defense against love, after all). To grow out of the shell of our "acorn" self, we need to become more and more aware of the ways in which we push love away even though we need and want it. For Eights it is imperative to actively examine the ways in which they may have given up on love. If they can reawaken their awareness of their desire for love, Eights can open themselves up to the trust and vulnerability true love requires.

The Inner Flow for Type Eight: Using the Arrow Lines to Chart Your Growth Path

In Chapter 1, I introduced an Inner Flow model of the arrow lines that define one dimension of the dynamic movement within the Enneagram framework. The connections and flow between each core Type, its "stress–growth" point, and its "child–heart" point map one kind of growth path described by the symbol. As a reminder, the arrow lines can be seen to suggest one kind of growth path for each type:

- The direction from the core point along the arrow line is the path of development. The "stress–growth" point ahead represents specific challenges perfectly suited to expanding the narrow focus of our core point personality.
- The direction against the arrow from the core point to the "child–heart" point indicates issues and themes from childhood that must be consciously acknowledged and owned so that we can move forward and not be held back by unfinished business from the past. This "child–heart" point represents qualities of security we unconsciously repressed, occasionally fall back into as a comfort in times of stress, and now must reintegrate consciously.

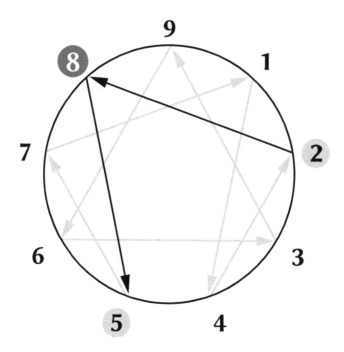

Type Eight Moving Forward to Type Five: Consciously Using the Five "Stress–Growth" Point for Development and Expansion

The Inner Flow growth path for Type Eights brings them into direct contact with the challenges embodied in Type Five, allowing for a balance between withdrawal and forward momentum and between thinking and acting as a way to marshal inner resources to develop "nonattachment." Not surprisingly, the Eight move to Five may represent an extreme response to an intense experience of stress, as it can be a mode of retreat that Eights are driven to when their normal reliance on power and action has failed. To the normally expressive Eight, the experience of Five may feel like a bunker where they take shelter when threatened or when conditions have dealt them a severe setback. The Five Point offers Eights a way to protect themselves through withdrawal to a remote place of safety where they can regroup rather than use power and strength. But this experience of Five, when consciously and mindfully managed, can help Eights develop a capacity for careful analysis conducted from a distance in place of overreliance on force, aggression, and bold (sometimes precipitous) action to get what they need.

The Eight working consciously in this way can make ready use of the tools healthy Fives use: analytical skills and economical use of energy and resources in support of self-protection and self-expression. The Five stance has a basis in observation, objective thinking, and a cautious focus on boundaries, and it can serve to balance out Eights' tendencies toward impulsivity, excess, and intimidation. Fives' judicious use of inner resources can help Eights focus more intentionally on self-regulation and moderation in the things they do. The mental activity, conscientious research, and planning characteristic of Fives can remind Eights to think more thoroughly about what they want to do before they move into action. And the way in which Fives automatically prioritize their own safety, maintaining a safe distance from danger, can help Eights develop a more conscious ability to take care of their "inner child." Valuing their need for time alone, energetic self-regulation, and personal space balances the Eights habitual reliance on brute force and over-action.

Type Eight Moving Back to Type Two: Consciously Using the "Child–Heart" Point to Work through Early Issues and Find Security in Support of Moving Forward

The path of growth for Type Eights calls for them to reclaim their ability to actively open up to their empathy for others and their need to be appreciated. Eights' early impulses to be seen and loved by others were not particularly recognized and supported in childhood. As children, Eights may have felt that they had to decide between the vulnerability of needing affection and the power of not needing anything from anybody – and they chose to take refuge in a position of strength.

Without awareness around the move to Type Two, Eights can act out the Two habits of "giving to get" and seducing through charm and helpfulness. They may compulsively and expansively do things for others, give advice, or express physical affection as a way of forging connections. Eights may go to Two in anxious ways—in an unconscious search for the comfort of relationship when they are stressed—or as a way to act out the disowned need for love they usually don't allow themselves to feel. As Sandra Maitri observes, "within the tough and no-nonsense Eight who delights in testing her grit… dominating and controlling life, and triumphing over adversity, lies a needy, clingy and lonely little Two-ish child who is desperate to be loved and held."[37]

Navigated consciously, however, Eights can use the move to Two developmentally, to reestablish a healthy balance between attuning to others' feelings and needs and asserting their own needs. Eights can focus on the qualities of this "child–heart" point to understand the needs they may have had to deny in themselves in their youth in order to get along in the world. Moving back to Two can thus be a way for Eights to consciously re-engage a lost sense of their needs for comfort, love, and care, and their desire to adapt to and please others as a way of relating. Eights often pride themselves on their independence and on the fact that they "don't care what anyone thinks of them." But this habitual posture is a defense adopted as a protection against an insensitive world. For this reason, the move to Two can be both a way for Eights to search for a sense of security through love and a way for them to embrace and reintegrate important parts of themselves they had to deny.

By reincorporating Type Two qualities, Eights can consciously remind themselves that it's okay to care about what other people think and feel about you; and that it's important to value your needs for love, understanding, affection, and acceptance. Instead of hiding their need for love and connection in a pose of strength and autonomy, Eights can seek to embody the high side of Two and open up a channel to loving and supportive relationships. They can use the wisdom of Two to adapt to meet the needs of others and to express their care and affection to other people more consciously. In this way, Eights can balance their talent for acting boldly in the world with the capacity for experiencing the vulnerability of needing support and care. They can use their Two "child–heart" point as a way of reclaiming their inner child's need for care and affection and opening up to a deeper participation in the give-and-take of loving relationships.

The Vice to Virtue Conversion:
Accessing Lust and Aiming for Innocence

The developmental path from Vice to Virtue is one of the central contributions of the Enneagram map because it highlights a usable "vertical" path of growth to a higher state of awareness for each type. In the case of Type Eight, the Vice (or passion) of the type is lust; its opposite, the Virtue, is *innocence*. The theory of growth communicated by this "Vice to Virtue conversion" is that the more we can be aware of how our passion functions and consciously work toward the embodiment of our higher Virtue, the more we can free ourselves from the unconscious habits and fixated patterns (the "acorn shell") of our type and evolve toward our "higher" side or "oak tree–Self."

As Eights become more familiar with their experience of lust and develop the ability to make it more conscious, they can take their work further by making efforts to focus on enacting their Virtue, the "antidote" to the passion of lust. In the case of Type Eight, the Virtue of innocence represents a state of being that Eights can attain by consciously manifesting their higher capacities.

Innocence is a way of being that is free from guilt, pure of heart, and naturally connected to the flow of our animal wisdom and nature as a whole. This higher Virtue encompasses the ability to wake up to the animal or instinctual level of our functioning and to see and feel how it comes from a pure source in the natural order of things.

Type Eight, like the "id" or the "libido," represents the raw sexual and instinctual energy that animates the lives of all animals and allows us to tap into the powerful energy of our physical selves. When this energy is put to work in service of the ego, however, it gets limited and distorted through its participation in the defensive personality structure. As a part of the conditioned personality, lust activates the energy that fuels the drive we all have to get what we need to survive as a species. However, in modern society, there's more than a hint of "badness" behind this drive to energetically go for whatever you need without restriction. The idea of "sin," and the fear of unrestricted instinctual impulse, has fueled cultural ideas that make us label sex and other urges as somehow wrong, when nothing is more fundamental than following our inherent animal wisdom. And it is this kind of cultural repression or judgment of our animal drives that the Eight personality naturally moves against.

Innocence, then, represents our ability to become conscious of the activity of our animal drives and our instinctual impulses for physical satisfactions, and to free up the life energy that can become trapped in defending our egos through the push-pull around our instinctual movement. Through mindful awareness of the ways in which we rebel against the repression of our instincts, we allow ourselves to experience ourselves more in the natural "flow of reality" regarding our physical drives.[38]

Embodying innocence as an Eight means that you have examined how your lust drives you. You have worked on being more aware of your unconscious tendency to go against others and the rules they create and to lose contact with your deeper sense of emotional truth and purity as a result. Achieving a state of innocence means you are directly connected with your own life force on all levels—the intellectual, the emotional, and the physical—so that you don't have to take refuge in a show of power or strength to assert yourself. Rather you can deeply trust in the purity of your impulses and intentions as you interact with others to get what you need.

Maitri cites Ichazo in defining innocence as an experience of reality and the connection to its flow, and the innocent being as one who "responds freshly to each moment, without memory, judgment, or expectation."[39] For Eights, releasing lust and aiming to inhabit a state of innocence means that they allow themselves to align with the natural flow of reality and be in the present moment without fearing being too much, wanting too much, receiving too little, or re-experiencing the hurts of the past. By aspiring to innocence, Eights release themselves from any guilt or pride connected to their desires, and they open up to a direct experience of their own life force and its connection to themselves, others, and the world around them.

Specific Work for the Three Type Eight Subtypes on the Path from Vice to Virtue

Whatever type you are, the path from observing your passion to finding its antidote is not exactly the same for each set of subtypes. The path of conscious self-work has been characterized in terms of "grit, grind, and grace:"[40] the "grit" of our personality programming, the "grind" of our efforts to grow, and the "grace" that comes to us from doing our work in conscious and positive ways. According to Naranjo, each subtype has to grind, or exert effort, against something slightly different. This insight is one of the great benefits of understanding the three distinct subtypes of each of the nine types.

Self-Preservation Eights can travel the path from lust to innocence by learning to allow for a wider range of feelings; expressing more of their thoughts and emotions with others; and developing more of a sense of trust related to the fulfillment of their needs. Self-Preservation Eights often feel a sense of urgency around their need for the resources required to live a good life. They usually feel like they have to "go it on their own" and work hard to get the things they want and need. In line with this drive, they naturally develop the skills and abilities they need to be strong, self-reliant, and self-supporting. But this stance can intensify rather than alleviate their sense of insecurity around getting their needs met. And this (usually unconscious) insecurity may be denied and overcompensated for when they work excessively hard in the belief that they have to be autonomous. If you are a Self-Preservation Eight, you can grow toward an experience of innocence by slowing down, learning to rely on others more, and having more faith in your ability to get what you need without having to expend so much effort and energy. Expand your ability to communicate what you need and want to others, whether it is about money and resources or love, care, and companionship.

Social Eights can travel the path from lust to innocence by learning how to take care of themselves in the same ways they feel moved to take care of others. Social Eights focus on protecting and supporting others as a way of acting out their own denied needs for protection and support, so it's important for them to embody innocence by being more actively and regularly aware of their own inner child and its needs for love and safety. These Eights grow in direct proportion to the degree to which they can see how they displace their need for love and support into taking action to be powerful in the world. It may be important for them to actually think about themselves as innocent children, as we all understand that all children deserve love, care, and protection—and that all children are naturally innocent. Opening up to the innocence involved in allowing themselves to be loved, taken care of, and vulnerable—which may have been impossible when they were young—allows Social Eights to reintegrate the child inside them that they had to abandon when they needed to get big fast in order to deal with the world.

Sexual Eights can travel the path from lust to innocence by reminding themselves that they are lovable and "good enough" as they are, and that they don't need to be provocative, superior, or extraordinary in order to be worthy of other people's devotion. It may help these Eights to explore the reasons behind their need to rebel and to possess everyone's attention. The Sexual Eight's pattern of being powerful and charismatic often serves to cover over a hurt child who didn't get the love and attention he or she deserved. If you are a Sexual Eight, and you can allow yourself to own and reintegrate the lonely, needy child inside you, you can take the charge out of your defensive need to have control over what happens and to be the center of everything. You have so much to offer in terms of your strength and your passion and your emotional energy, but you can be even more potent and present in the things you do and the relationships you build when you can allow yourself to have an ongoing sense of the innocence and purity of your deeper feelings, needs, and intentions. This is the true heart and the powerful potential of innocence. When you can bring that spirit into the things you do and share more of your energetic space with others in conscious ways, you can be truly powerful.

Conclusion

JUST AS THE EIGHT POINT REPRESENTS the way we become big and powerful to get what we need when it doesn't work to be small and vulnerable, the Eight path of growth shows us all how to transform the lustful energy behind our instinctual drives into a conscious sense of purpose and trust about who we are and what we can be. In each of the Type Eight subtypes, we see a specific character who shows us what is possible when we can turn lustful rebellion against limitations on our animal power into an awakened ability to feel, own, and integrate our most vulnerable emotions and innocent needs for love. In this way, Type Eights teach us all about the beauty of innocence when they can embody a state of being that flows in ease and harmony with the natural world through the alchemy of self-observation, self-development, and self-knowledge.

CHAPTER 5

The Point Seven Archetype:
The Type, Subtypes, and Growth Path

If you can't dazzle them with brilliance, baffle them with bull.

—W. C. Fields

Men are only as loyal as their options.

—Bill Maher

TYPE SEVEN REPRESENTS THE ARCHETYPE of the person who seeks pleasure in different forms as a distraction from the discomfort, darkness, and downside of life. This archetype's drive is to defend against the experience of pain using intelligence, imagination, charm, and enthusiasm, and to avoid fear through an optimistic outlook.

The Jungian concept of the "puer" or the "divine child" is another form of this archetype. It represents a "symbol for future hopes…the potentiality of life, newness itself… frivolity, pleasure, and play."[1] Jung characterizes this archetype as the "Eternal Child," who resists growing up as a way of trying to avoid taking on responsibility, along with its commitments, encumbrances, and difficulties.

This archetypal character predominantly focuses on the lighter sides of life, the "enlivening, charming, and refreshing elements of human experience,"[2] avoiding the darker Shadow aspects of human experience. The Type Seven personality and the puer archetype embody a highly positive idealism, a youthful enthusiasm, and a focus on future hopes. This archetype's dark side reflects the opposite of these qualities in its unconscious unwillingness to face the pain of separation, aging, and mortality.

Type Sevens represent that tendency in all of us to focus on the positive parts of life, on the upside, on the light instead of the dark. In much the same way that the Enneagram's Type Four represents the human tendency to focus on the Shadow—on what's missing or feels bad—Type Seven typifies that part of us that looks to the light as a way of avoiding the Shadow. This attraction toward positive feelings like excitement and happiness, and the difficulty of experiencing uncomfortable feelings like sadness, fear, or pain, is a universal human experience. As Sandra Maitri explains, "aversion to pain and attraction to pleasure is hard-wired into our physiology."[3] We all, to one extent or another, seek refuge in pleasant feelings as a way of evading painful emotions.

In a larger sense, from the point of view of the esoteric wisdom tradition behind the Enneagram, much of what we label as "good" and "bad" or "positive" and "negative" is defined in neutral terms. (We sometimes think of someone who is angry a lot as "bad," when anger is not intrinsically negative.) The value judgments we place on these different emotional states are a result of our cultural conditioning and our animal instincts. Our attraction to pleasure and our aversion to pain are universal human drives. But if we cannot develop an awareness of the ways we automatically distance ourselves from the "bad" and the "painful," we will impede our ability to grow.

Pain is part of what motivates the desire for personal development, and conscious suffering represents a key part of the growth process. Most people decide to do the difficult work of the "inner journey" in order to ease their suffering and find happiness. We must necessarily face our fears and childhood pain in the course of this journey, like an acorn in the Chapter 2 analogy has to "go underground and have its shell crack open." For any of us to become all that we can be—expand into the "oak tree" of our higher Self—we have to find the courage to see wisdom and truth in the darkness as well as the light. To truly develop, we must face our fears and our Shadow parts. This hard truth is what the Seven's path of growth teaches us.

The Seven archetype expresses several dimensions of the personality's movement toward pleasure and away from pain. Sevens automatically retreat into their intellect to rationalize away difficult emotional states. They actively seek out fun and stimulating experiences as a way of avoiding the darker side of life. Sevens move and think at a fast pace, allowing them to outrun or outwit whatever discomfort may arise.

In the Enneagram framework of personality, Type Sevens are typically playful, optimistic, inventive, adventurous, fun-loving, and imaginative. As one of my Seven friends has frequently noted about himself, he is "fun at parties" and "has a way with the ladies." Sevens have a gift for seeing the best in people and in situations, and they bring excitement and enthusiasm to the things they do. They are also creative, innovative, and flexible thinkers with a natural facility for generating multiple ideas and options. They are characteristically upbeat, friendly, and energetic. The specific "superpower" of Type Seven is the power of positive thinking—the ability to see interesting ideas and positive possibilities almost anywhere.

As with all the archetypal personalities, however, Type Sevens' gifts and strengths also represent their "fatal flaw" or "Achilles heel," as their talent for reframing "negatives" into "positives" can cause them to ignore important data that doesn't fit their positive frame. Although they are fun and enjoyable companions, Sevens have difficulty in relationships when called on to confront problems and deal with the pain or discomfort of conflict. And while they excel at brainstorming, their dislike of the routine and mundane aspects of life can lead them to be avoidant, distracted, irresponsible, and noncommittal in long term projects. Sevens often find it hard to move forward in life because they resist dealing with deeper emotions and sticky situations. And they frequently take refuge in a superficial or overly optimistic way of viewing things that discounts the hard realities involved. However, when Sevens can balance their positive and enthusiastic view of life with an ability to engage more deeply and with the full range of emotions, they can be enlivening, inspiring, and dedicated partners and friends.

The Type Seven Archetype in Homer's *Odyssey*: Aeolia and Aeolus, the Master of the Winds

When Odysseus and his men reach Aeolia, they find a place that epitomizes the Type Seven personality. This sumptuous island has no fixed location; it moves with the wind, which its ruler, Aeolus, controls. The Aeolians enjoy continuous feasting and festivities as they float about. Life is easy, fun, and comfortable—by design.

Aeolus has an easy and comfortable solution to Odysseus's problem, of course. He ties all the winds but the West Wind into a sack and has Odysseus store the bag in the hold of his ship so "there should be no wrong breath of wind"[4] to blow them in the wrong direction. Then he sets the West Wind free to blow Odysseus and his ships on their way west toward home.

Thus aided, the Greeks sail continuously for ten days until they have Ithaca within sight. Odysseus is exhausted from working the ropes day and night, and he succumbs to his fatigue. While he is sleeping, his men get curious about that bag of winds, thinking there might be treasure inside:

The crews began to mutter among themselves...sure I was hauling troves of gold and treasure home..." Look at our captain's luck—so loved by the world...Heaps of lovely plunder he hauls home from Troy, while we who went through slogging just as hard, we go home-empty handed."[5]

The crew opens the sack while Odysseus sleeps, thinking that Aeolus has given him gold and silver and they will take some for themselves. They unleash all the "blowing winds" inside, creating a furious wind-storm that blasts them all back to Aeolia.

Now, however, the Greeks' return to Aeolia is only spoiling the party. It proves that these men are the worst kind of unpopular: the gods hate them. Odysseus's pleas fall on deaf ears, and he and his men are ejected from the otherwise carefree island.

Certainly, the creative optimism and innovative spirit the Type Seven personality exudes can put a breeze in anyone's sails. New encounters, sensuous pleasures, and pleasant experiences are a big part of what makes life worth living. But as Odysseus's crew found out, focusing only on getting our share of the comforts of life causes trouble. No one can truly have their own private Aeolia, where the cares of the world are intrusions to be dispatched or avoided. Bobbing on the surface in a land of endless festival will always be just another way of drifting.

The Type Seven Personality Structure

LOCATED ON THE LEFT SIDE OF THE ENNEAGRAM, Type Sevens belong to the "head-based" triad, associated with the core emotion of fear and a central concern with safety. Although Sevens are part of the "fear triad," they usually don't act afraid and may not feel much fear at all. Within this group of three types, Sixes overdo fear, Fives stave off fear by skillfully avoiding it, and Sevens underplay their fear. They defend themselves with mental intelligence, and their main coping strategy operates to move them away from fear and related feelings.

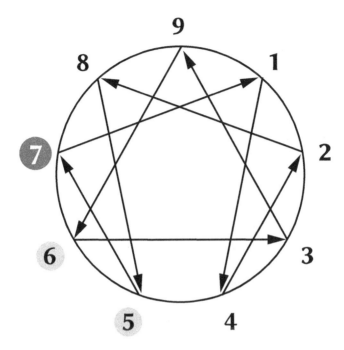

As mental types, Sevens have a distinct pattern of thinking, sometimes referred to as "monkey mind." This style is characterized by a rapid switching from one line of thinking to another according to the associations forming quickly and automatically in their minds. Another way of describing this predominant Type Seven quality would be to say that they have "synthesizing minds" that allow them to easily find links and commonalities among seemingly different subjects.

Sevens do share the other two head-based personalities' underlying concern with safety, but they avoid anxiety and fear by moving toward happy feelings, a positive outlook, and pleasurable experiences. Their main focus is seeking pleasure, which can take the form of fun activities, sensual enjoyments, or interesting things to think about.

The Early Coping Strategy: Type Seven

Sevens often report having had a good experience early in life, and most recall having a generally happy childhood. And their early life may indeed have been pleasant and carefree—but certainly for some Sevens, selective recall makes it better in memory than it really was. This rosy recollection is not surprising because Sevens' central coping strategy is to automatically reframe negatives into positives—to avoid the dark side and focus attention on the bright side. As Naranjo suggests, sometimes "memory in such a case supports fantasy to deny suffering."[6]

While Sevens often do experience a prolonged period of childhood satisfaction, many say that they experienced some sort of fear-inducing event, which they felt ill-equipped to deal with. Often there was a "fall from paradise" at a particular point in time, an experience that motivated the child to unconsciously cope with his fear by withdrawing back into an earlier stage of development in which he felt secure and omnipotent. By psychologically backing up and reverting to a slightly earlier stage in which they felt good and had a sense of control, Sevens take refuge in a happier, safer-feeling experience. From then on, when feelings of anxiety, fear, or pain threaten to emerge, Sevens employ a similar strategy: they automatically move away from trouble and toward thoughts, feelings, or imagined experiences that are stimulating, fun, and pleasant—often without having the conscious awareness that they are making this shift.

Type Seven individuals thus adopt the unconscious survival strategy of pulling back from distressing aspects of reality by moving toward what's positive in terms of pleasurable thoughts, fantasies, and plans. This defense provides the child (and later, the adult) with an effective strategy for avoiding pain and other uncomfortable emotions. It also leads Sevens to develop skills and strengths like an active imagination, a positive temperament, and an inventive mind. But avoiding harsh realities makes it hard for Sevens to handle (or even register) difficult emotions in naturally challenging situations. Automatically avoiding such things becomes habitual and unconscious. As the thinking behind this Seven life strategy goes, why would you choose to be sad (or anxious or uncomfortable) when you could be happy instead? Feeling good rather than bad seems to Sevens like a choice they can continually decide to make—and the thought of doing otherwise seems absurd to them.

In the history of many Sevens, often there was a good relationship with one parent, usually the mother, and a more challenging relationships with the other, usually the father. As Naranjo explains, the Seven most commonly had an authoritarian father "whose excessive dominance and sternness was experienced as lovelessness and not only contributed to an implicit judgment to the effect that authority is bad, but to the experience of an authority that is too strong to be met head-on."[7] A typical familial pattern for Sevens with regard to mothers, or mother figures, is that they are often experienced as "overprotective, permissive, and indulgent."[8] However, the gender roles may be reversed in some cases, with the mother playing the "paternal" authoritarian role and the father being perceived as more loving.

Based on their parental experience, Sevens get the idea early on that authority equals limitation and control from the outside. And Sevens, along with Type Eights, are among the types who most dislike being told what to do.

Sevens respond by retreating into the mind—and, more specifically, into imagining a positive future, best-case scenarios, and stimulating ideas and options. This distraction functions as a way of turning away from a potentially negative reality that might evoke unpleasant emotions. Thus, Sevens develop a talent for reframing a troubling present into a more positive and intellectually stimulating experience. In this way, as Naranjo suggests, Sevens "defend themselves through intelligence."[9]

Having learned to view fun and pleasure and "soft" forms of rebellion as strategic ways of meeting the dangers of being controlled and avoiding bad emotions or getting stuck in discomfort of any kind, the Seven becomes a pleasure-seeker and a good talker. More than just open-minded and exploratory, their search for stimulation through interesting and engaging experiences represents a way to defend against present discomforts: it "takes them from an insufficient here to a promising there."[10] They automatically avoid dealing with the threat of immediate unpleasantness by thinking about what they have to look forward to. They develop a mental focus on future possibilities and options as a way of distracting themselves from a deeper fear of getting stuck in unpleasant feelings and being limited by circumstances beyond their control.

Sam, a Type Seven, describes his childhood situation and the development of his coping strategy:

Sam was the youngest of Seven children and his mother's favorite. He was eight years younger than his nearest sibling. His mother had wanted to have him as a way to repair her difficult marriage with his father. Sam remembers his early life as one in which he was in caught in the middle between his parents' conflict. He had the sense that his mother really loved him, but his father was very angry and always yelling. Often they would fight over him and he would be put right in the middle of their battles. In this difficult situation, Sam retreated into the world of his mind. He read a lot and dreamed of places he would go and things he would do.

One time, after a particularly bad fight, he remembers his mother taking him to a hotel to get away from his father. As his mother cried, he recalls focusing on looking out the window and deciding he would enjoy the rain that was falling. He got intensely fascinated by beauty of the rain drops.

When his mom died when he was nine years old and he was left with a father who didn't want him around, his underlying insecurity increased and he continued to take refuge in his imagination. To this day he doesn't like controversy and conflict. Although he draws on his high energy and quick mind as assets in confronting people in court as a lawyer, he acknowledges that he doesn't deal very well with conflict in his personal life. If he is alone he will simply ignore any anxiety he might feel, and when he is out with friends he will get "charismatically nervous." He still reads a lot and he still retreats to his imagination and embellishes things in his mind as a way to escape from what might be happening in his life that feels uncomfortable.

The Main Type Seven Defense Mechanisms: Rationalization and Idealization

Type Sevens' characteristic ease with reframing things into positive terms is connected to their primary defense mechanisms, *rationalization* and *idealization*. Rationalization as a defense entails finding good reasons for doing whatever you want to do, seeing things however you want to see things, or believing whatever you want to believe. Naranjo cites Ernest Jones as saying that "rationalization is the invention of a reason for an attitude or action the motive of which is not acknowledged."[11]

All of us rationalize to create theoretical support for what we do or what happens to us. This allows us to buffer ourselves from the pain we might feel when something unfortunate happens to us or when we want to do something even though it's not good for us. If we've suffered a setback, we can think, "it was a good learning experience," which may make it easier to avoid feelings of defeat or failure. If we want to eat another piece of cake, but we know we shouldn't for health or diet reasons, we can say to ourselves, "it's just a small piece," or "it's okay because I will run five miles in the morning."

Using rationalization, Sevens can find good reasons for whatever they want to do, think, or feel. And while finding a rationale for what you are doing serves as a defense in protecting you from having bad feelings connected to your behavior, it also keeps you from direct contact with your real motives and the feelings connected to the things you do.

Seeing things in largely positive terms—or, more specifically, *needing* to see things in positive terms—also leads Sevens to use the defense mechanism of idealization. Idealization allows Sevens to perceive people and experiences as being better than they are, imbuing them with superhuman or super-positive qualities; this allows Sevens to avoiding reckoning with any flaws those people or things might have or any less-than-positive emotions they might inspire.

In some ways, of course, idealization can be a normal component of loving someone. Children idealize parents when they want to believe that someone loves them and will keep them safe. But when the Seven idealizes, they often do so to defend against feelings they might naturally have about the real person they are with. When this happens, idealization can keep them in a fantasy relationship instead of the one they are actually in. This can lead Sevens (often without their knowledge) to stay on the surface in a relationship and avoid a deeper experience of who the other person is, lest they tarnish the idealized (highly positive) version they have created in their heads.

The Type Seven Focus of Attention

Sevens tend to be self-referencing. In contrast to other types, like Twos and Nines, that focus more on other people, Sevens focus primarily on their own inner experience and needs, and, especially, their own thoughts. Since the main mode of psychological defense for the Seven is the escape into fantasy and positive mental possibilities, Sevens tend to focus their attention inward, on their own plans and preferences. This habit is essential to managing their experience by directing their internal thought processes. It can also lead Sevens to (often unconsciously) use their (mental) intelligence to manipulate others, as they naturally assert their own agenda by automatically focusing on their own wants, needs, and self-interest.

Sevens automatically pay attention to the positive data in a situation and can accentuate and expand it in their minds in a glass-half-full way until they see a best-case scenario unfolding. Unconsciously motivated to avoid pain, they want to feel good and stay upbeat and so tend to overlook or downplay the negative data in the environment, instead focusing on what will help them stay positive.

Characteristically pleasure-seeking, Sevens see the world as their oyster. They want to keep the mood as high as possible as much of the time as possible, so Sevens focus on experiencing the best of what life has to offer: the finest foods, the best wines, the most exciting locations and activities. Sevens happily earned their other descriptions as "the Epicure" or "the Adventurer." They perceive life in terms of endless opportunities and have an easy time imagining and moving toward stimulating experiences and possibilities. Their enthusiasm and readiness to be fascinated makes them very active people who energetically pursue a range of different hobbies or personal interests.

Sevens are the most optimistic of all the Enneagram types, and they habitually focus their attention on what is possible in the future. They can be charming visionaries with a thirst for new and stimulating experiences. Sevens sincerely believe that they can actualize all they can imagine for themselves—that they can attain whatever they aspire to.

Being future-oriented in this way allows Sevens to live in an imagined reality that's based on a positive vision of how they would like things to be. This idealized vision operates as a buffer against being or feeling in the present: Sevens think about future plans so they don't have to experience any potentially boring or negative reality that might be occurring in the present. A good Seven friend of mine says that as he goes through his day he "always needs to have something to look forward to."

Sevens also like to have a lot of options for enjoyable things to do so they can choose the most desirable option on the fly. With multiple possibilities in play, their attention automatically shifts to the best option if a particular plan becomes untenable or less desirable. This flexibility can make Sevens hedge their commitments—when you ask them to make a commitment, they may (enthusiastically) say "yes," but they often really mean "maybe." As they mentally sort for the best option, sometimes they need to bail out of a commitment at the last minute when another possibility offers a better experience. Sevens dislike limits, especially real-life constraints inhibiting their ability to move away from potential discomforts. Sevens have a kind of soft anti-authoritarian stance, for example one that might look to equalize authority within hierarchies to prevent those below them or above them from controlling them in any way.

Sevens' resistance against constraints also takes the form of an intense dislike of routine chores like paperwork or housework, which are inherently constraining. Their aversion to tedium also makes them gravitate toward work that doesn't involve repetition or a focus on boring details. Whenever possible, Sevens will define (or reframe) work tasks as fun so that even work gets turned into an enjoyable way to spend their time. The Seven habit of avoiding boredom or stagnation also fuels a tendency toward multitasking. They usually have several things—lines of thought and activities—going at the same time.

The Type Seven Emotional Passion: Gluttony

The "passion" or "chief feature" associated with Type Seven is *gluttony*. But gluttony as an Enneagram passion is not defined as a desire to consume large portions of food (according to the usual meaning of this word). In the context of the Enneagram, gluttony suggests an (often insatiable) hunger for stimulating experiences of all kinds, such as good meals, pleasurable interactions with others, interesting conversations, or exciting travel plans. Naranjo points out that all of the passions operate as an attempt to fill up an inner emptiness. Gluttony in this sense represents a desire to take in as many novel and superlative experiences as possible in an attempt to compensate for a feeling of underlying fear or insecurity. Maitri points out that gluttony motivates a desire to taste as many things as possible; that it is a "wanting more" that leads to taking in but not filling up. As "consuming rather than digesting is the focus," Sevens' gluttony for experience usually leads to a sense of dissatisfaction, which leads to (and is masked by) the pursuit of further stimulation.[12]

Naranjo describes gluttony as a "passion for pleasure." He explains that if we understand gluttony more broadly, we see that it constitutes a kind of hedonism and a generalized susceptibility to temptation that can end up inhibiting Sevens' growth. And while all of the passions have this quality of being both a key motivator and an eventual trap, it may be hard to see gluttony as an obstacle at first, especially because Sevens tend to be so charming and convincing in their pursuit of pleasure. It is as if they are asking, "What could be so wrong with wanting to have a good time?"

The passion of gluttony motivates Sevens to crave more and more—more pleasure, more of what feels good, and more thrilling experiences. Their pursuit of fun and pleasure can have a romantic cast, as an idealistic and excited search for more unique and extraordinary forms of fun and adventure. And while this can make the Seven attractive to others, who may get drawn in by their conviction that more is better and life is an exciting world of possibilities, it can also make it difficult for the Seven to establish deep relationships. The problem with this gluttony for pleasure-filled experience is that "insatiability [is] veiled over by an apparent satisfaction" and "frustration is hidden behind enthusiasm."[13] While Sevens' gluttony for experience arises from a desire to avoid suffering and emptiness, gluttony actually *is* their suffering.[14] Their gluttony for happiness is a way of running away from fear, especially the fear of pain.

So, while gluttony drives Sevens to continually seek out new and better forms of entertainment and stimulation, this compulsion to "want more" ultimately leaves Sevens emotionally empty. Pursuing pleasure doesn't lead to a satisfying feeling of contentment, because the strategy is mainly a defense against emotions Sevens don't want to feel. Despite their desire not to be limited, they constrain their own emotional life by experiencing things "from the safe remove of their minds."[15] They act out the fear they don't let themselves feel through a gluttonous search for mental stimulation that at the same time comforts them and prevents them from engaging with their authentic emotions. Even as Sevens talk about wanting deep engagement, they also fear it: their gluttony drives them around in circles.

The Type Seven Cognitive Mistake:
"Believing I'm Okay and You're Okay Isn't Always Okay"

We all get stuck in habitual ways of thinking that influence our beliefs, feelings, and actions, and this continues even after the mental models that create our overall perspective aren't accurate anymore. While the passion shapes the personality's emotional motivations, the "cognitive fixation" or "cognitive mistake" preoccupies the personality's thought processes. Type Sevens' cognitive stance centers on beliefs that support the passion of gluttony by focusing on the idea that the best way to live is to keep your mood up, have options, and be optimistic.

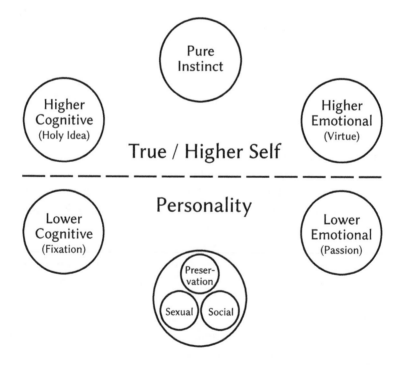

Under the sway of their personality's life strategy and patterns, Sevens sincerely hold beliefs that keep them focused on the positive and help them mentally defend against getting close to their pain. This cognitive approach to life expresses a deeper (often unconscious) fear that if they don't have options—and if they don't expend energy to stay happy—they will get stuck in a painful experience they don't believe they could tolerate. Underneath their positive mental attitude and their cognitive focus on happiness and pleasure, Sevens fear getting stuck in feelings of boredom, anxiety, sadness, depression, discomfort, or pain.

Thus, the following organizing principles underlie and support Type Seven's focus of attention.[16]

- I must always have pleasant options of fun things to do and think about so that I will feel good and not bad.
- If I am not focused on planning for and having positive experiences, I will get stuck in a painful feeling that I would much rather avoid.
- I must avoid experiencing pain, discomfort, or boredom, because if I allow myself to experience these emotions, I will likely become stuck in them for a long time, perhaps even forever.
- Being trapped in a negative emotional experience is something to be avoided at all costs.
- I can avoid pain and other negative emotions if I stay focused on the positive and seek out pleasant experiences.
- Limitations of any kind lead to negative feelings, and they should and can be avoided.
- By moving from one stimulating experience to another, I can keep discomfort at bay and keep life exciting.
- Why would anyone want to dwell in discomfort if they could be happy instead? Being happy and staying upbeat is a sensible, reasonable, and worthy goal.
- I won't be able to tolerate feelings of frustration, sadness, or pain, and thus must avoid them by always looking on the bright side.
- Life is about sampling as many good and fun things as possible.

While some of these Type Seven core beliefs are positive and life-affirming, they can be just as harmful and limiting in the end as any of the more obviously negative sets of mental organizing principles. In a way that might seem counterintuitive, Sevens can have a "maladaptive" or self-defeating belief in the need to stay positive. Their excessive positivity is really a coping strategy designed to perpetuate the illusion that we can live our lives to the fullest even as we avoid the inevitable pain of living.

The Type Seven Trap:
"Focusing Exclusively on Happiness Can Lead to Unhappiness"

As it does distinctly for each type, the cognitive fixation for Type Seven leads the personality in circles. It presents an inherent "trap" that the limitations of the personality cannot resolve. As Sandra Maitri observes, Sevens' "movement away from pain…ends up creating its own kind of anguish."[17]

Given their coping strategy and its associated focus of attention, Sevens typically end up caught in the conflict between the habit of avoiding pain through pursuing pleasure and the reality that you can't outrun your pain forever. The defensive maneuvers Sevens employ to avoid discomfort can, in the end, leave them depressed when they eventually realize that avoiding difficult feelings and realities doesn't make them go away.

In trying to avoid pain by focusing on pleasure, we inevitably create more pain for ourselves. When you avoid the bad stuff, it doesn't go away—it just gets swept under the carpet where someone can trip on it later. When we don't deal with problems in the present because we can't bring ourselves to focus on life's difficulties, we are bound to make life more difficult for ourselves when our challenges inevitably mount up and overflow.

Although we can all understand the appeal of wanting to avoid the pain in life, Sevens perpetuate their discomfort and underlying fear by trying to ignore the darker aspects of life. In the same way that light always casts a shadow, the light side of life that Sevens celebrate so well always has a corresponding dark side, which they often refuse to see.

When your life strategy is based on the illusory idea that focusing on the bright side will make the dark side go away, you set yourself up for surprising disappointment and failure. Keeping things light is an attractive option for fun and ease of movement, but when it's used to avoid facing the challenges inherent in human life and relationships, things have a way of taking a turn for the heavy or the dark anyway. And without experiencing the bad, how can we ever fully appreciate the good?

The Key Type Seven Traits

Self-Referencing

In the Enneagram system of personality types, the focus of each character's style can be self-referencing or other-referencing, or both. This distinction means that each personality has a focus of attention aimed at either what is going on inside their own self, what is going on with other people, or both.

In the case of Type Seven, the focus of attention is the Seven's own inner experience—their thoughts, preferences, desires, needs, and feelings. This pattern of attentional focus has the description "self-referencing" because the contents of the Seven's inner world is their primary focus. This habit makes Sevens tune in primarily to what they want, need, and do in an immediate way. Like any other essentially neutral trait, this tendency can be a good thing: for instance, Sevens tend to know what they want and need, which makes it much easier for them to get it. And as with anything else, this self-focus can also present problems, especially in relationships, when Sevens prioritize what they want to the extent that they fail to perceive and respond to the needs of others.

Positive Reframing/Optimism

Sevens excel at positively reframing situations that might be perceived in less-than-positive terms. Habitually oriented to keeping their mood upbeat, and automatically attentive to "the bright side," they are relentlessly optimistic; they easily reframe negatives into positives without much conscious effort.

Reframing comes naturally to Sevens, given their tendency to idealize their experience of the world. Framing things in positive terms goes hand in hand with the tendency to amplify positive data and minimize the negative, a strategy that allows Sevens to see things and people as better than they really are.

Like most elements of characterological coping strategies, reframing has its "positive" uses. It can be a highly effective way of maintaining a perspective that motivates people, for example, especially when external conditions make it hard to keep morale up. And it can also highlight important truths about what is good in a situation that some might initially view as negative.

But, like most habitual patterns, reframing can also be taken too far—especially by Sevens, who reframe reality to defend against seeing something real and important that they might label as "negative" because it gives them bad feelings. Positive reframing can cause Sevens to suspend criticality just when a critical eye is most needed. It can be a way of making everything all right and denying a real need to cope with something difficult. And it can eliminate "negative" data that may be vital to a deeper understanding of what is going on and what can or should be done to ensure a positive outcome.

Finally, the optimism and idealization common to Type Sevens can lead them to confuse imagination with reality. They so naturally and automatically see whatever is occurring through the positive vision of their imaginations that they can misread or ignore important elements of events or people that don't fit into that positive picture. Because looking on the bright side is socially acceptable—and it seems like common sense to many people—it is important for Sevens to see how this seemingly benign (or worthwhile) activity can also be taken too far in the context of the human ego. Since personality patterns are, by definition, unconscious, Sevens may not see the problems inherent in continually reframing what is happening in positive terms.

Hedonism

In the Seven's focus on hedonism, the goal of a pleasure-filled life rationalizes the avoidance of suffering. If one of your central values is that seeking pleasure in itself is an important and desirable goal, you can avoid questioning the deeper motivations that drive the "gluttonous pleasure bias."[18]

When hedonism becomes normalized, you have a ready rationale for the ongoing movement away from pain and into pleasure. And to the extent that Sevens' pleasure-seeking activities distract them from important emotions they don't want to feel, hedonism becomes a valid end in itself, justifying all manner of inspired avoidance practices. In this way, Sevens create a philosophy about the value of living for pleasure that supports their illusion that they can banish suffering and still manage to lead a full and fulfilling life.

In fully accepting the hedonistic attitude, Sevens may also habitually confuse pleasure with love, as Sevens typically came to feel loved through the experience of pleasure and indulgence in childhood.[19] As a result, Sevens regularly engage in self-indulgent experiences that they (unconsciously) take for love. Perpetuating this false equality between real love, which necessarily involves an active willingness to experience a whole range of feelings and not just the happy ones, and pleasure invites Sevens to believe that the hedonistic mode of living can supply an experience close to love—which it can't. In this way, fixated Sevens can believe they are having deep experiences of love when in reality they are just skimming along the hedonistic surface of what is possible in a relationship.

Rebelliousness

Given that Sevens want to do what they want to do when they want to do it—that they don't want to have limits imposed on them by other people—it follows that, like their fellow head-based types, they are essentially anti-authoritarian. However, because they dislike open conflict and the associated unpleasant feelings it may stir up, Sevens display more covert forms of rebelliousness.

Naranjo describes them as having an "anti-conventional orientation"[20] rather than an "anti-authoritarian" stance, as they adopt an attitude toward authority that is a form of "implicit rebellion," which manifests through their "keen eye for conventional prejudices" and often finds a "humorous outlet."[21] Their rebelliousness is thus "not confrontive or direct, but sly."[22]

Being anti-conventional allows you to question authority implicitly without feeling compelled to openly oppose it. Sevens would rather charm their way around a limiting authority figure through humor, intellectual manipulation, and seeming acquiescence than pick a fight that might lead to unpleasantness. An anti-conventional viewpoint also allows Sevens to question typical ways of doing things without having to abandon conventional behavior completely. Open opposition has the possible negative side effect of attracting more potentially limiting authoritarian attention, something that the morally flexible Seven excels at avoiding. As Naranjo points out, this makes Sevens the ideological forces behind revolutions rather than the activists.[23]

Generally, Sevens are kind and friendly people who "do not pay very much attention to authority and...implicitly assume authority to be bad."[24] Type Seven individuals are not so much engaged in an obvious struggle against authority, like Type Sixes or Type Eights, "they simply do not heed it."[25] They want to be free to indulge themselves—something that is often not possible in daily life when we are subject to the potentially inhibiting influences of parents, spouses, bosses, or subordinates—so they live in what Naranjo calls a "non-hierarchical psychological environment."[26] Sensitive to being constrained by outside authority, Sevens adopt an attitude that is "diplomatic rather than oppositional."[27]

Seven individuals don't take authority too seriously; they have confidence in their own ability to make potential tyrants into friends, so authority figures don't infringe excessively on Sevens' ability to indulge themselves. Similarly, Sevens find *being* the authority uncomfortable, preferring instead to exert influence through mental creativity and comradeship, "while at the same time assuming the garb of modesty."[28] They allow themselves and others a great deal of freedom; "their motto is 'live and let live.'"[29]

Lack of Focus/Discipline

The Type Seven tendency to avoid limits also leads to difficulty in maintaining focus and self-discipline. Sevens' ability to shift their mental focus very rapidly leads to a heightened ability for creative thinking, but it also means they have a difficult time focusing on one thing at a time. Sevens tend to be permissive with themselves and also highly distractable—both by internal and external stimuli. As a result, Sevens characteristically find it hard to focus on something for the full amount of time it takes to work from start to finish on something mundane.

Sevens view the world through an idealized lens instead of seeing it as the often limiting and frustrating place it is. This fantasizing about the future and intolerance for frustration and boredom in the present is a recipe for distraction. Besides, Sevens do not like to postpone pleasure. If there is something fun to do now, it can be easy for them to find a way to rationalize putting off a (less obviously enjoyable) work task in favor of doing something pleasurable.

The Type Seven Shadow

Sevens have blind spots related to the pain and discomforts inherent in life, and especially the potential *value* of feeling painful emotions. In many ways, Sevens' Shadow is the archetypal Shadow: they focus on the light and don't want to see the shadow of darkness that it casts. Their personality's perspective represents the reluctance many of us feel about facing the darker aspects of our experience and the desire most of us have to avoid feeling painful or frightening emotions. Sevens model the basic human impulse to retreat from pain and other bad feelings—a reaction that forms the basis of all our psychological defenses.

Many Sevens report a fear of getting stuck in fear or depression or other painful feelings; they express a belief that if they allow themselves to open up to feeling their deeper pain, they will become trapped in it forever. This underlying, sometimes unconscious, fear keeps the potential value of the conscious experience of pain—especially in the service of personal growth—in the Shadow, and it motivates the Seven's focus on pleasure, options, visions of the future, and freedom. Their conscious focus on pleasure helps them avoid unpleasant experiences; their conscious need for many options allows them to have potential exit pathways through which they can maneuver around uncomfortable situations; their attention on future possibilities helps them get away from difficult feelings in the present; and their preoccupation with freedom assures them that they won't be forced to stay in a particular painful reality.

Most of all, fear and anxiety themselves remain blind spots for Sevens, even though those emotions might drive many of their behaviors. Although Sevens belong to the "fear triad" of Enneagram types, they often report not feeling afraid (though more self-aware Sevens may sometimes be conscious of a vague or underlying sense of anxiety). When fear is kept in the Seven's shadow, it gets acted out in the search for mental stimulation, fun things to do and think about, and future adventures. In these ways, Sevens habitually avoid having regular contact with their pain—and, by extension, their emotional depths.

Related to the fear of fear, Sevens have a strong aversion to boredom—but this often expresses a resistance to becoming aware of experiences, like emptiness and discomfort, that Sevens relegate to their Shadow. Sevens are known for keeping up a fast pace in life. They tend to be fast talkers and quick thinkers. They like to keep moving, and this can reflect a desire to avoid whatever they might label as "boring." But behind their desire to not be bored is a potentially unconscious fear of having to slow down or sit still in the experience of stillness, which might cause uncomfortable feelings to arise.

While Sevens put their conscious focus on levity, fun, and happiness, they may also be sensitive to to not being taken seriously by others. Their need to be "light" can make it seem to other people that they are "lightweight," creating a situation in which they want to be seen as substantive and engaged but people perceive them as superficial or noncommittal. This perception in turn can make Sevens deny their own capacity for seriousness, or cause them to remain blind to their actual resilience in the face of discomfort. Their gluttony for positive experience and pleasure thus often hides a fear of what they might have to feel if they did not fill themselves up completely with what feels good.

The Shadow of the Type Seven Passion:
Gluttony in Dante's Underworld

The passion of gluttony, like lust, is a sin of indulgence. The gluttonous Shadow of Type Seven habitually subjects reason to this comfort-loving, thrill-seeking, pleasure-chasing appetite. In the *Inferno*, gluttony leads earthly souls to a diametrically opposite punishment based on an experience of complete deprivation:

> *We walked across this marsh of shades beaten down by the heavy rain, our feet pressing on their emptiness that looked like human form. Each sinner there was stretched out on the ground, except for one who quickly sat up straight the moment that he saw us pass him by...I said: "The pain you suffer here perhaps disfigures you beyond all recognition: I can't remember seeing you before. But tell me who you are, assigned to grieve in this sad place,*

afflicted by such torture that—worse well there may be, but none more foul."[30]

Dante's images show the arrogance and excess of the gluttonous appetite for pleasure being punished in the perpetual discomfort of filthy muck. Pressed together like paving stones, howling with hunger, the Gluttons' only excess now is the stinking slime coating them, and they suffer extreme discomfort under a constant storm of filthy rain and hail.[31] As Dante the Pilgrim observes, other passionate fixations might have more painful consequences, but none could be more humiliating than the miseries inflicted upon unrestrained appetite. Thus Dante symbolically communicates the dark side of gluttony: when your unconscious gluttony for pleasure runs amok, it inevitably leads to discomfort. The appetites of the lower self (personality) are insatiable, and we only become fulfilled when we can leave behind our passionate excess and ascend to a higher state of being.

The Three Kinds of Sevens: The Type Seven Subtypes

THE THREE SEVENS EACH REPRESENT a different way of expressing or responding to the passion of gluttony. The Self-Preservation Seven finds security through a gluttonous search for pleasure, satisfying opportunities, and cultivating a network of allies. The Social Seven expresses a kind of anti-gluttony by being of service to others. The Sexual Seven channels gluttony into an idealistic search for the ultimate relationship and the best imaginable experiences.

The three subtypes of Seven therefore represent three different manifestations of gluttony, each one depending on the dominant instinctual drive. When the drive for self-preservation dominates, we see a Seven character whose gluttony motivates him to find security and opportunities for well-being in a close network of family members, friends, and associates. When the social instinct is prominent, we see a Social Seven who goes against gluttony by sacrificing his own needs for the good of others. And when the drive for sexual or one-to-one connection dominates, the Seven character is expressed through an exceedingly enthusiastic personality whose gluttony for pleasurable experiences creates a tendency to view reality in an extremely positive way.

The Self-Preservation Seven: "Keeper of the Castle"

Self-Preservation Sevens express gluttony through the formation of alliances. They typically collect around them a kind of family network, in the sense of banding together with trusted others and creating a good "mafia" or partisan group through which they can get their needs met. They rely mostly on those they trust. These Sevens create a kind of surrogate family of people they value—a family in which they typically occupy a privileged position.

These Sevens are very practical, good at networking, and skilled at getting what they want and finding a good deal; they tend to be opportunistic, self-interested, pragmatic, calculating, and clever. They readily recognize opportunities for creating an advantage for themselves. In this way, Naranjo explains, gluttony expresses itself in the Self-Preservation Seven in an excessive concern with making a good deal at every opportunity.

Self-Preservation Sevens always have their nose to the wind for good opportunities. They find ways to get what they need and want, and they have an easy way of finding pathways to making things happen for themselves— whether it's finding the right people, the most advantageous connections, or a fortuitous career opportunity. They have their ears to the ground and are socially adept.

These Sevens make business connections and network easily because they are alert and mindful to the opportunities that come along that can support their survival. They hold the position that if you are not alert to opportunities, you will lose out. This Self-Preservation theme is expressed well in the proverb "The alligator that sleeps becomes a bag." There's an element of self-interest in the alliances the Self-Preservation Seven makes that may or may not be denied by (or unconscious in) someone with this subtype. Naranjo says there is a kind of reciprocal interest in these relationships, expressed in the idea that "I will serve thee, and thou will serve me." On the low side of this kind of arrangement, an element of corruption can be present.

Stylistically, Self-Preservation Sevens are cheerful and amiable, with traits that resemble a hedonistic, "playboy" or "playgirl" type. They tend to be warm, friendly, and talkative. (They love to talk.) They can express a kind of greed and impatience that reflects their desire to consume as many pleasurable experiences as possible; they want to eat everything. They expend a lot of energy on controlling everything, handling things without being noticed. And most of the time, they get away with getting what they want.

The dominant traits of the Self-Preservation Seven subtype stand out as a love of pleasure and a self-interested focus on getting what they need to feel secure. In seeking security, however, they can often confuse desires with needs.

These are people who usually feel a need to have a lot of resources, including money and other supplies that support survival, and they may panic if they feel a sense of scarcity.

According to Naranjo, the three main fixations of the Self-Preservation Sevens are strategy, rebellion, and isolation, though it may be hard to see these characters as isolated because they tend to be very popular. But their strategic and mental nature, together with the prominence of their self-interest, can isolate them from others at a deeper level.

Self-Preservation Sevens cultivate a sense of being kind and generous—they like to feel that everyone depends on them. They may feel omnipotent and they may sometimes use people. They may also feel that normal rules don't apply to them—that for them, there is no law, and they can do what they please. This kind of assertion of their freedom and their ability to do whatever they need to do to support their self-interest helps them feel safer in the world.

Self-Preservation Sevens' desire for pleasure and hedonistic self-indulgence can sometimes be seen as a kind of retroactive compulsion to return to the womb—they dedicate their lives to the pursuit of a kind of primordial or utopian paradise state of perfect pleasure. In pursuing positive and stimulating experiences, they may use sex, food, and drink as an escape from the more difficult parts of life.

The Self-Preservation Seven and the Sexual Seven should be easy to tell apart, as they represent two opposite ends of a continuum, from pragmatic and materialistic (Self-Preservation) to idealistic and ethereal (Sexual). The Self-Preservation subtype is more earthy and sensuous—more gluttonous in the literal sense of the word—while the Sexual Seven is more "heavenly" and enthusiastic, more "upward-looking" in terms of both positivity and high ideals. While both of these two characters focus on distinct kinds of excess, the Self-Preservation Seven is the most sly, cunning, and pragmatic personality among the Sevens, while the Sexual Seven is more of a light-hearted enjoyer.

In contrast to the Sexual Seven, the Self-Preservation Seven is not so much idealistic as they are cynically distrustful. They're not gullible people who are easily hypnotized (as the Sexual Seven is); they are more practical and concrete. The Self-Preservation Seven is the most astute and strategic character of the three Seven subtypes. They may display elements of Type Six in that they can at times be fearful or even paranoid, though this is not their regular mode. And perhaps paradoxically, the Self-Preservation Seven is more actively flirty, seductive, and sexual than the Sexual Seven, who often focuses more on an imagined, idealized kind of communion than actual sex. While the Self-Preservation Seven character resembles a "playboy" or "playgirl" type of person—an enjoyer of food and sex—the Sexual Seven can be content with the perfume of things.

Self-Preservation Sevens may experience less difficulty than other Sevens with making commitments. For instance, many Self-Preservation Sevens report that they have been married for many years or that they have had a solid relationship with a partner for a long period of time. When they participate in groups, however, it may be so they can feel a sense of having access to resources if they need something at some point. Often, having close relationships is something they view as an investment, like putting money in the bank—you always have someone you can call on if you need some specific kind of help. For that reason they tend to be very active in the groups they join and the networks they are affiliated with.

Naranjo explains that spiritual aspiration is not so common in Self-Preservation Sevens; they often reject religion and tend not to believe in anything. They're more practical, more materialistic, and more rebellious than the other two Seven subtypes. They're very cheerful and friendly, but also disconnected from their emotions. They are sensuous, earthly, worldly characters who can be very entertaining and who display a light-hearted lack of seriousness—though when it comes to finding security through making money and establishing a network of associates, they display keen self-interest.

When Self-Preservation Sevens have the Sexual instinct as their second most dominant instinct, they can look more like Sixes (more isolated, overly careful, and strategic), and when they have the Social instinct in second place, they may look more like magnanimous Eights (people-oriented and impulsive). However, unlike Sixes, they tend to be relentlessly positive and to find security through pursuing their self-interest; and in contrast to Eights, they tend to be motivated by a survival fear or anxiety deeper down, even if they aren't always aware of it.

Joe, a Self-Preservation Seven, speaks:

There is a gluttonous element in me that I believe stems from an early understanding in childhood that life is inherently evanescent. Opportunities missed are not easily regained. In that light, as I approached my graduation from middle school and prepared to go to high school, I realized that it was time to weigh my priorities and start planning for a career and a life maximally lived. So, at thirteen years old, I prioritized:

1) living and enjoying life to the fullest while it was possible; 2) helping others do the same; 3.) not hurting others along the way. That was in eighth grade.

The road to medical school and beyond involved painful sacrifices in regards to quality of life. I endured a decade of deferred pleasure and buried myself in my studies by making the most of my intellectual interest in medicine and the awesome experience of becoming a surgeon. What got me through the hard work was the clear vision I had of a complete life: weighing the short-term missed experiences against the long-term pleasures and security over the span of a full life as a plastic surgeon helped me see that the hardships involved in becoming a doctor were worth it. To keep things balanced, I played hard during my brief breaks from work and tried not to miss a minute of fun with friends on weekends or nights off.

While the sacrifices involved in becoming a surgeon weren't easy, I now find myself in the most wondrous position of having fulfilled my "mission statement"—I've done the most good with the least harm while reaping additional quality-of-life benefits. I love my artist wife beyond words. We sail and grow organic vegetables together. I enjoy the challenges of growing grapes and making wine, and we are creating an aesthetically beautiful and self-sustaining homestead. I relish the rewards of time at work and even more at play. What could be better than or wrong with that?

I am aware, however, that I am less in touch with my emotions than might be ideal, as experiencing life more intensely on many different levels makes sense to me. I enjoy the experience when love, empathy, and other emotions well up into my consciousness, but I usually function quite happily on a more cerebral plane. Other times, fear or anxiety may enter the room, but I am less eager to tolerate their presence. I have learned to listen to my intuition and emotions, but unless they present an actionable warning, I prefer not to dwell on negative moods.

The Social Seven: "Sacrifice" (Countertype)

Social Sevens represents a kind of a pure character that, as the countertype of the Type Seven subtypes, expresses a kind of "counter-gluttony." Social Sevens go against the Seven passion of gluttony in that they consciously avoid exploiting others. Naranjo says it's as if they can sense the tendency within themselves toward gluttony and decide to instead define themselves as anti-gluttonous.

If gluttony is a wish for more, a wish for taking advantage of all you can get from a situation, there is a hint of exploitation in gluttony. But as the countertype, the Social subtype wants to be good and pure and *not* act on their gluttonous impulse. This is a person who wants to avoid being excessive or excessively opportunistic, and who works against any unconscious tendency they may have to exploit others.

Gluttony may thus be difficult to recognize in Social Sevens because they strive to hide it in altruistic behavior. This purifies them of the guilt of feeling an attraction toward pleasure or toward acting in their own self-interest in ways that cause them to take advantage of others.

Social Sevens avoid focusing on their own self-interest or advantage by pursuing an ideal of themselves and the world. They sacrifice their gluttony to become a better person and to work for a better world in which there is no pain or conflict. As Naranjo explains, they defer their own desires in pursuit of an ideal.

In their efforts to work against gluttony, Social Sevens can actually be too pure. Their efforts to attain purity can extend to worrying about their diet, their health, and their spirit. Interestingly, Naranjo notes, these Sevens are often vegans.

In striving for purity and anti-gluttony, they express a kind of ascetic (or Five-ish) ideal. They make a virtue of getting by on less for themselves. In trying to prove their goodness, they typically give others more, and take less for themselves, as a way of going against their gluttonous desire for more. Even though they might want the biggest piece of cake, they go against that impulse and take the smallest one instead, leaving the larger portions for others.

Social Sevens take on a lot of responsibility in the group or the family. In doing this, they express a sacrifice of gluttony for the benefit of others. They postpone their own desires in order to enact an ideal of service. As the name of this subtype suggests, "Sacrifice" means a willingness to be of service.

But where is the ego reward in this seemingly pure, unselfish personality strategy? Part of the ego strategy of this subtype is that they want—crave—to be seen as good for their sacrifice. They have a hidden gluttony for the acknowledgment of their sacrifice—are hungry for love and recognition—and this hunger can be insatiable. These Sevens use their sacrifice to cover up defects and shortcomings and to invite recognition and admiration or love, because they don't feel right legitimizing and acting on their desires and whims. Their sacrifice and service is the price they pay for their neurotic need for admiration.

In addition to inspiring appreciation and recognition in others, Social Sevens want to have a good image, to reduce conflicts, and to create debts in others. However, these motivations can lead these Sevens to enter into relationships that are relatively superficial.

In line with their need for recognition of their sacrifices, there is a tendency in this Social subtype to adopt the role of helper, to be of service, and to be concerned with the alleviation of pain. But while they are drawn to alleviate others' pain, they don't like to feel it themselves, and so helping others may also be a way for them to project their pain somewhere outside themselves and try to relieve it at a safe distance. They are always "being" for the other. This is an indulgent and generous character capable of managing projects and mobilizing energies for a particular purpose. They tend to deliver the services they provide with a lot of dedication.

Social Sevens experience an inner taboo on selfishness and want to be seen as the "good child" or the "good person." They experience repressed guilt for hiding their self-interest in the guise of good, and they may project their disowned guilt for their unacknowledged gluttony onto others, then judge them for not being committed or dedicated enough. These Sevens may also distrust themselves because they know they mix up altruism and self-interest; they may judge their own deeper motivations as "bad" or "self-interested."

Social Sevens are very idealistic, but their idealism is a mix of illusion, good intentions, and ingenuity that function together as an "intellectual drug" that motivates action. They're very active, moved in an ongoing way by the ideals they want to translate into life to improve the world, but they need their idealism to help them to activate—they invest a lot in altruism, idealism, dedication, and sacrifice to make them feel more acceptable. They also tend to use the defense of rationalization to support the things they do in the name of altruism and idealism. Their idealism is in part based on rationalizing ideologies so that if any of their beliefs are proved wrong, they can simply replace it with another rationale and then explain this change as evolution. Given this, they may have an underlying sense of panic about losing their idealism, as they fear that would ultimately lead to apathy and emptiness.

Social Sevens' focus on motivating themselves through idealism can take the form of a feeling of being on a mission—they may want to be "The Savior." They may at times criticize themselves for being naive and unrealistic, for wanting too much of mankind—and the Social Seven does have some youthful or adolescent qualities: they are provocative, enlightened, can be simplistic, and can get lazy when the task becomes too demanding. And in addition to this, they may not be conscious of their own laziness, love of comfort, and narcissism.

Naranjo explains that enthusiasm, idealism, and social skills are the three pillars of the Social Seven personality. These Sevens are also visionaries: they imagine a better, freer, healthier, more peaceful world. (New Age culture is a Social Seven culture.) They often express excessive enthusiasm about their visions and may have fantasies of a perfect future. They have a tendency to manipulate through enthusiasm. On the surface, they appear very joyful, and they avoid dissonance and conflict.

In relationships, Social Sevens may feel challenged when they get caught between their strong desire not to cause another person pain and their fear of commitment. In keeping with their desire to be pure and maintain their idealistic stance, they look for a kind of romantic love that is pure and perfect. They unconsciously put themselves in an arrogant position of being "better" or more pure than their partners and then expecting them to evolve toward perfection. They may also have difficulty navigating the deeper emotions that get stirred up by intimate relationships.

Because of their enthusiasm and joyfulness, as well as their prominent desire to help and be of service, Social Sevens can look like Twos—but while Twos focus primarily on others and don't have as much of a connection with their own selves, Social Sevens are still primarily self-referencing, not other-referencing, so they will usually know what they need, even if they decide to sacrifice it. Their desire to help is born of the need to go against a sense of self-interest, not just a desire for approval, so they have a more direct experience of their own needs and wants despite their tendency to make efforts to serve others or a higher good. These are people who are very pure—and in this way they can also look One-ish—but theirs is a goodness for applause, a desire to reach an ideal of perfection or purity that's based on social consensus (as opposed to Ones' internally generated sense of what is "right").

Rusty, a Social Seven, speaks:

The easiest thing to forget about Sevens is that fear drives us and safety is what all the options are for. We are practiced at not showing our desperation on the surface. As a Social Seven, "Sacrifice" plays out without too much trouble for me, because in the vast array of possibilities, any treasure is expendable as long as there is some other nugget to gloat over. This goes for any cause or endeavor, no matter what the seemingly altruistic reason or the secret self-reward.

Idealism and the desire to be seen as a good person rather than a greedy person has led me to join a long series of philanthropic groups. I love the feeling of safety and certainty I get in groups, even though I generally join groups in which I don't exactly belong. No matter how committed I was to breathing life into the touring theater company, in the final analysis it was the fact of hating to perform soliloquies that allowed me to leave that safe haven for something else. While we Social Sevens can look like Twos, my deep impulse to stop nodding and agreeing (along with not having a truly deep need-anchor of my own) is what has allowed me to leave just about as many groups as I have joined, no matter how devastating the wreckage left behind. Or how still the pond without a ripple.

Grappling to own the Four-ish/Seven-ish fact of narcissism, I balked until it clicked that seeing too much of both goodness, virtue, and beauty and wickedness, evil, and inadequacy in my reflection ultimately leads down the same rabbit hole of overexamining myself. So, in many efforts to get outside myself, for my own good, serially joining and leaving has put me on many peaks and in many corners. With myriad projects, plans, and escape hatches comes that ability to illuminate and stitch together odd similarities and unique insights, always from way out of left field: for instance, I have been the only person at the logging camp carrying a dulcimer, the guy fresh from Wyoming managing an A&D showroom on Madison Avenue in NYC, the Quaker in a Presbyterian church choir, the token straight man in a gay men's chorus, and so on. I like to sneak in the side door, stir things up, make contributions large or small, grab several magpie points for virtue, and then I've gotta go.

The Sexual Seven: "Suggestibility"

Individuals with the Sexual Seven subtype are gluttons for things of the higher world—for optimistically seeing things as they could be in the ideal world of their imaginations. Sexual Sevens are dreamers with a need to imagine something better than stark, ordinary reality. These Sevens have a passion for embellishing everyday reality, for being too enthusiastic, and for idealizing things and seeing the world as better than it actually is. Their gluttony gets expressed as a need for idealization.

Sexual Sevens are not as interested in the things of this world as they are in the things of a more highly advanced dimension. They look at the sky as an escape from the earth; they are more "heavenly" than "earthy." People with this subtype are light-hearted enjoyers with a need to dream and to idealize and embellish the ordinary. In line with this tendency, they can be very idealistic and somewhat naive.

These Sevens tend to look at things with the optimism of somebody who is in love. Everything looks better when you are in love, and the Sexual Seven takes refuge in this kind of ideal, positive experience as a way of unconsciously avoiding what might be unpleasant in life. They focus on a highly positive view of life to distract themselves from the uncomfortable or scary emotions they would rather remain unaware of.

It is said that "love is blind." Naranjo contends that Sexual Sevens may be said to be blind in this same sense: they display a bit too much enthusiasm and optimism and pay disproportionate attention to the positive data in a situation. These Sevens can fall in love very intensely, and they relate to their world through dreaming and imagination. They imagine what the world could be, and they can believe that this optimistic view is real.

In this way, Sexual Sevens express a need to fantasize, a need to dream, or a need for rose-colored glasses. These Sevens have a tendency to be *too* happy. They display a need to live in a charmed reality, to fantasize—to live in a world they create in their minds rather than the actual external world. This can be seen as an overcompensation that reflects an unconscious desire to deny or avoid the painful or boring or frightening parts of life. Sexual Sevens tend to experience an underlying fear of getting stuck in these kinds of feelings and so take refuge in optimism.

This Seven's need to dream is a form of idealization—a passion for viewing life as it could be or as they imagine it to be; a tendency to live for the sweetness in a dreamed-of or imagined world rather than for the ordinary and not-so-interesting reality. They don't want to pay attention to anything bad or difficult that might be happening.

Sexual Sevens think, "I'm okay, everything's okay." Naranjo points out that this way of thinking is very therapeutic for everyone who is *not* a Seven. Sexual Sevens often had some sort of painful experience growing up and they've adopted a sense of lightness as a defense against feeling their pain. They defensively take refuge in a happy, or excessively happy, and expansive mood that operates as a way of unconsciously diverting themselves from recognizing and feeling a deeper pain. It's like walking lightly above things or hovering at an elevated level as a means of escaping the uncomfortable emotions.

The name given to this type is "Suggestibility," which implies a readiness to be mentally flexible and imaginative—but it also has to do with being gullible, easy to hypnotize, and susceptible to the infection of enthusiasm. Naranjo points out that Sexual Sevens' cognitive defenses are shaped as suggestion, fantasy, and illusion. They can naively believe that people are what they say they are, and they can be very trusting, seeing the world and people in beautiful, perhaps overly positive, terms. They run to an idyllic future and away from a potentially uncomfortable or painful present. They display a prevalence of thought and imagination over feeling and instinct.

In terms of personal style, Sexual Sevens are people who like to talk a lot. They are verbose and excited by their own discourse, and their speech is characterized by a flow of "wonderful ideas and possibilities." They can also play the role of the carefree clown whom nothing seems to affect. People with this subtype tend to use ironic humor, which can be escapist, and they test limits through seduction and humor. They seek acceptance, appreciation, and recognition, and they manipulate through seduction.

Sexual Sevens plan and improvise a lot. They believe that they can do everything, and they feel a need to plan or mount successful strategies that will ensure their pleasure. They may experience anxiety, however, about the difficulty of engaging in many scenarios at once and having to give something up. They can have a restless and anxious energy, which can take the outer form of doing things on many fronts and engaging in many activities at the same time. Their excitement and anxiety can cloud their perception of reality. At times they may rebel through passive-aggression, which they tend to do by living in their imagination—relating to situations as they would like them to be and not taking action in the real world.

Sexual Sevens see the world as a marketplace of outstanding opportunities: the more you take, the more you can enjoy. These Sevens express excitement about the possibility of consuming many experiences—everything is exciting and spectacular—like someone who goes to a bakery and wants to try a bit of everything. They find a sense of satisfaction in being able to have it all, in not missing or losing out on anything.

Contrary to what we might expect from this "Sexual" Seven subtype, this Seven is not so much focused on sex as they are on the essence of love. Sexual Sevens fall in love very easily, but they're not as interested in having sex with someone as they are in attaining a kind of idealized ultimate connection. Sexuality itself stays primarily in the head for these characters. It's a normal sexuality on one hand, but it's a promise for a bigger opening to a mystical union on the other.

Sexual Sevens are gluttons for things of the higher world, and this makes them dreamers. They often feel an attraction to spiritual or metaphysical experience, as well as to extraordinary or esoteric things. Earthly, mundane things can be very hard to bear for a person who lives in a more idealized mental reality, and so this individual can have an intense dislike for activities they find routine, tedious, or boring.

For the Sexual Seven, earthly things take effort, and can therefore feel boring or tedious, whereas the mind works so easily and without friction. It's so much easier to imagine doing something than to actually do it. So, this Seven finds comfort—indulging a kind of worldly laziness—in imagining instead of doing.

Adam, a Sexual Seven, speaks:

I deeply resonate with the description of the Sexual Seven. While I have never been a glutton for things or substances, I have been a glutton for idealization, learning, and good energy. In order to feel okay, I have generally needed to feel positively "stoked." In fact, my nickname in high school was "EnthusiAdam." I was very excited about most facets of my life, and my enthusiasm was contagious. This characterization of me has remained fairly constant, although I have mellowed somewhat as I've aged.

I have also thought of myself as a serious romantic, and much of my thinking is consistent with an enneatype of Four: I love deeply, I love being in love, and I have always longed for love. As such, I was very careful about who I chose as my wife. I needed to be unequivocal about this important decision—and, thankfully, I chose well. I have been madly in love with her for the now more-than-eleven years we've been together. What is now a reality was previously a dream that I spent much time visualizing and fantasizing about, and I'm now aware that these activities are consistent with this subtype.

I have a strong dislike for the mundane. I find mindless chatter difficult to bear, and I really, really can't stand housework. The only way I can do housework is by distracting myself with an MP3 of a stimulating lecture and being left alone while I do my chores. Then, at least, I'm learning—the time is not a total waste and my gluttony for learning is satisfied.

Lastly, I have spent a great deal of time fantasizing about my ideal retirement. For me, that retirement would involve traveling with my beloved wife, plenty of intellectual stimulation, endless fun, and tons of time for deep connection with her.

"The Work" for Type Seven: Charting a Personal Growth Path

ULTIMATELY, AS SEVENS WORK ON THEMSELVES and become more self-aware, they learn to escape the trap of pursuing more superficial pleasures and avoiding the enjoyment of a deeper experience of themselves. They do this by slowing down and allowing themselves to be present, appreciating the value of their fear and their pain, and finding the joy in personal connections that comes when they connect with their own depths.

For all of us, waking up to habitual personality patterns involves making ongoing, conscious efforts to observe ourselves, reflect on the meaning and sources of what we observe, and actively work to counter automatic tendencies. For Sevens, this means observing the ways they avoid the deeper parts of themselves (and life) to stay comfortable; exploring the ways they lose contact with themselves when they defend against pain and seek out pleasure; and making active efforts to reconnect with themselves and reengage with life on a deeper and more immediate level. It is particularly important for them to learn to endure the pain involved in inner work with the understanding that true joy, contentment, and aliveness come from facing what we tend to run away from and integrating what scares us.

In this section I offer some ideas of what Sevens can notice, explore, and aim for in their efforts to grow beyond the constraints of their personality and embody the higher possibilities associated with their type and subtype.

Self-Observation: Dis-Identifying from Your Personality by Watching It in Action

Self-observation is about creating enough internal space to really watch—with fresh eyes and adequate distance—what you are thinking, feeling, and doing in your everyday life. As Sevens take note of the things they think, feel, and do, they might look out for the following key patterns:

Focusing on pleasure as a way to escape pain

Observe what happens when you speed up and head toward an experience that promises to be pleasurable. Try to get clearer about your motives when you feel driven toward a particular experience of pleasure. Ask yourself if you might be moving toward fun as a way of avoiding the threat of feeling something uncomfortable, and what, exactly, you might be trying to get away from. Notice if you change the subject during a conversation to avoid an unpleasant topic. Tune in to the ways you may flee when a painful feeling threatens to arise. Observe what is happening when your enthusiasm rises or the pace of your activity or planning increases. What are you moving toward? What might you be running away from? Think about what is motivating you when your search for fun intensifies or you distract yourself with stimulating ideas while trying to focus on something less interesting. Inquire into your feelings if something objectively painful happens, and notice what you do in response. Notice the way you devalue specific experiences by framing them negatively, thereby justifying (or rationalizing) the act of avoiding them.

Confusing indulgence and freedom from limits with love

Observe what happens when you engage in "soft rebellion." Note how you experience the "authorities" in your life, even if this includes your partner or a friend who has expectations of you. Notice how you deal with options and how you respond to constraints others place on you. What kinds of things do you feel limited by? How do you react to these perceived or actual limitations? Try to tune into any fear or anxiety connected to your experience of feeling constrained by others. Notice any fears related to being trapped in discomfort, and think about what that might be about. What do you imagine that fuels your fear of limits? Observe the ways in which you might indulge in pleasure when what you really want is love. Notice the ways in which you indulge yourself as a way of finding comfort. Note if you equate limitation with a lack of love and indulgence with love and think about why. Tune in to what is happening inside you if some sort of painful experience seems to intensify your quest for pleasure. Think about what you really want from the people you are closest to, and note if you push them toward engaging in fun with you when what you really want is love or attention.

Living for or in the future as a way of avoiding being present now

Observe what is happening when you are focused on the future. Inquire into your deeper motivations if you feel a compulsion to plan for a future adventure. Notice what your visions of the future look like and how they might function as a way to escape (or compensate for) what's happening in the present. Think about what is going on *now* when you are focused on what is going to happen *then*. Observe any tendency you might have to imagine an excessively utopian or optimistic future scenario. What motivates you at a deeper level when you create these positive, futuristic pictures? What, exactly, is so good about your imagined future? Is there something specific you are trying to get away from? Try to slow your pace and observe what happens, especially if any emotions or sensations arise.

Self-Inquiry and Self-Reflection: Gathering More Data to Expand Your Self-Knowledge

As Sevens observe these and other related patterns in themselves, the next step on the Enneagram growth path is to *understand* these patterns better. Why do they exist? Where do they come from? What purpose do they serve? How do they get you in trouble when they are intended to help you? Often, seeing the root causes of a habit—why it exists and what it is designed to do—is enough to allow you to break out of the pattern. In other cases, with more entrenched habits, knowing how and why they operate as defenses can be a first step to eventually being able to release them.

Here are some questions that Sevens can ask themselves, and some possible answers they can consider, to get more insight into the sources, operation, and consequences of these patterns.

How and why did these patterns develop? How do these habits help Type Sevens cope?

In understanding the sources of their defensive patterns and how they operate as coping strategies, Sevens have the opportunity to become more aware of how and why they avoid deeper and darker experiences and hover more at the surface of things. If Sevens can tell the story of their early life and look for ways in which they may have needed to retreat from fear and pain as a way to cope, they can have compassion for their young self, who may have developed that strategy in order to stay happy. Exploring the "how and why" of the development of their habitual patterns can also provide Sevens with a larger perspective on how their pursuit of happiness paradoxically prevents them from having a fuller and richer experience of life. Gaining insight into how their need for levity actually masks important aspects of experience helps Sevens realize how their personality style helps them stay comfortable and blocks them from contact with their deepest inner sources of vitality. Seeing how needing freedom to escape pain worked as a protection early on enables Sevens to see how they can become trapped in the limiting "acorn shell" of their personality, even while they believe they are free.

What painful emotions are the Type Seven patterns designed to protect me from?

For all of us, the personality operates to protect us from painful emotions, including what psychological theorist Karen Horney calls our "basic anxiety"—a preoccupation with the emotional stress of not getting basic needs fulfilled. For Sevens, however, their specific "false self" personality is exactly designed to help them avoid an awareness of their painful emotions. The Seven personality often develops as a response to not having enough protection—or the right kind of protection—early in life; it operates defensively to distract the Seven individual from having to feel difficult emotions like pain, sadness, fear, anxiety, envy, and inadequacy. The Seven personality is the prototype of the way all the personalities—to one extent or another—protect us from bad feelings by helping us focus on and generate good feelings. And while this is often necessary in childhood, in order to have healthy relationships and to become all we are meant to be as adults, we must see how our early defenses against pain have come to represent obstacles to a fuller expression of who we are.

Why am I doing this? How do the Type Seven patterns operate in me now?

Through reflecting on how their patterns operate in the present, the three kinds of Sevens can begin to have a greater awareness of how they distract themselves when they feel uncomfortable, or how they make plans with escape hatches. If they can consciously catch themselves in the act of avoiding making a commitment, they can wake up to the deeper motivations that drive them to seek comfort in positive stimulation. It can be eye-opening for Sevens to see how they deprive themselves of a deeper sense of their own aliveness and connection to others when they automatically divert their attention to the pursuit of amusement. By tracking their habits of mind, they can see how actively remaining stuck in old patterns prevents them from having an ideal experience of all they can be, even if those patterns are about promising fun and excitement. Sevens open a door to a more complete sense of fulfillment when they can see how and why their personality patterns inhibit them in an ongoing way.

What are the blind spots of these patterns? What do Type Sevens keep themselves from seeing?

To really increase their self-knowledge, it will be important for Sevens to remind themselves about what they *don't* see when their personality's programming is driving the show. Sevens tend to focus on what feels good and serves their interests. But when they pay attention to their own priorities as a way of asserting their freedom and staving off limitation, they may not always pay sufficient attention to what other people need and want. And while their intentions toward others are often pure and positive, their reluctance to tune into their own deeper feelings means they unconsciously avoid empathizing with others. In addition to this, Sevens' habit of moving away from the difficult feelings they keep in their Shadow may keep them trapped in exactly the kinds of painful experiences they try to avoid. When you don't see the value in contacting your own pain and discomfort, you can't effectively deal with it in ways that can support your growth and expansion. If you have a blind spot where your sensitivities, your fears, and your sadness would normally be, how can you forge an effective and enlivening connection with your depths? When you fail to see your own deeper feelings—when you can't allow them to surface because you fear getting trapped in them—it's hard to wake up to all of who you are. Focusing on looking for what you don't see may help you get out of the habit of always needing to feel good and allow you to realize your capacity to feel whole.

What are the effects or consequences of these patterns? How do they trap me?

The irony of the Seven strategy is that by trying to remain happy all the time, you limit your ability to grow and to experience the full range of human emotion. When you are only interested in being happy, you can't do the inner work of growing beyond the limited constraints of your ("acorn") personality because you don't have the desire or the fortitude to "go underground" and allow your shell to break open. As discussed in Chapter 2, for all of us, the

path of growth to a higher state of being necessarily passes through a full engagement with our fear, our pain, and all the emotions we learn to avoid when
we adopt a coping strategy to survive in the world. When we (consciously or
unconsciously) decide we are only going to experience the positive side of life,
we prevent ourselves from going through the "dark night of the soul" that is
a part of any inner journey of waking up and coming home to the true self.
If you can't face your darker emotions by feeling them all the way through,
receiving the information they bring about who you are, and letting them go,
you can't break the acorn shell open to reveal the future oak tree inside.

Self-Development:
Aiming for a Higher State of Consciousness

For all of us who seek to wake up, the next step in working with type-based
knowledge of the personality is to begin to inject more conscious effort into
everything we do—to begin to think, feel, and act with more choice and
awareness. In this section I provide some ideas for Sevens about "what to do"
after they've observed the key patterns and done some investigation into their
sources, operation, and consequences.

This last section is divided into three parts, each corresponding to one of
three distinct growth processes connected with the Enneagram system: 1) "what
to do" to actively counter the automatic patterns described above in the "self-
observation" section, 2) how to use the Enneagram's Inner Flow arrow lines as
a map of growth, and 3) how to study your passion (or "Vice") and consciously
seek to embody its opposite, the antidote, the higher "Virtue" of the type.

The Three Main Type Seven Personality Patterns:
"What To Do" to Address Them

Focusing on pleasure as a way to escape pain

Make yourself more mindful of the movement from pleasure to pain. Only
when Sevens consistently observe how they automatically move away from
pain and toward pleasure, can they see this escape route as the illusion it really
is. The first step to being able to stick with discomfort is to slow down the
process of the flight into pleasure and watch how it happens. The more Sevens
can mindfully watch themselves as they deny, avoid, or otherwise move away
when they get a whiff of pain, the more they open the door to being able to
make the conscious choice to stay with difficult experiences and learn that
they can survive and grow from them.

Don't mistake a bag of wind for a bag of treasure. Just as Odysseus and his crew got blown all the way back to Aeolia when the sailors got greedy for the pleasure that they thought a bag of treasure would bring them, Sevens are in danger of creating more pain for themselves when they focus so single-mindedly on pleasure.[32] Often, the pretty pictures we elaborate in our minds as imaginative escapes into fabulous possibilities don't really amount to anything. Just because you can focus on pleasure and imagine something greener on the other side of the proverbial fence, doesn't mean that you don't have to experience the pain sometimes involved in real life if you really want to live. As long as Sevens believe they can avoid dealing with difficult emotions by immersing themselves in pleasurable experiences, positive mental pictures, and party plans, they won't be able to make very much progress on their inner journey.

Recognize the pleasure of your pain and the pain that comes from living only for pleasure. Fond as they are of reframing, Sevens can wake up to an important truth when they realize the pleasure in their pain and the pain of too much pleasure. Paradoxical as it might seem, allowing yourself to face your fears and touch into your pain can lead to more pleasure in life and relationships, and too much of a good thing usually leads to some sort of pain. Regular reminders to this effect help Sevens reverse the belief that they have to avoid pain through pleasure to be okay and allow them to engage in the work of becoming more open to traversing all of their inner terrain.

Confusing indulgence and freedom from limits with love

Recognize anxiety as a side effect of liberation. The philosopher Soren Kierkegaard famously said that "anxiety is the dizziness of freedom." Sevens can use this idea to remind themselves that anxiety is an inherent part of being free, not something you escape by seeking unlimited freedom. Walking toward anxiety instead of away from it (and understanding its sources) can help Sevens to work through it and truly become free of it.

Learn the difference between love and pleasure. Sevens can confuse love and pleasure if receiving pleasure was one of the only ways they felt loved early on in life. While Sevens often focus on pleasure as a way to be "happy" in relationships, real love and relationships require bringing all of yourself to your experience with others, not just the happy or pleasurable parts. Sevens can grow by noticing when they are using the pursuit of fun and pleasure as a substitute for love. Modern psychologists have moved away from "the pleasure principle," Freud's idea that humans are mainly motivated by a drive toward pleasure. While pleasure is a primary motivation for Sevens, post-Freudian theorists wisely suggested it's not pleasure but the quality of our contact with others that's primarily important in human fulfillment.

Reference others as a way of balancing freedom and connection. As discussed above, Sevens primarily "reference," or pay attention to, their own needs, feelings, and desires. Learning to consciously focus more on others helps them to balance out the compulsive need for freedom with a stronger ability to be present for and with other people. While Sevens are quite relational and are actively drawn toward others, they can seek contact with people out of the same defensive drive for pleasure that motivates many of their key personality habits. It is important for Sevens to allow themselves the opportunity to learn to sink more deeply into their connections, not as a way of finding refuge through stimulation but as a way of bringing the fullness of their own experience into more intimate contact with all of someone else. Often this is fun and exciting, but many times it isn't. Sevens grow through learning to really "be with" their friends' and partners' down moods and painful struggles as well as with their joys.

Living for or in the future as a way of avoiding being present now

See all the ways you go to "then" to escape from "now." Just as it is important for Sevens to observe and examine the ways in which they move toward pleasure to distance themselves from pain, they can also become more conscious by noticing how they focus on the future as an escape from the present moment. If you are a Seven, when you notice yourself becoming absorbed by a futuristic fantasy, try to see how you could bring what you are longing for into the present moment. Try focusing on today instead of tomorrow or next week. Realize that the urge to plan a getaway or take an idealized journey in the future is a sign that you may be having a hard time accepting "what is" in the present. One my favorite poets, T. S. Eliot, emphasizes the importance of being able to live in the present moment in his four-poem cycle "The Four Quartets." In these poems, he beautifully communicates an idea Sevens might do well to heed—that we deprive ourselves of life when we avoid the present moment, the only "place" in which we can truly live, by focusing exclusively on "memory or desire." Eliot writes, "Time past and time future / Allow but little consciousness," of the present moment, which he calls "the still point of the turning world." Eliot poetically illustrates this dangerous tendency to escape from the "now," and thus our only possibility of consciously living and loving, when he writes, "Desire itself is movement / Not in itself desirable; / Love is itself unmoving, / Only the cause of end of movement."[33]

Allow for a fuller experience of pain and other uncomfortable emotions. What drives most people to do inner-growth work is an experience of their pain. As a psychotherapist who seeks to help people in the most direct and effective ways possible, I have been advised by more senior therapists to "follow the pain." If you can't allow for a full experience of your painful emotions, it's very difficult to have the motivation necessary to do the work entailed in growing up. This reluctance to fully feel pain is thus part of the character of the Seven-like archetype of the "puer," also portrayed through the depiction of Peter Pan as an "eternal child." And it's true that one aspect of the Seven personality is a desire to not have to "grow up." All of the personality types have their own prototypical ways of resisting the growth process, and in Sevens it takes the shape of wanting to stay with the good feelings and not enter into the bad ones. So, knowing this, Sevens will need to make a concerted effort to find ways to more fully engage with the pain that will motivate their journey "home" to becoming all they can be. Whether through meditation, through the support of others, or a combination of supportive practices, Sevens benefit greatly when they can learn to feel their pain.

Risk living in the present. One simple (and yet not always easy) way Sevens can begin to make more room for their painful emotions is by practicing living in the present. Reminding themselves continually to come back into their bodies and to ground themselves in their breath, or checking in to how they are feeling, can help Sevens take the risk of not running away from what's happening now. Consciously noticing when they get caught up in a fantasy based in the future and challenging themselves to see what's wonderful in the present helps support Sevens' efforts to slow down and "be here now." And if this kind of thing is difficult (or "boring"), it will be important for Sevens to seek out the help of others to support them. As Sevens learn to be more still and present, they may then want to find further support for the difficult feelings that might arise from that practice. It may help them to see that it is exactly their deeper experience of (all) their embodied feelings in the present moment that provides them with a portal to the higher capacities and greater joys of their "oak tree–Self."

The Inner Flow for Type Seven: Using the Arrow Lines to Chart Your Growth Path

In Chapter 1, I introduced an Inner Flow model of the arrow lines that define one dimension of the dynamic movement within the Enneagram framework. The connections and flow between each core Type, its "stress–growth" point, and its "child–heart" point map one kind of growth path described by the symbol. As a reminder, the arrow lines can be seen to suggest one kind of growth path for each type:

- The direction from the core point along the arrow line is the path of development. The "stress–growth" point ahead represents specific challenges perfectly suited to expanding the narrow focus of our core point personality.
- The direction against the arrow from the core point to the "child–heart" point indicates issues and themes from childhood that must be consciously acknowledged and owned so that we can move forward and not be held back by unfinished business from the past. This "child–heart" point represents qualities of security we unconsciously repressed, occasionally fall back into as a comfort in times of stress, and now must reintegrate consciously.

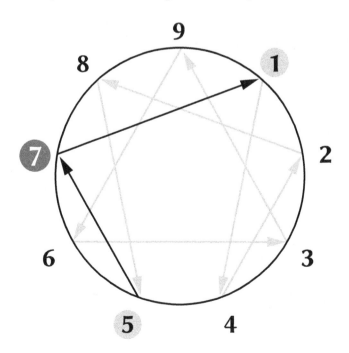

Type Seven Moving Forward to Type One: Consciously Using the One "Stress–Growth" Point for Development and Expansion

The Inner Flow growth path for Type Sevens brings them into direct contact with the challenges embodied in Type One: allowing for a clearer perception of what is ideal and "right" in a larger sense as a way of stabilizing a focus on taking action in service of a higher good. Not surprisingly, Sevens can find the anxiety and frustration they might feel as they move to One (and potentially become perfectionistic or self-critical) uncomfortable. But an experience of Type One managed mindfully, can help Sevens move out of their dreams and fantasies, and into a more realistic acceptance of standards and limits. When done unconsciously, this shift may involve an anxious resistance or adherence to the constraints imposed by rules and routines; but when done more consciously, it can open Sevens up to the possibility of a supportive structure based on standards and precision that can help Sevens actualize their ideals. Instead of getting caught up in living for an imagined or idealized future, Sevens can find ways to accept the specific constraints that will allow them to put their plans into action in more pragmatic ways in the present. Sevens can thus be inspired by the high side of the One Point in ways that both help them express their impulse toward creative invention and ground what they actually do in larger notions of the "good" or the "perfect." Sevens' focus on planning and play can, in the extreme, prevent them from moving forward in serious and disciplined ways; moving to One can help Sevens make the possibilities they imagine more practical, achievable, and polished.

The Seven working consciously in this way can make ready use of the tools healthy Type Ones use: diligence, discipline, responsibility, and an intuitive sense of the use of structure for constructive purposes. Ones' idealistic dedication to the larger social good—rather than their own self-interest—can inspire Sevens to balance out their healthy self-interest with selflessness, so that their visions can more usefully fit in with and serve higher causes. Ones' natural appreciation of order, structure, and rhythm can help Sevens implement their plans and creative ideas, providing routines and processes through which they can bring their dreams into reality. While Sevens moving to One may defend against what they might perceive as the boredom or tedium entailed in the One's focus on detail, a conscious incorporation of the higher side of the One Point can support them in learning to blend enthusiasm with practicality as a way of making things happen. And although freedom-loving Sevens may at first feel discomfort with potentially embodying the One-ish tendency toward judgment and evaluation, Ones' natural knack for objective, critical analysis can help them structure their imaginative visions and rein in their rebellion against all limits.

If Sevens can thus moderate the stress-induced tendency to become anal and controlling through the move to One—if they can find a sense of power in their One-like ability to stick to schedules and work within structural (and supportive) constraints—they can achieve a higher integration of their talent for creative thinking with an appropriate sense of control and discipline. When they can balance the potential for over-control at the One Point and the under-control natural to the Seven, they can achieve the "perfect" blend of seriousness and lightness that can represent a higher and healthier level of development.

Type Seven Moving Back to Type Five: Consciously Using the "Child–Heart" Point to Work through Early Issues and Find Security in Support of Moving Forward

The path of growth for Type Sevens calls for them to reclaim healthy restraint and the ability to withdraw and reflect that is characteristic of Type Five. Sevens may have had the experience in childhood that their need to retreat to a private space as a way of avoiding fear wasn't okay. They may have felt like their natural sense of fear and the associated desire to retreat was unacceptable, so they became more active in managing the outside world through charm to disarm the limiting potential of outside authorities. For one reason or another, it may not have been safe or desirable for Sevens to show their fear or express their need to hold on to precious resources. Sevens may thus "go to Five" under conditions of stress or security as a resource point to which they can withdraw to find to a safe place to rest or to consolidate their position and generate internal support. The move to Five can thus represent a desire to be less social and less "out there"—to be more boundaried and safely removed from the social whirl.

For these reasons, "moving back to Five" can be a way that Sevens retreat from others and moderate their need to be excessively social. Consciously drawing on the high side of the Five Point can help them find a healthy way be more internal and more involved in their thoughts in a less manic way. But because the Five point represents a natural part of Sevens that they had to repress in childhood and thus may return to compulsively, Sevens risk getting stuck in the back-and-forth between the overly optimistic, excessively enthusiastic gregariousness of the Seven and the total withdrawal of the Five. When Sevens return to the Five Point in an anxious or unconscious way, it's likely that Sevens are not so much reclaiming a healthy sense of privacy and inner calm as they are temporarily shutting down as an escape from over-commitment and excessive activity. In addition, as Sandra Maitri suggests, the usually happy-go-lucky Seven experiences the move to Five as a childish sense of inner scarcity motivated by the fear of loss and inner emptiness.[34]

Navigated consciously, however, a Seven can use the move to Five developmentally, establishing a healthy balance between the desire to be involved in the stimulation of the social world and the need to rest and reinvigorate through a healthy withdrawal from the social scene. Sevens can focus on the high-side-Five qualities of the inner child they may have had to repress—such as the need to relax and not have to manage the outside world through diplomacy and humor—by consciously honoring that part of them that might need to withdraw, hide out, and enjoy private pleasures, without fearing inner depletion. Sevens can choose to consciously remind themselves that it's okay to retreat once in a while and consolidate their inner resources. When they can reassure themselves in this way, they can reintegrate the Five impulse for inner quiet that supports their move forward on their growth path to the One Point. In this way, Sevens can consciously shift their attention from the external world to the inner world and make more objective, thoughtful, considered decisions about how they want to spend their energy and how they might be more economical in doing it—how they can more mindfully take care of themselves. This will allow Sevens to honor their occasional need for solitude as a means of being thoughtful about what is going on in their lives without becoming distracted. In this way, they can draw on what they may have needed to downplay in the past as a source of inner support that can serve them in taking on the growthful challenges involved in the conscious move to One.

The Vice to Virtue Conversion:
Accessing Gluttony and Aiming for Sobriety

The developmental path from Vice to Virtue is one of the central contributions of the Enneagram map in highlighting a usable "vertical" path of growth to a higher state of awareness for each type. In the case of Type Seven, the Vice (or passion) of the type is gluttony, and its opposite, the Virtue, is *sobriety*. The theory of growth communicated by this "Vice to Virtue conversion" is that the more we can be aware of how our passion functions and we consciously work toward the embodiment of our higher Virtue, the more we can free ourselves from the unconscious habits and fixated patterns of our type and evolve toward our "higher" side or "oak tree–Self."

As Sevens become more familiar with their experience of gluttony and develop the ability to make it more conscious, they can take their work further by making efforts to focus on enacting their Virtue, the "antidote" to the passion of gluttony. In the case of Type Seven, the Virtue of sobriety represents a state of being that Sevens can attain by consciously manifesting their higher capacities.

Sobriety is a way of being that is free from the pressure of the insatiability of the desire for more. The personality is structured around a need to fill up an inner emptiness; to ease a sense of basic anxiety or insecurity by helping us get what we think we need in order to feel okay. Type Seven demonstrates a desire we all have to feel good and avoid feeling bad. The search for pleasure typified by the Seven is a way for us to defend against the fear that we aren't safe and secure enough; through following an impulse to get more and more of what we believe we need to feel good—food, sex, fun times, intellectual stimulation—we hope to feel a sense of inner satisfaction. The problem is, this satisfaction never comes. The Type Seven dilemma illustrates how we seek and seek for what makes us feel good, but it never satisfies us because we can never get what we really need to feel content when our view of life is hemmed in by the limited view of the personality (the "acorn shell").

In light of this, sobriety represents the higher attitude that answers the personality problem illustrated by Type Seven character. Through becoming sober, we rise above the addiction to pleasure and the need to escape from pain. We see the falsity of personality-based belief that we will find what we need by trying to fill ourselves up with more and more of what feels good. As Sandra Maitri explains, "rather than relating to ourselves as an emptiness needing to be filled, we begin to relate to ourselves as the journey *itself*."[35]

For Sevens, then, focusing on sobriety means they work to let go of the quest for enjoyable experiences in favor of being with the truth of their experience. Instead of moving away from pain and running toward pleasure, they allow themselves to be aware of whatever is real and true in the moment without needing to reach out to try to get more or get away. Sobriety inspires Sevens to let go of seeking out the "highs" of pleasurable experiences, whether they are related to physical appetites, intellectual activity, or spiritual process. So although the word "sobriety" is usually applied to not drinking alcohol or ingesting other mind-altering substances, as the virtue of the Seven, it's larger than this. Maitri quotes Ichazo as describing sobriety as giving the body "its sense of proportion," and as being in a state "firmly grounded in the moment, in which you take in no more and no less than you need."[36]

Embodying sobriety as a Seven means you have examined and worked hard to be conscious of your hedonistic gluttony bias to the point that you can make the choice to temper the drive for pleasure that takes you from "an insufficient here to a promising there."[37] Achieving sobriety means you can be more grounded in the here-and-now reality of your true feelings, thoughts, and sensations, and that you have begun to understand that true satisfaction lies in valuing your authentic experience of yourself rather than seeking ephemeral pleasures.

When Sevens can do the "Vice to Virtue" work of noticing how they feel driven to feel good as a way of not feeling bad, they have the power to wake up to the fears and insecurities that may fuel their need to grasp for what's positive. In owning and fully experiencing their fear, and any other painful emotions they may have, they model for all of us how to overcome the pressure to defend against pain and instead open up to the deeper truth of who we are, trusting that we can find a sense of joy and well-being through being present to our own wholeness.

Specific Work for the Three Type Seven Subtypes on the Path from Vice to Virtue

Whatever type you are, the path from observing your passion to finding its antidote is not exactly the same for each of the subtypes. The path of conscious self-work has been characterized in terms of "grit, grind, and grace:"[38] the "grit" of our personality programming; the "grind" of our efforts to grow; and the "grace" that naturally comes to us when we sincerely work toward the higher virtue of our type. Naranjo explains that each subtype has to grind, or exert effort, against something slightly different. This insight is one of the great benefits of understanding the three distinct subtypes of each of the nine types.

Self-Preservation Sevens can travel the path from gluttony to sobriety by observing and owning the way self-interest in support of the drive for security can lead you to unconsciously close yourself off to a greater realm of experience. If you are this Seven, be aware of how you may narrow your focus on what's important in life based on fears and anxieties you may not be aware of and then work to open up to experiencing the presence of these deeper motives. You can aim for sobriety by noticing how you stay alert for opportunities and seeing that tendency as a potential sign of a deeper fear that you won't have enough to survive or stay comfortable. When relating to others, work to be conscious of all the motives and underlying feelings that influence your actions. Surface any anxiety and pain as a first step to tempering your drives for self-preservation and pleasure. Recognize when your pursuit of your needs and your self-interest may impact others in negative ways, and explore

the ways in which you might rationalize doing whatever you want and getting whatever you need, even when it narrows your perspective or allows you
to justify harm you might (unintentionally) do. Allow yourself to sink more
deeply into an enjoyment of the people you are close to by connecting more
consciously with all of yourself. As you work to accept and allow all of your
feelings, you will be reminded that the greatest joy comes from a total and
complete openness to the full experience of yourself and others.

Social Sevens can travel the path from gluttony to sobriety by making the motives behind the things they do more conscious. If you are a Social Seven, try
to be more aware of the desire to be recognized for your sacrifice or helpfulness—for being "good"—without judging yourself for being selfish or self-
centered. Observe and work with the glutton/anti-glutton polarity within
you, and try to be open to seeing what fears and needs might underlie that
internal dynamic. Watch out for feelings and motives you might not own that
drive you, and support yourself in accepting all your needs and feelings as
valid and important. Allow yourself to see how you might criminalize selfishness and avoid internal conflict and darker motives. Challenge yourself to be
honest about the ways in which you may confuse altruism and self-interest.
Surface the truth about your deeper motives while at the same time making
an effort not to judge yourself as "bad" for any self-interest you uncover. Don't
let your fear about not being seen as "good" get in the way of being more
conscious of what's really true. Recognize how you may manipulate through
enthusiasm and use your idealism as an intellectual drug. And allow yourself
to see how you might cling to your idealism and your ideals of service to the
group as a way of staving off an inner sense of emptiness. Support yourself
in feeling and being with any fears you might have about your worth or your
essential goodness. Give yourself credit for your good intentions, and make
room to see all your intentions and your limitations with compassion.

Sexual Sevens can travel the path from gluttony to sobriety by noticing when
they are living in their imagination rather than in reality and allowing themselves to explore why they're doing so and what's happening inside them when
they allow this. If you are this Seven, learn to distinguish between fantasy and
reality. Work on understanding your need to embellish reality and idealize
people and things, and explore the motives and feelings behind those tendencies. Be alert to identifying "logical arguments" and rationalizations that support fantasies that prevent you from growing and moving forward. Recognize
when a rose-colored view of something is masking a deeper frustration or fear,

and work to unearth those deeper feelings. Work on learning how to tolerate frustration so you can get more of what you want and need in the real world and don't have to subsist on fantasy. Notice if you are engaging in passive-aggressive rebellion of any kind, and investigate what might be motivating it. Work to get in touch with your deeper feelings, including fear, sadness, or anger. Be honest with yourself when you think you are working on a relationship but you are actually just "working on it" in your imagination. Be open to recognizing when you get disappointed in the reality of something; when it doesn't measure up to your idealization of it; and when anxiety may be clouding your vision of what's happening. Support yourself in getting in touch with any anxiety you might be feeling instead of acting it out through enthusiasm and a drive for pleasure.

Conclusion

Just as the Seven Point represents the way we avoid feeling pain and focus on pleasure in order to cope with a world that seems to threaten to trap us in fear and bad feelings, the Seven path of growth shows us how to use an awareness of our pain to fully awaken to the "good" and the "bad" of all that we are so that we can grow into all we can be. In each of the Type Seven subtypes we see a specific character who teaches us what is possible when we can turn our fear of fear and our unconscious aversion to pain into a fully awake ability to live from the reality of who we are and how we feel, opening up to our higher capacities through the alchemy of self-observation, self-development, self-acceptance, and self-knowledge.

CHAPTER 6

The Point Six Archetype:
The Type, Subtypes, and Growth Path

*In the best of times, "security" has never been more than
temporary and apparent.*

—Alan Watts, *The Wisdom of Insecurity:
A Message for An Age of Anxiety*

*Courage is not simply one of the virtues,
but the form of every virtue at its testing point.*

—C. S. Lewis

TYPE SIX REPRESENTS THE ARCHETYPE of the person who, given the fear of impending threat, seeks to find safety through the protection of others or by taking refuge in their own strength. The drive of this archetype is to scan for danger in a scary world and defensively manage fear and anxiety through fight, flight, or friends.

Type Sixes are thus the prototype for that tendency in all of us that needs to find a sense of security in the world in the face of the fears that naturally arise as part of being human—fears we feel (especially) as we seek to dis-identify with our personality. All the personality types feel afraid in different ways, but the Six's placement on the Enneagram map communicates the idea that "as long as we are identified with our personality structure, we live in fear."[1] The "acorn-self" doesn't know a life without fear; only the "oak tree–Self" grows beyond fear and anxiety.

As part of the foundational inner triangle of the Enneagram, the Six Point represents a basic step in the path of transformation we all must take in order to transcend the ego. After observing our habitual patterns so that we can dis-identify with, or separate from, our ego-personality (symbolized by the Three

Point), we must all do the work it takes to find a way to face our fears, work through the anxiety that arises from losing our egos, and contend with the emotions our personality arose to defend us against in the first place.

The Six Point sheds light on the psychological fear of letting down our defenses—the anxiety that inevitably occurs when we courageously allow ourselves to be vulnerable and unguarded, but which must be overcome if we are to grow toward union with our true selves. Sandra Maitri highlights the fact that while today we are "far less centered around survival than in previous eras," as many of us no longer have the search for food and shelter as the main focus of our lives, "this has not diminished our fear."[2]

Sixes thus represent the prototype for the universal human tendency to contract in fear and develop a personality that will protect us when we are young—a response to the understandable fear associated with being a small person in a big world. Psychologists talk about "basic trust" as an early stage of growth necessary to feeling a sense of well-being in the world.[3] If we can't achieve a certain level of faith and trust in our environment, it's hard (or impossible) to live our lives and develop our inherent capacities.

The Six archetype, like the widely known phrase "fight or flight," illustrates the basic range of normal human reactions to fear. (Sometimes "freeze" is also included as a basic response to fear, as in "fight, flight, or freeze.") As in all animals, it is clear that fear represents a vital survival mechanism in humans, in that it alerts us to the presence of danger. In the three Type Six subtype personalities, we see how three basic, but distinct, responses to fear shape the personality.[4]

The three kinds of Sixes reflect specific reactions to fear, both in the natural world and in civilized society: when we feel fear, we can either run away, get tough and fight, or seek the protection of someone we perceive as stronger. This makes it challenging to describe Type Sixes in terms of one set of characteristics. It also explains why the three Type Six subtypes differ so markedly. The complex emotional, thought, and behavioral patterns associated with fear are at the center of what motivates the three Six personalities in three very different ways.

In society, we find the theme of the Six archetype expressed in power dynamics, "us against them" attitudes, authoritarianism, and all forms of hierarchy. Naranjo connects fear with authority and power because it stems from an experience in childhood of being small in the presence of our parents, who, in the eyes of a child, seem like giants. The father figure is the archetypal symbol—if not the real executor—of authority in most homes, and so the father-child relationship serves as a template for our experience of power relationships (relations between a superior and an inferior) from then onward.[5] As Naranjo puts it, "Fear is therefore a passion that leads in the social world to the existence of the bossy and the bossed."[6]

Sixes have excellent analytical minds and they can be extremely loyal and steadfast friends to those they trust. They are good strategists, troubleshooters, and problem-solvers. Practiced in living with an underlying sense of anxiety, Sixes can be calm and effective in a crisis. They can be courageous rebels against exploitive authorities or sincere advocates for underdog causes. Naturally intuitive, they read people well and their specific "superpower" is their talent for seeing through false pretenses and detecting ulterior motives and hidden agendas.

As with all the archetypal personalities, however, Type Sixes' gifts and strengths also represent their "fatal flaw" or "Achilles heel:" while Sixes are great critical thinkers, they can get stuck in doubt, endless questioning, and overanalysis. They excel at planning and preparation, but can focus too much on worst-case scenarios and what might go wrong, so much so that they can fail to move forward and take action. They can trip themselves up by worrying too much, allowing anxiety to drive them, or by denying their fear through aggression and risky behavior. They may question authority in important ways, or fixate on doubt, mistrust, or rebellion with respect to authorities. They can get stuck in contrarian thinking and become indecisive. And they can confuse accurate intuition with the projection of their own fears onto others.

When they can balance their tendencies to act out unconscious forms of fear and anxiety with true insight and clear-minded analysis, Sixes can be wise, deeply thoughtful, and faithful friends, allies, and counselors.

The Type Six Archetype in Homer's *Odyssey*:
The Laestrygonian Disaster

Although Odysseus and his men face many harrowing situations on their journey, the encounter with the Laestrygonians is the one that proves the most frightening—and the most disastrous.

After six days and six nights of rowing, Odysseus moors his twelve ships in a seemingly peaceful harbor. His landing party meets the daughter of the king, and she directs them to his castle. As the three men enter, they are horrified by the Laestrygonians' monstrous queen. She calls for her king, and the two giants attack the men, tearing one of them apart and eating him.

As the survivors flee back to the ships, hundreds of giant Laestrygonians race down to the harbor. They bombard the twelve ships with boulders. Only the strength born of abject terror saves the ship that Odysseus captains:

> 'Put your backs in the oar—now row or die!' In terror of death they ripped the swells—all as one—and what joy as we darted out toward open sea, clear of those beetling cliffs...my ship alone. But the rest went down en masse. Our squadron sank.[7]

The Laestrygonians are powerful enough to fear no one. But they react aggressively and immediately on the assumption that anyone approaching them must be an enemy. Like an outsized symbol of the low side of the Type Six personality, they are fixated on negative expectations and see only threats. The Laestrygonians are on the alert for trouble to the point of being paranoid, and they do not pause for rational explanation or an investigation of what's really true once fear takes hold.[8]

The Type Six Personality Structure

LOCATED ON THE LEFT CORNER of the Enneagram's inner triangle, Sixes are the "core point" of the "head-based" triad, associated with the core emotion of fear and a concern with safety. In a world they experience as dangerous and uncertain, their focus centers on thinking about what might go wrong and strategizing and preparing for potential problems. Their thoughts focus both on real possible pitfalls and the trouble they create in their heads through imagination; but in either case they often find it difficult to stop worrying about their internally generated negative expectations.

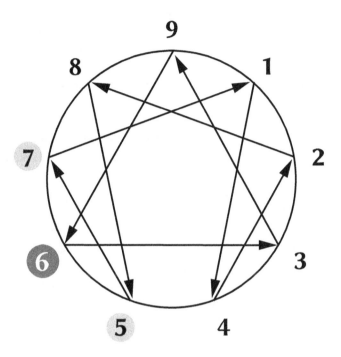

While fear represents both the core emotion of the head-based triad as well as the passion or "chief feature" of the Six, Sixes vary in their level of awareness that they act from fear—some Sixes may not be consciously aware that fear drives many of their defensive habits. Each of the three types based in the head center have a relationship to an early experience of fear that gave shape to their personality. Whereas Fives become detached and minimize their need for others, and Sevens focus on what is positive and exciting, Sixes try to understand threats and uncertain outcomes so that they can prevent something bad from happening.

The Early Coping Strategy: Type Six

The Type Six personality usually begins with a child who experienced some sort of ongoing threatening situation early in life. This is an individual who gets an early sense that the world is a dangerous place. Sixes often tell stories of living with a parent who was an alcoholic or mentally ill or violent or too weak to protect them. They may have experienced shifting expectations, objectively dangerous conditions, or periodic punishments.

Living with some form of untrustworthy, unpredictable, or inconsistent caretaker, the Six child develops a coping strategy centered on becoming an expert at picking up small cues that signal the presence of danger or threat. They specialize in detecting signs that help them know what is going to happen next, which allows them to prepare for and otherwise proactively deal with challenging or scary situations. This skill shapes the child's basic way of taking in and processing information from the outside world.

Sixes thus develop a way of absorbing and sorting information based on picking up on signs, subtle or not, of the negative or threatening intentions of others. Being able to predict when and if someone was going to hurt them was their way of trying to stay safe. Eventually, the automatic sorting process of a Six's mind gets attuned to detecting incongruities or whatever lies beneath the surface of things.

In conscious and unconscious ways, Sixes become focused on perceiving negative data in the world and looking out for and thinking about dangerous or problematic things that might happen before they happen. Through imagination, Sixes develop a radar for trouble that they can't turn off. While this habit makes them highly intuitive and analytical, these tendencies can also get skewed toward worst-case scenario thinking, projection, and self-fulfilling prophecy. Sixes get good at detecting what may lie beneath a false presentation, but they also mentally manufacture dangers that don't exist to confirm their internal sense of threat or doubt.

As mentioned above, Sixes' survival responses to fear are analogous to "fight or flight" reactions. The "flight" (or fearful, "phobic") strategy is to run away, to hide or somehow withdraw, or to seek the protection of others. The "fight" (or fear-denying, "counter-phobic") strategy is to move toward the perceived source of danger and manage it through strength or intimidation. In the middle of these two ends of the fear-response spectrum is a third fear-based survival strategy that represents a mixture of phobic and counterphobic reactions and constitutes finding safety in obeying or adhering to an authority. While this authority may be an actual person, it is very often the "impersonal" authority of a set of guiding rules or reference points—a system of knowledge or an ideology about how one should behave.

In light of their history with inconsistent or threatening authority figures, Sixes both wish for a truly good authority (sometimes unconsciously) and question and rebel against the authorities in their lives. Being habitually suspicious of anyone who might have power over them, the defensive strategy of the Six involves a wariness or skepticism toward unfamiliar others in general, and especially authority figures. Importantly, however, the three Six subtype characters vary with respect to their approaches to authority. The Self-Preservation (phobic) Six tends to be the most quietly avoidant; the Social Six the most yielding and compliant; and the Sexual (counter-phobic) Six, the most competitive and rebellious. Despite this, however, all three have the tendency to be suspicious and anti-authoritarian if the conditions call for it.

Often, Sixes' issues with authority grow out of an early experience with an authoritarian father or an overprotective mother. A threatening father figure reinforces a child's fear of rejection or punishment, and an anxious or overprotective mother can send the child a message that the world is not safe and that he or she does not have the inner resources to deal with external threats. However, a Six's father may have also been absent or weak—and the specific father a given Six had may influence their dominant subtype. Naranjo suggests that Sixes who are inclined toward hero worship and insecurity (Self-Preservation or Social Sixes) often display an excessive need for a good father they didn't have, while Sixes who tend toward grandiosity and a heroic view of themselves (Sexual Sixes) likely experienced a rivalry or competition with their fathers (or took the place of a weak father).[9]

The Six child thus often suffers from the lack of a good "first authority," someone who would have provided a model of confidence and security in meeting threats. In light of this, the Six coping strategy can be viewed as a compensation for the lack of a strong, protective, benevolent father figure.

Jack, a Sexual Six, describes his childhood situation and the development of his coping strategy:

Jack was the oldest of three children. From the time he was born, his mother suffered from migraine headaches. She usually managed to cope during the week, but would get a debilitating migraine every Friday. At that time, there were no medications available that would ease her pain, so she would be out of commission for the entire weekend. Jack's father (a Type Five) was very absent. With his mother often unavailable and his father not able to be present, Jack experienced life as uncertain and his authority figures as undependable. In this situation, Jack came to feel that he had to be independent because he could only really rely on himself.

Jack's mother was a phobic Six, and Jack internalized her belief that the world was an unsafe place. Her anxious focus on safety contributed to Jack having an underlying sense of fear. His father was not a good role model of strength and Jack would get angry when his mother would berate his father in front of other people and his dad wouldn't stand up for himself. He would feel mad at his mother for humiliating his father and pissed off at his father for being so passive. He can see that his drive to be strong and independent grew out of the painful experience of witnessing his parents' conflicts and needing to go off on his own as a way to escape them.

Jack learned early on that he had to be his own authority. While he really wants and looks for a strong authority in his life, he owns that he's very particular and he's always on alert and looking for incongruities in others' behaviors, whether in a potential authority figure or his other relationships. There have only been a few authority figures in his life that he's had a high regard for because he can't help believing they can't be relied on. He looks for good authorities and people he can trust, but keeps expecting them to let him down or prove themselves untrustworthy. Even in his friendships, he's always "waiting for the other shoe to drop." His wife is the only person in his life he's ever been able to be with and relax his habit of being vigilant.

The Main Type Six Defense Mechanisms: Projection and Splitting

The primary defense mechanism of Type Six is *projection*. As in the case of introjection, when someone engages in projection as a psychological protection, the psychological boundary between the self and the world disappears. When Sixes "project," they unconsciously disown something originating inside themselves and "project it onto," or experience it as belonging to, someone on the outside.

As psychologist Nancy McWilliams explains, "projection is a process whereby what is inside is misunderstood as coming from outside. In its benign and mature forms, it is the basis for empathy...In its malignant forms, projection breeds dangerous misunderstandings."[10] Oriented to detecting threats, Sixes psychologically defend themselves from their own internal sense of fear by unconsciously projecting it out or "getting rid of it," imagining that it originates in the outside world, often in another person. For example, if a Six is

feeling judgmental of or insecure about herself, she may imagine that someone else is judging her. By locating the fear as coming from someone on the
outside, she can avoid the pain of her own judgment or insecurity and then
manage (or seek to control) the pain of inner judgment by relating to that
other person in particular ways.

Just as Fours use the defense mechanism of introjection to manage an
outside threat by experiencing it as being inside themselves so they can better
control it, Sixes deal with uncomfortable feelings like fear and self-doubt by
experiencing them as being caused by someone else. By attributing the motives, feelings, or thoughts they do not want to acknowledge in themselves to
another person, they expel them from their internal experience and feel safer
on the inside. If someone else is causing them to experience a bad feeling,
they can move away from them or be nice to them. For Sixes, managing a
bad feeling that comes from the inside can be harder or more threatening to
address. Thus, projection allows Type Six individuals to escape the blame and
threat related to their feelings and thoughts by placing those feelings outside
of themselves, thereby allowing the Six to believe that uncomfortable feelings
are caused by other people.

Although projection serves as a defense, easing a sense of inner threat, it
can also cause many problems, as McWilliams notes: "When the projected
attitudes seriously distort the object on whom they are projected, or when
what is projected consists of disowned and highly negative parts of the self, all
kinds of difficulties predictably ensue. Others resent being misperceived and
may retaliate when treated, for example, as judgmental, envious, or persecu-
tory."[11] The habit of projecting fear and other inner experiences onto others
also leads to feelings and behaviors that can be said to be suspicious or paranoid in nature, because when you habitually locate the source of your own fear
and discomfort in other people, you unconsciously create reasons to suspect
them, mistrust them, or regard them as dangerous and potentially threatening.

In addition to projection, Sixes also make use of a second primary defense mechanism: *splitting*. Splitting originates in an early stage of childhood
and relates to the infant's need to organize its perceptions of "objects" (others
in the outside world) in terms of "good" and "bad." Developing at a time
before young children can comprehend the fact that good and bad qualities
can coexist in one person or one experience (this is called *ambivalence*, and is
achieved at a later stage), splitting operates defensively to reduce anxiety and
maintain self-esteem.[12]

We can see evidence of splitting—both in an individual and on a collective level—when someone makes one person or group all bad or all good. This

happens in politics when one side demonizes their opponents, and in wars when we perceive the enemy as completely evil. In individual psyches, and, more specifically, within the psychology of a Type Six individual, a person can use splitting to clearly demarcate who is good and who is bad as a way of feeling less fear—they locate the "badness," or the source of fear, in a clear way so as to more easily cope with it. If you see yourself as bad and others as good, you can try to be better and rely on others to protect you. If you see yourself as good and others as bad, you can maintain your self-esteem and use your positive internal resources to protect you from a specific, localized threat from the outside.

Splitting is the psychological reason why many Sixes experience a large degree of guilt and self-accusation, and a firm belief that they are somehow bad. It can go both ways, however, with the Six viewing some other person—someone whom they dislike or see as untrustworthy—as all bad, even when that other person objectively possesses both "bad" and "good" traits.

The Type Six Focus of Attention

Sixes develop a way of being in the world based on the habit of paying selective attention to potential threats and imaginatively elaborating what might happen as their defensive basis for coping with danger. They tend to be alert to the complexities of things and to focus their analytical minds on perceiving and understanding all the varied aspects of situations and people. The focus of Type Sixes also centers on doubting and questioning themselves, other people, and data in the outside world—the specific focus of their doubt varies by subtype.

Driven by an underlying need for safety in what they experience as a world full of potential dangers, Sixes focus on the negative data in their environment (or their own heads) that might signal the presence of threats to their security. When encountering others, Sixes tend to harbor an initial attitude of wariness and mistrust, questioning the other people's motives until they get a read on what their intentions are. People are watched until they earn the Six's trust through experience or evidence. In looking for danger by perceiving and intuiting the "negative" data in a situation—in focusing on the search itself—Sixes sometimes end up creating it.

If something the Six perceives stirs up suspicion, their thoughts can move to creating worst-case scenarios. Generally, Sixes tend to trust their own radar for trouble and their intuitive ability to pick up on small amounts of information in the environment to determine what might happen and what preparations might be needed. Sometimes this habit of attention leads to an accurate and insightful reading of a situation or a deep or intuitive understanding of what is going on; at other times, however, Sixes can fill in the gaps in the objective data they've collected with fear-based thoughts about what is happening. In other words, they can unknowingly (unconsciously) project their fear-based, imagination-fueled thinking to create a threat where none exists.

Sixes tend to focus attention on authorities, either looking for a good authority to guide their actions or regarding people in positions of authority with suspicion. They often feel suspicious about people who wield power, questioning whether they will use it well or not. Sixes also tend to naturally focus positive attention on underdogs and underdog causes because they understand what it's like to feel vulnerable and threatened by authority figures who might seek to dominate or oppress others.

Focusing on and taking a "devil's advocate" or contrarian stance is another aspect of the way Sixes pay attention. Sixes typically question or oppose people who express strong opinions. They habitually focus on alternative views or contrary positions as a way of getting to the truth, fleshing out the complexity of an issue, or challenging or testing people by promoting a view that has been denied or left out. Continually questioning and analyzing everything can make Sixes feel more secure, because they are gathering more data to generate or confirm certainty. They look for holes in an argument, both to push others to prove their trustworthiness (or their deeper intentions) and to get to the truth. This habit of taking the role of a devil's advocate and noticing what might go wrong makes Sixes good troubleshooters, a role they often play in the workplace.

To people with other personality types, Sixes may appear to dwell on the negative, or to be suspicious, paranoid, or pessimistic, but Sixes usually do not see themselves as having a pessimistic outlook. Rather, they tend to perceive themselves as realistic, or even idealistic, in that they are trying to achieve the best-case scenario by performing a thorough analysis of each situation and assessing what might go wrong.

The Type Six Emotional Passion: Fear

Fear is a universal emotion central to assuring survival in all animals—and it's the passion of Type Six. As the emotional passion that gives shape to the Six personality, fear can take many forms and can be more or less conscious. It can take the form of a fear of the unknown; it can motivate anxiety and obsessive worrying about potential threats to well-being; or it can feel like self-doubt and uncertainty. It can be experienced as guilt and shame related to your sense of self, or it can surface as a conviction that someone means you harm or can't be trusted. Fear can be constant and paralyzing; it can motivate obedience to rules and order to maintain control and safety; or it can manifest as a forceful counterreaction of aggression born of a desire (or impulse) to attack when afraid.

Closely related to fear, anxiety is also a central characteristic of the Type Six personality. Anxiety is a state of "apprehension, tension, or uneasiness from anticipation of danger."[13] It is differentiated from fear in that fear is seen as an emotional response to a "consciously recognized and usually external threat or danger," whereas anxiety is primarily of "intrapsychic origin"[14]—that is, anxiety is something we create in our heads in response to an unknown or unrecognized threat.

Often, anxiety occurs even when there isn't a clear sense of imminent threat, because anxiety often stems from a fear of fear itself or of something that we imagine or only dimly perceive. Naranjo likens anxiety to a "frozen fear or a frozen alarm before danger that has ceased to threaten (though it continues to be imagined)."[15] Sixes tend to feel anxiety related to fear when they imagine fearful scenarios or anticipate that they will be endangered or threatened. Often, anxiety can attach to social situations, and Sixes may fear that they will be judged, criticized, or otherwise threatened by other people. Their hesitance or discomfort with regard to social situations may be related to self-doubt or a habit of suspecting others' motives and judgments. Doubt or the inability to act in the face of anxiety can further intensify their anxiety, and thus the anxious tendencies of a Six can become cyclical, self-reinforcing, and hard to break out of.

Whichever form fear and anxiety take, these emotional experiences, and Sixes' internal efforts to cope with them, give rise to a defensive structure based on patterns designed to find ways to survive in the face of threats, whether they are commonly felt as overwhelming or only vaguely sensed.

The Type Six Cognitive Mistake:
"Thinking the World is a Dangerous Place Makes It More So" or "Just Because I'm Paranoid Doesn't Mean Someone Isn't Out to Get Me"

We all get stuck in habitual ways of thinking that influence our beliefs, feelings, and actions, and this continues even after the mental models that create our overall perspective aren't accurate anymore.[16] While the passion shapes the personality's emotional motivations, the "cognitive fixation" or "cognitive mistake" preoccupies the personality's thought processes.

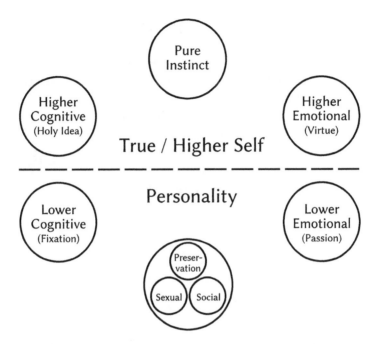

From the outside, the thoughts and beliefs that typically drive Sixes may seem overly negative. However, they seem to Sixes like smart ways to prepare or strategize to meet problems should they arise, giving them a (potentially false) sense of control. Type Sixes' core beliefs reflect themes of what it takes to perceive and manage threat and risk; create safety and find security in the face of real dangers in the world; and cope with the anxiety inspired by having an active, fear-fueled imagination.

To support the passion of fear, Sixes hold the following core beliefs as psychological organizing principles:

- The world is a dangerous place, and you must be alert to and aware of signs of trouble in order to stay safe.
- By imagining the worst thing that could happen, you can prepare for it and thus potentially protect yourself or ward it off in advance.
- By expecting and anticipating what might go wrong, you can guard against making mistakes, getting hurt, or becoming trapped in a bad situation.
- Imminent catastrophe could strike at any time, and if you aren't prepared, you will be less able to prevent it or deal with it.
- Searching for certainty and gathering information in an uncertain world is one way to feel safer.

- It's difficult to completely trust anything (or anyone) because there's always room for doubt.
- It's good to be on guard about how people might threaten you, hurt you, or take advantage of you, so you won't be taken by surprise and unable to protect yourself.
- Phobic: By focusing on the ways in which I am vulnerable to others, I can take steps to minimize my vulnerability.
- Counterphobic: By focusing on the challenges I must meet as I move through life, I can think about ways to overcome those difficulties by proactively meeting them with strength and forcefulness.

Although the Six's preoccupation with thoughts of managing risk and danger are originally resorted to as a way of maintaining a sense of safety—giving them a sense of control in an uncertain, fearful environment—in adulthood, they can actually lead to more anxiety and stress, as it can seem impossible for the Six to ever feel certain or safe enough.

The Type Six Trap:
"When You Expect Something to Go Wrong, It Usually Does" or "Danger is Where You Find It"

As it does distinctly for each type, the cognitive fixation for Type Six leads the personality in circles. It presents an inherent "trap" that the limitations of the personality cannot resolve. Given their life strategy and focus of attention, Sixes experience a conflict between their habits, which are designed to help them feel safe in a threatening world, and the fact that these defensive maneuvers actually work to keep them stuck in anxiety, fear, and insecurity.

Sixes' core beliefs keep them fixated in a threatening world because their unremitting focus on fear and related imaginings can have the effect of intensifying, rather than diminishing, their perceptions of threats. Sixes' over-focus on thoughts about what might go wrong can lead to self-sabotage and self-fulfilling prophecies, as creating fearful scenarios in your mind and acting on them can have the unintended effect of manifesting your fears. To the extent that our reality tends to be shaped by our beliefs and perceptions, Sixes can inadvertently create more danger through the mental activity that is designed to help them escape it.

The Key Type Six Traits

Hypervigilance

Closely related to Sixes' anxiety is their trait of hypervigilance. With fear as a central characteristic, whether conscious or not, it follows that the Six individual is motivated to frequently be "on alert" to signs of danger or threat or things going wrong. By nature suspicious and overly cautious, the Six's disposition tends to be characterized by a hyperalertness to clues that might reveal hidden dangers. What Naranjo describes as a "state of chronic arousal" serves as a way to gather data to reduce uncertainty, to protect oneself against negative surprises, and to interpret a potentially dangerous reality in an ongoing way.

By continually watching for signs of problems and other negative data, the Six engages in a habitual defensive behavior; being in a constant state of vigilance makes sense to a person who tends to imagine that the worst could happen. Being highly alert all the time is a natural consequence of the belief that we live in a dangerous world. And often this belief is supported by painful experience. Just as people who suffer from post-traumatic stress disorder (PTSD) tend to remain hypervigilant and anxious about experiencing a repeat of a trauma they actually experienced, Sixes can maintain an alert focus based on a fear of something they suffered in the past happening again.

Theoretical Orientation

Fear contributes to a lack of certainty about what to do and how to act, so the Six continually looks for good data to base decisions on, then processes that data mentally, applying logic, reason, and rationality as a way to make the best decision about what to do.

As Naranjo points out, the Type Six "is not only an intellectual type, but also the most logical of types, one who is devoted to reason." He goes on to say that "in his need for answers to solve his problems, type VI is more than any other a questioner, and thus a potential philosopher."[17] The Six lives in the realm of intellect, not only as a method of solving problems, but also as a way of "problem-seeking" in an attempt to feel safe.

The tendency to focus on the theoretical provides Sixes with a mental means of combating fear and indecisiveness; it also represents a consequence of a fearful holding back. The Six attempts to find safety in the thought process itself—through their excessive orientation to thinking and the abstract—but can frequently get stuck there, trapped in an endless cycle of thinking and applying logic and then questioning their conclusions, which then necessitates further thinking and reasoning. Sixes thus seek refuge in the abstract and theoretical, but this tendency also represents a trap that can prevent them from acting in the world.

Orientation to Authority

The orientation to authority is one of the most distinct Six traits. Usually as a result of the echo of early experiences with authority figures—parents, generally—Type Six individuals have specific attitudes toward authorities that vary according to the three Six subtypes. Sixes live in a hierarchical world, and they both love and hate authorities, reflecting the early experience of both loving a parent and hating being dominated or somehow punished by that same parent.

Naranjo summarizes how experience with parental authorities archetypally structures the three distinct variations of authority issues displayed by the three kinds of Sixes:

> What the aggressive [Sexual], the dutiful [Social], and the affectionate [Self-Preservation] safety maneuvers have in common is their relevance to authority. We may say the fear of enneatype VI was originally aroused by parental authority and the threat of punishment by the power-wielding parent—usually the father. Just as originally this fear led to sweetness [Self-Preservation], obedience [Social], or defiance [Sexual] (and usually ambivalence) toward his parents, now he continues to behave and feel the same in the face of others to whom he assigns authority.[18]

Most Sixes, including the Self-Preservation Six (who may not openly oppose authority), report that they feel some anti-authoritarian feelings. Usually Sixes describe experiencing some sort of suspicion, questioning, and mistrust in relation to authority figures, and some may also frequently rebel or work against authority. Of course, this skepticism toward authorities can be a strength—some authorities may not be benevolent, and Sixes can show great courage in challenging unjust authority figures—but at other times, on the low side, this characteristic can indicate paranoia and an inability to accept any authority, even a well-intentioned one. With the tendency to question what is happening, and a natural distrust of those in power, there may be few authorities in a given Six's life who can pass the trust test.

Doubt and Ambivalence

Having a "doubting mind" is a key characteristic of Type Six. Built in to the way a Six thinks is a tendency to doubt and question nearly everything. This reflects both an anxiety about the intentions of others and a need to feel secure through testing and mentally evaluating people and ideas. Prone to both self-doubt and doubting others, the Six coping strategy of being alert to signs of threat relies on the habit of doubting what is true as a way of attempting to find safety. In this way, Sixes can be seen to both invalidate themselves through constant self-doubt and doubt others through the expression of suspicion, with the different subtypes doing one more than the other.

Naranjo describes the situation of a Six in doubt when he states, "he doubts himself and he doubts his doubt; he is suspicious of others, and yet he is afraid that he may be mistaken. The result of this double perspective is, of course, chronic uncertainty in regard to choosing a course of action, and the consequent anxiety."[19] Beyond the attitude of an "accusatory inquisitor" of self and other, the role of doubt in the Six character reflects the uncertainty of the Six in regard to his views: he both invalidates himself and he props himself up. Individual Sixes may feel both persecuted and grandiose.

Ambivalence and indecisiveness are natural outgrowths of doubt in that doubting leads to an inability to emerge from ambivalence and to clarify ambiguity. As Naranjo points out, despite the fact that ambiguity causes anxiety in a Six, they are the most explicitly ambivalent of all the character types. Ambivalence is an early theme for Sixes: when you both love and fear a childhood authority, it can lead to a profound sense of ambivalence. Thus, doubt and ambivalence reflect the ongoing inner conflict a Six experiences between pleasing others and rebelling against them, admiring others and trying to invalidate them.

Contrarian Thinking

Another manifestation of doubt and the search for certainty is evident in the Six habit of contrarian thinking. This characteristic is evident in Sixes' tendency to voice an opposing idea to whatever the dominant opinion of the moment is. As a way of looking for the right answer and defending against heedlessly accepting someone else's power to dominate, when Sixes hear a statement or an opinion, they often automatically speak to the other side. This is why the Type Six is sometimes called the "Devil's Advocate" or the "Contrarian."

It can feel dangerous to Sixes to immediately buy into someone else's point of view, so their habit of contrarian thinking constitutes a defensive strategy—a way to prevent being quickly taken over by someone else's wrong idea.

By instantaneously being able to argue the other side of any argument, the Six tendency to engage in contrarian thinking allows them to go up against others who would try to persuade them as a way of attempting to dominate them.

Contrarian thinking also creates a scenario in which doubt (and, potentially, unconscious fear) motivates a kind of forced investigation through an immediate argument about what is really true. Both as a way to avoid domination and a way to search for the right answer, contrarian thinking allows Sixes to feel like they will not be easily taken over or influenced in a way that might be dangerous.

This kind of thinking also underscores the intellectual, logical nature of the Six personality. If you have an orientation to the theoretical and the abstract, you can naturally generate opposing arguments quite easily. However, like doubt, the tendency to engage in contrarian thinking can cause the Six to get lost in the endless back and forth of debate. And while this style of thinking can be useful in forestalling easy domination of one point over another, it often fails to bring about certainty, and only leads to more argument.

Self-Fulfilling Prophecy

Because Sixes have the habit and primary defense mechanism of projection, which is rooted in fear, they also have the tendency toward self-fulfilling prophecy. Here's how this works: the Six experiences a feeling that is threatening—perhaps a fear about himself, a feeling that he is too weak or that people don't like him—and to protect himself from the pain or fear of this feeling, he unconsciously projects it out onto someone else. So, the Six starts by doubting himself and feeling fearful about his own inadequacies, and then he projects that fear and corresponding negative self-evaluation onto someone else. The Six then perceives that other person, the projectee—who may not have been feeling negatively toward the Six at all—as having negative thoughts about and threatening feelings toward him, and he bases the way he acts toward that person on this perception/projection. In response to the way the Six is acting, the other person then develops negative feelings about the Six. In this way, the Six's initial feeling experience, which at the outset is not real, becomes real—becomes a self-fulfilling prophecy.

In this way, the fear and anxiety characteristic of the Six personality can have the effect of actually creating problems and negative circumstances where none existed in the first place. The influence of Sixes' fear and self-doubt (and aggression, in the case of the Sexual Six) on other people and external situations can actually cause Sixes' fear-based suspicions and expectations to be fulfilled.

The Type Six Shadow

As with many other dimensions of the Type Six personality, what is relegated to the Shadow varies according to what subtype we are talking about and the preferred strategy of the different subtypes for dealing with fear and anxiety.

Generally, however, Sixes focus on their fear and thinking and worry about how to handle threats, which may leave their own courage, faith, power, and self-confidence in their Shadow. Being preoccupied with imagining what might go wrong as a way of exercising control in the world means they don't always recognize their own authority, strength, and capability when it comes to handling problems. (This is especially true of Self-Preservation Sixes.)

Even the counterphobic Sexual Six—who may not be aware of feeling fearful and who takes refuge from anxiety in strength—may only *look* confident and courageous. Naranjo says that the "courage" of this Six may be the courage of "having a weapon," not a deep sense of confidence that things will be okay. With the Sexual Six, vulnerability and fearfulness may be in their Shadow because of their need to appear intimidating and strong. This is in contrast to the Self-Preservation Six, who gets caught up in self-doubt and consciously feels very vulnerable, and so may have blind spots with regard to his power, self-confidence, or aggression. Social Sixes focus consciously on obedience to an impersonal authority, such that a healthy sense of doubt and ambivalence may become blind spots.

Living primarily in their heads and relying on thinking and analysis as a first line of defense may mean that for some Sixes, many emotions, along with their capacity for "gut knowing," can be part of their Shadow. Their habit of trying to think their way through problems by relying on logic and rationality can mean that they don't own their emotional truth and gut (or instinctual) "wisdom." Self-Preservation Sixes may avoid being aware of their more aggressive emotions; Social Sixes may not live from their uncertain or sentimental feelings; and Sexual Sixes may have their more tender emotions in their Shadow.

Naturally skeptical, Sixes may also not be very conscious of their internal capacity for trust and faith, preferring instead to consciously doubt, test, and question what people say as a protection against putting faith in the wrong person or idea.

Whatever a Six projects onto others may be, by definition, unconscious and thus part of the Shadow. Often, Sixes project their power onto others instead of owning it themselves. Naranjo explains that self-accusation and guilt are key features of the Type Six personality in that the inner habit of making themselves "bad" (as perhaps they were made to feel bad by threatening authorities) contributes to the insecurity that motivates their fear.[20] They may act out the effects of this underlying assumption of their own "badness," fearing that bad things will happen to them because they somehow deserve it, without ever realizing the extent to which this kind of guilt and "self-opposition" drives them.

Sixes also may be blind to the ways in which fear fuels their imagination of what's happening. When perceiving danger and risk, Sixes often believe they are just seeing what's out there, and assume that whatever fears are fueling them are realistic and evidence-based. However, they may not fully see how active their imaginations can be in catastrophizing or seeing threats that aren't really there. Similarly, they may not fully see how they get caught up in feedback loops—how, when their fears cause them to perceive reality in a particular way, that stimulates more fear, which affects their perception of what is real and what isn't.

The Shadow of the Type Six Passion: *Doubt* in Dante's Underworld

Fear (like anger) is a basic human emotional response that is entirely appropriate in some contexts. So fear as such is not punished as a separate sin in Dante's *Inferno*. But the underworld does punish the passion of fear in a way that rings true for the shadow side of the Type Six personality.

The Vestibule (or outer ring) of the Inferno punishes the compulsive doubters, those too fearful to ever be truly faithful to anything:

> I looked and saw a kind of banner rushing ahead, whirling with aimless speed as though it would not ever take a stand; behind it an interminable train of souls pressed on, so many that I wondered how death could have undone so great a number...These wretches, who had never truly lived, went naked, and were stung and stung again by the hornets and the wasps that circled them.[21]

The reflexive doubt of the Type Six Shadow is like being caught between the impulse to risk vulnerability and the sharp fear that accompanies it. Sixes are forever trapped in the habit of wanting to trust or act and finding reasons not to. In Dante's underworld, this indecision is final. Relentless stings now force these shades to mindlessly chase a banner, expressing allegiance that stands for nothing, symbolizing they way they failed to overcome their doubt and take a stand in life.

The Three Kinds of Sixes:
The Type Six Subtypes

EACH OF THE THREE SIX SUBTYPES expresses a different approach to dealing with the passion of fear and related anxieties. Self-Preservation Sixes feel a need for protection and so deal with fear by making connections with people. Social Sixes cope with a social fear that makes them afraid of doing the wrong thing in the eyes of authorities by consulting rules and reference points. And Sexual Sixes deal with fear by denying their vulnerability and combating fear from a position of strength.

Naranjo observes that the variance between the three subtype characters is particularly noticeable in Type Six. In fact, he states that in Sixes more than in any other type, it is "difficult to speak of a single character."[22] While all three Sixes share an early history of having to deal with anxiety, the Self-Preservation Six copes with it through a "desire to form reciprocal protection alliances," the Social Six through the "wish to find an answer to the problems of life through reason or ideology or other authoritative standards," and the Sexual Six "through a wish to be bigger and intimidating to others."[23] As a result of the dominance of the three different instincts and their corresponding ways of dealing with fear, the three Six subtype personalities have different "energetic temperatures:" Self-Preservation Sixes are warm, Social Sixes are cool, and Sexual Sixes are hot.

The Self-Preservation Six: "Warmth"

In the Self-Preservation Six personality, fear manifests as insecurity. Self-Preservation Sixes have a fear related to survival—a fear of not being protected that fuels a driving need for protection through friendship and other kinds of alliances with others. This is the most phobic of the three Six subtypes; this is the Six subtype who feels fear the most.

Perceiving the world as dangerous, Self-Preservation Sixes seek friendly connections and alliances, and to do this they endeavor to be friendly, trustworthy, and supportive—as good allies are supposed to be. As Naranjo clarifies, "not trusting themselves enough, they feel alone and incapable without outside support."[24] Self-Preservation Sixes want to feel the embrace of the family, to be in a warm, protected place where there are no enemies. They search for an "idealized other" for protection, and they can have issues that look like separation anxiety. Like a child who needs to hold on to the mother, these Sixes don't feel confident in defending their own self-interests and survival.

These Sixes seek to escape anxiety by seeking the security of protection; therefore, they become dependent on others. They have a passion for compensating for the fear of separation, which manifests as a warm and friendly temperament. Their driving need is therefore for something like (neurotic) friendship or warmth, which makes this subtype the warmest of the Sixes. They tend to be in a good mood and have a generally pleasant disposition. They look for a bond of intimacy and trust in their relationships, and they fear disappointing others, especially those who are closest to them. Being warm is their way of getting people to be friendly so they won't be attacked.

Self-Preservation Sixes fear anger, aggression, provocation, and confrontation. Being afraid of other people's aggression means they can't let their own aggression out. As Naranjo explains in describing this Six, making people like you means being good, and being good means not being angry. Naranjo asserts that "the taboo on aggression that results from the needs of dependency weakens this Six in the face of others' aggression and contributes to their insecurity and their need for external support."[25]

There is a lot of hesitation, indecision, and uncertainty in the Self-Preservation Six personality. These Sixes ask many questions, but they don't answer any. They doubt themselves, and they doubt their doubt.[26] Feeling uncertain, and unable to find a satisfying sense of certainty, Self-Preservation Sixes have a difficult time making decisions. They see the world in terms of ambiguity—as "gray" rather than "black and white." People with this subtype can't dispel their sense of doubt and uncertainty. Because of their fundamental sense of insecurity and their habit of questioning and doubting, they never feel ready or able. They also feel a lot of blame and guilt, even assuming or feeling the blame of others.

There are two realities for Self-Preservation Sixes: an external reality of warmth, tenderness, serenity, and peacefulness, and an inner reality of fear, guilt, anguish, and torment. Their head and heart are separated—they feel heart-centered on the outside, but are head-centered internally.

As the most phobic of the three Sixes, the avoidant Self-Preservation subtype equates love with protection, and in looking for love they search for a source of security to compensate for an inner sense of insecurity. This Six wants to find a strong person to lean on, and they may be excessively friendly and giving as a way of preventing an attack from outside. In order to feel the strength they are lacking, the Self-Preservation Six attracts the affections or protection of somebody strong—the more forceful presence of another helps them to feel safer.

Self-Preservation Sixes can thus look like Type Twos in that they are warm and friendly and put a lot of energy and attention into the development of relationships with others. Like Type Twos, these Sixes tend to lead with affection and accommodate others as a way of forging connections—but unlike Twos, their deepest motivation is to create safety, not to gain approval in support of pride.

Linda, a Self-Preservation Six, speaks:

I live in a small community governed by a homeowners' association. Initially, I was comforted that we could come together as a group to create guidelines and rules that I assumed would make for less conflict between neighbors and more security. I made it a point to meet and establish a comfortable relationship with each of them. I volunteered to be on the board, and even offered to lend my professional expertise to work with the entire group on our community values and vision.

Over time, though, I saw that compliance to the governing principles was lax and enforcement was selective or nonexistent. Four years ago a situation arose in which my rights were being violated by a neighbor, and for reasons unbeknownst to me, the board sided with the neighbor. In one fatal stroke my carefully nurtured allies became dangerous enemies, rendering me defenseless because of my fear of invoking further attack should I try to defend myself or my interests.

My shock and anger at their betrayal quickly devolved into a sense of guilt, shame, and anxiety so profound that I could no longer attend homeowner meetings, speak with my neighbors, or even walk around the block because of my fear of being "attacked." I became obsessed with phantom conversations in my mind, composing just the right speech that would win them back or what I would say or do to these people for revenge, if only I had the courage to do so. On the outside, I try to act friendly, but on the inside I feel fearful and contemptuous. This dissonance is exhausting. All I want to do now is sell the house and escape from this place and these people.

The Social Six: "Duty"

Lacking either trust in themselves (like the Sexual Six) or other people (like the Self-Preservation Six), Social Sixes deal with the passion of fear and its related anxiety by relying on abstract reason or a specific ideology as an impersonal frame of reference. They find safety by relying on authorities, or on the "authority" of reason, rules, and rational thinking.

The name given to this type by Ichazo is "Duty," which doesn't mean they "do their duty" (though they often do) as much as it means that they focus on "what their duty is." In coping with anxiety, the Social Six consults the guidelines associated with whatever authority they adhere to. They focus on knowing what the benchmark is and on obeying the rules of the game. They feel a need to know all the points of reference—what the party line is, who the good guys are, and who the bad guys are.

Consciously or unconsciously, Social Sixes fear the disapproval of authorities and believe the way to be safe is to do the right thing as determined by an authority. And knowing what the right thing is means having clear rules that tell you how you should think and act. This orientation has the effect of developing the philosophical mind, because when you don't know how you should live—when you don't trust your intuition or your human sense of life to guide you—you have to become very intellectual. But this sense of duty also becomes a way to structure your life: someone gives you the rules, and you follow them.

Archetypally, the guidelines of whatever system a Social Six follows become a kind of replacement authority for the first authority—the parent, usually the father. While they may have rebelled against or been disappointed by their actual father, they look for a good authority in life as a way of finding security. Total submission and obedience to authority (and the rules associated with authority) helps them feel safe in the world. Naranjo points out, however, that choosing the wrong authority can be a problem for Social Sixes: "Instead of believing in the person who is right, they tend to believe in people who speak as if they were right, and who have the special gift of making themselves believed."[27]

The Social Six typically represents a mixture of phobic and counterphobic expressions. This Six is a cooler character than the Self-Preservation Six. They find safety in being precise about how one should conduct oneself. They have a lot of anticipatory anxiety—they believe that everything will go wrong. So they rely on precision in following the rules as a way of coping with their anxiety. They feel most secure when they have clear minds and when things are in clear categories. Social Sixes are good Boy Scouts and Girl Scouts, dedicated to adhering to the group code and to a competent way of doing things based on that code.

The Social Six is a stronger character than the Self-Preservation Six, and this greater strength has to do with having more certainty than uncertainty.

The Self-Preservation Six is an insecure person—they hesitate because they are not sure. The Social Six is someone who, in defense against the insecurity associated with not being sure, becomes *too* sure. They can—in the extreme— become "true believers" or fanatics. In the counterphobic Sexual Six, fear is turned into its opposite when the person adopts a stance of strength, but in the Social Six, "it is not fear that is turned into an opposite, but doubting."[28]

The Social Six can also be very idealistic, structuring life through an adherence to high ideals. This is a character who holds tight to ideologies and a particular view of things as a way of feeling safe.

In contrast to the Self-Preservation Six, who gets stuck in ambivalence and can't make decisions, Social Sixes have an intolerance of ambiguity. They fear ambivalence and have little tolerance of uncertainty, because to them, uncertainty equals anxiety. As a result, they have a love of precision and see things more in terms of black and white than gray.

The Social Six is also a bit of a legalistic character; they have the mind of a lawgiver, and they like clear categories. Culturally, the Germans provide a good example of this archetype in that they like precision, order, and efficiency. Social Sixes have a strong sense of duty, they idealize authority, and they display a generalized dutifulness—an obedience to law, a devotion to fulfilling responsibilities as defined by external authority, a tendency to follow rules and to value documents and institutions, and a kind of rigidity and organization.

Social Sixes both fear making a mistake and long for certainties: a person with this subtype "wants to be talked to in a certain manner so that he or she may feel that the speaker knows, the speaker is right."[29] They have a highly intellectual orientation, and their patterns of thinking can take the form of diagrams and flowcharts.

These Sixes are not very spontaneous; they live a more scripted life. As a result of being so much in their heads, they don't have very much contact with their instincts or their intuition. They tend to be shy and have little ability to socialize or to be moved or touched by something or someone. They may feel uncomfortable with experiences related to unrestricted animal instincts or sexuality.

Social Sixes can tend to be controlling, impatient, judgmental, and self-critical. They demand a lot of themselves, and may insist on everything being done according to their codes and viewpoints. Others may perceive Social Sixes as cold or cool, as they can be very formal in the things they do.

Individuals with this subtype can have many characteristics in common with Type Ones, especially Self-Preservation Ones. Like Ones, they follow rules and tend to be controlled, critical, hardworking, punctual, precise, and responsible. However, while Ones are guided in a confident way by a sense of their own internal standards, Sixes' fear of making a mistake has more to do with getting in trouble with an external authority.

The love of precision and the efficiency of this Social Six subtype can also make them resemble Type Threes; however, the main motivation of this Six is to avoid anxiety by finding a sense of authority in reference points, not to accomplish goals and look good through efficiency.

A. H., a Social Six, speaks:

Some of my happiest moments as an adult have come after aligning myself with a system for how to live. When I was thirty, I discovered the work of Ken Wilber and found myself ease into a sense of clarity and peace because everything finally made sense. All my confusion about how different things related to each other suddenly dissolved. Here was a system I could trust. The same thing happened a few years ago, when I was shocked to find that my body fat percentage was nearly 25 percent. I immediately researched how to improve this. Once I found a system of eating and exercising that seemed trustworthy, I latched on to it. In both cases, it wasn't just that I had rules to follow; it was that the rules actually brought me in touch with a sense of purpose and comfort.

Now, the other side of the story is that I have an internal set of rules about how to stay physically safe, and I get upset when other people don't follow them. I can't tell you how many times I've said to my wife, "Watch his head!" while she carried my infant son through a doorway. In such situations, my body's threat response goes into high gear. Not only do I perceive danger—I can see that someone isn't following the rules on how to avoid it. That's when the cool guy can get mean and even cold.

The Sexual Six: "Strength/Beauty" (Countertype)

The countertype of the Type Six subtypes, the Sexual Six is the most counterphobic Six, the one who turns against the passion of fear by assuming a stance of strength and intimidation. Instead of actively feeling fearful, these Sixes have an inner belief that when you are afraid, the best defense is a good offense. As Naranjo explains, anxiety in this Six is allayed by skill and readiness in the face of a possible attack. They often appear bold and even fierce. They go against danger assertively, and even aggressively, as a way of denying and coping with their (often unconscious) fear.

Through denying their feelings of fear to one extent or another, Sexual Sixes go against danger from a position of strength; therefore, they have a passion for searching for or securing a position of strength. And it's not just a strong character they seek, but the kind of strength that makes somebody else afraid—they want to assume a powerful enough stance to hold the enemy at a distance. These Sixes display a forcefulness that comes from not wanting to be weak, and they don't allow for weakness in themselves.

Sexual Sixes' strength is often physical. They may develop this physical strength through sports or exercise that serve to build muscles and make them feel strong in their bodies. They tend to have marked control over their bodies as a way of cultivating a sense of inner strength to guard against feeling the chaotic emotions associated with the release of rage or other impulses.

These Sixes also seek to be strong in terms of endurance; they seek to feel tough in the face of fatigue, repression, humiliation, and pain. (In this aspect, they may resemble the Self-Preservation Four.) For the Sexual Six, strength is often directly connected to an illusion of independence and a sense of being able to remain "unscathed" by trouble. They may also have a feeling of being somehow "bad" inside, and their strength protects them from their own inner attacks on themselves.

Sexual Sixes have a need not just for strength but for intimidation. As Naranjo suggests, this expression of intimidation is very much the essence of the character: if they appear strong, they won't be attacked. While Naranjo explains that Ichazo's title for this subtype, "Strength/Beauty," originally meant "strength" in men and "beauty" in women, it may also be true that being beautiful is a source of strength in both male and female Sexual Sixes.

These characters walk around with the idea that anyone can become dangerous, so they do everything they can to not feel cheated, manipulated, taken advantage of, or attacked. If you are someone who thinks and feels this way, you need to be prepared to be strong and mount a resistance. That's why Sexual Sixes not only develop strength but also intimidation— in the service of resistance, of being prepared to scare someone off, rebel, or be contrary.

Sexual Sixes give off the impression that they could get violent with anybody at any time, but that doesn't mean that they have no fear. It is precisely out of a sense of fear that their anticipation of an attack comes—there is a somewhat paranoid imagining of danger, a belief that anyone can turn into a threat. However, these Sixes usually do not look afraid; their visible character could hardly be called "fearful" from the outside.

In contrast to the Self-Preservation Six, who backs away from threats, the counterphobic Sexual Six tends to move toward risky situations, feeling a sense of safety in actually confronting danger rather than hiding from it or avoiding it. They convince themselves (and others) that they are not victims of fear; they are convinced that fear is an emotion that should be eliminated systematically.

Despite being aggressive as part of their effort to intimidate through strength, Sexual Sixes tend not to acknowledge their aggressive side and may not be aware of it—or at least of the intensity of it. Their aggression is expressed mostly in the social arena and not as much in their private lives, as they will usually have needed to develop some level of trust with those they are close to. They also tend to separate their emotions: aggression is disconnected from fear, and sex is disconnected from feelings of love and intimacy.

The fact that these Sixes regularly move against danger (or perceived danger) can, at times, give them the appearance of a rebel, a daredevil, a risk-taker, an adrenaline junkie, or a troublemaker. In some cases, Sexual Sixes may be prone to megalomania or having a "hero complex." In their own way, they seek to be "good guys" to avoid being punished. They may have the illusion that they are spontaneous, but they tend not to be.

Sexual Sixes tend to be very contrarian: they always have an argument at hand to refute and contradict an opinion. Instead of thinking in terms of "best-case" or "worst-case" scenarios, they think in terms of contrarian scenarios—if the trend is for others to focus on the worst, they will focus on the best; but if everyone is focusing on the best, they will assert the worst.

Although they may seem certain in their assertiveness, Sexual Sixes may hold doubt in their minds for a long time—doubting which road to take and so getting caught between choices. They often believe that there is only one truth, and they prefer concrete and pragmatic ideologies because they feel safe and allow control of the world. They fear making an error, and the consequences of doing so.

The Sexual Six can look like a Type Eight because both types can appear intimidating, strong, and powerful. However, in contrast to the Eight, who tends to be fearless, the Sexual Six is motivated by an underlying fear, even when they don't consciously feel it or show it. Also, while Eights like to create order, Sexual Sixes often like to disrupt order by stirring up trouble. Sexual Sixes can also look like Threes in that they are action-oriented, fast-moving, assertive, and hardworking. They differ from Threes, however, in that they have more paranoid fantasies and their assertiveness has its basis in fear rather than in the need to achieve and accomplish goals in the service of looking good.

Richard, a Sexual Six, speaks:

For me the world is a dangerous place and as a result I maintain a constant vigilance. Scanning and looking for inconsistencies in people and the world around me is an ongoing and never-ending task. Dealing with the outside world is exhausting as a result.

Social occasions are especially taxing. On a recent night out with my wife, we went to a party where there were twenty to thirty other couples in attendance. Everyone was in a fun and festive mood...including myself. However, I quickly noticed that while my wife was easily approached and engaged by the new people around us, I, on the other hand, seemed to maintain a three-foot "No Fly Zone" around me for at least the first hour.

I've realized that my automatic and unconscious approach to dealing with uncertain and potentially threatening situations is to present myself as a potential threat. I don't literally threaten people, of course; it's more of an energy, or an aura, I create around myself without always knowing I'm doing it. I often wonder how others experience me when I'm in that mode: reserved and somewhat stoic, critical and watchful, and physically intense. From the inside, I have the sense that I'm ready to spring into action at a moment's notice. Recently, through therapy, I've realized how important it has been for me to squash fear (and even potential hints of fear) aggressively, assertively, and with prejudice.

"The Work" for Type Six:
Charting a Personal Growth Path

U<small>LTIMATELY</small>, <small>AS</small> S<small>IXES</small> <small>WORK ON</small> <small>THEMSELVES</small> and become more self-aware, they learn to escape the trap of intensifying their fear (through their attempts to reduce it) by doing the following: seeking to embody faith and courage, becoming aware of how they create self-fulfilling prophecies, learning to trust themselves (and others) more, and owning their power and authority instead of projecting it out onto others.

For all of us, waking up to habitual personality patterns involves making ongoing, conscious efforts to observe ourselves, reflect on the meaning and sources of what we observe, and actively work to counter automatic tendencies. For Sixes, this process involves observing the ways they cope with fear and anxiety; exploring the ways they behave when they are scared (and the motives behind their behavior); and making active efforts to develop trust, faith, and courage.

In this section I offer some ideas about what Sixes can notice, explore, and aim for in their efforts to grow beyond the constraints of their personality and embody the higher possibilities associated with their type and subtype.·

Self-Observation: Dis-Identifying from Your Personality by Watching It in Action

Self-observation is about creating enough internal space to really watch—with fresh eyes and adequate distance—what you are thinking, feeling, and doing in your everyday life. As Sixes take note of the things they think, feel, and do, they might look out for the following key patterns:

Trying to find a sense of control and security in a dangerous world by watching, doubting, testing, and questioning

Observe your tendency to scan for danger and to be hypervigilant. How does this manifest in you in terms of your behavior, your energy, and the ways in which you relate to others? What kinds of things are you watching out for? How might this function as a stress-inducing way of "looking for trouble" instead of helping you to relax and feel safe? Observe your doubting mind in action and notice the patterns of thinking involved. Note your habit of questioning yourself and others. What does it help you to do? How might it also hinder you? Notice the ways you might test other people. Does this tendency help clarify things for you, or does it put up barriers that prevent you from connecting with others? Examine your thinking to see if you get caught up in circular patterns and explore why it may feel hard to escape this kind of mental loop.

Projecting fear, anxiety, and power out onto others, especially authorities

Projection may be a difficult activity to witness in yourself, but try to catch yourself in the act of disowning your fears and your power. When might you imagine that your fear is caused by an outside source? In other words, when do you look for people and situations to which to attach your anxiety so that you may convince yourself they are somehow to blame instead of owning your feelings and the reasons behind them? Are you dwelling on thoughts of someone as the cause of your problems and thinking about what they are doing that's bad as a way of distracting yourself from the anxiety inside you? Pay close attention to how you feel, think, and relate to authority figures. What might you be projecting onto them—both in terms of your fears and your disowned power—and how might these projections be influencing your perceptions and what is happening?

Acting out fear in different ways instead of owning it, being with it, and managing it

When we remain unconscious to the emotions that drive our behavior, we tend to "act out" those emotions in order to avoid feeling things that may be hard to feel. This can get us in trouble because we remain unaware of the true motives behind the way we are seeing and handling things. Sixes may act from fear when they overthink situations, create worst-case scenarios, build negative fantasies about others' bad intentions, become indecisive and unable to take action, or procrastinate. If you are a Six, it will be important for you to consciously notice how you see fear and anxiety motivating your behavior and look for signs that you may be acting out your fear unconsciously rather than fully experiencing it. Note if you feel fear and anxiety and what forms it takes. Notice also if you don't feel much fear or anxiety, as that may indicate that you are expressing it in other ways, through inhibitions, avoidance, imaginative or paranoid fantasies, projections, overanalysis, or overintellectualization.

Self-Inquiry and Self-Reflection: Gathering More Data to Expand Your Self-Knowledge

As Sixes observe these and other related patterns in themselves, the next step on the Enneagram growth path is to *understand* these patterns better. Why do they exist? Where do they come from? What purpose do they serve? How do they get you in trouble when they are intended to help you? Often, seeing the root causes of a habit—why it exists and what it is designed to do—is enough to allow you to break out of the pattern. In other cases, with more entrenched habits, knowing how and why they operate as defenses can be a first step to eventually being able to release them.

Here are some questions that Sixes can ask themselves, and some possible answers they can consider, to get more insight into the sources, operation, and consequences of these patterns.

*How and why did these patterns develop? How do these habits help Type
Sixes cope?*

Through understanding the sources of their defensive patterns and how they
operate as coping strategies, Sixes have the opportunity to become more
aware of how their main strategies for coping with fear and anxiety operate
in their life to help them try to find a sense of security. If Sixes can tell the
story of their early life and understand how and why they developed their
habitual ways of coping with fear, they can have more compassion for themselves. Examining the habitual patterns that help them exert control as a way
to meet fear can help Sixes gain insight into how tendencies like hypervigilance, doubt, overanalysis, and paranoia have developed to support the specific
coping strategies they use to manage fear, risk, and threat.

What painful emotions are the Type Six patterns designed to protect me from?

For all of us, the personality operates to protect us from painful emotions, including what psychological theorist Karen Horney calls our "basic anxiety"—
a preoccupation with the emotional stress of not getting basic needs fulfilled.
Ironically, the strategies Sixes use to try to gain some control in a scary world
may both mask deeper feelings of fear and anxiety and exacerbate them, as
these strategies keep Sixes focused on threats but often don't succeed in fend-
ing them off, especially as habits like questioning and doubting become circular traps. Depending on the Six's subtype, some of the typical Six patterns may
also serve as protection against feelings of anger, sadness, guilt, or loneliness.
Self-Preservation Sixes in particular may feel a taboo on their own aggression,
and their defensive habits may reinforce their inability to access anger. Their
focus on fear may also be a way to avoid feelings of guilt or shame, which
Sixes tend to experience on a deeper level as a result of having felt early on
that they were not worth being protected.

Why am I doing this? How do the Type Six patterns operate in me now?

By reflecting on how these patterns operate, the three kinds of Sixes can begin
to have a greater awareness of how their defensive patterns happen in everyday life—and in the present moment. If they can consciously catch themselves in the act of getting stuck in doubt, questioning, mistrust, or suspicion
as a way to feel safe, they can wake up to the deeper motivations that drive
them in their sometimes self-defeating attempts to reduce risk and manage

threat. It can be eye-opening for Sixes to see how they may *increase* their sense of insecurity through their efforts to cope with problems and dangers. By understanding exactly what is motivating them to enact recurring patterns like being hypervigilant, contrarian, rebellious, and even paranoid, they can gain a great deal of useful and actionable self-knowledge.

What are the blind spots of these patterns? What do Type Sixes keep themselves from seeing?

To really increase their self-understanding, it will be important for Sixes to become more aware of what they *don't* see when their personality programming is driving the show. While Sixes' blind spots will vary according to subtype, it will help Sixes to grow if they can begin to develop more consciousness around the areas of their experience their defenses may keep hidden, like the true nature and sources of their fear, anxiety, and aggression. Sixes tend to keep themselves from seeing the extent of their fear and the reasons behind it, as it could intensify their anxieties. Sixes that tend to respond to their underlying fear with counterphobic patterns may be blind to their more vulnerable feelings and fears; conversely, more phobic Sixes will actively avoid seeing and owning their aggression, power, and authority. Since Sixes tend to project their power onto others, it can help them to see and own the power and self-confidence they have unconsciously disowned.

What are the effects or consequences of these patterns? How do they trap me?

Because of the potentially circular nature of doubt, questioning, self-accusation, and insecurity, Sixes' efforts to cope with fear and anxiety are often self-defeating. If you can't help but doubt and question everything out of a need to find some safety in certainty, and you even doubt your own doubt, it may be hard to stop the questioning and actually locate a solid sense of something you can be sure of. Alternatively, Sixes who become too certain as a way of combating the insecurity of ambiguity and doubt may ally themselves too quickly, too completely, or too rigidly with the wrong authority. Being too uncertain and weak, too easily seduced by an authoritative system or person, or too aggressive and intimidating as a way to ward off threats are all patterns that can create more problems than they solve. Projecting fears onto others and creating mental pictures of fearful scenarios can undermine the security Sixes are trying to find in ways that may lead to self-fulfilling prophecies.

Self-Development:
Aiming for a Higher State of Consciousness

For all of us who seek to wake up, the next step in working with type-based knowledge of the personality is to begin to inject more conscious effort into everything we do—to begin to think, feel, and act with more choice and awareness. In this section I provide some ideas for Sixes about "what to do" after they've observed their key patterns and done some investigation into their sources, operation, and consequences.

This last section is divided into three parts, each corresponding to one of three distinct growth processes connected with the Enneagram system: 1) "what to do" to actively counter the automatic patterns of your core type described above in the "self-observation" section, 2) how to use the Enneagram's Inner Flow arrow lines as a map of growth, and 3) how to study your passion (or "Vice") and consciously seek to embody its opposite, the antidote, the higher "Virtue" of the type.

The Three Main Type Six Personality Patterns:
"What to Do" to Address Them

Trying to find a sense of control and security in a dangerous world by watching, doubting, testing, and questioning

Recognize that uncertainty is an inevitable part of life. Just as Type Ones benefit from accepting that imperfection is inherent in human life, Sixes can help themselves by acknowledging that uncertainty is a part of life. Sixes have very facile analytical minds, so it will be impossible or nearly impossible to eradicate all uncertainty—as Sixes well know, the nature of reality is also radically contingent upon circumstances, so efforts to achieve an ideal of certainty are most likely futile.

Instead of allowing yourself to get caught up in a relentless cycle of questioning as you look for proof that something is true, remember that the search itself lets you know that you are afraid. Instead of all the continual mental testing, take yourself out of your head and watch what you are doing from a distance. Look into your heart to ask yourself what you are feeling and what you need emotionally. Listen to what your gut is telling you. Remind yourself that the search for certainty won't get you anywhere, so it's important to consciously shift your attention away from that futile vortex.

Remember that we tend to find what we seek. In some ways, the habit of vigilantly watching for signs of danger may lead you to see danger everywhere. To the extent that we create our own reality through the lens we use for looking at the world, Sixes may find trouble because they are looking for it. They may see the world in terms of problems because their minds habitually seek problems to fix. Therefore, it can be important for Sixes to notice when they are fixated on looking for threats and problems and consciously shift their attention to the more positive data in life. While Sixes tend to see themselves as realists, others can perceive them as pessimists because their pattern of looking for problems to solve can make them seem like they are focusing on only what's negative. Instead of seeing the glass as half-empty (or looking for the holes in the glass), try seeing the glass as half-full.

Get out of your head and into your body. Sixes can be very head-based and intellectual. They generate fear and anxiety through their tendency to think, imagine the worst, and plan for what to do if the worst happens. Fear lives in the Six's head as anticipation of the negative, even if they frame this kind of proactive expectation as a good thing. So, one way to work against all that preparatory thinking and the anxiety and negative cycles it can spawn is to get out of your head altogether and into your body. Physical exercise can help you to ground your awareness in a "present moment" experience of your bodily self, shifting you out of the default mode of mental activity that keeps you stuck. Make a point of exercising regularly, consciously breathing from your belly, and putting your attention in your gut center as a way of reminding yourself that you need to visit other parts of your self in order to balance out all that thinking.

Projecting fear, anxiety, and power out onto others, especially authorities

Learn to discern the difference between intuition and projection. Sixes are both naturally intuitive and habitual projectors, so it is important for them to learn to discern the difference between information based on inner knowing versus information based on what they disown and attribute to others. Sixes project as a way of separating from, and defensively relating to, a threatening element or feeling. When they confuse projection for intuition, they may *think* they know what someone else is doing or saying, but they really don't. By unconsciously blaming others for their own feelings, they remain unaware of their own blind spots and disowned emotions and relate to others in potentially paranoid or alienating ways. So it will be important for Sixes to continually check in and ask themselves, "Is this something I intuitively know or something I am projecting?" Then they will need to examine the evidence as objectively as they can—and ask trusted others for input on reading the evidence if it still seems difficult to decide. If you are a Six and you think someone is mad at you or judging you, ask them directly before you make up a whole story about it.

Consciously claim whatever you are projecting. Sixes can work against projecting fear, power, and other things onto people by noticing the ideas they have about others and looking to see how they might reflect their own disowned emotions, experiences, and qualities. If you are a Six and you have a heightened sense of judgment, anxiety, or upset toward someone else, inspect the stories you are making up about what they are doing. Explore why you may be projecting onto them as a way of explaining why they are dangerous and you are innocent. Alternatively, notice when you are projecting your power onto someone and viewing yourself as powerless; consider that you may be underestimating your own strength as a way of finding a hero or a threat outside yourself.

Work to be more aware of your authority issues. As Naranjo points out, all three of the Type Six personalities have authority issues—they both want and mistrust authorities, both love and hate them. So, hierarchical and authority relationships are important areas for Sixes to develop a greater level of awareness of their defensive habits. They will want to pay close attention to the feelings and thoughts that get stirred up in their relationships with the authorities in their lives, and either try to trust more (when the evidence warrants it) or own their own independence, power, and wisdom. It can help Sixes along their path of conscious growth toward their more naturally powerful "oak tree-Self" if they can refrain from displaying an overreliance on an outside authority as a compensation for their own insecurity and own their own power, vulnerability, and the power that comes from being able to be vulnerable.

Acting out fear in different ways instead of owning it, being with it, and consciously managing it

Recognize "fight," "flight," and "freeze" as fear reactions. If you learn to see your specific reactions to fear when they arise, you can develop a clearer sense of when you feel afraid, what you are inclined to do in reaction to fear, and how you can have more conscious choice about how you respond when you get afraid. If you can create more clarity, space, and compassion for yourself around the specific ways in which fear shows up for you, you will have a much easier time navigating fearful experiences with consciousness. Whether you run away and hide, get paralyzed by overthinking or overreliance on rules, or rebel, it pays to become more and more conscious of how fear shows up in your experience, and to develop an ability to read the clues to know exactly how fear is driving your thoughts, feelings, and actions.

Learn to feel, manage, and let go of fear. Working with fear is a part of growth work for Sixes. Observing and reflecting on how your fear arises (or gets avoided) and on your relationship to fear and its consequences is key in watching how your personality operates. When feeling fearful, check out the evidence. What is really (objectively) happening? It will be important for you to honestly evaluate whether your concerns are misplaced or invented rather than a true representation of reality. As you learn to recognize how fear arises, you can more consciously examine it, explore it, modulate it, or calm it.

Some Sixes don't relate to having a prominent experience of fear. These Sixes may be more conscious of angry feelings or the ways in which they act from fear without understanding that it's fear that drives them. They may be working hard on something, or anxious about something, or moving aggressively on something, without being clear what emotions are driving their actions. In these kinds of situations, it will be important for Sixes to look underneath any active efforts, aggression, or defiant feelings they are having that may signal underlying fears they are avoiding by acting against them, and to work to understand and manage these responses.

Have more faith in response to fear. Just as fear is an anticipatory feeling that something will go wrong, faith is the ability to let go of fear and trust that things will generally be okay. If, as a Six, you can get out of your head and into your gut or your heart, you can consciously shift your attention away from mental analysis—get out of a thinking mode and into emotions and gut knowing, which provide other kinds of data and so can help you break your reliance on the intellectual search for certainty as a way of self-soothing.

The Inner Flow for Type Six:
Using the Arrow Lines to Chart Your Growth Path
In Chapter 1, I introduced an Inner Flow model of the arrow lines that defines one dimension of the dynamic movement within the Enneagram framework.

The connections and flow between each core Type, its "growth–(through)–stress" point, and its "child–heart-(security)" point map one kind of growth path described by the symbol. As a reminder, the arrow lines can be seen to suggest one kind of growth path for each type:

- The direction from the core point along the arrow line is the path of development. The "stress–growth" point ahead represents specific challenges the nature of our core point personality places in front of us.
- The direction against the arrow from the core point to the "child–heart" point indicates issues and themes from childhood that had to be disowned must be consciously acknowledged so that we can move forward and not be held back by unfinished business from the past. This "child–heart" point represents qualities of security we unconsciously repressed, occasionally fall back into as a comfort in times of stress or security, and now must reintegrate consciously.

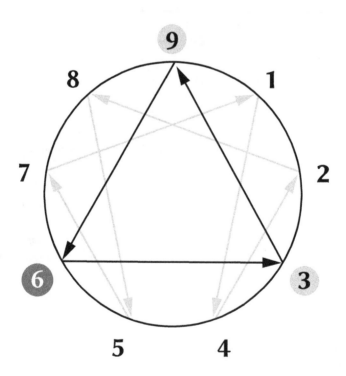

Type Six Moving Forward to Type Three: Consciously Using the Three "Stress–Growth" Point for Development and Expansion

The Inner Flow growth path for Type Sixes brings them into direct contact with the challenges embodied in Type Three: developing an ability to use goals and relationships as supports to overcome fear, take action, and achieve results. In extremely stressful situations, Sixes may defensively act out the "low side" of Three by engaging in frantic action or anxious striving. However, by engaging the Three Point in a conscious way and seeking to embody the higher Type Three qualities of productivity, honesty, and hope, Sixes can work against the fears that hold them back. In light of their tendencies to become paralyzed by fearfulness and overanalysis or throw themselves into nervous hard work, Sixes can use the Three Point to shift their attention away from their fears and anxieties and focus instead on the worthiness of their goals, the positive aspects connected to impressing others with their good work, and sincere pride in achievement. As getting stuck in fear can, in the extreme, threaten Sixes' well-being, it serves them to learn to use the natural motivation Threes feel toward forward movement and the accomplishment of goals to counteract their habit of getting caught up in inaction or indecisiveness.

The Six working consciously in this way can make ready use of the tools healthy Type Threes use: self-confidence, an ability to manage feelings, and dedication to results. The high side of the Three stance has its basis in honest self-expression, the enjoyment of activity in the service of making things happen in effective ways, and the hopeful expectation that they will be rewarded for their sincere efforts. These Three aspects can serve to balance out Sixes' preoccupation with what might go wrong, which can weaken their ability to act in the world. By focusing on realizing the higher capacities associated with Type Threes—actively focusing on the drive, industriousness, hopeful outlook, and healthy desire for recognition of the Three Point—Sixes can counter their tendency to undermine themselves through insecurity, doubt, and the fear of attracting attention and becoming a target. Instead of expending energy scanning the outside world for danger or battling internal anxieties, they can invest their energies in efforts that support their ability to express themselves in the world, balance their fear and doubt with hope and confidence, and contribute productively to society in active ways.

Type Six Moving Back to Type Nine: Consciously Using the "Child–Heart" Point to Work through Early Issues and Find Security in Support of Moving Forward

The path of growth for Type Sixes calls for them to reclaim their ability to relax in their connections with others and go with the flow of life without having to worry about threats in the environment or something bad happening. Sixes may not have been able to find inner support through connections with others because those others may have been threatening, punishing, unpredictable, absent, or ineffectual. Instead of being able to blend with others and find a comfortable sense of merger in relationships, Sixes usually had to move away from others in order to protect themselves from dangerous people or find safety in independence. Nines often say they trust others easily, but many Sixes did not have this luxury when they were young, and so have become stuck in mistrust and suspicion as a survival strategy.

Sixes may return to their "child–heart" point of Nine as a way of finding a sense of security through merging with something or someone safe—by taking refuge in a comfortable place or a connection with another. Sandra Maitri explains that within every Six is a lazy, Nine-ish child "who just wants to stay under the covers, doesn't want to go out and face the world, wants only to be comfortable and entertained."[30] The Nine Point may then represent a place of security and comfort that Sixes can retreat to in order to find safety in a dangerous world—but also a way of getting further stuck in inactivity when stressed. Sixes who go to the low side of Nine and don't consciously integrate the Nine qualities they've had to repress in order to survive may devolve into inaction, inertia, and unconscious merger with others when their anxieties drive them to withdraw from life and shut down.

Navigated consciously, a Six can use the "move to Nine" developmentally by establishing a healthy balance between watching out for dangers to their well-being and being able to relax in the security of supportive relationships. Sixes can focus on the attributes of this "child-heart" point to understand what they may have needed from their early relationships that they didn't get enough of, and then seek those things out as a way of tempering the fear and mistrust they had to develop to survive. "Moving back to Nine" can thus be a way of recovering their lost sense of comfort in merging with the agendas and the wills of others, allowing them to find more comfort in relationships instead of having their guard up. In this way, Sixes can call on the Nine Point to work through their need to push away from others to fend off threats and learn to see more deeply into others' points of view. If they can reincorporate some of the high-side aspects of the Nine Point, it can free them from some of the fear-based habits that inhibit their progress toward the Three Point.

By re-engaging with the natural Type Nine qualities of trust and comfort with others, Sixes can consciously remind themselves that it's okay to let their guard down and relax some of the time. Instead of needing to protect themselves from being hurt by others by remaining watchful, they can reclaim their ability to open up to others more and cultivate an appreciation for others' perspectives and approaches to life. In this way, Sixes can balance out their fear of others' hidden intentions with an ability to find security in a deeper sense of being and connection with other people.

The Vice to Virtue Conversion: Accessing Fear and Aiming for Courage

The developmental path from Vice to Virtue is one of the central contributions of the Enneagram map in highlighting a usable "vertical" path of growth to a higher state of awareness for each type. In the case of Type Six, the "Vice" (or passion) of the type is fear, and its opposite, the Virtue, is *courage*. The theory of growth communicated by this "Vice to Virtue conversion" is that the more we can be aware of how our passion functions and consciously work toward the embodiment of our higher Virtue, the more we can free ourselves from the unconscious habits and fixated patterns of our type and evolve toward our "higher" side or "oak tree–Self."

As Sixes become more familiar with their experience of fear and develop their ability to make it more conscious, they can take their work further by making efforts to focus on enacting their Virtue, the "antidote" to the passion of fear. In the case of Type Six, the Virtue of courage represents a state of being that Sixes can attain through consciously manifesting their higher capacities.

Courage is a way of being that is awake to the dangers inherent in the world and at the same time able to access a natural sense of confidence in meeting them. This higher Virtue encompasses our ability to face our deepest fears and anxieties secure in the knowledge that we have what it takes to cope with them. Courage also represents the inner support we provide ourselves such that we can let go of our ego defenses and grow beyond the narrow, confining (acorn shell) structure of our personalities. Ichazo defined courage as "the recognition of the individual's responsibility for his own existence," and as the body's natural movement to preserve itself.[31] Courage doesn't require thinking or vigilance or aggression; rather, it comes from a deep source of inner knowing that we can take care of ourselves.

Embodying courage as a Six means you have the ability to face outside dangers with confidence, but it also means you have the ability to open up to and explore your inner territory. As Maitri points out, because of the powerful pull of unconsciousness (symbolized by the Nine Point), one of the most difficult things we can do as humans is to commit to getting to know our inner reality. Courage thus represents the quality we inhabit when we do whatever it takes to pay attention to what is going on inside us despite the constant temptation to stay comfortable and avoid whatever pain and fear we might feel. It is so easy for us to go to sleep to ourselves, and so hard to stay engaged in the process of knowing ourselves, that we have to have courage to remain aware and awake to ourselves, especially because waking up inevitably entails encountering our suffering. Courage means having the will to know who you really are and who you may become, even when this leads you through your fears and all the other painful and scary emotions you had to go to sleep to (and relegate to your Shadow) in order to survive when you took on your personality in childhood.

All of us feel the inertia of wanting to stay asleep and the fear of putting down our protective defenses; and all of us must have the courage to try to stay awake to the deeper pain and fear that we put aside early on. Becoming more courageous allows Sixes (and all of us) to face our fears and our suffering head-on such that we can really grow. The Virtue of the Six Point represents this kind of deeply felt ability to engage more deeply in life with confidence. The Six virtue of courage thus reflects both a real inner resource inherent in who we are and a model of what we can develop and own more consciously as we try to let go of the protective defenses associated with the conditioned personality. As C. S. Lewis said, "courage is not simply one of the virtues, but the form of every virtue at its testing point."[32]

Specific Work for the Three Type Six Subtypes on the Path from Vice to Virtue

Whatever type you are, the path from observing your passion to finding its antidote is not exactly the same for each of the subtypes. The path of conscious self-work has been characterized in terms of "grit, grind, and grace:"[33] the "grit" of our personality programming, the "grind" of our efforts to grow, and the "grace" that comes to us when we our work toward embodying our higher virtue in conscious and positive ways. Each subtype has to grind, or exert effort, against something slightly different. This insight is one of the great benefits of understanding the three distinct subtypes of each of the nine types.

Self-Preservation Sixes can travel the path from fear to courage by saying things directly instead of being vague; making decisions instead of staying lost in questioning; and having the fortitude to fulfill their own needs rather than always looking to others for support and protection. If you are a Self-Preservation Six, you can work toward embodying courage by giving voice to your aggression in conscious, constructive ways. Take the risk to learn that you can draw on your own aggression and confidence more actively in support of yourself. Challenge yourself to break out of the compulsion to always need to be good and docile, and practice allowing yourself to be angry. Have the courage to say more clearly what you really think, especially when you fear others might disapprove. State your opinions and preferences, not from a place of reactivity under duress, but from a calm place of confidence that's more connected to your power and strength. Risk being "bad," getting mad, and expressing more of who you are without apology or doubt. Have the courage to own your power and authority in the world without needing to project it onto others. Rather than expecting support from others, own your many positive qualities such that you can be more confident in yourself. Work to have a more conscious sense of your strength and strength of purpose, knowing you have the courage to support yourself in the world in whatever ways you might need to.

Social Sixes can travel the path from fear to courage by forgetting about what their duty is or isn't and connecting in a more purposeful way with their own instincts, their own intuition, and with life in general. If you are a Social Six, recognize that living from the intellect only gets you so far; your head is not necessarily the right organ to tell you how to live fully. Allow yourself to get a little crazy and forget all the rules and reference points. You can grow toward courage more if you can learn to let go of your system of thinking, your ideas about what your duty is, and your clear categories, and develop the ability to become your own authority. Explore the ways in which you may be making an ideology—or even "rationality" itself—an impersonal authority that you rely on as a source of support or a parental surrogate, and take the risk of owning your own power instead. Realize and become more aware of how you may be compensating for a father figure who let you down, so you don't need to draw so heavily on whatever you are using as a guiding authority in your life. Don't be guided so much by your intellectual maps; act more from instinct. Have the courage to pursue pleasure rather than duty, knowing that connecting to your own power and satisfaction on all levels is the royal road to manifesting your higher capacities.

Sexual Sixes can travel the path from fear to courage by learning how to be more vulnerable. If you are a Sexual Six, you may at times feel courageous, but don't mistake aggression and "strength" born of fear for real courage. As Naranjo says, the courage of the Sexual Six is the courage of having a weapon. Put down your weapons and learn to tap into your vulnerable emotions as a source of real strength, real power, and real courage. Notice how being strong masks your fear and other vulnerable feelings, and work to get in touch with those instead of always taking refuge in your ability to squash fear and look strong on the outside. Work toward having the courage to be able to let your guard down with more people more often. Allow yourself to feel pleasure without ambivalence and tenderness without reserve. Notice how the fear of losing your freedom and independence may lead you to push people away, and work on learning to trust people more with your more vulnerable feelings. Allow yourself to be guided more by instinct, intuition, and softer emotions so you can expand the ways in which you relate to yourself and open yourself up to others. Recognize that you can be liberated from the fear that keeps you locked inside the hard shell of your "acorn" self by seeing and accepting that you don't always have to be so strong and so vigilant.

Conclusion

THE SIX POINT REPRESENTS the way we guard ourselves from others and the world out of a need to feel safe. The Six path of growth shows us how to transform our fear and all its manifestations into the courage and strength of purpose that allow us to find a greater sense of security within ourselves so that we can do the work of waking up to all we may become. In each of the Type Six subtypes we see a specific character who teaches us what is possible when we can turn our fear into a fully awakened capacity to have the courage to face what scares us—on the inside and the outside—through the alchemy of self-observation, self-development, and self-knowledge.

CHAPTER 7

The Point Five Archetype:
The Type, Subtypes, and Growth Path

He travels the fastest who travels alone.

—Rudyard Kipling

I have never found a companion that was so companionable as solitude.

—Henry David Thoreau, *Walden*

Understanding is a kind of ecstasy.

—Carl Sagan

TYPE FIVE REPRESENTS THE ARCHETYPE of the person who withdraws into thinking and detaches from feeling as a way of taking refuge in the inner world. This functions as a way of finding privacy and freedom in a world that seems intrusive or neglectful or overwhelming. The central drive of this archetype is to find security by minimizing needs and using resources economically so that external demands can be limited and controlled. In Fives, the natural human need for people can be displaced into a thirst for knowledge, such that internal support comes through information and firm boundaries instead of social connections.

We see a major characteristic of this archetype in Jung's concept of "introversion." While being introverted, or oriented primarily to the inner world rather than the outer world, is a general attitude that any of the personality types may have, "the introvert" as described in Jungian psychology closely mirrors the defining traits of the Point Five archetype.

According to Jungian analyst and author June Singer, the introvert "is directed primarily toward an understanding of what he perceives."[1] The introvert's attention is focused mainly on "his own being," which is the "center of every interest." People on the outside are important because of the way they may affect the introvert, and the introvert's "interest in self-knowledge prevents him from being overpowered by the influence of his objective surroundings."[2] The introvert "defends himself against external claims, consolidating his position"[3] of security. In Naranjo's words, introversion consists of "a movement away from the outer to the inner, and sensitivity to inner experiences."[4]

Type Fives are the prototype for that tendency in all of us to see ourselves as separate and disconnected from everything else, which causes us to feel the need to withdraw and hold on to whatever we have to survive.[5] We all identify with our egos, and so can believe that we are isolated individuals rather than part of an interconnected whole, which leads us to become attached to the things we think we need to sustain ourselves.

In everyday life, this universal archetype may manifest in the need to have time alone to rest, or "recharge," away from the prying eyes and emotional needs of others. It represents that part of us that would rather observe than participate and likes to withdraw periodically to a place of refuge. The Five archetype represents the model for preferring the relative safety of the intellect to the rigors of social and emotional life and sees knowledge as the most secure and satisfying form of power. In the face of conflict, difficulty, or hurt feelings, this stance sees withdrawal and distance as the best strategy.

In describing the character of the Five archetype, Naranjo points to psychological theorist Karen Horney's description of the person who favors "resignation" as a solution to life's conflicts, finding inner peace through maintaining an attitude of "not caring" and declaring himself uninterested in what is happening in the social world.[6] Uncomfortable with moving toward or against others, this person removes himself from the "inner battlefield" of love and aggression and gives up the struggle to get what he needs, resigning himself to settling for less, which potentially initiates an inner "process of shrinking, of restricting, of curtailing life and growth."[7]

Fives have analytical minds and tend to spend a lot of time pursuing their intellectual interests. They often possess a great deal of knowledge and expertise in particular areas of study. Because they automatically detach from emotions, they are highly skilled at performing rational, objective analyses of issues or situations. This habit also makes them calm in a crisis. As they appreciate the importance of boundaries in relationships, they value and respect others' boundaries and confidences. While they typically don't have a large quantity of close friends, they make high-quality, loyal, and trustworthy friends to the people with whom they do form relationships. Naturally austere and laconic, Fives are minimalistic and economical in the things they do, which reflects their concern with making the most of what resources they have and an ability to get by on limited supplies.

As with all the archetypal personalities, however, Type Fives' gifts and strengths also represent their "fatal flaw" or "Achilles heel:" they can isolate themselves from others, feel inhibited in relationships, and be detached and withdrawn in social situations. While Fives excel at objective analysis, they can be overly analytical and unemotional to the point that it can be hard for them to connect with others. They maintain a calm demeanor, but may not be able to express themselves emotionally. They may have too many or overly rigid boundaries and seem indifferent or hard to reach. They may hold themselves back from social interactions out of a fear of having their energy depleted by social contact. However, if they can learn to balance their needs for time and space with a greater openness to others and their own emotions, they can be dedicated friends and partners who display both a respect for the value of healthy separation and an ability to engage in wise and thoughtful ways.

The Type Five Archetype in Homer's *Odyssey:* Hermes and Circe

Hermes and Circe each reflect the themes of personality connected to Type Five. First, each of them guards and uses secret knowledge. Hermes is the messenger of the gods and charged with keeping the gods' secrets. He is also a symbol of boundaries and the protection they provide. Hermes has the power to bring what is secret into the light of day if he chooses. (To this day, an airtight enclosure is said to be "hermetically" sealed and the process of discerning the meaning behind a literal text is called "hermeneutics.")[8]

Circe means "hawk," and this name invokes the image of a sharp-eyed observer watching from afar. She is a mysterious sorceress who employs a magic wand and secret potions. She knows the routes and dangers of the world far better than any human traveler: "She is that wise being who can offer any seeker authoritative guidance about the road ahead, if she is so inclined, and if one knows how to approach her."[9]

Circe lives in a palace hidden deep in a wooded glen. She is surrounded by her collection of animals, but she has no human companionship. Odysseus's scouting party interrupts Circe as she is singing and weaving, and she invites the men in. She soon transforms them into pigs—the symbol of greedy appetite—highlighting their human

hunger and the craving that leads them to cling to and gorge themselves on what they have out of a fear of losing it or going without.

Odysseus follows in search of his men, and, with Hermes's help in
creating an internal barrier to her potion, he outwits Circe. She is truly
amazed, perhaps for the first time ever:

> I'm wonderstruck—you drank my drugs, you're not bewitched!
> Never has any other man withstood my potion, never, once it's
> passed his lips and he has drunk it down. You have a mind in you
> no magic can enchant![10]

Again, thanks to Hermes, Odysseus knows better than to fall into
Circe's trap, designed to enclose him in a pig's greed. He extracts a
promise from Circe that she will never plot against him. The sorceress
makes the oath and restores Odysseus's crew to human form. She
then begins to reveal the secret knowledge he needs to continue his
journey home through the underground territory of Hades.

Like the Type Five personality, Hermes and Circe are self-contained
keepers of secret knowledge. They share their guarded wisdom strategically—and only with those they deem intellectually worthy. Hermes
shows Odysseus how to safeguard himself against being lured into
avarice and Circe rewards him with abundance when he has shown
himself able to resist the trap of greed, and provides him with guidance into the underworld. Symbolically, Odysseus has now passed
through two different experiences of fear—fear of large, scary mon-
sters and fear of being consumed by greed, entrapment, and the need
for secrecy—and now he is ready to enter his underground territory.

The Type Five Personality Structure

FIVES BELONG TO THE "HEAD-BASED" TRIAD associated with the core
emotion of fear and a concern with safety. The personality of each of the
three head types (Five, Six, and Seven) is shaped by its response to the early
experience of fear. The primacy of the use of the head center also means that
these types process information from the outside world mainly through their
mental function—through thinking and analyzing data from the environment. Sevens avoid fear and anxiety by overcompensating with the search
for stimulating and pleasurable experiences. Sixes become vigilant, wary,

suspicious, and strategic in the face of early fear. Fives, however, become introverted, walled off from others, and focused on the protection and economical management of their inner resources. Fives become adept at avoiding situations in which fear might arise.

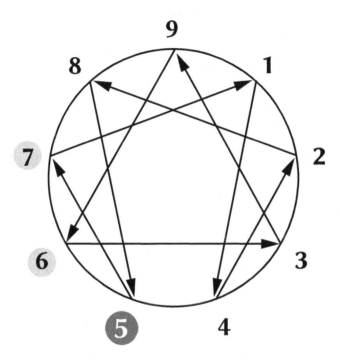

Type Five individuals "live in their heads" more than any of the other Enneagram personality types. They feel more comfortable when they are thinking and accumulating knowledge, and less comfortable with emotions. Fives can be very sensitive on the inside, despite their outward appearance as unsentimental—but they protect this sensitive inner core by creating thick boundaries that make them impervious to demands placed on them from the outside world. Fives adapt to their environment and manage early anxiety by automatically moving away from others, by protecting their inner lives and withdrawing emotionally from others when necessary.

The Early Coping Strategy: Type Five
Fives typically report that they had an early experience of being either neglected or engulfed by others at a time when they needed other people to survive. Caregivers were somehow not responsive to the Fives' needs, and they

learned that they could not achieve anything by force or seduction.[11] Because there was nothing to do but to live in privation, they learned to hold onto their meager resources.

To cope and find protection in a world that hasn't provided for their needs and to shield their young sense of self from external threats, Fives withdraw inside themselves. Finding other people either threatening or depriving, Fives essentially give up on receiving the sustenance provided by relationships and find satisfaction in knowledge and intellectual interests instead. Whereas some types cope by putting attention outward, seeking comfort through the approval or nurturing of others, Fives resolve to be self-sufficient and retreat from relationships as a way of saving themselves and protecting what little inner resources they believe they have.

To avoid needing other people and having to open up to dependent relationships, Fives minimize their needs and adopt an economical way of being. This leads to a tendency to withhold limited resources, and to a "greediness" or hoarding mentality when it comes to time, energy, information, and material supplies. They often pride themselves on having an ascetic or minimalistic way of life.

And to the extent that all coping strategies start with the need to adapt to some sort of deprivation or injury related to the need for love, Fives hold on to themselves and give up on relationships as a source of love and support. In this way, the Five coping strategy is based on a scarcity model—in the face of a lack of what they need, Fives unconsciously decide not to need very much from the outside and so turn inward, reduce their needs, and conserve their inner resources. This movement inward and toward independence as a solution to early deprivation (or intrusion) manifests as a sense of having a tight hold on one's inner life as well as a focus on the economical use of effort, energy, and resources.

This defensive strategy naturally leads Fives to acquire habits through which they distance themselves from others. This strategy can make Fives seem aloof and uncaring, but they are much more sensitive on the inside than they appear. This coping strategy involves not only distancing themselves from relationships and the need for relationship, but also separating themselves from their own emotions, in part because feeling their emotions might move them to reach out to others. In this way, through their compulsive avoidance of life and of others, they remove themselves not only from the "interfering world," but from themselves.[12]

Thomas, a Social Five, describes his childhood situation and the development of his coping strategy:

From a very young age I preferred my own company to that of others. I often read books or entertained myself with fantasy games. Figuring out how things worked was more important to me than playing with my siblings or other kids. I actually found it fun to read encyclopedias and other books that provided large amounts of information about the world. Although I was regarded as a clever child by those around me, I found it much easier to be a loner. The handful of friends I had as a kid were usually the other "loners" with whom I shared common intellectual interests.

I remember being nine years old and playing "thinking games" with my best friends. We would analyze the people around us, classify them according to sets of colors, animals, celebrities, and general archetypes, and write questionnaires to test out our theories. We created a secret language for what we wrote so we could communicate with each other privately through layers of encoded messages.

I never liked talking about myself and learned that by asking questions and listening carefully I could deflect other people's attention away from my own personal feelings and inner world. On one level, I felt inadequate, and on another, deeper level, there were precious layers of my identity that I needed to hold on to as much as possible. When my parents would take us shopping, I would always downplay my needs or choose the least expensive items out of a desire to avoid being a burden on them. I would hoard the sweets my mother would give to us in a big jar in my cupboard and not eat them.

The Main Type Five Defense Mechanism: Isolation

Psychologist Nancy McWilliams defines *isolation* as a defense mechanism in which people "deal with anxieties and other painful states of mind...by isolating feeling from knowing."[13] When using isolation as a defense, a person unconsciously separates out the emotion connected to an idea from the idea itself. Fives feel more comfortable with thoughts than emotions, so Fives automatically focus on the mental or thinking part of a situation and make any emotions related to what they are thinking about unconscious. Defensively reducing their awareness of their feelings protects them from experiencing troubling emotions and also limits their (potentially dangerous) need for the support of other people.

The defense mechanism of isolation, like many defenses, has a positive use: isolation can be of value in situations where experiencing feelings may be detrimental, as when a surgeon needs to distance herself from her emotions to be able to cut into someone or when a military general needs to plan strategy without being overwhelmed by the horror of war. However, isolation can also lead to an inability to feel feelings at all, especially as Fives overvalue thinking and underappreciate feeling. Fives also intellectualize—talking about feelings without actually feeling them.

To protect themselves from having to feel painful feelings like sadness or fear or loneliness, Fives withdraw from people who might stir up these feelings, separate their thoughts from their emotions, and identify themselves with their thinking function.

The Type Five Focus of Attention

Given Fives' early experience and the coping strategy that arises to deal with it, they focus on managing inner resources and potential impingements on their privacy from the outside. This contributes to a general stance of observing rather than participating, and a focus on the mental rather than the emotional or "gut" level of life.

On the inside, Fives focus on minimizing needs, analyzing, and thinking, and on the conservation and judicious use of energy and resources. One Five I know likens his sense of his energy to a gas tank. When he wakes up in the morning, he has a sense that he has a certain amount of energy in his "tank" that has to last for the whole day. Not wanting to run out of gas, but regularly fearful that he will, he has become an expert at knowing when someone or something might threaten to deplete his energy supply too much. Once he identifies people or activities that might overtax his energetic resources, he can take steps to avoid or otherwise neutralize the threat.

Fives like systems of knowledge and may become consumed by thinking about projects, hobbies, or particular areas of study that engage their interest. In a way that reflects their adherence to the idea that "knowledge is power," (and thus potentially a form of security) Fives seek to gain a kind of mental mastery over information—knowledge about the people and things happening around them, as well as specific topics that they enjoy knowing about.

Fives focus on protecting the inside, putting attention toward limiting intrusions and threats to inner resources and private space. Fives don't like surprises, and they dislike being subject to situations in which they might have to deal with the emotions or the emotionality of others. Whereas other types, like Twos and Nines, have difficulty erecting boundaries between themselves and other people, Fives have no problem putting up and maintaining boundaries—in fact, they tend to have the opposite issue: they can have too many boundaries. Most of all, they want to know that they have control over their boundaries, that they don't have to be put in the position of being intruded upon or invaded by others when they would rather be alone.

Characteristically introverted, Fives can assess very quickly whether or not they want to be involved with specific individuals. And when they do interact with others, they can get a lot out of a little—they can be present and sincerely engaged with others socially, but on a limited basis. In addition, they can be highly selective, because they want the energy they devote to social interactions to be limited to people they really like and trust—and also subject to time limits of their choosing.

The Type Five Emotional Passion: Avarice

The passion of Type Five is *avarice*, or greed. However, avarice as it applies to the Five personality does not necessarily imply a desire to hoard money or wealth or material goods, as greed is often commonly understood. For Fives, the central motivation of avarice is to hold onto what they have in light of an early experience of not getting much from others. Not having received enough love or care or responsiveness early on, Fives naturally fear being depleted, which leads to a defensive expectation of impoverishment. This poverty mentality in turn motivates Fives to reduce their needs and hold back from giving to others: "By giving the little they feel is theirs they feel that they will be left with nothing at all."[14]

A poignant story I once heard a Five tell highlights this situation: The main problem between him and his now ex-wife was that in their marriage she experienced him as withholding his emotions and his affection from her. He said that his wife was a Type Four, and if emotions were money, she would have been a millionaire, while he had only a few pennies. When he gave her six of his ten pennies, which was a lot to him, she saw it as nothing.

Fives' avarice thus represents a fearful grasping of time, space, and energy, motivated by an underlying, unconscious fantasy that letting go would result in catastrophic depletion. Behind the desire to hoard what little they have, there is a deeper fear of impending impoverishment that has its source in not having gotten enough nourishment.[15] At the same time, they may also have a fear of being overly encumbered by too many, or too onerous, commitments.

Under the influence of avarice, Fives get minimalistic and contract, withdrawing into themselves as a way of not letting others empty them out. They fear both not having enough and being weighed down/having too much to carry on their own. People may experience Fives as holding back or being aloof, and they may be perceived as not engaging fully. As a result, others may judge Fives as cold or unfeeling or arrogant, but behind this habit of holding back and holding in is a fear of not having enough of what they need to survive.

The Type Five coping strategy centers around avarice in that by minimizing interactions that may be energetically costly, Fives believe they can conserve their energy and hoard their precious resources. So, contrary to the usual understanding of avarice as the greedy acquisition of more and more potentially superfluous resources (like money and material goods), the Five passion of avarice manifests as a preoccupation with maintaining a grip on what minimal resources they think they have and feel in danger of using up or otherwise losing.

Where some passions motivate the personality to move toward others too intensely, avarice stimulates a move away from others. Avarice induces Fives to erect firm boundaries, withdraw from others, and otherwise avoid situations in which they might get depleted. Their desire not to be interfered with, invaded, or subjected to external demands becomes a passion, leading them to search inside themselves for what others look for outside themselves.[16]

The Type Five Cognitive Mistake: "Human Contact Exhausts Rather than Enriches"

We all get stuck in habitual ways of thinking that influence our beliefs, feelings, and actions, and this continues even after the mental models that create our overall perspective aren't accurate anymore.[17] While the passion shapes the personality's emotional motivations, the "cognitive fixation" or "cognitive mistake" preoccupies the personality's mental thought processes.

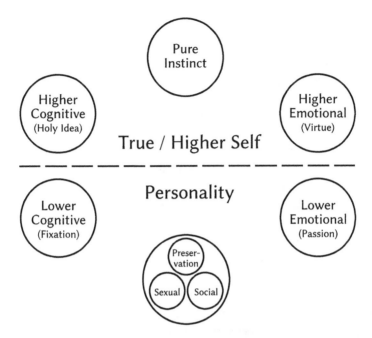

Type Fives' core beliefs reflect themes of isolation, emotional inhibition, energetic withholding, the value of knowledge, and inadequacy. These beliefs act as organizing principles that center around and reinforce the following general idea: in a world that is intrusive or unresponsive, you need to have the ability to withdraw inside yourself, take refuge in your mind, and exercise control over interactions with the outside; otherwise, you will be completely used up.

To support the passion of avarice, Fives hold the following core beliefs as psychological organizing principles.[18]

- People can be intrusive and threatening to my personal comfort.
- The world doesn't always provide what you need, so it pays to find ways to be self-sufficient.
- Other people want more from me than I want to give.
- I must protect my time and energy by having firm boundaries and maintaining my private space; otherwise, others will deplete me.
- The emotional demands others make on me will exhaust my inner resources and so should be avoided.
- If I open up to relationships, others will expect and demand more than I have to give. Having too many relationships with the wrong kind of people leads to the risk of feeling totally depleted.

- Commitments to others are burdens that are too heavy to carry with me. It's best to travel light.
- I am powerless when it comes to negotiating my needs and desires, and others may not listen anyway, so the safest course of action is to withdraw.
- Overall, separation from others feels more comfortable than the alternative.
- If I am spontaneous in my actions or feelings, others will disapprove, I will feel embarrassed, or I will feel out of control or expose myself in a way that seems intolerable.
- It's better and safer to feel my emotions when I am by myself (and not when I am in the presence of others).
- Knowledge is power.
- Knowledge is best attained through observation, research, and the collection and compartmentalization of data.

In reaction to a world that seems to want too much, Fives believe they are inadequately equipped to be present in an ongoing, engaged, and connected way, so it's better to avoid contact with others. By focusing on the demands of others as potentially exhausting and the wisdom of being able to withdraw from relationships, they continually confirm their conviction that the best and safest solution to the threat of inner depletion is to observe, detach from emotions, hoard their energy, and maintain boundaries to protect their private space.

The Type Five Trap: "Scarcity Breeds Scarcity," or "The Fear of Depletion is Itself Depleting"

As it does distinctly for each type, the cognitive fixation for Type Five leads the personality in circles. It represents an inherent "trap" that the limitations of the personality cannot resolve.

Fives' core beliefs keep them fixated in a world of scarcity because these self-limiting ideas sap their motivation to do the work it would take to realize the falsity of their underlying assumptions. Contrary to their thinking when under the sway of this fixation, the world does provide abundance, especially if you believe it does.

If you believe that emotional contact with the outside world can be supportive, you are more likely to allow yourself to open up to the risk of taking in sustenance from others. By not believing in abundance and the possibility of external support, Fives remain stuck in the mental patterns that make them feel safe. By cutting themselves off from potentially nourishing relationships with other people, Fives don't learn that their inner resources can be renewed and refreshed, not just depleted, by social contact. They deprive themselves through their adherence to a life strategy that cuts them off from replenishment as a response to deprivation.

The Key Type Five Traits

The Centrality of Thinking

Fives' "cognitive orientation" means that they "live in their heads" most of the time. They relate to the world primarily through their thinking function and tend to be very intellectual. A focus on thinking supports the Five's desire to observe and reflect on life instead of participate in it actively, in spontaneous ways. Naranjo thus likens the satisfaction Fives seek in thinking to a "replacement of living through reading."[20] Fives' thinking orientation also supports their sense that real power lies in acquiring intellectual knowledge. Intense thinking activity also serves the purpose of helping Fives prepare for life, a preparation that they always feel like they need to do more of because they never feel ready enough.

Thinking also feels comfortable to Fives because when you think, you can hide. Most people can't tell what others are thinking, whereas when we feel strong emotions, it often shows—we may share our feelings with others whether we want to or not. The emphasis on cognition together with the inhibition of feelings and action reflects Fives' preoccupation with being an observer of life—trying to figure out inside their heads what things mean and what is going on without having to commit to showing up for life and relationships. Feelings are not comfortable for the Five to experience and express, so they rely on thinking, which allows them to remain in their comfort zone.

Fives' thinking tends to focus on figuring things out, preparing for interactions, and engaging in mental classification and organization. They are also attracted to thinking because it supports looking competent, which can be a way of hiding or a way of communicating your value without revealing too much of yourself. Naranjo also highlights the fact that Fives tend to "dwell in abstractions while at the same time avoiding concreteness,"[21] and that this avoidance of the concrete is a way of maintaining their hiddenness—they are able to offer their perceptions to the world without having to betray the deeper substrate of emotional attachments, motives, and values underlying those perceptions.

Drawn to tools and systems of knowledge, Fives feel most comfortable when they are gathering data and figuring things out using their intellect. Because they are oriented toward collecting and organizing information, they often display a strong interest in science or areas of technical or specialized knowledge. One of the easier ways for them to form connections with others is through the sharing of knowledge and expertise—both as a way of demonstrating their competence and participating in a kind of connection that is less threatening.

Emotional Detachment and Feelinglessness

Fives automatically and unconsciously detach from emotions. This habit, born of an early experience of deprivation or intrusion, serves Fives' defensive structure in several ways. Emotional detachment allows them to avoid uncomfortable emotions and the cost in energy of feeling them; to remain aloof and separate from others (as feelings tend to connect people across space and time); and to repress the need for relationships. The habit of detaching from feelings helps Fives to avoid emotional burdens, the realization of their own needs, and "unwanted" relationships.

It's important to remember that Fives don't consciously unhook from emotions—rather, they experience a more automatic letting-go of emotion, a more generalized lack of awareness of feelings, or an unconscious interference with the generation of feeling.[22] More prominent in the Five's conscious experience is a desire to keep a safe distance away from undue emotional burdens and to maintain a sense of autonomy and control.

Type Fives' lack of engagement with their own emotions also causes them to have little tolerance for other people's intense emotions. And while this characteristic can make Fives seem cold, unfeeling, or unempathetic, this lack of obvious empathy simply reflects the Five's defensive stance, not an intentional or mean-spirited disregard. The lack of feeling expressed by most Fives represents a deep desire to remain hidden, to manage inner resources without being disrupted, and to maintain a safe distance in relationships.

Fear of Engulfment

Perhaps as a consequence of an early traumatic experience of feeling intruded upon or having their boundaries disregarded, Fives typically feel fearful of the possibility of being engulfed, taken over, or somehow used up by others. This usually half-conscious fear, like their (related) fear of being dependent on others, motivates Fives to avoid relationships. An anxiety can arise in Fives, perhaps in ways they only dimly experience, that causes them to hold onto what they have and to maintain strong boundaries by making sure they have the necessary privacy and alone time they need to maintain their independence. As Naranjo explains, "to the extent that relationship entails alienation from one's own preferences and authentic expression, there arises an implicit stress and the need to recover from it: a need to find oneself again in aloneness."[23]

Autonomy and Self-Sufficiency

Fives both feel a need for and idealize autonomy.[24] They highly prize self-sufficiency, a value that offers both a way of affirming and rationalizing their preference for distance from others. Fives' affinity for self-sufficiency also relates to the value system associated with their coping strategy of withdrawing from others: if you find it desirable to isolate yourself, you need to be able to do without external supplies or stockpile them yourself. As people who have given up on getting others to satisfy their desires, Fives need to be able to build up their resources on their own.

By needing and valuing autonomy, Fives both enact their characteristic coping strategy (designed to create distance in relationships to reduce the threat of depletion) and find theoretical support for the way of life they find most comfortable and attractive. Fives believe being alone is a good thing, as it enables them to get by on their own without having to depend on others or engage with them too much. Naranjo points out that this is the philosophy of life that Herman Hesse has Siddartha vocalize when he says, "I can think, I can wait, I can fast." And it makes sense that Siddartha, the young Buddha, expresses this idea, as Buddhism can be said to be a "Five" spiritual path, characterized fundamentally by head-based practices focused on the higher goal (the Five's higher "Virtue") of becoming non-attached.

Hypersensitivity

While Fives can appear detached or unfeeling on the outside, this stance reflects (and protects) a much deeper inner sensitivity that the Five defensive structure is designed to protect. Fives' emotional detachment arises out of a need to protect themselves from emotional pain, precisely because they feel so vulnerable to it.

Type Fives' habit of automatically detaching from feelings serves the function of guarding against the experience of the pain of loneliness, fear, hurt, powerlessness, and emptiness. The Five personality doesn't usually feel or acknowledge these emotions consciously in everyday life, but its defensive structure develops in response to them—or the fear of them. Naranjo points out that Fives' tendency toward internal conservation and minimalism contributes to their inner sensitivity to feeling deprived, since "an individual who feels full and substantial can stand more pain than one who feels empty."[25]

Fives can also be very sensitive toward others, though they usually don't show it. Their tendency to withdraw might be seen as a defensive reaction that expresses a desire to avoid having to feel the pain of others, since empathizing with others' pain can seem daunting and potentially exhausting in light of their hypersensitivity. Their unreserved acceptance of boundaries also displays this sensitivity, as Fives are mindful of others' needs for space based on their own concern with privacy and protection.

Because Fives do not live in their emotions, they may be more vulnerable to the effects of emotional pain; they have not built up a tolerance for or a comfort with their emotions and so may not know how to deal with painful feelings. In light of this, Fives may have less ability to feel and weather difficult emotions, and their seeming insensitivity might usefully be viewed as a reflection of the greater protection they need with regard to strong emotions.

The Type Five Shadow

Fives have blindspots related to their emotions, their need for love and relationships, the possibility of abundant resources, and their own strength, aggression, and power. Given their strategy of detaching from emotions and protecting their boundaries to preserve energy and maintain a safe distance from others, Fives may habitually separate themselves from their own feelings and other people such that their potential for relationship and connection remains hidden in their Shadow. Fives may undervalue their emotional life to the point that they give up on developing their capacity for feeling or expressing feelings. While they can be emotionally sensitive at a deeper level, it doesn't feel safe to express this, so they may stop believing in their capacity for deep feeling.

Fives feel safest when they can be autonomous and self-sufficient—when they can avoid having contact with their own need for people and for outside support. Instead of seeing this as something that they consciously avoid because it feels threatening, some Fives may believe they just don't like to be too close to too many people and so resign themselves to not being very connected to others—or to maintaining very few close relationships. As this tends to be what feels safe and comfortable, Fives may not feel motivated to challenge their limited need for people. They may not always recognize that, just like everybody else, they have needs for support, because their desire for the nourishment that relationships provide remains a blindspot.

While many Fives say they do want love and connection, most also focus on maintaining firm boundaries. They anticipate being depleted, and they don't see that they only perceive their energy as a scarce commodity because their defensive "self-system" has led them to believe in their inner energetic poverty and motivated them to wall themselves off and live on very little. Their potential for having abundant energy exists in their Shadow. The truth they don't see is that they have the capacity to generate more internal resources and a greater wellspring of energy, especially if they allow for more support and nurturance from the outside. Their belief in their inner scarcity blinds them to the greater possibilities for abundance in adulthood.

Conflict threatens to force Fives to expend energy they believe they don't have, so they avoid conflict and can disappear without walking away. While Fives can bring significant strength to bear in establishing boundaries, their sense of inner impoverishment can blind them to their (healthy) aggression, their true strength, and their personal power.

Naranjo writes that Fives "may suffer a great deal as a result of their incapacity to relate to others in overtly loving ways."[26] Being introverted, private, and unemotional, they may seem to others like they have no interest in love. And Fives may also see themselves as less loving than others. Feeling safest when alone, Fives' desire to receive love from others becomes dampened through the habit of minimizing any need related to being connected to or dependent on others. They typically do not believe themselves worthy of receiving love because their disinterest in others leads them to believe that they do not give enough.[27]

When Fives buy into their own limitations, they may experience themselves as not interested in relating to others in deeper ways, and that can become their reality. It is only the Five's conditioned personality that is limited in its ability to actively express and receive love, not their true self—but as long as Fives believe that their capacities for love and intimacy are limited, their true ability to love and be loved remains hidden from them in their Shadow

The Shadow of the Type Five Passion:
Avarice in Dante's Underworld

The passion of Type Five is a form of inner hoarding with the classical name "avarice." In the form of greed, it is a fixation on acquiring and holding onto material wealth and resources, though in the Five psyche, it connotes a withholding born of a fear of depletion. In Canto VII of *Inferno*, Dante shows the ultimate futility of clinging on to resources by punishing it in tandem with its opposite. Thus, the Miserly and the Prodigal—those who expressed avarice (mostly popes and cardinals) and those who spent without moderation—are condemned to move in an eternal circle, suffering the punishment of pushing against each other:

> [F]rom both sides, to the sound of their own screams, straining their chests, they rolled enormous weights. And when they met and clashed against each other they turned to push the other way, one side screaming, "Why hoard?," the other side, "Why waste?" And so they moved back round the gloomy circle.
>
> It was squandering and hoarding that have robbed them of the lovely world, and got them in this brawl: I will not waste choice words describing it![28]

The fundamental sin of the Miserly and its punishment in Dante's underworld expresses the dark side of the passion of avarice as he poetically comments on the heavy weight that material wealth can become when we focus on the threat of depletion.[29] Virgil explains that no one can counteract the dictates of Fortune that give some more than others, meaning that part of the mistake the Avaricious make is that they don't understand that "Fortune" or life brings us enough resources to sustain us; we don't have to mess with the natural order of things by holding on so tightly.[30]

Further, Dante highlights one more feature of the Type Five character, as he portrays the Miserly as "unrecognizable"—the Pilgrim cannot recognize anyone of these sinners because their concern with wealth left them undistinguished in life. Thus, Dante symbolically communicates the shadow effect of Avarice on the individual: by holding on and holding in, you end up carrying a heavier load (rather than a lighter one) and wind up being impossible to be seen and related to in the world of others.

The Three Kinds of Fives:
The Type Five Subtypes

THE PASSION OF TYPE FIVE IS AVARICE. All three Fives express a different sense of what they focus on to sustain themselves given the passion of avarice and the corresponding tendency to minimize needs and connections with others. The Self-Preservation Five acts out avarice by building and maintaining boundaries. The Social Five acts it out by adhering to specific ideals related to groups and ideas. The Sexual Five acts it out by seeking an experience of trust with a worthy partner and expressing romantic ideals.

Compared to some of the other personality types, like Fours and Sixes, the three Type Five subtypes are relatively similar to each other. As Naranjo explains, when it comes to the three instinctual subtypes, everything is more monochromatic with Fives. All three look somewhat alike, so it can be harder to tell them apart. The more intense Fours diverge more clearly in one direction or the other, and they wind up being distinct characters whose differences are easier to discern—but the Fives look more alike in their characterological expression. However, there are some differences between the three, including the fact, according to Naranjo, that Self-Preservation Fives and Social Fives are more removed from their feelings, whereas Sexual Fives are more intense, romantic, and sensitive inside.

The Self-Preservation Five:"Castle"

The Self-Preservation Five is the most "Five-ish" of the Fives. These Fives express avarice through their passion for hiddenness or for having sanctuary. The name given to this type is "Castle," which communicates this person's need to be encastled—to be able to hide behind or be protected by walls. Psychologically (and sometimes physically), Self-Preservation Fives build thick walls to protect themselves from the world and from other people.

Self-Preservation Fives have a need for clearly defined boundaries. This personality is the clearest expression of the archetype of isolation and introversion. They have a need to be able to hide behind boundaries they can control, and to know they have a place of safety they can retreat to, in order to avoid feeling lost in the world. In focusing on finding shelter, they learn to survive inside walls—and they want to have everything inside those walls so that they don't have to venture out into the world. To them, the external world can seem hostile, inadequate, and brutal.

Related to this need for the protection of clear boundaries, Self-Preservation Fives also focus a great deal of attention on how to survive free from the limitation of external shocks or surprises. They have a feeling of having to be on guard and a difficulty with expressing anger, though they may communicate anger passively by withdrawing and hiding or going silent.

Self-Preservation Fives' need for hiddenness can create difficulties with self-expression in general; this subtype is the least communicative of the three Five subtypes. Their passion for hiddenness also manifests in taking covert action: they act in secret so their actions do not compromise their ability to keep their guard up.

The problem with this stance, especially when it tends toward the extreme, is that living in an enclosure is not really compatible with having and meeting basic human needs. The Self-Preservation Five is the most withdrawn of the Fives, and, as a natural part of renouncing needs and wants, they try to get by on very little, especially when it comes to the emotional support that relationships provide. Self-Preservation Fives limit their needs and wants because they believe that every desire could open the door to their becoming dependent on others. Desires, then, are either sublimated in specific interests or activities or erased from consciousness. Self-Preservation Fives "live little," meaning they get by with few resources, which amounts to living small or poorly.

Naranjo explains that, normally, people have some ability to say, "I want that"—to express desires and do the work they need to do to get what they want—but these Fives cannot ask and cannot take. So they must rely on preserving what they are able to acquire themselves.[31]

You can see these Self-Preservation Five characteristics clearly reflected in the work of Franz Kafka (who was probably a Self-Preservation Five himself), especially in the books *The Castle* and *The Tremendous World I Have Inside My Head*, and in a story titled "The Hunger Artist," in which the main character becomes a specialist at renunciation.

In relationships with others, Self-Preservation Fives avoid creating expectations or dependent relationships. They also avoid conflict, which is another way they detach from people. They do, however, typically experience a strong sense of attachment to a few places and people. To prevent conflict and manage contact with others, they may adapt to fit in to not be seen.

One Self-Preservation Five I know who can seem outwardly quite sociable explains that she watches how other people interact and then acts in similar ways, modeling what she does on what she observes, using her ability to adapt to what is expected of her as a kind of camouflage. If people don't see her as especially reserved, she reasons, they won't challenge her boundaries. However, this need to adapt can cause Self-Preservation Fives to feel resentful when they feel like they have to expend energy to fit in with others.

While they may at times choose to share feelings with a trusted few people in their lives, Self-Preservation Fives have strong inhibitions against showing aggression in particular. They will very seldom show their anger. However, they do have a kind of warmth and humor that is both a genuine expression of their internal sensitivity and a defensive construction or social shield. In social interactions, this can give their superficial acquaintances the feeling that a bond has been established when the Self-Preservation Five has merely been studying or placating them, not necessarily initiating a relationship. As the most Fivish of the Five subtypes, it is unlikely that this Five would be mistaken for another type.

Stacy, a Self-Preservation Five, speaks:

I am often told that I am a good listener. The truth is that I have become an expert on asking just the right kind of questions—those that will keep the other person talking while at the same time allowing me to maintain a comfortable distance from any topic that might require me to engage more fully. Under most circumstances, I do not like talking about myself, and someone who pushes me in this regard will feel intrusive. Within a small circle of close and trusted friends, however, I will share quite deeply. These are the people whose perspectives I seek out and whose actions I study so that I can navigate my way through the emotional world.

I rarely ask for favors. While I am happy to help out a friend in need, the reciprocal nature of favor-doing feels suffocating to me. I work very hard to make sure that my life is organized and structured in a way that will require little assistance from others. Only in the most extreme of circumstances will I reach out for help, and then I will find myself immediately buying a thank you gift to absolve myself of any perceived indebtedness. In general, feeling needed by others just feels like the other person is being too needy.

My most peaceful moments are when I have limited obligations and can be on my own schedule, independent, and at home. Time by myself is rejuvenating—and spending time in my home is particularly restorative. Intrusions and unexpected visitors are difficult to manage. I keep neighbors at an arm's length and avoid the yearly block party like the plague. When we first moved into our home, a neighbor repeatedly asked me to join the book club comprised of women from our neighborhood. Honestly, it was as if she was asking me to run away with her and join a circus—the idea was that strange and unappealing. I still hide from her when I see her around.

The Social Five: "Totem"

For Social Fives, the passion of avarice is connected to knowledge. These Fives don't need the nourishment relationships provide because their passion for knowledge somehow compensates for what they might get from direct human contact. It's as if they have an intuition that they can find everything they need through the mind. Needs (for people and for emotional sustenance) get displaced into a thirst for knowledge.

The name given to this subtype is "Totem," which communicates their need for "super-ideals," or the need to relate to people who share their intellectual values, interests, and ideals. The image of a totem suggests both height and a character that is constructed (like an object) rather than a human being. These Fives do not relate to regular people in everyday life—they relate to easily idealized experts who share their ideals; to people who display what they see as outstanding characteristics based on shared values and knowledge and who they can keep at a certain distance. One Social Five I know says he "collects people" who share his interests and values.

For Social Fives, then, avarice gets acted out through a greedy search for the ultimate ideals that will provide a sense of meaning by connecting them to something special, thereby elevating their life. The Social Five's passion is the need for the essential, the sublime, or the extraordinary instead of what is here and now. In line with this need for relationships based on shared ideals, Social Fives have a tendency to look upward, toward higher values. According to Naranjo, they look toward the stars and care little for life down on earth.

In contrast to Sexual Fives, who are iconoclasts, Social Fives are admiring people—individuals who admire others that express their ideals in extraordinary ways. In looking for and adhering to super-values, they can be disdainful of ordinary life and ordinary people. The life of the mind feels more compelling, and the people at a distance who represent the extraordinary seem more seductive and interesting to them than the people they meet in everyday life.

Social Fives are looking for the ultimate meaning in life, motivated by an underlying (potentially unconscious) sense that things are meaningless unless the ultimate meaning is found. This Five's drive to find the extraordinary underscores a polarity they may perceive between extraordinariness and meaninglessness. They look for meaning to avoid a fearful sense that the world is meaningless, but in their search for meaning they orient themselves so much toward finding the quintessence of life—the extraordinary—that they may become disinterested in everyday life. They see a gap between the ideal and everyday life, and they burn in the longing for the ultimate meaning. For this

Five, motivated by the social instinct in the service of avarice, the common, ordinary self does not have enough value to satisfy their drive for meaning.

In their search for meaning, these Fives can become spiritual or ideal- istic in a way that is actually counter to real spiritual attainment, because it bypasses compassion and empathy and the practical level of how people con- nect to each other in ordinary life. This tendency is the prototype of what is sometimes called a "spiritual bypass," in which a person looks for and devotes himself to a higher ideal or a valued system of knowledge as a way of avoiding doing the emotional and psychological work he would need to do to grow and develop. They may believe they are transcending their ego, but their adherence to their spiritual values or practice is their way of escaping from their everyday emotional reality into a "higher" intellectual system that they have idealized. Any type can spiritually bypass, but the Social Five is the prototype of some- one who employs this as a defensive strategy.

Social Fives prefer not to feel. They can be mysterious and inaccessible, or fun and intellectually engaging. They may hide out in the pose of an expert, and they tend to have a sense of omnipotence through the exercise of their intellect. These Fives may imagine that they are superior to others because of their higher values and ideals. Although they would never (intentionally) show it, they seek recognition and prestige; they want to be someone impor- tant, and they often seek to fulfill this desire this by allying themselves with people they admire.

Social Fives can look like Type Sevens in that they can be fairly outgo- ing and display a great deal of excitement about interesting ideas and people. The Social Five is typically more "out there" than other Fives, in the sense of being more social and able to engage. Social Fives differ from Sevens, how- ever, in that they are more reserved, less self-interested, and less emotional than Sevens.

Scott, a Social Five, speaks:

When I first encountered the Enneagram, I thought I was a Seven. I consider myself very sociable, and I connect easily with people—but on deeper reflection, I realized that my connections are specifically with topic "experts" or people who share my interests. I would choose my friends based on their intellect, and the time we spent together would be focused on sharing ideas. I realized I was a Five and not a Seven because I categorize people and create barriers between myself and others by being invisibly secretive. I ask lots of questions about the other person to avoid being investigated by them. I often wonder, "Who am I? What is this mystery inside myself?"

As a young child I would read encyclopedias, "How it Works" books, and "Eyewitness" books all the time for fun. My inner fantasy world was a bigger focus for me than the mundane world outside of myself. On a long road trip to a holiday destination with my family, I would imagine rebuilding a city with huge statues of animals and architectural themes from Egypt. While everybody went to the beach, I just wanted to read my books.

I've always wanted to change the world on a large scale—to change it into the ideal world that I've imagined, irrespective of whether that is actually practical or realistic.

To make sense of the universe as a whole, I studied metaphysics, astrology, and different mystical, spiritual systems. I hoped that each new subject I studied would offer me a new piece of the puzzle I could use to find the meaning of life. Through a lot of self-development work, I eventually realized that the only real and meaningful experience is this moment, in the present.

The Sexual Five: "Confidence" (Countertype)

In the Sexual Five, avarice is expressed through an ongoing search for a connection that will satisfy their need for an experience of the most perfect, safest, and most satisfying (idealized) union. This Five may look like the other two Five subtypes on the outside, having all the regular Five inhibitions and introversion in the area of relationship, but the Sexual Five places a special value on one-to-one or intimate connections.

This Five has a passion for finding a special person they can connect with deeply, sometimes a person they cannot find or have yet to find. Like the Social Five, this Five also searches for a high ideal, but this Five looks for the ideal in the realm of love. This Five feels a need to find a high exemplar of absolute love. Like the search for the extraordinary of the Social Five, the ideal kind of connection this Five searches for represents a very high standard. Sexual Fives seek something like the ultimate mystical union—an experience of the divine in human relationship. And this can also happen with the search for good friends or a spiritual teacher.

While Social and Self-Preservation Fives are more removed from their emotions, the Sexual Five is intense, romantic, and more emotionally sensi-tive. This Five suffers more, resembles the Four more, and has more overt desires. This is the countertype among the Fives. It may not be completely ob-vious from the outside, however—they may seem very much like other Fives until you touch their romantic spot and inspire their romantic feelings.

While they can appear reserved or laconic on the outside, Sexual Fives have a vibrant internal life that is highly romantic. There are examples of Sexual Five artists—like Chopin, who Naranjo notes is the most romantic of the classical composers—who display extreme emotional expressiveness through their artistic creations but are cut off in many ways from others in the everyday world.[32]

Sexual Fives live in an inner world filled with ideation, theories, and uto-pian fantasies about finding unconditional love. They live for a couple's love as a kind of ultimate or ideal experience of connection. However, what they search for represents an idealized form of relationship that may not exist in the human world.

Trust is the basic issue with the Sexual Five. The name Naranjo ascribes to this subtype is "Confidence," which has a special meaning related to an ability to trust the other, and suggests a search for the person who will be with you no matter what, the partner (or friend) that you can trust with all your secrets. Confidence is the kind of ideal that makes Sexual Fives very romantic deep inside. They search for an idealized version of love and relationship as a source of meaning in life.

The Sexual Five's search for a high exemplar of connection is so exacting that it's very hard to pass their test with consistency if you are the person in relationship with them. It's very easy for the Sexual Five to be disappointed. This subtype has such a great need to trust in the other that the need is not easily satisfied, and so there can be a lot of testing in their relationships.

Fives tend to be a private people, but this Five has a great need for in-timacy under the right circumstances—if they can find a person they can really trust to love them despite their flaws. This subtype expresses a need to be completely transparent with their partner, and they need their partner to be very open as well—and this ideal of trust and intimacy is not easy to find. Because of this, Sexual Fives can get very picky about the people they have relationships with, and they can become frustrated when they discover that the other is human. If a partner does not live up to their expectations of transparency and openness, they tend to feel disappointed and—because they have a fear of being hurt by others—to isolate themselves.

Some Sexual Fives say that their search for an ultimate kind of connection does not only center on relationships with a lover or life partner. One Five said he related to the idea of "emotional promiscuity," saying, "I want ultimate contact with a lot of people," one at a time. And some Fives with this subtype report that although they feel guarded in the face of too much emotional intensity, they have a deep desire for intimacy with a trusted few. One Five with this subtype described especially appreciating the experience of "clicking" with someone—the feeling of having chemistry with another person—saying that when he felt this he could become infatuated very quickly.

Although the Sexual Five may look like a Type Four, this Five is still quite Five-ish, so is not likely to be mistaken for a Four. And while this subtype is the Five countertype and seeks to manifest an ideal of intimacy, it may be hard to discern the difference between this Five and the other two Fives, as all of the Five subtypes experience a need to withdraw. However, This Five has a need to find a special relationship that will provide both safety and an ultimate kind of love.

Stephen, a Sexual Five, talks about his subtype:

Full access to my feelings came after I started doing body work in my early 30s, and they were, and sometimes still are, very confusing and overwhelming—especially "softer" emotions like compassion. I'll find myself with tears welling up at times and need to look inside for the trigger, which can be as simple as the sight of a homeless person on the side of the road. My adult life has been a constant tension between my point's need to pull in and husband my (emotional, physical, intellectual, financial) resources, and a mostly stronger drive to reach out and connect, not merely with my intimate partner, but nearly everywhere.

The reaching out is an attempt to fill an existential-psychic hole that seems to have existed from a prenatal stage. I seek connections with others to avoid feeling that emptiness. The name of the subtype, Confidence, is about building a bond with another (or many others on a one-to-one basis). For instance, when I have to give talks to a group, I find a single person to be my focus, while appearing to address the group. Relationships are the most fearful of objects, yet the most needed.

I have been called out on Enneagram panels as not looking like other Fives—too flamboyant, too out, too willing to talk about the inner landscape and the demons that inhabit it. This is true, and in my youth it was (physical) camouflage. Now it is merely a way of being. I have learned that the desire to disappear into the background of my youth was a false hope, and since I cannot disappear, I might just as well be who I really am.

The most important thing that needs to be understood about the Sexual Five is that we are in a constant struggle between the withdrawing and withholding (stinginess) of the basic point, and the need to reach out and connect driven by the instinctual energy of the subtype. Behind this tension is an emotional sensitivity that is hidden to the outside world and also to the Five until they [we] allow awareness of emotions into their daily life.

"The Work" for Type Five: Charting a Personal Growth Path

ULTIMATELY, AS FIVES WORK ON THEMSELVES and become more self-aware, they learn to escape the trap of walling themselves off from the sustenance of emotional connections with others—thereby intensifying their inner sense of scarcity—by creating a stronger connection to their own emotions, learning to believe in their own abundance, and opening themselves up to receiving more love and support from others.

For all of us, waking up to habitual personality patterns involves making ongoing, conscious efforts to observe ourselves, reflect on the meaning and sources of what we observe, and actively work to counter automatic tendencies. For Fives, this process involves observing the ways in which they perpetuate their own sense of inner depletion; exploring the ways they maintain a sense of safety by erecting boundaries and limiting contact with others; and making active efforts to expand their comfort zone in social interactions. It is particularly important for them to learn to challenge their beliefs about inner scarcity, open up to receiving more nourishment from the outside, and regain a greater sense of inner aliveness and vitality through feeling and expressing more of who they are.

In this section I offer some ideas about what Fives can notice, explore, and aim for in their efforts to grow beyond the constraints of their personality and embody the higher possibilities associated with their type and subtype.

Self-Observation: Dis-Identifying from Your Personality by Watching It in Action

Self-observation is about creating enough internal space to really watch—with fresh eyes and adequate distance—what you are thinking, feeling, and doing in your everyday life. As Fives take note of the things they think, feel, and do, they might look out for the following key patterns:

Hoarding and withholding inner resources out of a perception of scarcity and fear of depletion

Observe your tendency to operate from the assumption that your time, energy, and other resources are scarce. What ideas do you have that you are basing this kind of thinking on? Notice any worry you feel or thoughts that arise about not having enough energy to do things or interact with people. Note what kinds of experiences make you fixate on your energy level. Observe any ways you hoard time, materials, or private space. Notice if you withhold yourself or your input from others, how you do this, and what you are thinking about (or feeling) when you do this.

Detaching from emotions and emotional life

Observe the ways in which you detach from your emotions (if you can see how this happens). Notice any situations in which you might feel something, but you don't. Can you catch yourself in the act of detaching from your feelings or distancing yourself from something or someone that might stir up emotion? Observe your inner territory for any signs of feeling or sensitivity with the same interest you might apply in observing others from a safe distance. Are there some emotions you feel more than others? Are there some emotions you avoid more than others? Notice when you delay feeling your emotions until you are alone. Are there specific emotions you feel more or less comfortable feeling in the presence of others? Notice especially the ways you rationalize not feeling your feelings and avoiding an acceptance and experience of others' feelings.

Distancing yourself from others through excessive boundaries, the need for control, and a fear of external demands

Observe the different ways you make boundaries with people. Notice how this happens and if you register any feelings that motivate you when you're establishing boundaries. Observe the way you try to control situations and what your thinking is behind your efforts to establish control. Notice when you distance yourself from others and how you do it. Are there some people you want more distance from than others? What ideas and factors do you base these choices on? Observe any fears that arise—or thoughts about how to avoid feeling fear—when you think about interacting with specific people in specific situations.

Self-Inquiry and Self-Reflection: Gathering More Data to Expand Your Self-Knowledge

As Fives observe these and other related patterns in themselves, the next step on the Enneagram growth path is to *understand* these patterns more. Why do they exist? Where do they come from? What purpose do they serve? How do they get you in trouble when they are intended to help you? Often, seeing the root causes of a habit—why it exists and what it is designed to do—is enough to allow you to break out of the pattern. In other cases, with more entrenched habits, knowing how and why they operate as defenses can be a first step to eventually being able to release them.

Here are some questions that Fives can ask themselves, and some possible answers they can consider, to get more insight into the sources, operation, and consequences of these patterns.

How and why did these patterns develop? How do these habits help Type Fives cope?

Although Fives are naturally curious, sometimes they don't get curious about the ways in which they limit themselves with the defenses associated with their personality. Unlike other Enneagram types, who may actively suffer as a result of their habitual patterns, many Fives feel relatively comfortable with their defensive posture because it allows them to feel safe and in control. It provides them with a way to get away from difficult feelings—both their own and other people's—and it helps them avoid having to feel fear. But the Five personality is a contracted stance that actively reduces Fives' connection to themselves and others, and thus constrains their ability to grow. It can be useful and enlivening for Fives to look deeper into themselves and their own history—to see how their patterns of thinking and behaving represent an ongoing overreaction to the legitimate need to protect their precious sensitivity early on.

While it may seem like "looking for trouble" at first, Fives can wake up to the ways in which they keep themselves cut off from life by hiding out in their "acorn shell" by examining how they came to need so much protection in the first place.

What painful emotions are the Type Five patterns designed to protect me from?

For all of us, the personality operates to protect us from painful emotions, including what Karen Horney calls our "basic anxiety"—a preoccupation with the emotional stress of not getting basic needs fulfilled. In response to an experience of stress, Fives adopt a strategy that centers on detaching from painful feelings and finding sanctuary in their heads. While inquiring into the painful emotions they might be avoiding goes against the main goal of their coping strategy, exploring what they might be missing in not having an ongoing connection to their emotions can potentially help Fives find more meaning, richness, and satisfaction in life. By at first thinking about, and then eventually and gently moving towards feelings they habitually cut themselves off from, Fives can reconnect with their own emotional vitality in a way that can be truly energizing. To know all that they can become, Fives must open themselves up to the fear, sadness, and anger they may not know they have inside.

Why am I doing this? How do the Type Five patterns operate in me now?

Through reflecting on how and why the Five patterns operate in the present as a protection in everyday life, Fives can increase their awareness of how they maintain boundaries and avoid engaging with the emotional part of life as a way of staying safe and undisturbed. It also can't hurt for Fives to revisit the deeper motives behind their patterns. Questioning the reasons they habitually protect themselves from a deeper engagement with life can help Fives to develop more self-knowledge about how they hold themselves back in ways that may not serve them. By watching how they steer clear of emotional entanglements and external demands to stay safe, they can examine how these habits might prevent them from growing. Rationalizing the desirability of the Five fixation can be part of the fixation, and it will be important for Fives to at least be honest with themselves about that, so they can make the conscious choice about whether they want to change or not.

What are the blind spots of these patterns? What do Type Fives keep themselves from seeing?

Some Fives may be okay with remaining within the safe confines of their "acorn shells." And this is understandable, given that the walls they build protect them from the pain of having needs and sensitivities in a world that can seem unresponsive or depleting. But it may be important for them to at least consider what they might be missing. The solution of distancing involves a kind of blindness to the value of feelings and the possibilities inherent in being more connected to your own power and aliveness. If you are a Five, the comfort associated with resignation may be distracting you from seeing how much better life might be if you allowed for greater contact with the right people. Whether or not anyone chooses to grow is up to them, but we owe it to ourselves to fully appreciate what our options are and what our defenses hide from us. If you are a Five, how good might your life be if you were able to take the risk to open up more and challenge the rigidity of your defenses?

What are the effects or consequences of these patterns? How do they trap me?

The trap involved in Fives' personality programming is that in building your life around a sense of scarcity and a fear of depletion, you intensify your experience of resource scarcity and the threat of being impoverished. While the Five coping strategy of employing "distance machinery" through "availing [yourself] of a good wall"[33] can lead to a comfortable sense of isolation, it may also intensify an ongoing fear of violation or intrusion. What Naranjo calls "the vulnerability and impotence involved in an exaggeratedly passive and unexpressive or unfeeling disposition"[34] can leave Fives feeling powerless and insecure. Fully exploring how their defensive patterns operate can open the door for Fives to reconnect with themselves on a deeper level, and it can lead them out of the trap of having to shrink themselves as the only way to feel secure.

Self-Development:
Aiming for a Higher State of Consciousness

For all of us who seek to wake up, the next step in working with type-based knowledge of the personality is to begin to inject more conscious effort into everything we do—to begin to actively think, feel, and act with more choice and awareness. In this section I provide some ideas for Fives about "what to do" after they've observed their key patterns and done some investigation into their sources, operation, and consequences.

This last section is divided into three parts, each corresponding to one of three distinct growth processes connected with the Enneagram system: 1) "what to do" to actively counter the automatic patterns of your core type described above in the "self-observation" section, 2) how to use the Enneagram's

Inner Flow arrow lines as a map of growth, and 3) how to study your passion (or "Vice") and consciously seek to embody its opposite, the antidote, the higher "Virtue" of the type.

The Three Main Type Five Personality Patterns: "What to Do" to Address Them

Hoarding and withholding inner resources out of a perception of scarcity and fear of depletion

Challenge false beliefs about scarcity. Fives benefit from challenging the false belief that they don't have enough resources to survive. Recognize that it only *seems* like you have limited time, space, and energy because of early pivotal and painful experiences. In reality, you have as many abundant resources as you believe you have (or let yourself have). And connecting more with other people actually increases the resources you have available to you because it expands your sources of support. Reminding yourself to have faith in abundance initiates a positive cycle of access to more and more of what you (falsely) think you don't have very much of.

Remind yourself that scarcity breeds scarcity. It's almost a truism these days that what we believe shapes our reality. When you view the world through a lens that sees everything in terms of the scarce resources that you have to hold on to, you may magnify your experience of scarcity. Focusing on what you have to grasp onto in order to survive only perpetuates the belief in and the reality of insufficiency. A scarcity mentality keeps you trapped in a mental model in which you have to get by on very little.

Find direct ways to fill yourself up on the outside. If you are a Five, it can be difficult to embark on a growth path because it goes against your grain to make efforts to feel more emotions, share more of yourself, and reach out to others more purposefully. But as Naranjo indicates, "being an observer of life naturally leads to a feeling of not living, and this may stimulate a desire for experience."[35] Turn up the volume on any desires you might have to experience more of life, and support yourself in taking the risk to find ways of experiencing the world that feed you and enhance your life. Whether it's getting a massage, letting someone take you out to dinner, or sharing more of yourself with someone you trust, allow yourself to increase the pleasurable ways in which you participate in the external world.

Detaching from emotions and emotional life

Become more aware of the choice to detach from feelings. An important first step in being able to connect more with your feelings and empathize more with others is noticing when you detach from your emotions or otherwise stop yourself from feeling. Recognize when you may be thinking about feelings rather than actually experiencing emotions. It may be important to think about feelings in the early stages of your self-work, but remember to discern the difference. Notice when you detect an absence of feeling when you might (logically) be inspired to feel something, and allow yourself to shift your attention to your body, with the intention of being open and alert to picking up subtle signs of emotion. Engaging in physical exercise can also be an important way to get out of your head and into your heart and your body.

Make efforts to feel more emotions more often. For Fives who feel a longing to connect more fully with others despite their defensive personality tendencies, growth entails making continual efforts to reattach to life—making it a practice to try to engage with and express feelings more regularly. Allowing for real needs and feelings to arise, and gently letting yourself open up to them, helps you to wake up to parts of yourself that you may automatically avoid. Start by trying to feel your emotions when you are alone and then expand your efforts to paying attention to your feelings when you are with others. And try to talk more about your feelings with people you trust.

Make a point to see the upside of emotions and emotional connections. Remind yourself of all the good aspects of connecting with your emotions, even if you don't fully believe there are any at first. If you do have a positive experience of connecting with someone else emotionally, keep this in the forefront of your mind as something to remember when thoughts about the disagreeability of feeling your emotions surface. Celebrate small victories of emotional connectedness, knowing that it's okay to take small steps toward a more positive view of the relational possibilities that become available to you when you can open up to feeling.

Distancing yourself from others through excessive boundaries, the need for control, and a fear of external demands

Recognize that your sense that there's nothing wrong is part of your fixation. Fives are so good at doing what they do that they can go to sleep to the fact that they may be severely limited by their personality's fixation. It can seem to

Fives who live safely behind carefully constructed barriers that there's nothing to fix. When in the grip of their personality, Fives typically feel a comforting sense of control. They are good at avoiding people who are needy and overemotional; they excel at maintaining boundaries; and they know how to control life so they can avoid feeling their fear. When I moderate panels of educated self-observers as a way of teaching the Enneagram, it can be hard to find Fives who can testify in a clear way about why their programming is something they might want to grow out of. Seeing the comfort and control that comes from a good system of protective barriers can be the first step to seeing the problems inherent in this strategy.

Get in touch with the fear that motivates distancing and wall-building. Although Fives are "fear types" within the Enneagram framework, because they hide, they don't connect with their fear very much. As Naranjo (a Five himself) points out, unlike Sixes, who feel their fear because they don't hide as much, Fives specialize in avoiding situations in which they will feel fear. If they can allow themselves to not hide as much, and get more in touch with fear, they can reduce the rigidity of the defenses they use to help them avoid the experience of fear altogether.

Move forward into life instead of withdrawing inside yourself. Although it goes against the Five's personality program, Fives who seek to grow must move forward into life more, find a deeper energy source inside, and reconnect with feelings, instead of hiding deep inside themselves. If you are a Five, when the automatic defensive impulse to distance yourself arises, as a first step, experiment with just staying still and not automatically disconnecting. Start to notice how and when you withdraw and, practice staying put instead. Whether in relationships, in conflict situations, or in your work life, play with the possibility of making the choice to move toward people and more into the flow of life. Remind yourself that learning to risk trusting the outside world is a big and wonderful step for you to take toward your own enlivenment.

The Inner Flow for Type Five: Using the Arrow Lines to Chart Your Growth Path

In Chapter 1, I introduced an Inner Flow model of the arrow lines that defines one dimension of the dynamic movement within the Enneagram framework. The connections and flow between each core Type, its "growth–(through)-stress" point, and its "child–heart-(security)" point map one kind of growth path described by the symbol. As a reminder, the arrow lines can be seen to suggest one kind of growth path for each type:

- The direction from the core point along the arrow line is the path of development. The "stress–growth" point ahead represents specific challenges perfectly suited to expanding the narrow focus of our core point personality.
- The direction against the arrow from the core point to the "child–heart" point indicates issues and themes from childhood that must be consciously acknowledged and owned so that we can move forward and not be held back by unfinished business from the past. This "child–heart" point represents qualities of security we unconsciously repressed, occasionally fall back into as a comfort in times of stress, and now must reintegrate consciously.

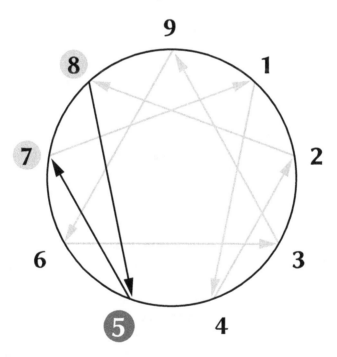

Type Five Moving Forward to Type Seven: Consciously Using the Seven "Stress–Growth" Point for Development and Expansion

The Inner Flow growth path for Type Fives brings them into direct contact with the challenges embodied in Type Seven: using levity, sincere intellectual interest, innovative thinking, and creative options as a way of interacting more directly with the outside world. Consciously drawing on the natural strengths of the Seven archetype can help Fives see how they can engage more fully with others without having to disappear. While Fives can move to the Seven Point in times of stress, causing them to act out their nervousness in social situations through anxious laughter or a manic way of talking, they can work to ease this tension with awareness by consciously embodying aspects of the high side of Seven. Fives can expand their ability to share more of themselves with others by intentionally using humor, playfulness, and intellectual curiosity to help them to manage any anxiety they might feel when opening up more socially.

The Five working consciously in this way can make ready use of the tools healthy Type Sevens use: creative thinking and an interest in people in support of an engaged focus on interacting more deeply with others. The Seven stance has a basis in generating options as a way of seeing different ways of dealing with situations, even in the midst of underlying anxiety. The mental habits of finding connections and enthusiastically participating in the exchange of ideas can provide a good model for Fives seeking to expand their comfort zone by sharing more of themselves with others. The quick and agile way of thinking Sevens use to connect their feelings and ideas with those of others can support Fives in finding more ways to link up their own ideas and emotions more with the outside world.

Type Five Moving Back to Type Eight: Consciously Using the "Child–Heart" Point to Work through Early Issues and Find Security in Support of Moving Forward

The path of growth for Type Fives calls for them to reclaim their ability to engage more actively, more fearlessly, and more powerfully in the world. The Eight Point can be a place of comfort for Fives who allow themselves more freedom to assert themselves and enforce the boundaries they need. The Eight archetype may also represent what didn't work for Fives in their early environment. Fives' early impulses to act in direct ways to get what they needed—the Eight-ish strategy of self-assertion—may not have been seen or supported in childhood, and they may have retreated when force didn't work. However, the Eight experience likely continued to be a place Fives moved to after childhood to find comfort in feeling free to act in powerful ways to protect themselves, erect walls, or push people away.

Navigated consciously, Fives can use the "move to Eight" developmentally—to reestablish a healthy balance between withdrawing and moving out into the world. Fives can focus on the qualities and high-side traits of this "child-heart" point to understand what they may have needed to repress to get along in the world, and what they can usefully reintegrate to support their growth toward the Seven Point.

Moving back to Eight with awareness can thus be a way for Fives to re-engage with their lost sense of their power and authority, a way for them to feel more strength in dealing with fear, engaging with their emotions, and interacting with others. Fives can support themselves in their self-work and expansion by consciously calling on the gifts Eights have in expressing anger in productive ways, making big things happen, and asserting themselves to impact people in positive ways. Instead of always having to survey what's happening from a safe distance and think before doing anything, they can act more decisively in the world.

By reincorporating Type Eight attributes, Fives can consciously remind themselves that it's okay to own your authority, express yourself more power-fully, and use strength to both make boundaries and open up to the vulnerability entailed in sharing yourself more with other people. Through owning these Eight abilities, Fives can heal any childhood hurts associated with having to hide out instead of express themselves more powerfully, and they can draw on a more present sense of their own authority to support the challenges entailed in embodying more of the idealism, optimism, and possibilities for expansion associated with the Seven Point.

The Vice to Virtue Conversion: Accessing Avarice and Aiming for Non-Attachment

The developmental path from Vice to Virtue is one of the central contributions of the Enneagram map in highlighting a usable "vertical" path of growth to a higher state of awareness for each type. In the case of Type Five, the Vice (or passion) of the type is avarice and its opposite, the Virtue, is *nonattachment*. The theory of growth communicated by this "Vice to Virtue conversion" is that the more we can be aware of how our passion functions and consciously work toward the embodiment of our higher Virtue, the more we can free ourselves from the unconscious habits and fixated patterns of our type and evolve toward our "higher" side or "oak tree–Self."

As Fives become more familiar with their experience of avarice and develop the ability to make it more conscious, they can take their work further by making efforts to focus on enacting their Virtue, the "antidote" to the passion of avarice. In the case of Type Five, the Virtue of nonattachment represents a state of being that Fives can attain by consciously manifesting their higher capacities.

Nonattachment is a way of being that is oriented toward letting go of the need to grasp what feels necessary to staying safe, and opening up to a deeper experience of the natural flow of life. For Fives, the virtue of nonattachment can inspire them to work toward releasing their need to control what happens and make sure the way is safe before moving forward. Nonattachment requires Fives to explore the ways in which they hold on to and hoard time, space, and energy, and to challenge their beliefs in scarcity. As fear types who cope by controlling precious resources, Fives' deeper anxiety manifests in the habits of holding on and holding back. By facing and working through their fear of depletion, they can work toward the higher goal of seeing through their false expectation that life won't support them. This, in turn, allows them to release their attachments to the things they think they need to survive all alone in the world.

Working toward embodying nonattachment means recognizing what it means to be attached, seeing what you are attached to, and having the faith to let go of what your acorn-self personality thinks you need to hold on to to survive. Sandra Maitri points out that the "attachment" that Fives must learn to let go of to grow is not the kind of "attachment" we commonly think of—"forming deep bonds with others"—but rather the opposite, a sense of "clinging to things" in light of a perception of a lack of such bonds.[36] As a guide to nonattachment, Maitri highlights Buddhist teachings that encourage us to see and release our attachments to possessions, beliefs, and, ultimately, our ego's need to control reality as a way of freeing ourselves from the suffering attachment inevitably causes. Achieving a state of nonattachment works in exactly this way for Fives. When they can wake up to the ways they cling to their ideas and assumptions about what they need to control to stay safe and supplied, Fives open the door to a deeper acceptance of life as it is. When they can do this, they can release the need for control and withholding and open up to a more enlivening engagement with the world.

In consciously letting go of attachments, their belief in their separateness, and their need for control, Fives can allow themselves to connect to the abundance that is available to them in the larger, interconnected world of nature and other people.

Specific Work for the Three Type Five Subtypes on the Path from Vice to Virtue

Whatever type you are, the path from observing your passion to finding its antidote is not exactly the same for each of the subtypes. The path of conscious self-work has been characterized in terms of "grit, grind, and grace:"[37] the grit of our personality programming, the grind of our efforts to grow, and the grace that comes to us from working toward our virtue in conscious and positive ways. Each subtype has to grind, or exert effort, against something slightly different. This insight is one of the great benefits of understanding the three distinct subtypes of each of the nine types.

Self-Preservation Fives can travel the path from avarice to nonattachment by taking the risk to relax boundaries and barriers to connection more often, and by making more efforts to share their feelings with other people, even when it opens the door to fear or anxiety. People with this subtype can usefully work to notice how their beliefs about what's possible or desirable in relationships and in the world hold them back from getting the recognition or support that might help them grow. Rather than becoming fixated in resignation, challenge your sense of what's possible and imagine all the ways you might allow yourself to grow and expand if you didn't feel like you needed such high walls around you. Remind yourself that you can open up to letting more people in more deeply and more often and still maintain a healthy sense of control in your life. Wake yourself up to ways in which you might be "living little," and realize that you don't necessarily have to make yourself smaller to feel okay. Open up to seeing ways you might share your gifts with the world if you were to spend more time outside the walls of your castle.

Social Fives can travel the path from avarice to nonattachment by broadening their focus of attention from knowledge and information to a greater sense of emotional engagement with real people. If you are a Social Five, notice when your devotion to high ideals displaces an openness to what's happening in everyday life and actually causes you to close yourself off to others. Recognize when you may be idealizing or overidealizing experts and a narrow set of (potentially distant) individuals—getting your relational needs met indirectly rather than taking the risk of interacting more directly with the people in your immediate environment. Notice and work against the tendency to connect only through shared ideas by intentionally sharing more of your emotions and gut feelings with others. Examine the ways in which you might be attached to trying to create meaning and avoid a deeper fear of meaninglessness through specific values and ideals; challenge yourself to more fully experience your fears as a first step on the path of letting go of those attachments. Appreciate the joys of everyday life and the full range of human expression as a way of expanding your focus to allow for a richer experience of what life has to offer you.

Sexual Fives can travel the path from avarice to nonattachment by noticing and working against the tendency to hold others to high standards as a way of avoiding intimacy. Recognize when you are testing others or adhering to impossible standards of connection as a way to avoid your fear and defend against your own fear of exposure. Notice the ways in which you might close yourself off to contact even as you long for it. Work toward achieving the intimate connection you desire—not through an attachment to an ideal of what love can be, but through taking the risk to express your real feelings to the people in your life. Allow yourself to feel into and work with the fear that arises as you open yourself up to deeper relationships and authentic expressions of your emotions. Release your preconceived ideas about what connecting with others is supposed to be about, and challenge yourself to just allow contact to happen. Let yourself be surprised by life, and communicate the beauty of your deeply romantic feelings and desires more frequently and in more ways.

Conclusion

THE FIVE POINT REPRESENTS the ways we close ourselves off to contact with the world as a way of staying safe and in control. The Five path of growth shows us how to transform our fear of fear and impulse to withdraw into the will to share more of who we are and connect in deeper ways with ourselves and others. In each of the Type Five subtype personalities, we see a specific character who teaches us what is possible when we can turn our fearful desire to remain separate and contracted into a fully awake ability to connect with who we are and what we may become, thereby engaging more deeply in the flow of life through the alchemy of self-observation, self-development, and self-knowledge.

CHAPTER 8

The Point Four Archetype:
The Type, Subtypes, and Growth Path

Man only likes to count his troubles; he doesn't calculate his happiness.

—Fyodor Dostoyevsky

I have the true feeling of myself only when I am unbearably unhappy.

—Franz Kafka

Sorrow prepares you for joy. It violently sweeps everything out of your house so that new joy can find space to enter.

—Rumi

TYPE FOUR REPRESENTS THE ARCHETYPE of the person who experiences an inner sense of lack and a craving for that which is missing, and yet can't allow for the attainment of what might provide satisfaction. This archetype's drive is to focus on what is lacking as a step to regaining wholeness and connection, but through an over-focus on the experience of a flawed self they become convinced of an inner deficiency that prevents fulfillment. While this entails an understandable frustration with regard to deprivation, an overidentification with the frustrated, deprived state leads to an inability to take in that which would provide fulfillment.

This Four archetype can also be found in Jung's concept of the "shadow," defined as "the inferior parts of the personality."[1] While Type Threes overidentify with the persona, or the positive aspects of ourselves we highlight in the "public face" we show to the world, Type Fours overidentify with those parts of ourselves we'd rather others don't see. Although Fours may also recast their sense of deficiency as being "special" or "unique" as a way of valuing themselves on a surface level, they identify with a deficient self more than an idealized self.

The Four archetype also represents the archetype of the tragic artist who suffers in the service of artistic self-expression. It suggests an idealistic vision of the value of emotions, especially the way in which authentic emotions are usefully expressed through art in a mode that inspires, moves, and unites people.

The Four's resonance with the Shadow can also be seen in the fact that they have a natural gift for understanding the deeper emotional level of experience and seeing the beauty in darker emotions that other types would rather not feel, much less acknowledge. This can make them feel dangerous to others on an unconscious level, as Fours may raise the issue of authentic emotions that others would often rather not deal with.

Type Fours are thus the prototype for that part in all of us that feels dissatisfied with who we are. We all have the capacity to feel bad about what we see as our flaws, and to grieve and long for what we see as lacking in our lives. We can all become depressed in the face of feeling inadequate when we don't fit the idealized image of what we believe we have to be to get the love we want. This archetype thus represents the tendency we all have to develop an "inferiority complex," which makes it difficult to feel good about ourselves and take in what is good from the outside.

The natural strengths of Type Fours include their large capacity for emotional sensitivity and depth, their ability to sense what is going on between people on the emotional level, their natural feel for aesthetics and creativity, and their idealistic and romantic sensibility. Relatively unafraid of intense feelings, Fours value the expression of authentic emotion and can support others with great care, respect, and sensitivity when they are experiencing painful emotions. Fours are highly empathic and can see the beauty and power in painful feelings that other types habitually avoid.

Fours' "superpower" is that they are naturally emotionally intuitive. Fours' regular contact with their own emotional terrain gives them a lot of comfort and strength in being with intense feelings and empowering others to feel and accept their emotions. Although it would be wrong to think that all Fours are artists or all artists are Fours, they do have an artistic impulse that enables them to see and respond to the poetry in life, and to highlight for others the way everyday experiences can be viewed and communicated in creative and even transcendent ways.

As with all the archetypal personalities, however, Type Fours' gifts and strengths also represent their "fatal flaw" or "Achilles heel:" they can overdo their focus on pain and suffering, sometimes as a way of avoiding a deeper or different kind of pain. While they have a gift for emotional sensitivity, they can become attached to their feelings in a way that can prevent them from thinking objectively or taking action. They can see what's missing so clearly that they may be blind to what is good or hopeful in a situation, often to their own detriment. However, when they can wake up to the ways in which they dwell in suffering or dramatize their emotions as a way of distracting themselves from their deeper need for love, they can express a special kind of wisdom that is informed by deep emotional truth.

The Type Four Archetype in Homer's *Odyssey*: Hades and The Sirens

When Odysseus asks the goddess Circe to help him on his journey home, Circe tells Odysseus he must go to Hades and perform blood rituals so he can speak with the spirit of Tiresias, who will give him further guidance. In return for Odysseus's blood sacrifice, the blind prophet tells him his future, good and bad to the very end:

> *Glorious Odysseus, what you are after is sweet homecoming, but the god will make it hard for you...But even so and still you might come back, after much suffering, if you can contain your own desire,... Death will come to you from the sea, in some altogether unwarlike way, and it will end you in the ebbing time of a sleek old age. Your people all about you will be prosperous.* [2]

Odysseus hears from other spirits in the Land of the Dead, but their common message is a litany of regret for their choices in life and envy for those still living. Hades thus represents "the land of what might have been, a place we are all destined to visit at one time or another." However, Hades also conveys a message about the role of longing and regret in human life. We can potentially get stuck in a "Hades" of our own making if we don't just visit our internal spaces of grief, but live our whole lives around "the aching sense of loss and failed dreams."[3] After this visit to the underworld, Odysseus can more mindfully choose life, having spoken with the ghosts of his past who symbolize the cravings and unfulfilled longings of the psyche—his shadow aspects—that he must make peace with and let go of to move ahead in his journey home.[4]

The next destination further reveals the nature of longing. After leaving Hades, Odysseus and his crew sail past the Sirens' Island. The Sirens can feel the unique anguish of each individual. They enchant whomever comes their way, seducing travelers with their melody so they have no prospect of getting home. They sing to Odysseus that they know all the pains he suffered in the Trojan War. And they promise him wisdom if he will listen to his heart's content. They will reveal to him the meaning underlying his own suffering. "What song could be sweeter? *Who wouldn't die to listen?*"[5]

Odysseus makes a voluntary personal decision to listen to the Sirens' song and know the depth of human longing and temptation. He knows in advance he will encounter these temptresses. He knows their exquisite singing draws sailors to their deaths, dashed against the rocks. First, he protects his men by fitting wax into their ears. But he also orders them to tie him to the mast and ignore his impassioned pleas until they have passed the danger.

Only careful planning saves Odysseus from his own irresistible longing for this experience. Otherwise, the temptation to explore unfathomable emotional depth would have ended, as it so often does, in total self-destruction.

Hades and the Sirens are a dark passage of the Odyssey reflecting the pain and wisdom of Type Four. Longing, envy, and regret are seductive emotions from which some can never escape. But these emotions also bring us the unvarnished truth about our own needs and pains if we are brave enough to receive it. And facing these important emotions is an important part of the journey home to the true self.

The Type Four Personality Structure

LOCATED AT THE LOWER-RIGHT CORNER of the Enneagram symbol, Fours belong to the "heart-based" triad associated with the core emotion of sadness or grief. While Type Twos are in conflict with their sadness and Threes underdo grief, habitually numbing out their feelings so they don't get in the way of their goals, fours overdo an attachment to grief. The three heart types also share a central concern with image—a self-consciousness about how they might appear in the eyes of others. While all three types in this triad have a formative, underlying need to be "seen," they each act this out differently based on the ideals they try to fulfill in order to be recognized and appreciated by others.

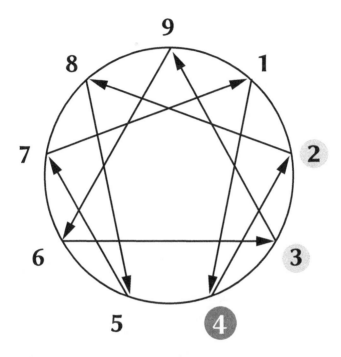

The sadness at the core of the heart type personalities reflects their feeling of not being loved for who they are and their grief over having lost touch with their real selves because they've disowned who they really are and created a specific image to try to get the love (or approval) they need. All three heart types have core issues related to unmet needs to be deeply seen, accepted, and loved for who they are. Their respective coping strategies are designed to gain approval from other people in three distinct ways as a substitute for the love they seek but fear or believe they can't get as they are. While Twos strive to have a likable, pleasing image, and Threes create an image of achievement and success, Fours present themselves as unique and special.

In many ways, Type Fours are the most comfortable of all the types with the experience of emotions. They value connections with others based on authentic feelings. A Type Four's relationship to their emotions is both primary and complicated, as the Four coping strategy involves an attachment to some emotions as a protection against the experience of others. As Naranjo points out, while Type Threes identify with an idealized image of the self, Fours identify with that part of the psyche that "fails to fit the idealized image, and is always striving to achieve the unattainable."[6] As part of the "heart triad," of which Type Three is the "core point," Type Four individuals express a version of the Type Three passion of vanity in wanting to be seen and loved by others; but Fours' desire for admiration leads to a sense of failure because of an inner sense of "scarcity and worthlessness."[7]

The Early Coping Strategy: Type Four

Most Fours report having suffered some sort of actual or perceived loss of love early in life. Things usually started out well, but at some specific point in time the Four child experienced some sort of abandonment or deprivation, and to make sense of this loss—and to achieve some sense of control in light of it— the young Four unconsciously became convinced that they somehow caused it. While this is almost never true in reality, it gives the Four child a feeling that they can do something to regain what was lost through their own efforts, even while their mistaken sense that something about them caused the rejection persists as a inner sense of unredeemable deficiency.

To cope with the pain of this loss, Fours adopt a strategy of focusing on and longing for that which was lost, and at the same time making themselves "bad" as a way of explaining and controlling it. They dream of finding an idealized, special love connection that will make up for or reverse their loss. But because they can't help feeling hopeless about ever regaining what they lost— both as a natural response to feeling deprived and a defense against being disappointed again—they often get stuck in feelings of grief, melancholy, and shame, which makes it difficult or impossible for them to really open up to receiving the love they long for.

The memory of something valuable that was lost also causes Fours to dwell on the past and continue to mourn what they once had. As Naranjo explains, "unlike other people who forget and resign themselves, [Type Fours] harbor a keen sense of 'lost paradise.'"[8]

Fours thus end up seeing themselves as "not good enough" to be loved as a way of defending against opening up to the possibility of love, because allowing themselves to hope for love leaves them vulnerable to the worst kind of pain: the re-experience of that early loss, and the confirmation of their worthlessness that goes with it. They dwell in painful feelings of hopelessness and melancholy to protect themselves from the sadness and shame that comes from believing they are essentially unlovable and so will never get the love they need and want.

At the same time, Fours can't help yearning for an ideal or special kind of love and recognition that will prove they are worthy after all. Looking for an idealized love connection that will redeem their inner sense of lack quells the sense of shame they may feel as a result of the sense that their inadequacy somehow caused their initial experience of loss. But even while they fantasize about being loved as a way to soothe themselves, they thwart their attempts to receive love in the real world because they are so convinced that they aren't worthy of actually being loved. They tend to pursue unattainable people and engage in "push-pull" patterns in relationships: they idealize and move toward the perfect partner in fantasy, but reject the possibility of connection in actuality when they perceive the reality of it as too mundane or flawed.

Overidentification with feelings of hopelessness and melancholy, together with the search for confirmation that they are special or superior, distracts Fours from the real way out of their particular defensive trap: actively taking the risk of hoping for real love and opening up to receive it. While they long for the love and acceptance they need, Fours habitually prevent themselves from realizing their quest for love because their false self (personality) firmly believes they can't get what they are looking for.

All of the Enneagram personality types put up defensive obstacles to attaining what they need out of a fear of repeating the experience of the early pain of not getting it. Fours do this by harboring negative beliefs about themselves and over-identifying with feelings related to loss or abandonment, closing themselves off from the possibility of finding satisfying and nurturing relationships. Allowing for the possibility of being loved for who they are feels like a dangerous setup for further loss and further shame-inducing experiences.

For non-Fours, the Four coping strategy can seem counterintuitive, as it rests on feeling bad about yourself as a way to avoid feeling worse about yourself. As Naranjo points out, this is a strategy of "seeking happiness through pain." By hiding out in suffering, by having a need to suffer, Fours distract themselves from the inner work they would need to do to open up to receiving what they really want—what they incorrectly, but defensively, believe they can't have.

Grace, a Type Four, describes her childhood situation and the development of her coping strategy:

My first critical loss of safety and holding occurred in my early infancy. At ten days old, while being fed, I aspirated, turned blue, and almost died. I was rushed to the hospital and spent the night in the ICU.

The fifth child of seven, I was two and a half when the twins were born. Up until then, I had enjoyed a lot of love and attention as the first girl after four boys. I have a picture of my mother sitting on the edge of the bed with two infants in her arms while I stand nearby with my face contorted, desperately looking up at her, confused and heartbroken. She's turned away from me, offering a strained smile for the camera.

With two infants to tend to, my mother was too busy for me; my day in the sun was over. I was no longer the object of her love and adoration. With six siblings vying for attention, and both my parents overwhelmed and distracted, I learned early on to suppress my sensitivity and needs. On the outside I was independent and assertive. On the inside I was painfully insecure and felt a lot of shame. I had to develop a thick skin and use my anxiety and anger to be heard amongst the chaos and to protect my tender heart.

The Main Type Four Defense Mechanism: Introjection

Introjection is the Four's primary defense mechanism. It is a psychological defense through which Fours internalize painful feelings as a way to protect themselves. As psychologist Nancy McWilliams explains, "Introjection is the process whereby what is outside is misunderstood as coming from inside."[9] Introjection is the inverse of projection, the primary defense mechanism of Type Six.

Introjection operates as a defense mechanism by allowing an individual to identify with and "swallow" another person whole. When you "introject" someone, you take that person inside you, and whatever that person represents to you becomes part of your identity. Through introjection, you give yourself a feeling of being able to control that person and whatever they do or stand for. For instance, if someone important criticizes you and you introject that person, you now experience that person's criticism as coming from inside yourself. And while you are still being criticized, at least you have a sense of control—the illusion that you can do something about it—since the critic is now a part of you. What was coming from the outside is now coming from the inside, giving you the feeling that you can manage it instead of being subject to it (or being a passive victim of it).

The appeal of this usually unconscious process is the implicit desire to exercise more control over the whole interaction. If we have been criticized, through introjection we can both take charge of the criticism and try to do better.

In seeing how this defense operates, we can gain insight into something we all do: take what we experienced as being done to us early on and do it to ourselves. If you were criticized, you criticize yourself. If your needs weren't met, you neglect your own needs. For type Fours, this means that they continue to subject themselves to experiences that were painful from the inside, both as a way of taking it in and trying to manage it and as an effort to protect themselves from being reinjured in a similar way.

The Type Four Focus of Attention

Fours primarily focus their attention on their internal experience, their emotions, the emotions of others, and interpersonal connection and disconnection. I once asked a Four whether she put her attention more on herself or more on others, and she said she put her attention "on the space between us." That said, Fours are more self-referencing than other-referencing, meaning their attention is aimed more at their own inner experience than at what is going on with other people. At the same time, Fours naturally tune in to the state of their connections and to their perception of the underlying emotional tone or status of their relationships.

Fundamentally, Fours focus on thinking about and expressing what they are feeling. Fours also focus on what others may be thinking or feeling about them, and whether or not they are achieving authentic connections with the people around them. While Fours have an innate gift for being able to sense and appreciate a wide range of emotions, Fours can focus too much on their own feeling state at times, and they have the tendency to get lost in a narrow band of emotions—especially feelings of loss, longing, sadness, melancholy, or hopelessness. By paying a lot of attention to what they are feeling, they tend to over-identify with their emotions, and when absorbed in this way, they may find it difficult to shift their attention to other aspects of their experience.

In relation to others, Fours have a tendency to both feel like a misfit and want to stand out as unique and special. Focusing on the ways in which they don't fit in can lead to fantasies of being judged negatively and found lacking, and focusing on being special often leads to fantasies of garnering praise from important people for their unique qualities.

Fours also tend to focus on what is missing in any given situation. In a relationship or in a specific circumstance, like a job or a class or a social gathering, Fours will automatically focus on what they see as ideal and absent—on what is missing that would make the situation better or what isn't working well because something specific is lacking.

Sometimes Fours can get stuck either focusing on the outer world or on their inner world; they may find it difficult to switch back and forth. They frequently become preoccupied with a sense of envy: comparing themselves with others, thinking about what others have that they don't have, and focusing on their imagined deficiencies (while sometimes attributing this perception to others). Alternatively, they may also become fixated on their inner state and over-identify with specific feelings. They may then have difficulty with shifting their attention to other aspects of their experience, especially more positive emotions and perspectives.

In line with this, sometimes the Four might think, "If the outside environment would just give me what I need, things would be better." In the face of feelings of dissatisfaction, they often lack a sense of agency. It may feel hard to them to change their feelings or the world through their own efforts or force of will. While they tend to focus on what isn't working, it can be hard for them to take action, even though taking action might help them break them out of the focus of attention that is holding them hostage.

Creating drama can also be a way that Fours amplify what they feel is going wrong as a way of distracting themselves from painful emotional truths. They may also create drama because they don't like to pay attention to what seems mundane or ordinary. They can inject drama into everyday experiences or the expression of their emotional state as a way of amping up the mundane aspects of life that may depress them or make them feel ordinary or deprived. Because of this, others may find Fours excessively dramatic.

Finally, Fours tend to focus on the past. They may replay old hurts or disappointing experiences over and over again, and they may dwell on pivotal moments in their own history as a way of explaining what they see as their suboptimal state in the present. One Four friend of mine used to return again and again to talking about how his parents set his life on a negative course when they denied him the opportunity to become a professional golfer. He found solace or a distraction from his own lack of effort in believing that if only that condition of his life had been different—if only someone else hadn't held him back—his whole life would have been better.

The Type Four Emotional Passion: Envy

Envy is the passion of Type Four, and it organizes the personality around a sense that what is valued and needed is outside of you and somehow unavailable. Envy grows out of a sense of personal deficiency—a belief that "others have something that I want that I don't have." Fours can also have a perception that "things come easily to other people, but not to me."

This tendency to compare themselves with others contributes to Fours' painful sense of lack and shame. Naranjo points out that while the emotional state of envy is an understandable reaction to early frustration and deprivation, Fours' envy ends up being a self-frustrating factor in the psyche, because the intense "craving for love that it entails never answers the chronic sense of inner scarcity and badness, but on the contrary, stimulates further frustration and pain."[10]

This sense of envy contributes to a longing for love and acceptance on the one hand and a sense of shame for needing and not feeling worthy of love on the other. Fours' sense of inner lack also contributes to a painful cycle in that it intensifies their sense that something good—and outside of them—must be sought and gained, even as they believe that they don't deserve or can't attain what is needed because they are somehow deficient. Envy thus keeps Fours focused on what they don't have, and this focus fuels their sense of lack, which only perpetuates their envy.

The specific experience and expression of envy in Fours, however, differs by subtype. The Social Four dwells in a sense of deficiency and shame heightened by actively envying others; the Self-Preservation Four denies envy by strenuously pursuing whatever is seen as lacking; and the Sexual Four gets competitive, striving to prove themselves as superior, in response to feeling envious.

The Type Four Cognitive Mistake: "I Dream of Getting the Love I Won't Ever Have"

We all get stuck in habitual ways of thinking that influence our beliefs, feelings, and actions, and this continues even after the mental models that create our overall perspective aren't accurate anymore.[12] While the passion shapes the personality's emotional motivations, the "cognitive fixation" preoccupies the personality's thought processes.

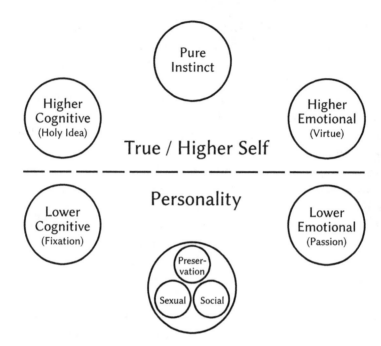

Type Fours' cognitive mistake centers on the underlying belief that they are lacking in some important quality that would make them worthy of love. Fours hold beliefs and ideas related a sense of personal deficiency and the inevitability that they will be rejected or abandoned because they are flawed. These beliefs, which act as organizing principles for the personality, structure Fours' experience and expectations.

If you believe that you are lacking in important personal traits that would make you attractive and acceptable to others (and thus worthy of love), then it logically follows that you won't want to risk rejection or abandonment by opening up to being loved. If you expect others to reject or abandon you—if you anticipate negative results—you end up creating an external reality that confirms your negative expectations.[13]

Here are some key beliefs and assumptions characteristic of the Type Four personality that support the passion of envy:

- I am lacking some essential qualities of goodness, and so I will inevitably be rejected or abandoned by others.
- Since I lost the love of someone I loved and needed in the past, it must mean there's something fundamentally wrong with me.

- Others have what I want, but I can't get it because there's something wrong with me.
- What I want eludes me, and what I can have seems somehow boring or lacking something essential. What is here and now is mundane and boring; what I desire most is ideal and at a distance.
- If someone does love me or want to be with me, there must be something wrong with them.
- My intensity makes me special.
- What I most want is love, but I won't be able to get what I want because (experience has proven) I am not lovable.
- I lack some basic attributes that would allow others to really love me. But if I could find the ideal person who realizes how special I am, then maybe I could really experience what I long for.
- I am special, but others don't recognize it.
- No one understands me. I am destined to be misunderstood.
- I will never be able to fit in because I'm unique (or special or deficient). I feel as if I don't belong.
- I expect that eventually, most people will abandon me.

These common Four beliefs and recurring thoughts support and perpetuate the Four's worldview that they can't have what they most want. They typically have many different flavors of self-rejecting thoughts. A belief in your own inner deficiency can't help but perpetuate feelings of hopelessness, melancholy, or depression. Given these beliefs, it makes sense that Fours both search for the love that will prove them wrong and prevent themselves from being open to love in case they are proved right.

The Type Four Trap:
"Envy Fuels a Craving for Something You Don't Let Yourself Have"
As it does distinctly for each type, the cognitive fixation for Type Four leads the personality in circles. It presents an inherent "trap" that the limitations of the personality can't resolve.

Naranjo states that in Type Fours, "love is sought as a compensation for a lack of self-love, a condition of intense, chronic self-rejection and frustration."[14] But while Fours seek love as a way of regaining what was originally lost—motivated by a fantasy that it will finally provide proof of their worth and specialness—their firm belief in their own lack won't allow them to take in the love they think might redeem them.

Type Fours paradoxically "seek happiness through pain"[15] and get trapped in the various ways they generate pain as a defense against the fear of not getting the happiness they want. And while they long for love and understanding, they habitually prevent themselves from receiving the love they seek—rejecting themselves as unworthy, invalidating the love they do get, creating drama and suffering as obstacles to healthy relationships, and proactively abandoning their efforts before they are abandoned.

The Key Type Four Traits

Inferior Self-Image
It may be clear already how envy sets the stage for the Four's tendency to have an inferior self-image. Believing goodness exists on the outside means that Fours view themselves as lacking important and positive traits and qualities. Their sense of goodness or satisfaction as something that has been or is being withheld from them leaves them with a sense of unworthiness on the inside.

These beliefs develop early on in Fours in response to real circumstances, and they also evolve throughout their lives as a kind of protection against hoping that the situation will change for the better. An inferior self-image operates as a kind of protection within the personality because it defends against new and surprising revelations of your own lack: if you already believe you aren't worthy, you won't be confronted with the unexpected and painful experience of further rejection or frustration.

Focus on Suffering
Naranjo explains that Fours have "a need to suffer." Fours' pattern of hoping they will earn or attract love through their pain results in a tendency to be masochistic or to (unconsciously) move toward painful experiences.

Fours' focus on suffering can serve several purposes within their personality. It can, as Naranjo suggests, represent an unconscious hope that through suffering, they will attract the attention and compassionate love of a parent or other important person who will appreciate their depth of feeling and unique brand of sensitivity. The hope may be that if someone can understand the way the Four has suffered, the Four will be rewarded with a special kind of understanding and appreciation.

Suffering can also function as a defense in that if you are already focused on a specific source of suffering, you can avoid or distract yourself from a deeper source of suffering. If you are already hopeless, you won't be disappointed or shocked by bad news. This is depression as a defense: if you are preoccupied with feeling bad about not being understood in a specific situation, you won't notice and suffer your more profound sense of inadequacy or the lack of love in your life.

Suffering can also be an expression of the Four's unique capacity to feel things deeply and to endure pain and to comfort themselves through making contact with their pain. The archetype of the artist who suffers for his art, or the romantic poet on a tragic quest for unrequited love, creates something beautiful and special out of the experience of pain, and is thus redeemed or valued for his or her ability to suffer (and express that suffering through art).

Emotional Sensitivity and Empathic Ability

Along with Type Twos, Fours are the most emotional of the Enneagram personalities. In contrast to Twos, however, Fours tend to be more introverted and are sometimes more intellectual. Fours are also more likely to feel and be comfortable feeling a wider range of emotions, including hate and anger, whereas Twos repress these feelings out of a persistent desire to avoid offending others.

Fours value emotional intensity and authenticity, they tend to feel emotions deeply, and they find more comfort in feelings like melancholy or sadness than most other types do. According to the Four perspective, emotions point to the inherent depth and truth of your experience of yourself, and so authentic emotions shouldn't be denied, as they reflect what is special and uniquely you.

Perhaps more than any other Enneagram type, Fours possess the gift of empathy. They make great therapists and friends for people who might need emotional support. Unlike some other personalities, who may urge you to "look on the bright side" when you are feeling down, Fours have the experience and the emotional courage to be with darker emotions like sadness and pain. Fours have a natural comfort with a wide range of feelings, from joy to rage to fear to sadness, though of course they may avoid feeling some of their emotions for defensive reasons at times. Their ability to feel their own feelings at a deep level gives them both a familiarity with and an understanding of the intense emotional experiences of others.

Fours also automatically tune into the emotional level of social interactions—they have the natural ability to intuit what is happening below the surface of things on a deeper, emotional level.

Aesthetic Sensibility

Fours have a natural ability to see the aesthetic qualities and possibilities of a given situation. Both because they have an emotion-based disposition and because they have an affinity for artistic process as a way of communicating emotional truth, Fours easily see the beauty inherent in things. The archetype of the Four also resembles that of the suffering artist who sees the beauty in pain and uses his sense of the tragic and the romantic to express deep feeling through artistic creation.

Push-Pull Pattern in Relationships

Fours typically demonstrate a "push-pull" pattern in relationships. When a loved one is at a distance, the Four idealizes that person, focusing on what is positive and pleasing about the loved one and longing to be with them. However, when that same person comes close—when the person is relating to them intimately in the present moment, right in front of them, on a regular basis—the Four then typically focuses on what is missing or undesirable or even intolerable in the person, and feels motivated to push them away. This "push" part of the pattern represents a proactive abandonment or rejection based on a fear of abandonment and rejection, which can be experienced as a straightforward aversion to the partner. The "pull" portion of the pattern represents the tendency to idealize what seems unavailable or is at a distance and is longed for—and it also represents the Four's real desire for closeness, a desire that can seem dangerous once someone actually comes close to the Four.

This dynamic explains why Fours often feel a deep sense of ambivalence in relationships: they may both appreciate or love a person and want to be close to them, but also have an acute perception of what is missing or flawed about that person, which makes it hard for them to fully embrace them.

The Type Four Shadow

The Type Four personality itself is a kind of archetypal representation of the Shadow. Fours typically focus their attention on the kinds of emotional experiences that other personalities avoid or deny being aware of. Fours actively feel—and may even take comfort in—feelings like anger, disappointment, fear, grief, and shame, emotions that most people prefer to deny or avoid.

In contrast to some of the other personality types, then, Fours' *positive* aspects and attributes represent a big part of their personal Shadow. It is the good things about themselves that Fours relegate to unconsciousness and don't own or see.

One of the main challenges Fours face is that their tendency to focus on what is missing or lacking in situations can get them stuck in a negative cycle in which they can't make the transition to accepting what is satisfying and "good enough" in the present. They don't recognize and acknowledge their own positive qualities, like their capacities for growth (and positive change), their inherent lovability, and their beauty and power. And because they focus much of their attention on the past and the future, they tend not to see and take advantage of what is positive in their immediate, present lives.

As the passion of Type Four, envy also functions in part within the Four Shadow in that it creates an illusion of everything "good" being on the outside. Although many Fours are very conscious of feeling envious, envy also operates at an unconscious level within the Four personality to motivate much of what can keep them stuck in a vicious cycle of negativity and hopelessness. Naranjo describes the unconscious activity of Fours' envy as an "over-desiring." Fours' insatiable desire or hunger for love grows out of their deeper sense that they have been deprived of the love they need to survive and their unconscious fear that they are not "good enough" to be able to deserve it or receive it.[16]

While the passion of envy may be obvious to the Four, and so not very "shadowy," it nonetheless creates an unconscious conflict for Fours that can be hard to make conscious and resolve: an intense desire for love and connection from the outside, and a corresponding sense of shamefulness and inner lack that makes them unable to take in what they need and want the most. Fours' tendency to have a poor self-image and focus on suffering represent unconscious ways they lock themselves into not getting what they desire, even while they are preoccupied with the need for it and fantasies of getting it.

In these ways, Fours' "positive" Shadow—the ways they don't see, own, and make conscious the facts that they are just as deserving of love and capable of being loved as anyone else—keeps them from being able to access that part of themselves that could more confidently open up to fully participating in the kind of love connections they dream about. Their conviction that they are unworthy operates as an unconscious block to owning and acting upon their inherent lovability and ability to love. As a result, Fours may not only fail to see their own natural goodness, they may also take on Shadow aspects of their family or group, unconsciously carrying the Shadow—the darker feelings and parts of reality that others don't want to acknowledge—of the larger collective. And this may intensify their inability to see themselves in a positive light.

Fours make good targets for unconscious group projections of the Shadow, not because they are actually bad in some way but because they are highly sensitive to emotions like grief and pain. They make effective targets for others' projections because they can't help but be aware of—and voice—the negative aspects that others don't want to see or own. This is why many Fours become the "identified patient" in their families. And this whole dynamic can work to reinforce the Four's defenses, which in some ways cause them to take refuge in their "badness" as a way of avoiding the positive aspects of themselves that might lead them to open up to the dangerous prospect of being seen and loved.

The Shadow of Type Four Passion: *Envy* **in Dante's Underworld**

The darker side of the Type Four Passion of Envy can fuels a focus on competition, superiority, sorrow, and contempt. This envy is not simply wanting, it is a deep melancholy that reflects a need to suffer and a vision of life based on what is lacking and how you stack up against others. In Dante's *Inferno* people are judged mostly for their deeds. In the Inferno, we see the dark side of envy in Dante's portrayal of "the Suicides," who are punished for going against the natural order of things, indulging their "laments," and seeking to escape from scorn by killing themselves.

Each soul that surrenders to despair in this way becomes a barren tree in a black underworld forest. These trees are described only in negatives, and their branches have only thorns. Half human- half bird harpies torment them by snapping their twigs and branches, causing "pain, and for the pain an outlet."[17] These wounds bleed briefly, releasing pleas for pity from the soul trapped inside. One shade admits that he killed himself specifically in reaction to envious slander:

> 'That courtesan who constantly surveyed Caesar's household with her adulterous eyes, mankind's undoing, the special vice of courts, inflamed the hearts of everyone against me, and these, inflamed, inflamed in turn Augustus, and my happy honors turned to sad laments. My mind, moved by scornful satisfaction, believing death would free me from all scorn, made me unjust to me, who was all just... If one of you should go back to the world, restore the memory of me, who here, remain cut down by the blow that Envy gave.'[18]

Like the shadow side of Type Four, the Suicides do violence to themselves by making their own pain paramount. One of these spirits tried to get "scornful satisfaction"[19] through winning back people's good opinion by ending his life. In this way, we see a character who copes with looking bad in the eyes of others by plunging further into misery. It results in an existence that is dismembodied (because they denied the sanctity of their bodies on earth) and trapped within itself, emotionally barren and tormented. Tragically, in the underworld, these shades cannot see the envy within themselves.

The Three Kinds of Fours:
The Type Four Subtypes

THE PASSION OF TYPE FOUR IS ENVY. All Fours have an exaggerated focus on suffering (related to envy), but it's different for each subtype. Fours' suffering grows out of the habit of comparing themselves to others and feeling deficient—enviously thinking that something outside of them is better or more ideal, and experiencing a sense of inner lack. The Self-Preservation Four internalizes and to some extent denies or suppresses suffering; the Social Four lives in it too much and wears it on his or her sleeve; and the Sexual Four projects it out onto others to evacuate (and thus defend against) a painful sense of inferiority.

Naranjo notes that the contrast between the three Four subtypes is among the most striking of the nine types. The three different Fours vary significantly from one to another, and so they appear more differentiated than some of the other subtype groups.

In Fours, according to Naranjo, the passion of envy combines with each of the three fundamental human instincts to create a situation in which the Four feels a specific kind of driving need to suffer. Each of the three Type Four subtypes, then, is motivated by a different need related to suffering: the Social Fours suffer, the Self-Preservation Fours are long-suffering, and the Sexual Fours make others suffer.

The Self-Preservation Four: "Tenacity" (Countertype)

The Self-Preservation Four is the countertype of the Four subtypes, and so it may be difficult to identify this person as a Four. Although this Four experiences envy like the other Fours, they communicate their envy and suffering to others less than the other two Four subtypes do. Instead of talking about their suffering, these Fours are "long-suffering" in the sense of learning to endure pain without wincing. These Fours are more stoic and strong in the face of their pain.

Envy is less apparent in the Self-Preservation Four because instead of dwelling in and expressing envy, this Four works hard to get what others have that he or she lacks. Instead of hanging out in their longing in a way that prevents them from taking action, they strive to get "those distant things" that give them the feeling of being able to obtain that which was lost. Whatever they get, however, never feels like enough.

Self-Preservation Fours do not communicate sensitivity, suffering, shame, or envy, though they may feel all these things and they have the same depth and capacity for feeling as the other Fours. They learn to swallow a lot without complaining. Endurance is a virtue for them, and they hope their self-sacrifices will be recognized and appreciated, though they don't talk about them very much.

Like the other Fours, Self-Preservation Fours feel a need to suffer in the unconscious hope that this will bring them love and acceptance; but unlike the other two, they suffer in silence. Their willingness to suffer without complaint is their way of seeking redemption and earning love. Thus, this Four makes a virtue of toughing out difficulties without talking about them, hoping that others will see this, admire them for it, and help them to meet their needs. Instead of displaying the need to suffer, they have a tendency to deny their envy and bear too much suffering and frustration as a result.

As Naranjo explains, the other two Four subtypes are too sensitive to frustration. They either suffer too much or they make you suffer too much (as a compensation for their suffering). The Self-Preservation subtype is the countertype Four because they go to the other extreme, developing a high capacity to internalize and bear frustration. They make a virtue of resistance to frustration.

Self-Preservation Fours demand a lot of themselves. They have a strong need to endure, so they develop an ability to do without. They put themselves in situations that are tough. They test and challenge themselves. One of my clients with this subtype says that she "throws herself into the fire." These Fours have a passion for effort—they engage in intense activity, and may often appear strained and tense. They may experience distress if their activity level slows down, and they can be compulsive about making efforts to achieve what they need to survive, even if their efforts don't take them anywhere. In some cases, they may not know how to live without the stress and pressure they put on themselves. They don't allow themselves the experience of living in or from their fragility.

Just as the (countertype) Self-Preservation Three wants to be seen as successful but displays humility about the work they do because they believe outward displays of vanity make them less worthy of respect, Self-Preservation Fours internalize their suffering and strive to get what they want in a more autonomous way than the other Four subtypes.

This Four tends to be a humanitarian with an empathic and nurturing disposition, someone who protests for the sake of others and is sensitive to the needy, the dispossessed, and victims of injustice. This is their way of projecting their pain outward, addressing it through others' suffering instead talking about their own. They try to take care of others' pain or work to ease the "suffering of the world" so they don't have to fully deal with their own suffering.

While the other two Four subtypes can be dramatic, the Self-Preservation

Four is more masochistic than melodramatic. For this subtype, masochism is the ego or personality's strategy for getting love. Self-Preservation Fours devalue themselves in important ways, which can make it even tougher for them to do all the work they do to try to get the security and the love that they long for. Their attachment to enduring can be seen from the outside as masochistic, but it stems from a desire to earn love and acceptance through being strong and resilient. The motivation of this subtype stems from a desire for the parent to see that the child is *not* complaining, and instead is being a good boy or girl through not asking for very much.

These Fours may also masochistically enact a need to prove themselves by working against themselves: they make efforts to get what they need and want, but unconsciously work against themselves at the same time. They can be impulsive, but they will control and inhibit their impulses to get recognition. They may want to be happy, but they experience an unconscious taboo around happiness. They spend a lot of energy on being afraid of what's happening instead of dealing with problems and making improvements, so they habitually postpone actions necessary to achieving what they want and then blame themselves for doing so. They wear themselves out seeking and striving in ways and places where they know they'll fail, which ensures the perpetuation of a cycle of effort and devaluation. They may be ambitious, but they deny and work against their own ambitions.

Formerly called "Reckless/Dauntless," but more recently referred to by the name "Tenacity," these Fours move toward activities that require a large capacity for endurance as a way to earn love, without regard for the pain or the danger they may entail.

This Four subtype resembles a One or a Three. Self-Preservation Fours' focus on autonomy, self-sufficiency, and working hard may make them look like a One; however, this Four feels a wider range of emotions—more ups and downs—than Ones, even if they don't always express their feelings. Self-Preservation Fours can also look like Threes, especially Self-Preservation Threes, in that they work hard to achieve a sense of security and may be anxious; however, in contrast to Threes, these Fours will often work at cross-purposes, unintentionally thwarting their own efforts, whereas Threes tend to achieve what they are working toward. Fours also feel their emotions more than Threes do.

Interestingly, this subtype can also look like a Type Seven, which in some ways is the opposite of Type Four, because some Self-Preservation Fours express a need to be light. With all the enduring and efforting these Fours do, they may at times display the high energy characteristic of Sevens, and they may also have a need for fun and playfulness as an escape from having to tough things out all the time. This may account for the fact that there are some Fours who do not seem as melancholy as others—Fours that appear more "sunny" and lighthearted. However, these Fours can be distinguished from Sevens in their greater access to their emotions.

Marcy, a Self-Preservation Four, speaks:

For much of my life it was difficult for me to feel my true emotions because they were so buried; it just wasn't okay to express emotions when I was growing up—the phrase I internalized from my childhood was, "Just suck it up and move on." Plus, I've always had a stubborn streak, as if I'm the only one who knows how to do something right. My colleagues used to think I was a One because of my need for perfection. And it has sometimes been really difficult for me to connect with the passion of Envy in a meaningful way. But one day when I was thinking of someone I admired and how I came up short by comparison, and I heard my internal voice say "You're not good enough," I knew I was a Four. I really got the Envy bit then. Now my emotions arise more freely, in small impulses and bursts though, not like the bigger, wilder swings of emotions that you hear about with a lot of Fours.

Although I've meditated for many years, it's still difficult to relax and to be calm in daily activity. It just seems like a waste of time not to be doing or accomplishing something. Even now when I feel my feelings, I catch myself trying to figure out what I can DO with them. I've always pushed myself to work hard to be successful because I wanted to prove myself by being really good at whatever I do and I have been fortunate in being rewarded for my hard work.

I also see the idea behind the former name of the Self-Preservation Four, Reckless/Dauntless, showing up in my behavior. In a way that seems counter to "self-preservation" I have a penchant for spending money to buy fine things and help others out, sometimes more money than I make. (My mother used to say that I thought money grew on trees.) It's like I get this reckless feeling that money will always be there, so why not spend it on what I love? Plus, I tend to make snap decisions without really thinking it through. For instance, I left my job of 18 years and my 20-year marriage within a month of each other. Of course, the result was some pretty tough years but at least I began to feel my feelings!

The Social Four: "Shame"

The Social Four appears emotionally sensitive (or oversensitive), feels things deeply, and suffers more than most people. For this Four, there is a desire to be witnessed and seen in their suffering. They hope that if their suffering is sufficiently recognized and understood, they might be forgiven for their failures and deficiencies and loved unconditionally.

Naranjo explains that Social Fours are people who lament too much and who often put themselves in the victim role. They can appear self-sabotaging when they broadcast their suffering and their victimhood as a way of engendering sympathy in others, but they also undermine themselves by being too attached to the causes of their suffering.

In this Four, envy fuels a focus on shame and suffering by providing a constant source of pain: a feeling that others have what the Four wants. However, they believe that their suffering is also what makes them unique and special—there is a kind of seduction of others through suffering.

Fours' motivation for dwelling too much in suffering and sensitivity seems to be connected to an idea that suffering will be the shortest path to heaven. Like the child that cries to attract the mother's care, they have the idea that the way to happiness is through tears. While there is some truth to the idea that the path of transformation requires difficulty, this higher ideal gets put to use in justifying the expression of dissatisfaction as a way of attracting the help of others. Social Fours rationalize their attachment to suffering instead of doing something about it, and they depend too much on their needs being fulfilled by others. They express the idea that if you convey the intensity of your need in painful enough terms, someone will finally come to your aid and fulfill that need.

Whereas envy motivates Self-Preservation Fours to work to get what they want, it motivates Social Fours to focus on their emotional dissatisfaction and internal lack. For the Social Four there is a sense of comfort and familiarity in suffering—the sweet sadness of poetry, the rich meaning and painful beauty in melancholic music—and an unconscious hope that their suffering will somehow redeem them.

The central issue of the Social Four, however, is not just suffering—it's inferiority. For this subtype, there is a need for self-abasement and self-recrimination, for turning against oneself, for self-weakening. The Social Four's envy is expressed through a passion for comparing oneself with others and winding up in the lowest position. To others, the extremity of their mindset and insistence that "there's something wrong with me" can be surprising. They have a poor self-image that they themselves perpetuate. They also engage in self-sabotage a lot: they regularly underestimate themselves and always feel "less than" in comparison to others.

As Naranjo indicates, the Social Four may evoke a response in others that makes them want to ask, "What's wrong with you that you think there's something wrong with you?" A person with this subtype may be competent, attractive, and intelligent, and yet still tend to focus on and identify strongly with suffering and a sense of deficiency.

Social Fours tend to feel a sense of shame about their wants and needs, and their experience of desire is associated with more guilt than other people's. The Social Four feels guilty for any wish. Shame puts their internal focus on intense and dark emotions such as envy, jealousy, hatred, and competition. They are too shy to express desires, except through a display of suffering. They don't feel entitled to have their needs met but at the same time may believe that the world is "against" them or that "no one gives me what I want or what I need."

Social Fours don't compete with others (like Sexual Fours do) as much as they compare themselves to others and find themselves lacking—almost as if by showing themselves to be lacking they can call forth what they need from others. Underneath, however, they experience a fierce competitiveness that may be largely unconscious: a competitiveness for recognition, being unique and special, and wanting to be in first place. This is more hidden and subtle in the Social Four, however, than it is in the Sexual Four.

Social Fours explore the pain of the past repeatedly as a way of attracting someone who will take care of them and satisfy their wants. They criminalize their wants, as many of us do, but they suffer more keenly for turning against themselves.

Fours with this subtype tend to think with their emotions—they get entangled in "emotional" thoughts, caught up in and identified with intense emotions to the extent that they can't take action even when it would be good for them to do so. They tend to be generous and to do for others, but they do not take responsibility for their own lives and may dramatize problems to distract themselves from doing something to find a solution.

In public, Social Fours repress "frowned upon" emotions like anger or hatred and may appear sweet, friendly, and soft—but in private, they may express the emotions they store up in social situations and become aggressive. Generally, they prefer to swallow their own poison rather than externalize it to the people around them, and they typically have difficulty finding their place in a group and in society. These Fours may experience themselves as misfits, and yet they also tend to generate social situations of rejection to confirm their shame. They see themselves as victims and may view others as "perpetrators," and they don't always take responsibility for their own actions or aggressiveness.

Social Fours are less likely to be mistaken for other Enneagram types than the other two Four subtypes, but they can look like Sixes in their focus on what's missing or wrong in their lives. However, unlike Sixes, they have a desire to be special (as opposed to Type Six's identification with the "everyman"), and they spend less time in fear and more time feeling emotions related to sadness, pain, and shame.

Elizabeth, a Social Four, speaks:

I've been called "hyper-sensitive" my entire life. My feelings have always been so easily hurt—even at the tender ages of three and four I often felt terribly misunderstood or forsaken. I remember crying in my room at four years old racking my brain trying to figure out what was going on such that my family didn't get me and could be so hurtful. I came to believe that there was something wrong with me and that I didn't matter. These have remained bedrock beliefs for much of my life.

Feeling different, misunderstood, and dejected were my constant companions and felt like home. Over time, I developed an attraction and attachment to my pain and suffering because that's what feels most real and resonant with the pervasive sense that something is really wrong (with me or the world around me.) Experiencing my pain leads to feeling more connected with myself, which then alleviates the pain of feeling disconnected and misunderstood. Thus when a dark feeling hits, my impulse is to hang out with it and get to the bottom of it. And I tend to get irritated and feel even more misunderstood when people suggest lightening up, getting some exercise, or going to see a funny movie. Melancholy has always been my favorite feeling. Not only is it comforting in and of itself, but it creates a portal to my depths, my creativity, and a feeling of being at home in myself.

Despite the tremendous amount of positive feedback I have received in so many areas of my life, I still wrestle with a poor self-image every day. My friends, loved ones, and associates are always shocked to discover the discrepancies between how they view me and how I view myself. As a student, I was always surprised to get my papers and tests back with very high grades and glowing comments. And even now when I share my creative or professional work I am startled to hear the heartfelt positive feedback from others. My barometer for assessing the quality of my work in any area is greatly skewed toward "this could have been a lot better." And then it's back to "Poor me—I have a broken barometer, can you help me fix it?"

The Sexual Four: "Competition"

In the Sexual Four subtype, the inner motivation is envy, and its manifestation as competition. These Fours don't feel consciously envious so much as they feel competitive as a way of muting the pain associated with envy. If they can compete against another person they perceive as having more than they do and win, they can feel better about themselves.

Sexual Fours believe it's good to be the best. Most people want to present a good image to others, but Sexual Fours don't care very much about image management or being liked. For them, it's better to be superior. They are highly competitive, and their intense focus on competition takes the form of actively striving to show that they are the best.

People with this subtype tend to have an "all or nothing" belief related to success: if success is not all theirs, they are left with nothing. This pattern leads to excesses related to their efforts to achieve success, and it also generates feelings of hate.

Sexual Fours are usually arrogant, despite having an underlying sense of inferiority. In the face of the pain of feeling misunderstood, an arrogant attitude is adopted as overcompensation—a means of being recognized. These Fours like to be part of "chosen" group, and they can be very elitist. They may refuse to feel indebted to anyone, and they may have the sense that they have the exclusive right to feel offended by the lack of consideration of others. Any criticism or reproach is seen as an affront or disqualification.

Envious anger dominates the expression of this subtype's unconscious instinctual impulses. Sexual Fours' deeper instinctual motivation is about a refusal to suffer the pain brought about by envy, and a need to reduce suffering by projecting the responsibility for meeting their needs onto others and minimizing others' accomplishments in comparison with their own.

Sexual Fours "make others suffer" because they feel that they have been made to suffer and so need some sort of compensation. They may seek to hurt or punish others as an unconscious way of repudiating or minimizing their own pain. Naranjo observes that this tendency of this Four can be summed up by the phrase, "Hurt people hurt people." Externalizing pain helps them ease their inner sense of inferiority. Their relationship to suffering can thus best be understood as a refusal to suffer. This gets expressed as an active insistence on their needs being validated and met. (They want with anger.) More shameless than shameful, Sexual Fours are vocal about expressing their needs; they rebel against any shame connected to their desires. This subtype follows the life philosophy that "the squeaky wheel gets the grease."

When others experience Sexual Fours as demanding, this can lead to a pattern of rejection and anger: Sexual Fours get mad when others don't meet their needs, but their demanding nature causes people to avoid or reject them, and then they get angry about being rejected. This type can thus get trapped in a vicious cycle when rejection leads to protest and protest leads to rejection.

The Sexual Four is more assertive and angrier than the other subtypes. Naranjo refers to this Four as the "mad Four" as opposed to the "sad" (Social) Four. These Fours can be very outspoken with their anger because expression of anger is their way of defending against painful feelings. When they unconsciously turn their pain into anger, they don't have to feel their pain anymore.

These Fours may even seek to hurt or punish others as a way of repudiating or minimizing their underlying pain. They feel justified in pointing to others as the source of their own deprivation or frustration, which serves as both a distraction from their own role in their suffering and a plea for help and understanding.

Naranjo says that this Four subtype can be the angriest personality among the Enneagram types. They may express envious anger as a way to establish or assert power when they feel inferior at a deeper level, which can be a way to manipulate situations to their advantage. (This kind of anger was the impulse behind the French revolution: "I envy the rich, so I'll organize a revolution.") And Sexual Fours can be very impulsive. They want things immediately and have little tolerance for frustration.

Naranjo calls this type "Competition," and Ichazo called it "Hate." While this type can be both hateful and competitive, it is important to remember that the competition and hate expressed by this Four represents a deeper need to project their sense of suffering and inadequacy outward. The painful sense of envy felt by the Sexual Four can motivate a wishing with anger, or a sense of "I've got to get what I need, both to convince myself that my needs aren't shameful, and to feel better about myself with respect to others." Their competitiveness and anger is a compensation for and a defense against the hurt they feel underneath.

These Fours like and need emotional intensity. Without intensity, everything can seem unbearably dull and boring. When Sexual Fours want somebody's love, they can be very direct about asking for what they need, or they can become "extraordinary"—make themselves seem special and attractive and superior—in an effort to attract it. In line with their natural intensity (fueled by both their heart-based emotional temperament and their sexual instinct), these individuals tend to be more present and available in relationships because they don't deny or avoid many of the factors that can inhibit others relationally, like anger, neediness, competitiveness, arrogance, and having to be liked all the time. However, at times it may prove difficult for them to maintain a loving attitude because they confuse sweetness and benevolence with being false or insincere.

Sexual Fours are most likely to be confused with Type Eights or Sexual Twos. Like Eights, they have easier access to anger than most types, but they differ from Eights in the wider range of emotions they regularly feel. Naranjo points out that Eights often don't need to get angry, whereas this Four frequently feels misunderstood or envious, so they may show anger more often. They can also look like Sexual "Aggressive-Seductive" Twos (because both types can be aggressive and seductive in relationships), but the Sexual Two is more oriented toward pleasing others.

Roger, a Sexual Four, speaks:

The all-too-cumbersome online tests often report I am an Eight or a Three, but I know full well that I am a Sexual Four. My greatest friend in the world, my Type Five elder sister, once leaned over at an Enneagram workshop and underlined the word "hostility" in a description of the Sexual Four with her finger and told me, "You need to work on that." I had to listen to her feedback because she has known me my entire life and so must be a reliable reporter. Of course, I had a finger to offer her regarding the work I thought she might have yet to address in her own life.

Instead of feeling anything vulnerable in my personal life, I will often go to anger. Instead of experiencing myself as ordinary or less-than in my professional life, I will often go to competition, aggression, or even hostility. I don't relate to the descriptions of the over-sensitive, complaining (Social) Four: I go after my enemies or perceived adversaries who I feel threatened by directly rather than hanging out too long in discomfort. I also go after my objects of desire directly, and there are many. It may seem Threeish and Eightish that I need to be on top professionally and personally. But although I pride myself on being direct and honest rather than nice, I know I am not an Eight because my Focus of Attention and my Achilles Heel is definitely Envy; it invigorates me to go after what I want (or take down the person who got what I didn't get). I know I am not a Three because I take more pride in being one-of-a-kind than in being successful. I own that I can come across as arrogant and even hostile if I feel threatened. This has not always served me well in either personal or professional relationships and this kind of response saddens me. Luckily, I have learned the value of staying with the softer feelings, experiencing my vulnerability, being with a great partner, and being one amongst many.

"The Work" for Type Four: Charting a Personal Growth Path

ULTIMATELY, AS FOURS WORK ON THEMSELVES and become more self-aware, they learn to escape the trap of seeking—but blocking—love to prove their worth by seeing what is good in themselves and not just what's missing; taking the risk to believe in their own lovability; and opening up to receive the love and understanding they long for.

For all of us, waking up to habitual personality patterns involves making ongoing, conscious efforts to observe ourselves, reflect on the meaning and sources of what we observe, and actively work to counter automatic tendencies. For Fours, this process involves observing the ways in which they devalue themselves to justify defending against the love they want; exploring the ways they get stuck in envy, shame, and inferiority; and making active efforts to see what is positive in the present as a way to allow themselves to open up to the good things that are available to them. It is particularly important for them to learn to stop believing in their own inner lack, to understand how they thwart their own efforts to achieve happiness, and to rise above their emotional defenses to open up to what they really want.

In this section I offer some ideas about what Fours can notice, explore, and aim for in their efforts to grow beyond the constraints of their personality and embody the higher possibilities associated with their type and subtype.

Self-Observation: Dis-Identifying from Your Personality by Watching It in Action

Self-observation is about creating enough internal space to really watch—with fresh eyes and adequate distance—what you are thinking, feeling, and doing in your everyday life. As Fours take note of the things they think, feel, and do, they might look out for the following key patterns:

Holding on to a strong belief in your own deficiency such that you close yourself off from others (and love and goodness) in the expectation of abandonment

Observe your tendency to engage in intense self-criticism and even self-loathing. What kinds of thoughts and beliefs do you have about yourself? What kinds of things do you tell yourself about yourself on a regular basis? Note all the ways in which you buy into and perpetuate negative beliefs about yourself and your worth. Notice if you engage in self-criticism and self-abasement, what that looks like, and how and when it happens. Observe the ways in which you focus on your flaws and devalue or dismiss compliments and positive feedback. Recognize the ways in which you generate negative feelings about yourself based on your own negative view of yourself and what you perceive as your flaws and deficiencies. Notice if you view yourself as special or unique or superior as a way of defensively compensating for a deeper belief in your inadequacy. Note the way this may be a back-and-forth pattern that doesn't shift, which ends up reinforcing your underlying belief in your own unworthiness.

Distracting yourself in various ways from your own growth and expansion through your attachment to various emotions

Observe the ways in which you create suffering for yourself through negative thoughts about who you are and then dwell in that suffering as a way to distract yourself from taking action to address the causes of your suffering. Notice if you use depression as a defense—if you focus on the hopelessness of things as a way to avoid deeper kinds of pain or won't do anything to generate hope and a more positive outlook. Look out for what you are avoiding when you get attached to your sadness. Observe any tendencies you have to amp up your emotions or create drama as a way of avoiding inner emptiness or grappling with the realities of your life. Notice if you avoid dealing with what's happening in the present by devaluing it as boring or mundane.

Focusing on what's missing such that nothing measures up and nothing can be taken in

Observe the way your attention habitually goes to what is missing in any given situation. Notice if this helps you to improve things such that you benefit from what's happening, or if it functions as an excuse to dismiss or devalue what is happening or as a way to avoid constructively engaging with your present reality. Observe the ways in which you apply this to people and generate ambivalence, distancing yourself or thwarting potential connections by focusing on others' flaws. Notice if you get stuck in ambivalence by focusing on what isn't good enough. Observe the ways in which you focus on the past as a way of devaluing what's happening in the present. Notice any push-pull patterns you see in your relationships, and think about why you push and why you pull. Note how you fixate on what's missing and "throw the baby out with the bath water" such that you don't take in the good parts of a situation or a relationship.

Self-Inquiry and Self-Reflection:
Gathering More Data to Expand Your Self-Knowledge

As Fours observe these and other related patterns in themselves, the next step on the Enneagram growth path is to *understand* these patterns more. Why do they exist? Where do they come from? What purpose do they serve? How do they get you in trouble when they are intended to help you? Often, seeing the root causes of a habit—why it exists and what it is designed to do—is enough to allow you to break out of the pattern. In other cases, with more entrenched habits, knowing how and why they operate as defenses can be a first step to eventually being able to release them.

Here are some questions that Fours can ask themselves, and some possible answers they can consider, to get more insight into the sources, operation, and consequences of these patterns.

How and why did these patterns develop? How do these habits help Type Fours cope?

In understanding the sources of their defensive patterns and how they operate as coping strategies, Fours have the opportunity to become more aware of how and why they undermine their ability to get the love they want. If Fours can tell the story of their early life and look for ways that indentifying with a negative sense of self, getting attached to particular feelings, and focusing on what's missing helped them to cope, they can begin to have more compassion for themselves and see how these patterns have operated to protect them. Generating insights into why they developed these patterns in the first place, and how these patterns work as defenses but also keep them stuck in their "acorn shell," can help Fours challenge their assumptions and pave the way for a more expansive view of themselves and their ability to grow beyond the limited perspective that keeps them trapped.

What painful emotions are the Type Four patterns designed to protect me from?

For Fours, answering these questions means looking at how they over-identify with some feelings to avoid or deny others. It will be important for them to ask themselves if being attached or over-involved with hopelessness and melancholy serves as a way for them to hold themselves in a familiar emotional space and at the same time avoid confronting a deeper experience of pain at not getting the love they needed. If hanging out in hopelessness or sadness is operating as a defense, what are these emotions actually defending you from feeling? Having the courage to locate and feel these deeper emotions can help to set Fours free from the defensive over-identification with emotions that keeps them stuck in a cycle of depression and longing. If you are amping up certain feelings or creating drama to distract yourself from what you're feeling at a more fundamental level, what is going on deeper down? Investigating their emotional territory in this way can be an important way for Fours to help themselves see through the potentially tricky ways they use some emotions as a defense against others.

Why am I doing this? How do the Type Four patterns operate in me now?

By reflecting on how these patterns operate, the three kinds of Fours can begin to have a greater awareness of how their defensive patterns surface in everyday life—and in the present moment. If Fours can consciously catch themselves in the act of focusing on what isn't working and how they don't measure up, they can become more aware of the ways they rationalize not opening up to love and acceptance. If they can explore the reasons why they get stuck in ambivalence, they can wake up to the deeper defensive motivations that keep them fixated in a pattern of actively not allowing in what they enviously see as missing. It is important for Fours to see—in real time—how they erect barriers to receiving the understanding and acceptance they yearn for, and how this contributes to a vicious cycle when they then feel hopeless about getting it.

What are the blind spots of these patterns? What do Type Fours keep themselves from seeing?

To really increase their self-knowledge, it will be important for Fours to remind themselves (repeatedly) about what they *don't* see when their personality is driving the show. Fours pay so much attention to what is lacking—in themselves, in other people, and in the good things that come to them—that they habitually avoid seeing all that's *not* missing, all the quality and value and goodness inherent in their selves and in others. If you have blind spots where your beauty, goodness, and power should be, how can you develop the confidence and faith in yourself to take action to get what you need and want? If you don't recognize the potential in others, give them credit for their good points, and appreciate the way they make efforts to love you even though they aren't perfect, how can you be receptive to the good stuff others want to give you? By focusing on what isn't there, you blind yourself to all that is there.

What are the effects or consequences of these patterns? How do they trap me?

The irony of the Four coping strategy is that by idealizing what you want as perfect and perpetually distant, you cut yourself off from getting what you want in everyday life. By dwelling on your own inadequacies, you convince yourself that you aren't good enough to get what you want and unconsciously prevent yourself from attaining it—your beliefs shape your reality. By over-identifying with certain emotions, you distract yourself from taking action to get what you need and want (and believing that's possible). Although you focus much attention on what, exactly, you want—and fantasize about the ways you might get it—your beliefs about the ideal conditions necessary for actually taking it in might not exist in the real world. As a result, even though you focus a lot of energy on longing for what you want, you unconsciously but actively frustrate your own efforts and keep yourself from getting what you want.

Self-Development:
Aiming for a Higher State of Consciousness

For all of us who seek to wake up, the next step in working with type-based knowledge of the personality is to begin to inject more conscious effort into everything we do—to begin to actively think, feel, and act with more choice and awareness. In this section I provide some ideas for Fours of "what to do" after they've observed their key patterns and done some investigation into their sources, operation, and consequences.

This last section is divided into three parts, each corresponding to one of three distinct growth processes connected with the Enneagram system: 1) "what to do" to actively counter the automatic patterns associated with your core type described above in the "self-observation" section, 2) how to use the enneagram's Inner Flow arrow lines as a map of growth, and 3) how to study your passion (or "Vice") and consciously seek to embody its opposite, the antidote, the higher "Virtue" of the type.

The Three Main Type Four Personality Patterns: "What to Do" to Address Them

Holding on to a strong belief in your own deficiency such that you close yourself off from others (and love/goodness) in the expectation of abandonment

Challenge your unwavering belief in your inferiority. Only by becoming aware of their vicious cycle of envy and need and inferiority and shame can Fours step out of the defensive patterns of thinking, feeling and acting they engage in that become self-reinforcing and self-frustrating. As long as Fours believe so strongly in their own inferiority, they can't realize and embrace the essential truth of their own goodness and lovability. By noticing, exploring, and then actively challenging this belief, Fours can realize it's a false belief and start to believe not in their own superiority, which is the other pole of this Four pattern, but in their own "goodenough-ness." By consciously comparing their belief in their own deficiency with the evidence available to them—and by challenging themselves to consider the positive evidence—they can realize the falsity of their belief and expand their view of themselves to include their real value. Challenge shame by focusing on all the ways in which you are good.

Actively work to reverse your self-debasing tendency through efforts at self-love. Another important aspect of development for the Four is learning to accept themselves and not beat themselves up for what they perceive as their deficiencies. It is crucial for Fours to gradually learn to find the love and acceptance they crave within themselves, to learn to appreciate who they really are, and let go of their consistent focus on the ways in which they are unworthy or bad. A big part of the chronic frustration Fours feel in not getting the love they want is that they don't love themselves. This lack of self-love is what keeps the whole Four defensive cycle going. Make active efforts to notice and embrace all the positive things about yourself. Catch yourself in the act of being harsh to yourself and work to stop it.

Recognize envy, competition, and masochistic behavior as danger signs. Fours tend to compare themselves to others and find themselves lacking. Then, depending on their subtype, they can either strive in masochistic ways to prove themselves, wallow in feelings of inadequacy, or get aggressively competitive. It will be important for Fours on a path to growth to see these behaviors as the hallmarks of excessive self-judgment and self-debasement and realize that the actual "cure" for feelings of deficiency is self-love and self-acceptance. If you are a Four, notice when you are engaging in behaviors based on an assumption of your inadequacy—and actively work to appreciate yourself and care for yourself. Sometimes consciously shifting your attention and your behaviors can help you to eventually turn around your beliefs and emotional attitudes.

Distracting yourself in various ways from your own growth and expansion through your attachment to various emotions

Observe and accept your emotions instead of over-identifying with them. Consciously identify and accept your emotions without becoming attached to or over-identified with particular emotions (or emotions in general). Some Fours, who may have been shamed for having feelings early on, may also need to consistently remind themselves that their feelings are valid and important, regardless of how others may have reacted to them in the past. Consciously notice when you get stuck in specific emotions, especially hopelessness, sadness, or regret. Recognize how this might be a way of avoiding moving through and mourning real losses and getting to the other side. Allow yourself to have your feelings, move through them, listen to the information they bring, and then let them go. Most importantly, recognize how the act of getting lost in your feelings operates to protect you from taking action or reaching out in productive ways to actually get what you need—make the choice to let go of your emotions after you've felt them sufficiently. Consciously shifting your attention from your feelings to thinking or taking action will help you avoid fixating on your emotions in unproductive ways, valid though the emotions themselves might be.

Notice and work against your desire to create drama and intensity. If you are a Four, notice when you are amping things up to avoid specific experiences—like boredom or emptiness—and challenge yourself to take the risk of accepting and valuing the "here and now," even if it feels ordinary and uninteresting initially. If you are intensifying your emotions to distract yourself from being with feelings and realities you may not want to accept, allow yourself to be with any feelings and experiences you may be avoiding, knowing that this is the way out of being trapped in your defensive emotional stance. Support yourself in accepting your present experience by consciously focusing on what is good and pleasurable in the here and now, and also by feeling through painful feelings you have been avoiding as a way of affirming your ability to work through them.

Learn to see hopelessness, suffering, and longing as a defense against living and opening up to possibilities. Fours tend to find comfort in the familiar feelings of hopelessness, disappointment, and longing—and their attachment to these feelings can be a kind of addiction. It is vital for Fours seeking to break out of their characterological trap to see that these feelings hold them back from finding ways to get the love and appreciation they crave. Remind yourself that it is just as possible and easy to focus on hope as it is to focus on hopelessness, or to focus on what makes you happy as opposed to what causes you to suffer. Then shift your attention to all the possibilities for love and connection that would be available to you if you could let go of your focus on specific feelings and see what positive options are available to you in the present.

Focusing on what's missing such that nothing measures up and can be taken in

Align your desires with what's possible. Naranjo points out that envy is an "excessive desiring." Fours' desiring is excessive because it grows out of an early and painful experience of frustration and because it "asks for more than can be expected."[20] Waiting for what's perfect or having unrealistic expectations of others can be ways of defending against opening up to getting the love you want. Without settling for less than what is truly satisfying, try to notice when you are asking for more than you can get as a way of defending against disappointment, and experiment with moderating your expectations and requests. Notice when you avoid accepting something good because you're busy finding fault with it, and challenge yourself to see all the things that could be satisfying and "good enough."

Apply your idealism to seeing the worth inherent in yourself and others. Instead of imagining that what you really need is only available through the attainment of some distant ideal, support yourself by being aware of and appreciating the worth inherent in yourself and others. Actively remind yourself that the worth something has for you can be based on how you perceive its positive aspects. If you focus on and idealize what's missing, you will be perpetually unsatisfied. But if you see what's ideal in everything, even the everyday, you can identify and receive the gifts in even mundane experiences.

Actively shift your attention to see the positive. Make it a constant practice to see the positive in everything—in yourself, in others, and in life. When you catch yourself focusing on lack as a way of justifying your frustration, allow yourself to make a list of all the good things that are happening, and support yourself in embracing and moving toward those things. To receive the love and understanding you want, you have to have the courage to shift your attention to how that might be possible rather than dwelling on impossibility.

The Inner Flow for Type Four: Using the Arrow Lines to Chart Your Growth Path

In Chapter 1, I introduced an Inner Flow model of the arrow lines that defines one dimension of the dynamic movement within the Enneagram framework. The connections and flow between each core Type, its "stress–growth" point, and its "child–heart" point map one kind of growth path described by the symbol. As a reminder, the arrow lines can be seen to suggest one kind of growth path for each type:

- The direction from the core point along the arrow line is the path of development. The "stress–growth" point ahead represents specific challenges perfectly suited to expanding the narrow focus of our core point personality.
- The direction against the arrow from the core point to the "child–heart" point indicates issues and themes from childhood that must be consciously acknowledged and owned so that we can move forward and not be held back by unfinished business from the past. This "child–heart" point represents qualities of security we unconsciously repressed, occasionally fall back into as a comfort in times of stress, and now must reintegrate consciously.

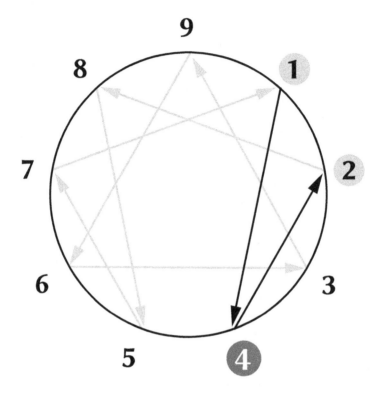

Type Four Moving Forward to Type Two: Consciously Using the Two "Stress–Growth" Point for Development and Expansion

The Inner Flow growth path for Type Fours brings them into direct contact with the challenges embodied in Type Two: allowing for a balance between self-referencing and other-referencing, between meeting your own needs and meeting the needs of others, and between being your authentic self and adapting to other people. Under stress, Fours can get defensive when pressed toward the Two point and act out the lower side of Two by giving compulsively in an effort to be liked, or giving up what they need in an attempt to buy others' love or acceptance. But when Fours can consciously manage the challenges embodied in the Two "stress–growth" opportunity, they can use the high side Two qualities to bring themselves out of their self-absorption, intense feelings, and isolation, find creative ways to express who they really, are and open themselves up to connecting with others.

The Four working consciously in this way can make ready use of the tools that healthy Type Twos use: a sensitivity to the needs and preferences of others, a positive view of what's possible in relationship, and the conscious management of feelings and needs in light of the feelings and needs of others.

The Two stance of adapting to please others can help Fours learn to be more adaptable and supportive of others in a way that also enlarges their view of their own worth and value to others. Fours can get lost in their own interior emotional worlds, but they can temper this tendency in service of their growth by reaching out more to nurture others. Finding ways to provide support and understanding to other people can be a good way for Fours to balance out their over-focus on their inner experience of lack or on a particular mood or emotional reaction. Consciously embodying an attitude of service to others can highlight Fours' qualities of optimism, generosity, and cheerfulness—attributes that they might not always see and value in themselves. Through consciously balancing self-referencing with other-referencing, and the ability to dwell in darker feelings with the ability to be light, Fours can use the Two Point as a way to embody a more full and more whole sense of who they really are, and work against the self-deprecating tendency of their "acorn" self.

Type Four Moving Back to Type One: Consciously Using the "Child–Heart" Point to Work through Early Issues and Find Security in Support of Moving Forward

The path of growth for Type Fours calls for them to reclaim their ability to use self-evaluation, self-discipline, and structure as ways to support themselves rather than as ways of devaluing and punishing themselves. As children, Fours may have had to downplay their natural ability to use their ideals and follow the rules as a way of taking action to feel good about themselves and be productive in the world. In response to early loss or deprivation, Fours more typically took refuge in a flawed self-image and an experience of longing for what might have been, which can pull their focus away from working hard to prove their worth. The strategy of trying to be good as a way of earning approval may not have worked if they had to cope with an overwhelming sense of loss or deep feelings of deficiency.

Fours tend to cope by attaching to a feeling of hopelessness or melancholy, to avoid being hopeful about things they believe might not happen. In doing this, they may have had to give up One attributes such as the active capacity to enact practical ideals and a belief in their ability to control what happens through hard work. They may not have been able to provide structure for themselves through routine and adherence to standards and rules because they had to focus on coping with a specific experience of loss or deprivation.

Fours can consciously draw on the strengths of the One Point, using them to gain the support they need in their growth toward the Two Point, by taking action to manifest their ideals. Being more perfectionistic—not by controlling or stifling emotions, but by actively improving themselves or their environment—can give Fours a sense of control and accomplishment. One Four I know, for example, likes to work in the garden to relax when he has time off. His rows of vegetables are perfect, and his garden is extremely beautiful. Working in his garden provides him with a structured activity that relaxes him, contains him, and lets him express his natural creativity.

Regular patterns and repetitive work can help a Four find peace and containment amidst a life in which they can get lost in the ups and downs of their shifting moods. By reincorporating their ability to work hard in support of improving themselves or others, Fours can take action and feel more powerful and confident, which can support their growth and development instead of holding them back in a search for something they lost in the past.

The Vice to Virtue Conversion:
Accessing Envy and Aiming for Equanimity

The developmental path from Vice to Virtue is one of the central contributions of the Enneagram map in highlighting a usable "vertical" path of growth to a higher state of awareness for each type. In the case of Type Four, the Vice (or passion) of the type is envy and its opposite, the Virtue, is *equanimity*. The theory of growth communicated by this "Vice to Virtue conversion" is that the more we can be aware of how our passion functions and consciously work toward the embodiment of our higher Virtue, the more we can free ourselves from the unconscious habits and fixated patterns of our type and evolve toward our "higher" side or "oak tree-Self."

As Fours become more familiar with their experience of envy and develop their ability to make it more conscious, they can take their work further by focusing on enacting their Virtue, the "antidote" to the passion of envy. In the case of Type Four, the Virtue of equanimity represents a state of being that Fours can attain by consciously manifesting their higher capacities.

Equanimity is a way of being that is both engaged with emotional life and above the ups and downs and pushes and pulls of being overly consumed with specific emotional experiences. When Fours are in a place of equanimity, they can feel their feelings but not be consumed by their suffering. They can let go of particular feelings without abandoning themselves. They can focus on important emotions without losing themselves. Equanimity is a way of viewing emotions from a healthy distance, with the wisdom and detachment of the inner observer that is part of the higher Self. Sandra Maitri describes equanimity as the ability to see the big picture of things such that "everything falls into perspective."[21] Explaining that "equanimity" literally means "equal mind," she describes it as a state of "emotional balance" that's characterized by a balanced view of ourselves and others, and which is developed as we "learn to keep our heart open through the changing circumstances of our life and practice."[22]

If envy is a state of emotional reactivity based on a perception that others have something you need and lack, equanimity is a place of openness and acceptance based on a larger view of the whole of ourselves, other people, and life. Embodying equanimity as a Four means you have learned to rise above your intense and shifting emotions, which are based in an experience of suffering brought on by the personality's experience of loss and deprivation. Embodying equanimity means you value your feelings for the way they reflect your emotional truth, but you also have the confidence and understanding to not get swept up in them or allow them to distort your view of who you are and what you are capable of. Equanimity is thus the antidote to the endless craving of envy because it focuses attention on the big picture, on the value of all emotions, and the importance of detaching from particular emotions or a sense of lack, allowing you to open up to an experience of abundance.

When Fours do the "Vice to Virtue" work of noticing how the painful emotions that envy inspires trap them in a vicious circle, the wider view of equanimity can wake them up to their own essential goodness, allowing them to see all emotions as equally valuable and leading them to an enlivening understanding of their fundamental wholeness.

Specific Work for the Three Type Four Subtypes on the Path from Vice to Virtue

Whatever type you are, the path from observing your passion to finding its antidote is not exactly the same for each of the subtypes. The path of conscious self-work has been characterized in terms of "grit, grind, and grace:"[23] the grit of our personality programming, the grind of our efforts to grow, and the grace that comes to us from doing our work in conscious and positive ways. Each subtype has to grind, or exert effort, against something slightly different. This insight is one of the great benefits of understanding the three distinct subtypes of each of the nine types.

Self-Preservation Fours can travel the path from envy to equanimity by relaxing into their feelings more and sharing them with others, thereby allowing themselves more sources of internal and external support. Envy leads

Self-Preservation Fours to believe they have to go it on their own, but by actively seeking out help from others, they can allow themselves to have more room to breathe and relax. By consciously seeking to embody equanimity, these Fours can develop a place of peace inside themselves—allowing them to feel through and let go of their pain, allowing them to live more from their fragility, and healing what needs to be healed. Self-Preservation Fours actively release envy by not working so hard to prove themselves and instead allowing for more lightness, fun, and pleasure. Rising above the need to suffer silently and tough everything out means going easier on yourself and allowing yourself to embrace all of who you are, not just your ability to endure.

Social Fours can travel the path from envy to equanimity by doing the work it takes to release their inferiority complex, own their positive qualities, and enhance their self-confidence. If you are a Social Four, it will help you to work on relaxing your self-judgments and negative self-perceptions—to take the risk to see what is positive about you and your life and not get stuck in envious comparisons and shame. Manifesting a sense of equanimity means valuing all your feelings equally, and also not getting over-identified with your feelings. It helps to consider that it's okay to be angry and express wishes and feelings directly, from a place of self-compassion, instead of seducing through suffering. Most of all, you can support yourself in embodying equanimity by considering all your feelings, consciously analyzing the whole situation, and taking action to get what you need and want instead of becoming so invested in your emotional suffering.

Sexual Fours can travel the path from envy to equanimity by strengthening their ability to be with their own suffering without needing to externalize it or project it onto others. If you are a Sexual Four, you can grow by seeing all your emotions as equally valuable and important, whether you are feeling envious and angry or sad and vulnerable. Your tender feelings are as important to consider as your competitive impulses. For you, equanimity means recognizing the value of who you are, even if you aren't the best or superior to anyone else. No one has to prove themselves to be the best to be worthy—we are all inherently good enough. Allow yourself to see your anger, frustration, and impatience as important clues to deeper feelings of pain that you might be experiencing or relegating to unconsciousness. By allowing yourself to experience all your feelings and remembering they are all important reflections of the emotional truth of who you are, you can develop more compassion for yourself and others and allow yourself to be more open to receiving love and acceptance from the people around you.

Conclusion

THE ARCHETYPE OF THE FOUR POINT represents the way we all fear abandonment when we feel imperfect and focus on our flaws as a way to control or defend against loss in a world that seems to require us to be special to be loved. The Four path of growth shows us how to transform our longing and suffering into a sense of confidence in our inherent lovability so that we can wake up to a fuller experience of who we are and what we can be. In each of the Type Four subtypes, we see a specific character who teaches us how equanimity can allow us to value our emotional truth and essential wholeness, thereby furthering our own evolution through the alchemy of self-observation, self-knowledge, self-development, and self-acceptance.

CHAPTER 9

The Point Three Archetype:
The Type, Subtypes, and Growth Path

The only lies for which we are truly punished are those we tell ourselves.

—V. S. Naipaul

TYPE THREE REPRESENTS THE ARCHETYPE of the person who seeks to create an image of value and success, and to gain the admiration of others, through active efforts in both work and appearance. This drive provides defensive protection in a world that rewards achievement and attractiveness and emphasizes what things look like on the outside.

This archetype also exists as Jung's concept of the "persona," the individual's "system of adaptation to, or the manner in which he assumes in dealing with, the world."[1] Taken from the term used to describe the mask worn by an actor, the persona is our conscious outer social face, the role we play or the image we show to others "to give form to our outward sense of self."[2] The persona takes its form and function from external, collective reality.

Type Threes are the prototype for the way in which we all adopt a personality as an external public face in order to survive in the world and mediate between the inner self and the social environment. It is the model for the desire we all have to "put on a good face" or wear a social mask as a means of both protection and a marketing effort. This archetypal stance prioritizes looking good and matching social ideals of value and status as a way of feeling accepted and earning approval.

This effort also necessarily involves inhibiting or covering over aspects of the "real self" that don't fit with the constructed social mask. Type Threes tend to lose contact with the deeper emotions they naturally have that might interfere with the design of the image they create for others, and thus may become overidentified with their persona and under-identified with who they really are.

We also find the Three archetype in American culture in the emphasis on the values of "the market:" the importance of packaging, advertising, and selling products; the central focus on "winning" in a competitive environment by attracting the most customers; and the driving force of profit maximization through prioritizing work and corporate interests. The "American Dream" as a "rags to riches" story of upward mobility through hard work, demonstrated by the acquisition of conventionally agreed-upon symbols of success (a house, a nice car, a vacation home), also reflects the core themes of this archetype. In the US mass media, the superficial attractiveness of things is emphasized, and depth is often sacrificed.

The Three archetype can thus be seen at the societal level in all cultures in which competition and winning are emphasized, and in mercantilism generally, where marketing and sales efforts are a central component of social interaction. The archetypal themes associated with the Three Point can especially be seen in the corporate world, where the focus is on competing and working hard in pursuit of success in the form of popularity, profits, and coming out on top.[3]

Type Three individuals work very hard and know how to make a good impression. They are extremely competent and effective doers who get a lot done and make it look easy (even though it requires much effort). Threes are skilled at using goals to motivate their efforts and are resourceful and productive in achieving those goals. They know how to present themselves to others and fit the image of whatever context they might be in. Their specific "superpower" is their ability to make things happen by finding the most direct path to their goal, removing obstacles that might get in the way—and looking good the whole time. They know how to assure their own success by working diligently, completing the tasks necessary to reaching their goal, and exuding an image of success and competence.

As with all the archetypal personalities, however, Type Threes' gifts and strengths also represent their "fatal flaw" or "Achilles heel:" they exhaust themselves by working too hard, and they lose sight of who they really are apart from the persona they've adopted to achieve their goals. And they can be hard-hearted and insensitive to others in their race to the finish line. However, when they can learn to balance their focus on work and achievement with a focus on the needs and feelings of their true self, they can blend their skill at actualizing goals with the creativity and depth of who they are, producing positive results that can enhance life for themselves and others.

The Type Three Archetype in Homer's *Odyssey*:
Sailing by Skylla and Charybdis and Landing at Thrinakia

The goddess Circe tells Odysseus that after he and his crew pass by the Sirens, they will sail through a narrow passage. Circe advises Odysseus to travel through this perilous strait as quickly and efficiently as possible, because she knows that he will have to sacrifice six of his men to Skylla's six heads as he passes through.

Odysseus faces many leadership challenges as he strives to return with his crew to Ithaca. In this pivotal section of the journey, we see both his single-minded focus on achieving his goal and the disastrous consequences of seizing power illegitimately.

Odysseus knows that he must steer his ship carefully between these two terrible obstacles: Skylla (a savage six-headed monster) and Charybdis (a deadly, inescapable whirlpool). He cannot avoid these obstacles, so he focuses on keeping his ship on course to achieve the dire but practical goal of getting through the dangerous straight between them. He decides not to tell his crew about Skylla, because he knows he must sacrifice at least six of his men to keep on course and avoid complete destruction in the whirlpool.

Odysseus is the right man for the job. He knows he must keep his ego in check and stay efficiently, consistently, and relentlessly on course toward his goal. He masterfully exercises his power to control information and make the key decisions. His crew does not hesitate to follow his orders at the crucial moments. Six crewmen die. Everyone else survives.

When they reach the island of Thrinakia, Odysseus gives his crew a very specific warning. He orders his men not to touch the prime cattle grazing there; they are the property of the sun god, Helios, "who sees and hears all things."[4]

The men comply until their food supplies run out. Then, as Odysseus sleeps, his second-in-command (Eurylochus) convinces the men that being killed by the gods at sea is better than starving to death. They feast on Helios's cattle, assuming for themselves the powers and privileges that belong only to the sun god.

Odysseus awakens, but it is too late. He orders them to sea as soon as the wind permits. Zeus himself promptly destroys the boat and crew, leaving Odysseus as the sole survivor.

These encounters symbolize the power and pitfalls of the Type Three personality. Odysseus's focused, authentic leadership saved as many men as possible under harrowing circumstances. In his absence, the men assumed power beyond their true nature and led themselves to their doom.

The Type Three Personality Structure

AS PART OF THE "HEART-BASED" or "emotion-based" triad of types, the personality structure of the Three is centered in the emotion of *sadness* or *grief.* Threes have a focus on creating a specific *image* of themselves. Each of the heart type personalities (Two, Three, and Four) relate to other people primarily through emotional empathy. The "feeling sense" these types share gives these individuals a heightened need to connect with others and an ability to read interpersonal situations well on the emotional-relational level. Relationships are in the foreground of their attention, and so the heart types are especially aware of the image they feel they need to present to attract the love or approval of others.

While Type Fours overdo an attachment to grief and Type Twos are in conflict with their sadness, Threes underdo grief, habitually numbing out their feelings so they don't get in the way of working to reach their goals.

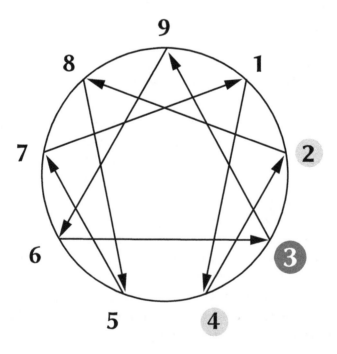

The sadness at the core of the heart type personalities reflects their feeling of not being loved for who they really are and their grief over having lost touch with their real selves because they've disowned who they really are and created a specific image to get the love (or approval) they need. All three of the heart types have core issues related to unmet needs to be seen, accepted, and loved for who they are. Their respective coping strategies are designed to gain approval from other people in three distinct ways as a substitute for the love they seek but fear they can't get as they are. While Twos strive to have a likable, pleasing image, and Fours present themselves as unique and special, Threes create an image of achievement and success.

Accomplishing things and looking good feels like the route to survival and well-being to Threes, who use their "heart intelligence" to automatically size up what others see as admirable and then become that. Performing well at tasks, reaching goals, and constructing a polished image—adhering to what is considered successful according to generally accepted standards—allows them to prove their worth to others.

The Early Coping Strategy: Type Three

Threes report that they received the message early on that they were loved for what they did. Whether implicit or explicit, perhaps due to well-intentioned parental praise for specific accomplishments, as children, Threes came to believe that the path to gaining support, approval, and admiration from others was performing and succeeding at tasks. Threes develop a sense that they are not loved for who they really are as individuals but for what they do. This leads them to adopt a coping strategy of conforming to parental expectations and conventional ideals of achievement. Thus, their need for admiration grows out of an early experience of being praised for achievements rather than affirmed for aspects of their "real self."

Alternatively, Three children may not have gotten the attention they needed, so they feel motivated to attract attention—to stand out and get noticed—by doing things to impress others. They become successful through the effort they expend in an attempt to avoid being ignored. Some Threes, for example, lacked parental support or protection as children, and they learned to be doers in order to survive. When a child loses a father in particular, he or she may feel a need to become supercompetent in order to fill the gap left by the absence of the archetypally masculine (active, protective, and productive) parental presence.

Faced with the perception that they must prove themselves to be admirable in some way in order to earn love, Threes develop a survival strategy in which they identify with and then become what others value. Type Three individuals possess a sensitive radar, or antenna, for what others like, admire, and view as successful. They turn themselves into a person who does or has whatever others associate with success and achievement. Similar to the Type Two's strategy of determining what others need and like and then shape-shifting into that, Threes shape-shift to match an image of competence, attractiveness, and high status. Thus, Threes are not only oriented toward attaining goals and looking good, they are also highly competitive and focused on winning.

Motivated by a need to feel affirmed in the face of an early lack of attention or a perception that approval is linked with performance, the Three coping strategy provides both a focus on performance and a defense against painful feelings. "Doing" thus takes precedence over "being" and feeling for the Three. Doing seems to bring the desired response of approval from others, while "being" becomes a blind spot, as feelings are avoided so as to not create any emotional obstacles to doing. This (understandably) leads Threes to be "human doings" instead of "human beings."[5]

Threes therefore cope with a world that doesn't offer them unconditional love by identifying with their image and their work, seeing themselves as equal to the image they create, and believing they are what they do. As their image and their work represent things they can control, Threes strive to match an image of what others admire; they work hard to earn approval by achieving a socially sanctioned definition of success and avoiding failure at all costs.

Candice, a Self-Preservation Three, describes her childhood situation and the development of her coping strategy:

My mother used to tell me I was such a good baby that she could leave me alone in my playpen for hours while she chased my older brother. Even as a child, I was proud of that. It was only when I saw how appalled others were at my mother's behavior that I realized my "pride" in self-sufficiency was misguided. I vacillated between being fearful about being ignored and feeling safe in my ability to fly under the radar of my mother's intrusive codependence. My brother was diagnosed as schizophrenic when we were in our early twenties and he committed suicide at twenty-nine. I've often felt that I hid behind him—being ignored and able to do for myself saved me. In those days, psychiatrists literally blamed mothers. My mom, who was a lot better than many, carried enormous guilt. My becoming industrious and reliable allowed her not to "worry" about me. This capacity has always trumped birth order in our family. When something goes wrong, my phone is the first to ring despite being the third of four children. I'm just back from helping my ninety-five-year-old father get settled at home after surgery. My younger brother and older sister had both been there before me. A friend of my father's said to me, "When you come to town, things get done."

As a Self-Preservation Three, I have an instinctual sense of what needs to be done and how to do it efficiently. It was hard to acknowledge that I've trained those around me to expect me to take over, so in more recent years it has been an interesting experience to step back. Before I jump in, I now ask the following questions: Does this have to done at all? Does it have to be done right now? Does it have to be done by me? It's been amazing to see how much wasn't needed but served my "doingitis."

"I'm fine" was my mantra for years. I always bristled at the descriptions of Threes as wanting to look good. When I read that Self-Preservation Threes want to look like they have it together but don't want to own their image-consciousness—that they have "vanity for having no vanity"—I knew I'd found my home. I wasn't happy about it, but I knew it was true. A recent broken ankle gave me an opportunity to observe myself and my reactions to offers of assistance. I can feel the "I'm fine" rising physically and have to consciously counteract it.

Another challenge I've faced is recognizing and feeling my emotions. I've often joked that "emotions are not aerodynamic and Threes don't like to be slowed down." One great find was The Book of Qualities *by J. Ruth Gendler. She describes dozens of emotions as if they are people. It helped me access a realm that I had avoided (originally) to help my mother not worry about me. It opened the gateway to truly feeling the loss of my brother, which carved a path for other emotions to pass through me. I am now fine not being fine.*

The Main Type Three Defense Mechanism: Identification

The defense mechanism associated with this early coping strategy is *identification*. By identifying with—by locating and matching a specific image or model—and becoming what others value, Threes attempt to satisfy their need for approval, which substitutes for their underlying need to be seen and loved. Threes create such a compelling image to defend against the pain of not being seen and loved as they are that they begin to mistake their image for the total-ity of who they are. They overidentify with the image they create as a way to control how people respond to them, and in the process they may forget that they are not equal to their image. This is why they represent the prototype of something we all do: identify with our personality such that we don't realize that we are more than our persona.

But how exactly does "identification" operate as a defense mechanism? It may seem strange that identification is even considered a psychological defense, as identifying with someone or modeling oneself after someone can seem like a normal, benign activity. And while it's true that some kinds of identification have few, if any, defensive components, many instances of iden-tification are motivated by a need to avoid anxiety, grief, shame, or other pain-ful feelings. Identification can also be a way to shore up a shaky sense of self or to generate self-esteem.[6]

Identification thus operates as a defense against painful feelings related to the early sense that love was conditional by allowing an individual to deliber-ately (though at least partly unconsciously) become like another person or an ideal of a particular kind of person. By adopting the characteristics of another person, or an image that others admire, you can reduce the threat of difficult feelings that grow out of a fear of not being seen and loved for who you are.

But what do Threes typically identify with, exactly? Naranjo explains that "central to type Three is identification with an ideal self-image built as a re-sponse to the expectation of others,"[7] which often starts with the defensive effort to match ideal characteristics their parents valued. Threes defensively transform themselves into what important others—people in their environ-ment whom they want to impress—admire and appreciate. By noticing and adopting characteristics that others regard as valuable, Threes seek to match an external model to assure approval.

The Type Three Focus of Attention

As a result of getting the message that love and approval is tied to perfor-mance, Threes focus their attention on achieving goals and tasks and on cre-ating an image of success in the eyes of others. Naturally able to focus like a laser beam on whatever tasks and goals will help them become what society defines as successful or valuable, most Threes achieve a high degree of worldly success. However, what gets sacrificed in the process is the Three's feelings and authentic sense of self, as Threes *don't* focus as much attention on who they are apart from their image. Threes are primarily other-focused, so they don't attend as much to what's going on inside them.

Threes become so focused on the things they have to do to make progress toward a goal that they tend to be hyperaware of obstacles that might block the path to their desired result. One Three I know described his vigilance about the potential for such obstructions as his tendency to quickly assess any "drag coefficients." Threes get so keenly focused on the path toward their goals that they automatically home in on and address any factors in the environment that may slow down their forward movement.

For Threes, even vacation and leisure time will be structured in terms of things to do. Frequent list-makers, Threes' attention is often focused on organizing their life in terms of the tasks that need to be accomplished, results that need to be produced, and the ways they will fill their time (such that they can avoid gaps in activity where feelings could emerge). Accomplishing tasks leads to the satisfying experience of checking items off the list after they are completed.

Threes often multitask; they are adept at splitting their attention over a range of activities. Experts at completing tasks in the most rapid and efficient way possible, Threes report that they find it both necessary and fairly easy to do many things at once, often at a fast pace, as moving quickly and efficiently enables them to accomplish the maximum number of tasks possible without wasting time.

The Three's focus of attention also goes to "playing to the crowd." Natural performers, Threes put their attention and thus their energy toward winning approval through focusing on other people and how they are responding to the Three's presentation. Naranjo describes the Three as having a "marketing orientation." A good marketer determines the needs and values of his target audience and then adapts the presentation based on his audience's responses. This is why Threes tend to be characterized as "chameleons." They have an automatic ability to match the perfect model of how someone should look in every context and every situation. Threes' talent for creating a persona in this way is their way of constructing an "acorn shell" that is protective and useful, but ultimately limiting if they can't break out of it.

The Type Three Emotional Passion: Vanity

The passion of Type Three is *vanity*. Vanity is a passion for "living for the eyes of others."[8] The passion of vanity motivates Threes to present a false image to others to inspire their admiration and to live life "in anticipation or fantasy of the experience of another."[9] Vanity thus moves Threes (unconsciously) to live for an insubstantial image—imagining how they will look to others from the outside—rather than out of their "true selves."

Vanity is understood here as the drive "to shine, attract attention, either through the development of sex appeal or through achievement or success"[10] based on established, universally accepted criteria. This involves a lot of effort, and Threes are action-oriented, striving people who do things well. They have "a talent for acting and a liking for display and applause."[11] When under the sway of vanity, which is oriented to external appearances, Threes have "little capacity for inwardness,"[12] and they have to be doing something all the time, such that they do not "leave themselves time for being with themselves."[13]

In the early Christian Contemplative tradition, where we see the earliest descriptions of the same passions we find in the Enneagram, vanity is called "Vainglory" and is described as involving "fantasizing about social encounters, a pretence of industriousness, the contrary of the truth…desire for privilege, the ultimate title, [and] slavery to praises."[14]

The Three's vanity expresses a deep need to be seen positively—a need the personality seeks to satisfy through the cultivation of a particular image designed to appeal to others by drawing on conventional values of attractiveness, quality, and stature. Living for and through appearances leads Threes to a constant preoccupation with how they look from the point of view of other people. They become good at playing a role or acting a part, marketing themselves through good packaging, and selling themselves as the kind of person people respect and admire.

The Type Three Cognitive Mistake: "When You Look This Good, Who Needs Feelings?" or "I Am What I Do"

We all get stuck in habitual ways of thinking that influence our beliefs, feelings, and actions, and this continues even after the mental models that create our overall perspective aren't accurate anymore.[15] While the passion shapes the personality's emotional motivations, the "cognitive fixation" preoccupies the personality's thought processes.

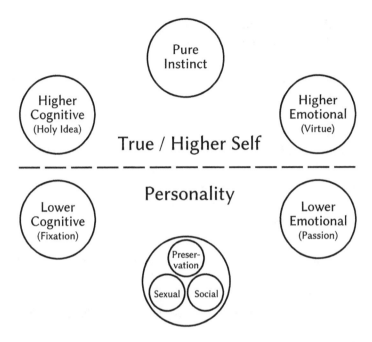

Deceit is the mental fixation of Type Three. This means that the key princi-ple that forms the Three's thinking is the "self-falsification" entailed in creating an image for public consumption. As part of the normal functioning of their personality, Threes "lie" to the world about who they are, but most of the time they don't do this intentionally. Instead, Threes' thought processes, like their core emotional motivations, are driven by the deep need to impress people.

Thus, much of the time, when Threes craft a specific image to show to the outside world, they are engaging in *self*-deceit. They automatically and un-consciously present a false front to influence the way people respond to them, and they often believe that their false image is who they really are. They may not always consciously see that there is a difference between the image they manipulate in order to impress and who they are inside. The lack of truthful-ness of the Three may not be what we typically think of as "deceit" in that the deception happens at a deeper level: Threes lie to themselves about who they really are because they so badly need to believe they are whoever they need to be for others to see them in a positive light.

The core beliefs, assumptions, and thoughts associated with this Three mental stance (or "trance") of deceit, or self-falsification, include ideas and rationalizations that support the central Three personality strategy of getting things done—being productive and effective—in the service of maintaining an image. The Three's mental organizing principles, or the key beliefs that guide their habitual patterns of thinking, feeling, and behaving include:

- People admire and respect success and achievement. To inspire admiration in others you must be successful and achieve.
- If you achieve high status, you are a valuable person in the eyes of society.
- Working hard to achieve specific goals enables me to control the things I do and makes me successful.
- Getting things done and being productive supports my well-being.
- Setting goals is an important way to stay organized, get things done, and achieve success.
- Reaching specific goals depends upon hard work. I work hard to do whatever it takes to reach my goals and remove any obstacles in the way.
- Image and appearance matter.
- How you look and what you've done tells people what to think and feel about you.
- It is important to have the right image for every context so that people will think well of you.
- Feelings aren't as important as getting things done. Feelings get in the way of getting things done and so can be a waste of time.

These common Three beliefs and recurring thoughts support and perpetuate the creation of a socially adept self-presentation designed to inspire people's positive regard. When Threes adhere more strongly to this mental stance—when they are "in the trance" of their type—it may be much harder to stop identifying with the personality and "come home" to the feelings and thoughts of the true self.

The Type Three Trap:
"I Have Such a Great Image, Even I Like it More than Me"

As it does distinctly for each type, the cognitive fixation for Type Three leads the personality in circles. It presents an inherent "trap" that the limitations of the personality cannot resolve.

When you create an image to get love, what gets "loved" is the image, not necessarily the person behind the image, which intensifies the Three's conviction that they can't be loved as they are (and necessitates the construction of an image to get the love).

Threes identify with an image of value in order to be seen positively in the eyes of others, but then they aren't "at home" in themselves to receive the love or appreciation they elicit. Threes disconnect from their feelings to do all the work they do to earn others' approval, and so they aren't rooted in their own experience and can't be present to relate to the people they have won over through all their efforts. By needing to work so hard and look so good, Threes turn themselves into something they aren't and lose sight of who they really are. They become what they think they need to be to forge positive connections with others; but because they live through an image of what they have become in order to be valued—and not their real selves—they often aren't available for real love and connection.

The Key Type Three Traits

Other-Directedness

It can seem to others that Threes must be fundamentally self-oriented because they get so much done to further their own interests, know how to present themselves to attract people, set goals and reach them, and seem easily able to manifest their personal desires.

At a basic level, however, the Three personality is shaped around playing to an audience. The strategy of creating an image for public consumption is based on the need to attract the attention of others and rests on Threes' ability to accurately read their audience and then reflect or become what others value. Thus, like any smart marketing expert, they do things and create an appearance designed to impress others, based on a careful evaluation of what others admire.

Achievement Orientation

Type Threes have an achievement orientation, meaning they are high achievers that work hard to set and reach goals based on social or cultural conceptions of what makes a person successful. A focus on achievement also means that Threes value efficiency and move at a fast pace to get as much done as possible without wasting time. For Threes, the drive to achieve can be so intense that they can become workaholics, unable to slow down or stop or take a vacation from all the "doing" they do.

Threes' formula for achievement really works. Unlike other personality types who may have habitual patterns that inhibit their functioning in the external world, the coping strategy at the heart of Threes' personality structure is more aligned with what Western culture sees as a productive (and thus a good) way to operate. Their goal and task orientation, their willingness to work very hard for long periods of time, their strong sense of ambition, and their optimism regarding their ability to achieve whatever they aspire to mean that Threes are usually successful at accomplishing their goals.

Focus on Success

Type Threes have a natural understanding of what constitutes success in a given culture or context, especially the outward signs of success. They hold the general view that if you know what it takes to be a success, why not just do it and enjoy the fruits of material achievements and the admiration of others that tend to go with it? A keen eye for what constitutes "success" and the willingness and drive to do what they need to do to achieve it makes Threes people who often embody whatever their cultural context views as successful.

In seeking to ensure that they are successful, Threes determine the short-est path between points A and B (the goal), and they do whatever it takes to get there in the most efficient way possible. To do otherwise just doesn't make sense to the Three. Why would you tolerate failure or halfway measures when you could work to accomplish your goals and achieve success? Why would you fail to do something you have established as a goal when you could just find a way to do it? The Nike slogan "Just Do It" effectively captures this common Three outlook.

Competitiveness and the Drive to Win

As a part of the drive to achieve, Threes can be ruthless and competitive, wanting to win at any cost and dominating situations in which they believe they must exercise their power to get things done. Pragmatic and practical, Threes specialize in targeting specific achievements and doing what it takes to make them happen. This means they play to win, they are extremely competitive, and they put a lot of energy and effort into coming out on top. In fact, Threes often report that they want to win so much that they simply don't engage in activities they know they can't win.

Image Manipulation and Self-Deception

Threes are so good at manipulating their image to ensure success on the public stage and the admiration of their audience that it can be very hard for Threes to see more deeply into themselves, beyond their image and achievements. Threes automatically tap into what others find appealing and create a perfect persona to match that picture. Whether at work, in the gym, or going out at night, Threes excel at wearing the right clothes and creating the perfect image for every setting. They acknowledge the importance of appearances and put thought and energy into understanding what others might want or expect.

In doing this, however, Threes not only (unconsciously) deceive others about who they really are, they also deceive themselves. Their intense focus on maintaining the right image (and disowning their feelings to support this false presentation) creates confusion about where the image stops and they begin. When Threes are "in the trance" of their personality's fixation, they mix up the reality of who they are—their feelings, needs, desires, and preferences—with the appearances they create to impact others. The deceit associated with this personality concerns the creation of a false pretense in place of a true self that might fail or be judged as flawed or inadequate.

An attractive and successful businesswoman friend of mine once said to me, in all seriousness, "I am what I do." Knowing the Enneagram and believing that she was a Three, I decided to argue with her. I said, "No, you aren't," (thinking to myself that she was much more than what she does). She said, "Yes, I am." I said, "No, you aren't." And she said, "Yes, I am." After we went back and forth like this a few more times, I decided to stop arguing with her. But I noticed I felt sad afterward. I knew she had good reason for thinking she "is what she does"—or for wanting to believe it. She had a good, high-level job, made a lot of money, and was seen as being very good at her chosen career. I could understand why she would want to see herself as equal to her success at work. But as objectively great as her career was, I knew she was much more than that.

The Type Three Shadow

Type Threes' natural strengths align with Western ideals of what it means to be successful, so it can seem to others like the Three has no internal challenges. But the biggest challenge for a Three is recognizing the difference between their authentic self and their image or role or job, because Threes have a blind spot where their "true self" should be. Threes tend to believe so much in their image that they consider their image and their real self to be one and the same thing.

As long as Threes take their image to be their real self, they can't really act in a personal way—can't act from their real feelings and needs. To live from the authenticity of your real self, you need to own your own feelings and realize that you are not the same as your public image.

Another Shadow element for Threes is how they feel emotionally. Threes regularly avoid experiencing their real feelings because they habitually suspend their emotions to get the job done. Because Threes rely on a coping strategy that involves avoiding emotions, they come to fear what will happen if they make space for feelings to emerge. Especially if Threes are busy and successful, they may see no need to feel their emotions, so the whole of their authentic emotional response to things can be in their Shadow. This is often reinforced by rationalizations that it takes "too much time" or "isn't productive" to have feelings.

Doing is often so much in the foreground of the experience of Type Three people that their own sense of "being" is an element of their Shadow. It can be extremely challenging for Threes to slow down and just allow for being—in fact, in can be difficult for them to even imagine "just being," because they get accustomed to doing and working all the time. It can feel strange, uncomfortable, or anxiety-producing to *not* do and just sit there. Some Threes become so oriented toward the constant "go, go, go" of producing and doing that they can't fathom what it means to just "be."

It can seem to others that Threes are "not at home" in themselves, that they are hard to connect with because they often aren't connected to their own being and their own inner world of feelings. Threes put so much attention and energy on shaping themselves according to what others see as positive and valuable, they end up experiencing a void in terms of their own sense of self. So much of their conscious effort is directed toward detecting what others see as successful and then matching that image (derived from others) that their real self remains a blind spot.

Related to this, Threes also have a blind spot with regard to their vulnerability. They focus so intently on competing to win that failure can feel intolerable to them. They put so much attention on how to succeed and avoid setbacks that they don't leave room for the conscious experience of insecurity, loss, or failure. And since Threes usually don't have much experience with failure, it can be devastating for them.

The Shadow of Type Three Passion and Fixation:
Vanity and *Deceit* in Dante's Underworld

The Passion of Type Three is *Vanity*. Vanity is a passion for "living for the eyes of others" by attracting and cultivating their attention and approval. Vanity feeds a fantasy of how one appears in other people's eyes. Vanity and the mental "fixation" of deceit are intimately related. The darker side of the Type Three personality's passion of vanity fuels a need to develop and present a false image to others to inspire admiration through deception.

Deep in the Inferno, in the "fraud" section—the last circle of the under-world before the final pit—Dante encounters the falsifiers. The sinners here built themselves up by deceiving others: alchemists, impersonators, counterfeiters, and strategic liars. Unlike anywhere else in the *Inferno*, the falsifiers' punishments come from *internal* torments rather than *external* ones. And in keeping with Dante's poetic device of making the "sinner" display the key problem of the specific unconscious issue he seeks to illustrate, the punishment associated with falsifying oneself makes the sinner externally repulsive. The alchemists all have leprosy, and the impersonators are rabid. The counterfeiters have dropsy, swelling them up with so much fluid that they cannot move. The infamous liars reek from a constant burning fever. The dark sides of vanity and deceit reach their extreme here, as Dante symbolically communicates the negative consequences of fraudulently presenting yourself as something you're not. Neglecting the truth and virtue of one's true self in favor of a deceptive outward appearance is revealed as an obvious internal rot. In this way, Dante dramatically cautions us about the shadow side of not being true to who we are.

The Three Kinds of Threes:
The Type Three Subtypes

THE PASSION OF TYPE THREE IS VANITY. The three distinct Type Three subtypes each express vanity through the need to achieve and maintain a successful image, but this manifests in three different ways. The Self-Preservation Three is an efficient, autonomous workaholic in the service of security who goes against vanity by trying to be good. The Social Three expresses vanity by wanting to be recognized on the social stage by creating, leveraging, and selling a polished image. And the Sexual Three is a charismatic pleaser who expresses vanity by being appealing to and supporting others and achieving through them.

The three Type Three subtypes represent very distinct types: the Self-Preservation Three is more focused on working hard to do things in the best way possible and less focused on being the center of attention; the Social Three likes to be on stage more than the other Threes and craves recognition for performance; and the Sexual Three seeks attention through attracting a romantic partner and promoting and supporting the important people in their lives rather than just manifesting their own achievements.

The Self-Preservation Three: "Security" (Countertype)

Following Ichazo, Naranjo calls this subtype "Security" because these Threes work hard to achieve a sense of security, both in terms of material and financial resources and knowing how to do things effectively. Self-Preservation Threes express a concern with security in that they have a need to feel autonomous and self-sufficient—to know how to take care of themselves and others.

People with this subtype often had a childhood in which they didn't have enough protection and resources. In response to those conditions, these Threes learned to be active and efficient doers, oriented to taking care of themselves without help from others. They have developed a special focus on autonomy in the face of a jeopardized sense of security.

This preoccupation with security can also extend out to others. This person emanates a sense of security; they are solid people who you might go to for advice. They seem outwardly calm and organized, like they have it all together, but they are anxious underneath. These are assertive people who specialize in solving problems and getting things done in a high-quality way—and while they work very hard, they don't show their stress. They are usually financially secure, highly productive, and "in control," but they also report feeling an underlying sense of anxiety related to the effort it takes to achieve the sense of security they crave.

Self-Preservation Threes strive to be the ideal model of quality in whatever they do. They want to be the best example of how to be in whatever role they play: the best parent, the best partner, the best worker, the best at whatever they do. They feel a need not only to be *seen* as good, but also to actually *be* good. They do this both to achieve a sense of security and to inspire admiration in others without being obvious about their vanity. They want to be admired because they do things well, and they want to do the things they do in the best way possible—not just to have a good image that people will find attractive, but also to live up to that image. Their tendency to adapt to a "model" also motivates them to forget their own feelings.

Following the perfect model of how things should be done means being virtuous, and being virtuous implies a lack of vanity. In this sense, the Self-Preservation Three "has vanity for having no vanity."[16] This means that while this Three wants to look attractive and successful in the eyes of others, they don't want other people to know they want this—they don't want others to see that they have actively created an image to look good to others. They don't want others to catch them in the act of wanting or working to look good because they have an ethic that says that "good," or virtuous, people are not vain. Some Self-Preservation Threes are aware (and will admit) that they want people to admire them for their good image—though, generally, they want to keep this a secret—but some Self-Preservation Threes believe so firmly that it is wrong or superficial to want the approval of others that they won't admit this desire even to themselves. These are people who want to be so perfect that it's not in their code of honor to allow for vanity.

In denying the presence of vanity, the Self-Preservation Three represents the countertype of the three Three subtypes—that is, this Three is the "counter-passional" type, the Three that doesn't necessarily look like a Three. Though these Threes are motivated out of vanity, just like the other Threes, they deny their vanity to some extent, and so their character is shaped more around going against the energetic pull of vanity. And there is a natural opposition between the vain desire to attract attention and a primary instinctual drive toward security and self-preservation. Unlike Social Threes, who will more openly brag about their accomplishments, Self-Preservation Threes avoid talking about their positive characteristics and high-status credentials because they believe it's bad form to advertise their strong points, even if they also want others to see them as successful. They may be either modest or falsely modest.

In terms of the mental habit of deception, this subtype is also anti-deception in that they try to tell the truth. The deception in this Three comes at a more unconscious level; when it comes to knowing their true motivations, Threes often confuse their image-based reasons for doing things with their real feelings and convictions.

Self-Preservation Threes display a strong workaholic tendency and are motivated to work very hard to achieve security. They have a compulsion to be self-reliant and to feel in control of their lives. They also feel responsible for making everything happen, and can even have a sense of omnipotence. Along with their need for control and their underlying anxiety, they may experience a sense of panic when they need help or lose autonomy.

The passion for security in this subtype leads them to oversimplification in life, reducing their focus and interest to what is "practical and useful." These individuals have an imperative need to know they can handle it all and that all will be good for everyone surrounding them. They don't show weakness. They may think things like, "I have to do everything, because I do it better." Situations that feel beyond their control can leave them confused and lost internally, causing them to freeze up, and in an effort to reestablish control, they can become invasive. These are the most rigid of the Threes.

With so much energy focused on work and efficiency and security, there can be little mental and emotional space left for these Threes to be able to engage deeply with others. Though they may work hard to maintain relationships, they may have trouble making deep connections. When Self-Preservation Threes—especially less self-aware Self-Preservation Threes—do make connections, they can be superficial. They can view feeling their emotions as a waste of time, and this inhibits their ability to connect in intimate relationships, since a true relationship comes through each person being in touch with their feelings and their "real self."

It can be hard for a Self-Preservation Three to be recognized as a Three. They may be easily confused with Ones or Sixes. This Three looks like a One in that the type is rigid, responsible, and self-sufficient. These Threes, like Ones, try to be a model of virtue in the things they do. They can be distinguished from Ones in that they move at a faster pace, pay attention to creating an image (even when they don't acknowledge it), and conform to a perfect model of how to be as judged by social consensus, not according to internal standards of right and wrong (as Ones do). They differ from Sixes in that they are fundamentally image-oriented and work harder in response to insecurity, while Sixes find protection in other ways. And while Threes may question their sense of identity, they generally don't allow their productivity to get slowed down by too much doubt or questioning.

Virginia, a Self-Preservation Three, speaks:

I've always been an achiever. In preschool I finished tasks so early that I was assigned to help others in order to stay engaged. By first grade, the school counselor explained to my proud parents that my insistence on perfect homework and exemplary behavior were early predictors of later anxiety. I have worked incredibly hard throughout my career and am now an officer of a Fortune 500 company. Married and divorced twice, my pattern was three to five years of being the perfect wife, followed by emotional exhaustion and an angry husband. Vulnerability or relying on others makes me uncomfortable. I love being counted on to tackle difficult challenges and strive to be hyper-responsible, fair, and generous. Although I crave admiration for these traits, I avoid seeming to care about superficial appearances. I need to be the good traits. When I first studied the Enneagram, I rejected the idea that I could be an image-conscious Three. I made myself a Six, even "performing" once as a model Six on an Enneagram workshop panel. My goal now is balance: vulnerability (versus fierce autonomy) and stillness (versus overactive doing).

The Social Three: "Prestige"

The Social Three has a desire to be seen and to have influence with people. This Three acts out vanity through the desire to shine before the whole world: Social Threes enjoy being on stage. This subtype is the most vain of the Threes, and the biggest chameleon.

The name given to this subtype is "Prestige," which reflects the idea of needing everybody's admiration and applause. This Three, more than the other two subtypes, likes and needs to be recognized, so they tend to be more out in front, basking in the spotlight. As children, it was typically important for Social Threes to "show" something, to look good and demonstrate competence in doing things, to get love. Support most likely came in the form of an approving "look" from parents.

Social Threes are socially brilliant. They know how to talk to people and how to climb the social ladder. These Threes feel a need to frame words carefully to get the maximum benefit, which is measured in terms of making the right impression, getting what they want, and reaching their goals. Their fuel is social success, though what exactly constitutes "success" can vary depending on the history and context of the individual Social Three. Some show intelligence, culture, or class; others have degrees and titles; and others have material symbols of social status—a nice house, an expensive car, designer clothes, or expensive watches.

The Social Three is very concerned with competition and winning. This is the most competitive Three. They are also focused on power, whether or not they are the one who has it. They tend to be demanding and authoritarian, though these characteristics may be hidden behind a presentation that is smooth, decorous, and humorous. Social Threes may view others in terms of how they potentially further or block the process of reaching their goals. They look at things in terms of how they can exert control over them, and they don't allow themselves to be surprised by life.

The Social Three is also the most aggressive of the Threes, possessing a strong and assertive character. Because they are good at numbing out their feelings, they can—in the extreme—be cold.

Social Threes have a corporate mentality and a passion for doing the job in the best way it can be done—especially in terms of outward appearances. They think about what is best for the group, especially in terms of what will sell, what looks good, and what will reflect well on them. Doing what works for the group also works to further their image of success. For the Social Three, image and moneymaking may override good intentions or virtuous actions. In the current age, corporations are primarily oriented toward making money above all else, and this is reflected in the Social Three's concern with finding an efficient way to meet corporate goals and enhance the bottom line, which may or may not take into account the destructive consequences for others in a wider sense.

This Three also has a lot of confidence in leading a group where they want to go. If a leader is not leading a group well enough, the Social Three can feel a strong desire to take over, as it can be frustrating for them to see the way forward and not be able to guide people in a more efficient or successful way. The Social Three enjoys being at the center of things.

These Threes have a highly developed talent for image-making and a strong ability to sell themselves (or whatever product they might want to promote). According to Naranjo, these Threes look so good, there's almost a sense that they have no faults. It's hard to see their flaws because they do such a good job at creating the right image. They look so good and seem to do things so well that any sense of there being a problem or of anything being left out is overshadowed.

However, Social Threes do feel anxiety about being overexposed. They feel vulnerable to being seen as having no worth. Because they place so much importance on making a good impression, criticism can be devastating to them, though they aren't likely to show it. Wanting to look good also means it can be hard for them to fully reveal themselves to others, so they may feel a need to keep people at bay. They want so much to be seen positively, and so they can fear that people might see through their image if they get too close. It can be hard for them to open up and let up on managing their image. This strong need to look good can also prevent Social Threes from knowing and being connected to their real selves and their real feelings.

Social Threes aren't likely to be confused with other types, as this Three is in many ways the most obvious Three, especially in terms of how Threes have historically been characterized in Enneagram books.

William, a Social Three, speaks:

When I was young, I lived with my grandmother and hung out with the older guys. I wanted to be accepted by them because of the prestige that came with the image. Whenever they chose sides for football, I was one of the first players chosen. One day during an intense neighborhood game, I was playing quarterback. I called a rollout right fake double reverse pass. I was supposed to hit my cousin Robert on a post pattern but I faked the pass, pulled the ball down, and started to run. One guy had a good angle on me, but I was faster. As he got close to me I made a cut and went behind him and scored a touchdown. I heard one of the older guys say, "Damn, Sonny is good!" I felt drawn to the game because I knew it was something I could do well. The praise from the older guys confirmed what I needed to hear and made me feel special. After that day, socially and athletically, I knew I wanted to be at the top of the food chain.

I continued to excel at football and eventually became a professional in the NFL. As a running back people often asked me how I could I take the punishment play after play. When you play football on any level, you can't do it half-assed, you have to be all in or not at all. Some call it internal fortitude or guts, others may equate it to will...I call it heart! I learned that it took hard work to come back again and again and succeed at the game on the highest level, and I was prepared to do it. The desire for this sense of being "Somebody" that came with playing football was huge. To be a part of something bigger, to get results and achieve success on that big a stage, was the fuel that drove me. Years later, through therapy and learning the Enneagram, I've changed a lot. I've realized authentic self-acceptance doesn't come through what I do or how I look to others; it's an inside job.

The Sexual Three: "Charisma"

The victory or goal that the Sexual Three subtype is interested in (that expresses this Three's vanity) is one of sex appeal and beauty rather than money or prestige—but they are just as competitive in pursuing these goals as a business executive is in work matters. In this Three, vanity is not denied (as with the Self-Preservation Three) or embraced (like the Social Three); rather, it's somewhere in between, being employed in the service of creating an attractive image and promoting important others.

The Sexual Three is sweet and shy and not as extroverted as the Social Three—especially when it comes to speaking about himself. It's hard for these Threes to promote themselves, so they often put the focus on others they want to support.

Although they are just as capable as the other Threes of achieving worldly success through competence and hard work, these Threes don't feel the need to achieve goals in the external world because their focus is much more on pleasing and making themselves attractive as a way of earning love. They see their accomplishments in the successes and happiness of the people around them.

Although Ichazo called this type "Masculinity/Femininity," Naranjo explains that this is not Hollywood-style masculinity or femininity, or even necessarily a very sexualized masculinity or femininity. This type is more concerned with having an attractive presentation as a man or a woman—and, subtly at times, with pleasing others by being attractive in a classically masculine or feminine way. And while Threes are heart types, in this subtype the pleasing may occur less through emotional connection or sexual seductiveness and more through a mental connection or enthusiastic support. Naranjo changed the name to "Charisma" to reflect the special way Sexual Threes motivate and excite the admiration of others through a quality of "personal magnetism."[17]

Sexual Threes achieve within relationships. These Threes are pleasers and helpers; they tend to work hard in support of someone else, expending a lot of energy in promoting others. Sexual Threes can be very ambitious and hardworking, but it's always to make someone else look good. Often this Three doesn't seem like a Three because they are not so focused on their own status and achievement, but for them it's more about being attractive and supporting others—it's enough for them to be beautiful; they don't have to achieve to get love. It's the pleasing that brings approval or love, so they don't have to be conventional achievers.

Sexual Threes put a lot of energy into seducing and pleasing others. They may have a fear of disappointing others, and so they justify themselves with excuses to avoid confrontation. People with this subtype may have fantasies about the "ideal partner," and they may want to change their partner to be like they would like him or her to be. They may have fantasies of waiting for "Prince Charming" (or "Princess Charming") and living "happily ever after."

These Threes tend to be oriented toward pleasing others in the sense of having a family or team mentality. They may focus narrowly on what is good for the family (at home or at work) and project the image of someone who is good in this way.

Because so much depends on their being attractive to others, Sexual Threes think they need to be good and perfect to be loved. They tend to be very helpful to prove their lovability—they aspire to have the image of the "best lover" or the "perfect wife."

Attaining love or desire from others becomes a goal, an achievement, a conquest for Sexual Threes. To support this, they have a passion for projecting a handsome, pretty, or sexy image. They feel an urgent need to be looked at and recognized as attractive by people they want to attract (romantically)—perhaps reflecting a lack of attention and admiration from their mother or father.

In this Three there is a sense of disconnection from feelings and from the real self. They often have no real contact with themselves or others. This disconnection is emotional, sexual, and physical. One Three with this subtype commented, "it's like we put out an 'Out to Lunch' sign." This is the main issue for Sexual Threes. They typically experience a feeling of emptiness, like a void. This Three experiences an empty feeling in terms of having a lack of a clear sense of self or identity. This is related to the fact that the Sexual Three experiences difficulty in being, feeling, and expressing authentically. While they may be very attractive, they may also have low self-esteem and be unable to love themselves. In the face of this, they may "put on a good face" and look sweet and complacent while hiding their strength as a way to look good for others.

The Sexual Three is the most emotional of the Threes, so you are more likely to see them expressing their feelings. This Three doesn't wear the kind of social mask that a Social Three wears. There is a deep sadness within the Sexual Three. They often had a difficult early life, and they use "disconnection" from themselves as a way to forget, or to make up for and minimize, past abuses. There is a lot of fear of feeling emotional pain and sorrow, and so they learn to disconnect from their deeper emotional experience. They also experience criticism as very threatening, as it destroys their mask of being a "perfectly good person."

Sexual Threes can look like Twos or Sevens. They can look like Twos because they seek to connect with others through being pleasing and attractive. They differ from Twos, however, in that they focus more on a specific image of physical attractiveness and less on shape-shifting, prideful self-elevation, and meeting emotional needs. They may be mistaken for Sevens in that they tend to be positive and enthusiastic in their support of others. They can be excellent cheerleaders. However, while Sevens are fundamentally self-referencing, Threes reference others as a way of determining how to be. Threes are more disconnected from themselves, while Sevens typically know what they need and want.

Tadeo, a Sexual Three, speaks:

Ever since I can remember, I have always done things with the intention of attracting the attention of others. Though I was somewhat shy, it was easy for me to dazzle people. I learned to draw others in without talking. We don't have cheerleaders in Argentina, but if we did, I'd have been one for sure. I strived to be charismatic, loving, pleasing, enthusiastic, and above all, an exciting and desirable person everyone wanted to be around.

I have to admit that all my life I've only looked at myself through the mirror of others. And one thing was pretty clear to me: nobody liked the ugly. As a child, people used to say I was perfect, cute, and pretty. I was like a doll that my parents showed the world—but as time went by, they were so over-whelmed with their problems (and three more children) that they stopped looking at me; especially my mom. From then on, I developed an extreme intolerance for going unnoticed. I had a neurotic need to please and be liked, and a neurotic vulnerability to flattery that made me "sell myself" to anyone who said nice things to me. Many times I engaged in abusive relationships without noticing I was being abused.

Thus arose my mania to present only what was beautiful about me and hide anything others might consider ugly. This led to self-alienation and to living in a fantasy in which I was the star of a Hollywood film. At the same time, my constant focus on the outside created a sense of hollowness inside, a void within myself that was impossible to bear. Looking only at myself from the outside in, I became totally disconnected from myself to the point of not knowing what I felt at all. On the outside I could be charming, sweet, and seductive, but on the inside (and in intimate relationships) I was cold, uncaring, hard, and totally lacking in empathy.

Finding the "ideal" partner became an obsession. I cared about success, image, work, and all those other things we Threes typically care about, but they didn't mean anything to me if I didn't have someone to share them with. I deceived myself into thinking that love was the answer to everything.

When I began my spiritual journey, the two biggest issues I faced were the meaninglessness of my life and my inability to feel the effects of the abuse that I had suffered years earlier due to my physical, emotional, and sexual disconnection from myself. It was painful to realize that I was like a cheap Easter egg: decorated with frosting on the outside and completely hollow on the inside.

"The Work" for Type Three: Charting a Personal Growth Path

ULTIMATELY, AS THREES WORK ON THEMSELVES and become more self-aware, they learn to escape the trap of cutting themselves off from the love they want and crowding out their real feelings by slowing down, making room for the vulnerability of "just being," and getting in touch with their real self.

For all of us, waking up to habitual personality patterns involves making ongoing, conscious efforts to observe ourselves, reflect on the meaning and sources of what we observe, and actively work to counter automatic tendencies. Sometimes it can be hard for Threes to recognize the necessity of self-work because the defensive patterns of their personality are so aligned with what society values. They may not see that they have cultivated an image that blocks them from growing, because that image is so successful in convincing everyone of their "worth." For this reason, the Enneagram can be an important way of seeing through the surface appeal of their personality to its limiting nature.

For Threes, growth work involves observing the ways they amp up their "doing" to avoid feeling; exploring the ways they live through their image and lose touch with who they are beyond their persona; and making active efforts to access what they really think and feel separate from the impression they want to make on others. It is particularly important for them to learn to access their real feelings, balance out doing with being, and appreciate who they really are and not just the images they construct.

In this section I offer some ideas about what Threes can notice, reflect upon, and aim for in their efforts to grow beyond the constraints of their personality and embody the higher possibilities associated with their type and subtype.

Self-Observation: Dis-Identifying from Your Personality by Watching It in Action

Self-observation is about creating enough internal space to really watch—with fresh eyes and adequate distance—what you are thinking, feeling, and doing in your everyday life. As Threes take note of the things they think, feel, and do, they might look out for the following key patterns:

Working hard to support a (narrow) focus on tasks, goals, and achievement

Observe how you prioritize work tasks and goals to the exclusion of other elements of life. Notice what seems most important to you as you go through your day and observe how attached you are to your "list of things to do." Note how driven you are to get to your goals, and what kinds of things you do to clear your path of obstacles. Observe your competitive tendencies and be honest with yourself about how important winning is and to what lengths you will go to be the best. Observe what role achievement plays in your everyday life and what you do to reach your goals.

Constructing and maintaining a specific image to impress others

Observe all the ways you evaluate your audience for the clues you use to design the right image. Notice when you need attention, and what it's about. Note how you strategize to construct a specific image. What kinds of things do you think about? What kinds of things do you do to manage your presentation? How might you falsify yourself (present yourself in ways that differ from what you really think or do) to conform to the image you want others to have of you? Observe how you feel when you succeed in getting a positive response to your image from others.

Doing without stopping to avoid feeling

Observe the pace at which you work and the ways you try to keep moving and avoid slowing down. Note when you speed up your activity level and what might be happening that drives that intensification of "doing." Notice what you do to avoid having any gaps in your schedule that might allow feelings to surface, and note any anxiety you feel if you have an inadvertent gap in activity. If there is a slowdown and feelings come up, notice what that experience is like and how you respond. Observe what happens inside you if or when feelings do arise. What is that like? Or, if you never (or almost never) allow deeper feelings to surface, note how you suppress them and what motivates you to keep your feelings at bay.

Self-Inquiry and Self-Reflection: Gathering More Data to Expand Your Self-Knowledge

As Threes observe these and other related patterns in themselves, the next step on the Enneagram growth path is to *understand* these patterns more. Why do they exist? Where do they come from? What purpose do they serve? How do they get you in trouble when they are intended to help you? Often, seeing the root causes of a habit—why it exists and what it is designed to do—is enough to allow you to break out of the pattern. In other cases, with more entrenched habits, knowing how and why they operate as defenses can be a first step to eventually being able to release them.

Here are some questions that Threes can ask themselves, and some possible answers they can consider to get more insight into the sources, operation, and consequences of these patterns:

How and why did these patterns develop? How do these habits help Type Threes cope?

Through understanding the sources of their defensive patterns and how they operate as coping strategies, Threes have the opportunity to become more aware of how and why they work so hard to achieve and maintain a particular image to attract attention and admiration. If Threes can tell the story of their early life and look for the reasons that motivate their drive to achieve and manage their image—perhaps to prove their value through an active implementation of a desired self-image—they can have more compassion for themselves and recognize how these patterns serve deeper needs. When Threes gain insight into why they work so hard and strive to look so good, it can help them see how these strategies operate as a protection, but also how they keep Threes trapped in a limited "acorn-self," even if their acorn shells look really shiny and attractive.

What painful emotions are the Type Three patterns designed to protect me from?

For all of us, the personality operates to protect us from painful emotions, including what psychological theorist Karen Horney calls our "basic anxiety"— a preoccupation with the emotional stress of not getting basic needs fulfilled. Threes adopt a strategy that allows them to avoid and "numb out" painful emotions so that they don't threaten their ability to work hard and achieve goals. Aside from impatience and anger, some Threes may not feel much at all. Difficult feelings related to needing attention and not getting it, not being *seen* in positive ways for who they are, and having to earn love can be conveniently bypassed through an unswerving focus on doing. By only acknowledging and expressing "correct" feelings, Threes steer clear of consciously attending to any feelings related to inadequacy or loneliness. By living for and from a desired self-image, Threes avoid real contact with the deeper part of themselves and the painful emotions that motivated their defensive patterns of doing and impressing in the first place.

Why am I doing this? How do the Type Three patterns operate in me now?

Through self-observation, the three kinds of Threes can begin to have a greater awareness of how and why their defensive patterns happen in everyday life—and in the present moment. If they can consciously catch themselves in the act of speeding up to stay away from their own emotions, or lying to themselves (or others) about who they are to maintain their outward appearance, they can reflect upon how these patterns work to keep them on task and focused on the central concerns of the defensive tendencies of their personality. If they can tap into their underlying needs for approval and admiration, they can see how their habits of looking good and being effective keep them focused on the limited goals of their "acorn-self:" staying safe through maintaining a positive sense of themselves (based on social consensus).

What are the blind spots of these patterns? What do Type Threes keep themselves from seeing?

As part of the self-reflection process, it will be important for Threes to remind themselves about what they *don't* see when their personality programming is driving the show. When Threes are caught up in compulsive doing, they distract themselves from seeing all of who they really are, which is actually more worthy of love and admiration, though they don't see this either. Threes actively keep themselves from seeing the inherent value of their own feelings, their human vulnerabilities, and their desire to connect with others in an authentic way. Perhaps because Threes' defensive patterns line up so perfectly with the values of Western culture, it can be difficult for them to see the flaw in the strategy of proving yourself through achieving and fitting whatever image garners the most admiration. Threes may be so blinded by the effectiveness of their own work ethic and image management that they totally miss the beauty and power of their real selves.

What are the effects or consequences of these patterns? How do they trap me?

The irony of the Three strategy is that by trying to win others' approval through hard work and the manipulation of their appearance, they actually distance themselves from the people they want to impress. It can be very enlightening for Threes to understand how their drives to achieve and look good actually keep them from expressing more of what's really true (and inherently good) about themselves. Threes can grow through seeing how the defensive patterns that seem so right in the eyes of society—working hard, gaining high status, and appearing attractive—actually hold them back from receiving the deep appreciation they really crave. By not living from a felt sense of who they really are, Threes trap themselves in the surface appeal of their acorn shells and prevent the oak tree of all that they can become from emerging. And they can be so convinced of the effectiveness of their socially sanctioned strategies that they may not even know what they are missing.

Self-Development:
Aiming for a Higher State of Consciousness

For all of us who seek to wake up, the next step in working with type-based knowledge of the personality is to begin to inject more conscious effort into everything we do—to begin to actively think, feel, and act with more choice and awareness. In this section I provide some ideas for Threes about "what to do" after they've observed their key patterns and done some investigation into their sources, operation, and consequences.

This last section is divided into three parts, each corresponding to one of three distinct growth processes connected with the Enneagram system: 1) "what to do" to actively counter the automatic patterns described above in the "self-observation" section; 2) how to use the Enneagram's Inner Flow arrow lines as a map of growth; and 3) how to study your passion (or "Vice") and consciously seek to embody its opposite, the antidote, the higher "Virtue" of the type.

The Three Main Type Three Personality Patterns:
"What to Do" to Address Them

Working hard to support a (narrow) focus on tasks, goals, achievement, and success

Embrace failure as a road to deepening your experience of yourself. Failure can feel intolerable to Threes, as it undercuts their whole coping strategy of earning love by achieving success and winning. If you are a Three, try to make some room to consider more thoroughly what might happen if you fail—how you would feel and what you would think and what you would do. And watch out for efforts to do a workaround—really try to confront what the possibility of failure means to you. And if you do experience a failure, have compassion for yourself around it; instead of seeing it as a bad thing, see it as an opportunity to be with your vulnerability and let in what you spend so much energy avoiding. Try to experience the feelings you have in response to failure more consciously.

Reframe your definition of success. Allow yourself to question your assumptions about what constitutes success. Open up to the idea that you can and should be loved for who you really are, not just for what you accomplish or for the outward, material signs of your success. Explore what you really want when you are competing to win or achieving as a way of attracting positive attention. Consider what a deeper sense of success might mean in terms of your need for love and acceptance, and allow yourself to move in that direction. Recognize that truer, more satisfying forms of "value" are achieved through authenticity, not status and worldly achievements.

Notice what gets left out when you are driving toward your goal. When Threes are focused on an important goal, they can put laser-like attention on what needs to happen to get to their desired result. While this can be a strength in many ways, it can also cause them to avoid paying attention to important facets of their experience, like what might be happening in their internal world that might impede their progress.

Constructing and maintaining a specific image to impress others

Question your focus on what others value as the basis for who you think you are. As Naranjo notes, Threes suffer from an identity problem. They may have the sense that they don't know who they are beyond their roles and tangible characteristics. And separate from pleasing others and performing effectively, they may not know what they want.[18] Although Threes may not actively worry about not knowing who they are, their defensive patterns represent a displacement of the inner sense of being with an outer search for approval; therefore, it can be helpful to them to examine the ways in which they construct an identity based on external ideals—to consciously question their use of specific values and characteristics as guiding principles in how they decide to design their public face.

Discern the difference between actions motivated by image-making purposes and those that address real needs and desires. Locate and solidify your sense of your real self by becoming more aware of when you do things for image-based reasons. Regularly ask yourself, "Am I doing this because I really want to, or because I believe it will enhance my image?" As Threes become more and more aware of their real feelings, needs, and desires, they will need to seek support in accepting and embracing who they really are, especially when it differs from what they think their image should be. It can help Threes to hear from others that they appreciate them even more when they take the risk to feel their feelings and express more of who they are.

Discover who you are separate from your image. With so much attention and energy going toward the development of your image, it can be difficult to realize that this image does not equal your total self. Actively practice discerning the difference between your image and who you really are. Work to ask and answer the question, "Who am I if I'm not my image?" Remind yourself that you don't have to give up your successes in life to manifest more of who you really are; you can be successful both in the world and on a deeply personal level. Reckon with any fears you might have about not being accepted by the world if you allow yourself to show up without the protection of a social mask. Remember that you can locate your real self through the channels of your emotions, your needs, and your vulnerabilities, and that what you might consider to be weaknesses can be sources of strength. Your "oak tree–Self" is fertilized when you embrace the power of your authentic emotions and your willingness to reveal who you really are.

Remember that only the real you can be present to receive love and acceptance. While you may think you are seeking love by creating an image, people want to experience and love the real you, not an attractive construction that stands in the way of you.

Doing without stopping to avoid feeling

Don't wait for a breakdown to alert you to the need for growth. Many times, Threes don't recognize the need for self-work until they experience a big failure or a breakdown of some kind. This can take the form of an unexpected bout of depression, when their deeper feelings of sadness or loneliness break through their relentless habit of doing. Or it can come in the form of a physical illness or a sense of "hitting a wall" when they finally exhaust themselves completely. Sometimes something objectively troubling happens, and they can't access their feelings in response to it. If you are a Three, notice and actively question your total focus on doing before that happens—especially if you are already feeling stress related to depression, exhaustion, or emotional numbness. Take the risk of asking for support from others who may not be able to see what you need because your image hides the fact that you are in trouble.

Reclaim and value your feelings. Notice how you avoid some feelings but not others. Allow yourself to be curious when you aren't feeling your emotions:

why do you avoid feeling, and what might you feel if you welcomed your emotions? Notice if doing accelerates when emotions threaten. Consciously allow yourself the time and space to access, own, and experience your emotions fully. Notice any fear and anxiety this brings up, and find the support you need to work through it. Keep an eye out for any loneliness that you might (understandably) feel related to the chronic frustration of having to be for others or the fact that whatever successes you have can be credited to a false self and manipulation.[19] Open up to seeing how fear drives you, whether it be a fear of failure, of exposure, or of rejection.

Increase your ability to just "be." For Threes, developing an ability to feel and "be" is part of the larger process of getting in touch with the real self. Challenge yourself by trying to meditate, or try to not do anything at all—just sit there and look out the window. If this is difficult, allow yourself to experience how difficult it is and think about why it is so challenging. Remind yourself that the real you shouldn't be measured or evaluated by how much you do—that it's much more important to allow for more being and less doing, because it will allow you to access your true ("oak tree") self.

The Inner Flow for Type Three: Using the Arrow Lines to Chart Your Growth Path

In Chapter 1, I introduced an Inner Flow model of the arrow lines that define one dimension of the dynamic movement within the Enneagram framework. The connections and flow between each core Type, its "growth-through-stress" point, and its "child-heart-security" point map one kind of growth path described by the symbol. As a reminder, the arrow lines can be seen to suggest one kind of growth path for each type:

- The direction from the core point along the arrow is the path of higher development. The "growth–stress" point ahead represents specific challenges perfectly suited to expanding the narrow focus of our core point personality.
- The direction against the arrow from the core point to the "child–heart" point indicates issues and themes from childhood that must be consciously acknowledged and owned so that we can move forward and not be held back by unfinished business from the past. This "child–heart" point represents qualities of security we unconsciously repressed, occasionally fall back into as a comfort in times of stress, and now must reintegrate consciously.

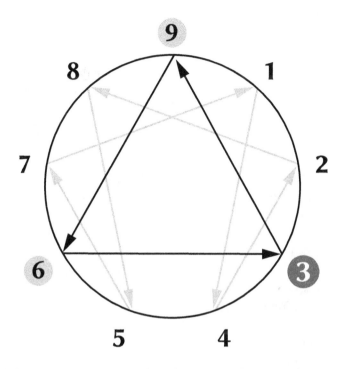

Type Three Moving Forward to Type Nine: Consciously Using the Nine "Growth–Stress" Point for Development and Expansion

The Inner Flow growth path for Type Threes brings them into direct contact with the challenges embodied in Type Nine: allowing for being without doing, prioritizing others and not just goals and tasks, and being connected to people without losing yourself. Threes can find the move to Nine difficult, and they often go there unconsciously in times of stress when they have worked themselves to the point of collapse. But considered consciously, Threes can use the Nine Point as a path of growth by learning to be more in their bodies, to include different points of view when completing a task, and to slow down and broaden their focus of attention. Nines are particularly good at "going with the flow," and Threes are not usually happy unless they are directing the flow and controlling progress toward a goal. Threes can use the Nine Point to consciously let go of their need to control things—to have things move forward at a certain pace in a certain way—and allow themselves to follow others more.

The Three working consciously in this way can make ready use of the tools healthy Type Nines use: a reliance on inclusion and consensus as important factors in getting the job done well, an ability to follow others' lead and not always have to be the center of attention, and a sense of "gut knowing" as a way to direct their efforts. The ability of conscious Nines to take "right action" based on both deeply understanding others' perspectives and taking their own gut knowing into account in directing forward movement can balance out the Three's tendency to forge ahead and rush toward a goal without stopping to consider a wider range of opinions. The more passive stance of Type Nine can usefully counter the active approach usually taken by Threes. And Nines' ability to relax and just be helps Threes learn how to slow down the doing and risk being.

Type Three Moving Back to Type Six: Consciously Using the "Child–Heart" Point to Work through Early Issues and Find Security in Support of Moving Forward

The path of growth for Type Threes calls for them to reclaim their ability to access their fears as a way of slowing down to more carefully consider the path to their goal. In response to a lack of protection early on, Threes often became doers, even if this required them to bury their anxieties as a way of finding security. Young Threes may have felt like they didn't have the luxury of feeling their fear, so they coped by getting active to accomplish things. A conscious return to Six can be a way for them to allow themselves to get in touch with the fears and concerns that can force them to slow their pace in helpful ways. Pausing to reflect on potential threats and problems gives them more space to pay attention to their feelings and intuitions. For these reasons, "moving back to Six" can be a healthy way for Threes to make space for thinking through more aspects of their plans than they usually leave time for.

Navigated consciously, a Three can use the move to Six to re-establish a healthy balance between moving forward and pausing for reflection. They can consciously insert a healthy round of questioning before moving ahead so quickly, and they can make sure to assess what is happening at a deeper level than they normally do. Focusing on what they are afraid of can be a way for Threes to tap into a deeper emotional level within themselves, which can also be a way to highlight their need to allow for support from others. Threes can relax more if they don't always need to be the one in control and can call on the high side of Six to have more faith in others, allowing someone else to take the lead in solving problems and providing protection. Questioning and self-doubt can be good for Threes in that it opens up a channel to the vulnerability they often hide behind an image of self-confidence.[20] All of these efforts to increase awareness of the move to Six can provide Threes with a grounding in a deeper sense of themselves that will better equip them in their forward progress toward the high side of Type Nine.

The Vice to Virtue Conversion:
Accessing Vanity and Aiming for Hope

The developmental path from Vice to Virtue is one of the central contributions of the Enneagram map in highlighting a usable "vertical" path of growth to a higher state of awareness for each type. In the case of Type Three, the Vice (or passion) of the type is vanity, and its opposite, the Virtue, is *hope*. The theory of growth communicated by this "Vice to Virtue conversion" is that the more we can be aware of how our passion functions within our personality and consciously work toward the embodiment of its opposite, the more we can free ourselves from the unconscious habits and fixated patterns of our type and evolve toward our "higher" side.

The work of Type Three centers around becoming more and more conscious of how different forms of vanity play a role in shaping the focus of attention and patterns of their personality. After Threes become more familiar with their experience of vanity and develop the ability to make it more conscious in everyday life, they can make further efforts to focus on enacting their Virtue, the "antidote" to the passion of vanity. In the case of Type Three, the Virtue of hope represents a state of being that they can attain through consciously manifesting their higher capacities.

Hope is a state of trust that all will be okay, that everything will work out. It is an experience of optimism, "an attitude of joyous openness and trusting receptivity to what the unfolding of Being presents to us."[21] In the "Paradise" section of Dante's *Divine Comedy*, the Pilgrim goes a step further in terms of the certainty that hope connotes when he states, "Hope is sure expectancy of future bliss."[22] Hope is the letting go of the egoic need to push things forward and see results, and the knowledge and trust that good things are going to happen.

Spiritual teacher and author A. H. Almaas further explains that hope is "the realization that Reality 'does itself,' independent of our imaginary autonomy."[23] As Type Threes learn to see their vanity in action as a way of controlling the way things happen and managing the way they appear to others, they can begin to work against their need to control the flow of things to achieve and impress and then they can relax into an experience of hope. This means they start to understand that the process of life will unfold as it will—that they don't need to rush it along or "do" so much. When driven by vanity, Threes know how to further their own interests, but implicitly don't trust that things will work out of their own accord or develop naturally.[24] When they understand the true meaning of the Virtue of hope, they can relax and stop working so hard, as hope inspires a sense of optimism and trust that what they desire will be fulfilled if they can stop doing and be receptive to the natural flow of things.

To embody hope as a Three means you are able to loosen your need for control, your need to force specific results, and your need to manage others' vision of who you are. It means you are open and receptive to what happens, because you have a sense of knowing that things will function as they should according to creative forces that we can't always see or understand. If we have hope, and if we can allow ourselves to let go and harmonize with the flow of things rather than take action according to the ego's preconceived notions of what works best, we can take a rest from all our efforting and still be fulfilled in the end. Hope is the antidote to vanity, because whereas vanity seeks to control events to serve the needs of the personality, hope allows us to see from a higher perspective—allows us to trust that everything will be okay.

Specific Work for the Three Type Three Subtypes on the Path from Vice to Virtue

The path from observing your passion to finding its antidote is not exactly the same for each of the subtypes. The path of conscious self-work has been characterized in terms of "grit, grind, and grace:"[25] the "grit" of our personality programming, the "grind" of our efforts to grow, and the "grace" that comes to us from doing our work in conscious and positive ways. Each subtype has to grind, or exert effort, against something slightly different. This insight is one of the great benefits of understanding the character of the three distinct subtypes of each of the nine types.

Self-Preservation Threes can travel the path from vanity to hope by slowing down and making room for experiencing more than just what's on their "to-do list." They aim for hope by leaving themselves more space to feel, and to express those feelings, so that they can tap into the rhythms of their own inner experience. As a Self-Preservation Three, it is important to notice when you create rationalizations for not allowing space for deeper emotions and relational needs. Allow yourself to find security through deep connections with other people, not just by relying on yourself and working hard. Allow yourself to realize that you don't have to be responsible for everything. Create safety through shared feelings of mutual trust, as opposed to going it alone and working so hard to be autonomous. Learn that your anxiety is a sign that you have deeper feelings and needs that aren't being addressed, and instead of working harder, take care of yourself by listening to your real self, allowing yourself to rest, and taking refuge in hope, the expectancy of future bliss that you don't have to make happen all by yourself. Allow yourself to be still, such that you can make room to have an experience of vulnerability and more of your true self.

Social Threes can travel the path from vanity to hope by making conscious use of setbacks, failures, and the experience of their own vulnerability to broaden their sense of who they really are. When Social Threes can relax their efforts to get recognition and learn to trust that people will see and appreciate their value if they just allow themselves to embrace more of who they are, they can release the need to control what happens and enter into an experience guided by hope. If you are a Social Three, aiming for hope means challenging any fears about exposure or rejection you might have and learning to see that you are much deeper and richer than your social mask permits you to be. Expressing more real feelings is an act of hope for this Three because it can be so hard to let go of an imagined or idealized self and risk that others will love who they really are. In line with this, it is important for this Three to see failures and setbacks as an invitation to a deeper experience of life—and a felt experience of the real self.

Sexual Threes can travel the path from vanity to hope by learning to live for themselves and not for a real or imagined partner. This Three moves toward hope by getting to know and experience more of their real self. People with this subtype are a paradox: beautiful, enthusiastic friends and supporters who don't love and support themselves the way they do others. This Three can move toward hope by learning to put the same faith and love toward their own self that they offer so generously to others. Launching an intensive search for the "real self"—finding a sense of identity and trusting that it will lead you in the right direction—is what hope is about for this Three. If you are a Sexual Three, consciously share your feelings with the people you support so well and know that hope will guide you toward establishing the deep connections you long for.

Conclusion

THE THREE POINT REPRESENTS THE WAY we all focus on and identify with a persona we mistake for our true self in a world that seems to reward a socially acceptable image. The Three path of growth shows us how to transform vanity into hope. By showing us the importance of learning to dis-identify from a limiting "acorn shell" personality, no matter how attractive or socially brilliant, the Three path of awakening through hope guides us in shaking off our outer coverings, breaking open to our real feelings, and becoming the "oak tree-Self" that we are meant to be. In each of the Type Three subtypes we see a specific character who teaches us what is possible when we can turn our vanity into a fully awake ability to let go of the need to manage how we appear in the eyes of others and just *be* through the alchemy of self-observation, self-development, and self-knowledge.

CHAPTER 10

The Point Two Archetype:
The Type, Subtypes, and Growth Path

Humility is not thinking less of yourself; it's thinking of yourself less.

—C. S. Lewis

TYPE TWO REPRESENTS THE ARCHETYPE of the person who seeks to please others as a way to evoke affection. The drive to win others' approval through indirect methods, such as seduction and strategic giving, is a way to obtain emotional and material support without having to ask for it. This strategy also provides a way to try to get others to take care of you while still defending yourself against the pain of having someone important reject a direct request to meet a need.

Twos can be of either gender, of course, but the Type Two archetype mirrors the Jungian concept of "anima," or the inner feminine. Jung described the anima as being like a "glamorous, possessive, moody, and sentimental seductress."[1] Related to the *Great Mother* or the *Great Goddess* archetypes, the archetypal feminine principle represents fundamental human ideas about the all-powerful, numinous woman who provides vital nourishment, and displays the feminine qualities of warmth, receptivity, softness, emotional sensitivity, and openness to the other.[2]

An element of this Two archetype can also be found in the caricature of the "Jewish mother" who is superficially selfless as a way to exercise emotional control over everyone close to her. It also fits the pattern of the classic "codependent"—the person who becomes addicted to supporting and enabling an addict. For each, below the surface, the giving is not an altruistic kind of helpfulness. These individuals find self-worth in being needed by those they value and (unconsciously) seek to get their own needs met in return. Their aid constitutes a strategic means of getting needs met through promises of reciprocal care, which sometimes involves promising more than can be delivered.[3]

Type Twos are thus the prototype for that part in all of us that adopts an elevated or idealized view of ourselves and our ability to make others like us. A tendency toward self-aggrandizement or self-inflation undergirds the Type Two's persona. Twos often appear boundlessly and indispensably generous, helpful, attractive, and supportive. The false self that Twos model is one seeking to create positive connections with others through an attractive and inviting front.

This false self engineers positive emotional alignment with people who then provide support for survival. Once a friendly relationship has been established, that human link may be used as a resource in a time of need. The Two archetype illustrates the idea that when you want something from others to support your well-being, "you can catch more flies with honey than with vinegar;" charm and helpfulness in the present provide a good groundwork for asking for favors in the future.

The natural strengths of Type Twos include their genuine ability to listen to others, empathize with their feelings, and meet their needs. They are usually cheerful, optimistic, warm, and friendly. Twos are naturally practiced in the art of using positive communication to create rapport. They can be very diplomatic and skilled at delivering messages in ways that people can hear. Twos' particular "superpower" is that they can be excellent friends and will often go to great lengths to take care of and support loved ones. Twos can also be driven and energetic, extremely competent people who get a lot of things done and strive to do things well, especially as a way to impress others.

As with all the archetypal personalities, however, Type Twos' gifts and strengths also represent their "fatal flaw" or "Achilles heel." Their focus on appearing to be powerful enough to "do anything" for others leads to self-inflation. This inflation is a form of pride—the passion of the Two. As we'll see, this pride also masks the Two's denial of the very needs that motivate seduction. As a result, they end up denying their own needs and losing a clear sense of how they really feel.

Twos can be upbeat, friendly, and genuinely giving. But at times they may get in their own way by overdoing their focus on shape-shifting to please others. For instance, Twos can't help imagining that other people are as sensitive to criticism as they are. So they may sugarcoat or shade the truth out of a fear of hurting someone. Other times, a Two's cheeriness can feel false, as it sometimes functions as an overcompensation to mask sadness, resentment, or disappointment.

To fully understand this archetype, it is important to understand the darker side of this "pleasing" character, who is similar to the beautiful, seductive, yet dangerous *femme fatale*. The help and support that Twos provide is *strategic* aid, though they are not always aware of their underlying motives. Reciprocity is the key to this survival strategy. Twos operate on the usually unspoken assumption that "if I take care of you, you will take care of me."

The Type Two Archetype in Homer's *Odyssey*: Calypso

At the beginning of *The Odyssey*, Odysseus is stranded on Calypso's island. It is the penultimate place he visits before he arrives home. As he tells his story, we learn that this island is the eighth location Odysseus has traveled to on his journey home after the Trojan War.

Homer describes Calypso as a "shining goddess," a "queenly nymph," and "bright among goddesses."[4] She is beautiful and elegantly feminine. Calypso is the archetypal nurturer. She pampers Odysseus, giving him the best food and supplying him with everything he needs. But she also wants something from Odysseus: she doesn't want him to leave. Odysseus wants to go home to his wife, Penelope, but Calypso wants to marry him and make him immortal like she is.

Until Zeus himself orders Calypso to let Odysseus go home, she detains him in her island paradise, providing him with all manner of sensuous pleasures. Her goal is to seduce him into giving up his dream of homecoming. Her support and hospitality are extraordinary, but they also imprison Odysseus. How could he want to return to his mortal wife, when he could have an immortal goddess? Why would he want to undergo the many hardships he has to endure to get home, when he could be the lord of Calypso's household and be immortal? Under the guise of helping, she wants to control him and own him forever.[5] But because Calypso's main motive in the relationship is something she wants for herself rather than the true interest of the other person, she can't get what she really needs.

When Calypso finally allows Odysseus to leave, she shows the high side of the Two archetype. With the understanding that he is leaving her, she nonetheless helps him prepare for his journey. With no strings attached, and knowing that he will not be reciprocating as she has wanted him to, she is finally able to love him in a more genuine way.

The Type Two Personality Structure

As PART OF THE "HEART-BASED" or "emotion-based" triad of types, the personality structure of the Two is associated with the emotion of *sadness* or *grief.* Twos have a focus on creating a specific *image* of themselves. Each of the heart type personalities (Two, Three, and Four) relate to other people primarily through emotional empathy. The "feeling sense" these types share gives these individuals a heightened need to connect with others and an ability to read interpersonal situations well on the emotional-relational level. Relationships are in the foreground of their attention, and so the heart types are especially aware of the image they believe they need to present to attract the love or approval of others.

While Type Fours overdo an attachment to grief, and Type Threes underdo grief, Twos are in conflict with their sadness.

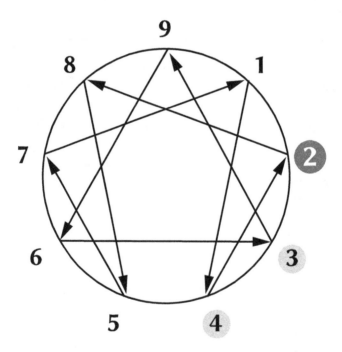

The sadness at the core of the heart type personalities reflects their feeling of not being loved for who they really are and their grief over having lost touch with their real selves. They've disowned who they really are and created a specific image to try to get the love (or approval) they need. All three of the heart types have core issues related to unmet needs to be deeply seen, accepted, and loved for who they are. Their respective coping strategies are designed to gain approval from other people in three distinct ways as a substitute for the love they seek but fear they can't get as they are. While Threes create an image of achievement and success, and Fours present themselves as unique and special, Twos strive to have a likable, pleasing image.

Pleasing the important people in their lives seems like the route to survival and success to Twos, who use their "heart intelligence" to actively and automatically (without thinking) "read" the people around them and align with what they perceive as their moods, needs, and preferences.[6] In lining up with or trying to create a connection with others by meeting their needs and accommodating their feelings, Twos strive to achieve positive relations with important others to support their sense of well-being.

Type Two is sometimes called "The Giver" or "The Helper," but they don't offer their "help" consistently or unconditionally to just anyone. Fundamental to this type is an often-unconscious habit of strategic giving to make people indebted to them. Twos naturally feel compelled to give to others, and they often believe they do so in a sincere and straightforward way. But the pattern of this personality is to give as part of a calculus in the service of seduction, self-elevation, and self-interest. Self-awareness for them involves recognizing how much of their giving reflects insecurity about their own perceived worth and lovability, rather than a simple desire to help without expectation of reward.

Understanding this dynamic of insecurity and "giving to get" puts us in touch with the sadness at the core of the Type Two character. For these individuals, this sorrow comes from having the sense that they are not loved for who they are but for what they do for others.

Like Calypso, Twos can free themselves from this pattern by humbly giving up their power to seduce others into meeting their needs. When they do so, they reveal the graciousness of true generosity and open up the possibility of receiving the love they have longed to know.

The Early Coping Strategy: Type Two
The archetypal story of the Two begins with an experience, often very early in childhood, of some crucial need not being met. For instance, this history often includes inexperienced or overwhelmed caregivers failing to provide some aspects of basic love and care. This failure could include all kinds of basic needs, but especially early emotional needs, like the need to feel recognized and loved unconditionally.

From this experience of unfulfilled need, Twos adapt to others based on the idea that their needs are too much for other people and that they can't be loved as they are. Twos develop a survival strategy in which they repress their needs in favor of tuning in to the needs of others. The effort of being super-supportive of others, they hope, will motivate others to meet their unstated needs in reciprocal fashion.

The whole Two personality can be seen as a strategic defense against the humiliation of having to acknowledge need. Twos' early experience that their needs are "too much" causes them to subconsciously conclude that because their needs are neglected, they themselves are somehow not worthy of love or care. From then on, any open refusal of need fulfillment can revive the early psychic pain caused by those needs going unsatisfied in the first place. Twos experience this refusal as humiliation because it confirms their image of themselves as unworthy.

This initial scenario also leads the Two to develop a range of unconscious strategies to get their needs met through indirect means so they can avoid the painful experience of their needs (and their "self") being directly rejected. On one hand, asking for needs to be met seems unthinkable to the Two, as it seems sure to invite further rejection. On the other hand, the Two finds that repressing these needs seems to both reduce the internal pressure of unmet need and make them easier for others to be around. (Thus, a Two might think: "If this person I want to connect with doesn't like angry people, I just won't be angry!" or "If the parent that I need to take care of me doesn't like sad people, I will get rid of my sadness.") By becoming what others want them to be in order to gain their approval or affection, the Two builds a personal network of positive connections to (hopefully indirectly) meet the needs they have so carefully hidden from view.

This early coping strategy protects the Two, but at considerable cost. Underneath their upbeat and friendly exterior, Twos often feel a deep sense of sadness that comes from believing that they are unlovable. This puts Twos in the unfortunate position of needing to disown parts of themselves to ensure that others like them. This habit of repressing needs can make Twos sensitive or even averse to being dependent on others, even in normal, nonintrusive ways. But as flattering and supporting others to earn love or approval becomes habitual, the Two gradually becomes more and more defended against the risk of potential rejection, and less and less able to open up and receive love from others in a genuine way.

Chris, a Type Two, describes his childhood situation and the development of his coping strategy:

I was an only child and the only grandchild on my father's side of the family. My grandparents took care of me a lot when I was very young because both of my parents worked full time. Two years after I was born, my parents and I moved out of the United States to pursue better economic opportunities overseas. This move involved leaving my father's extended family and moving to Greece. When we moved back to the U.S. again seven years later, I had to leave behind my mother's extended family that had raised me from the time I was two until I was nine.

While I don't recall consciously feeling the pain of specific unmet needs, I know that being passed to different grandparents, not always having my parents around to take care of me, and losing the support of two different sets of caretakers before the age of ten had an effect on me. On the one hand, I got a lot of attention because I was an only child, but on the other hand, I think I may have felt rejected or abandoned when my parents weren't around and when I had to leave people (twice) whom I had come to depend on.

My mother is a very critical Type One and my father is a very protective Type Eight. From early on, I adopted a strategy of pleasing people, primarily through entertainment (I could—and still do!—sing at the drop of a hat). This ensured I was the center of attention (and not ignored) and bonded to others in some way. (It also was my way of distracting people from the loud political arguments du jour.) I projected a happy exterior and learned to control my own anger based on the coaching my mom would give my Eight father—but this "tempering the temper" advice also caused me to hide or squelch my negative emotions. Not expressing negative feelings was also reinforced by my grandmother, who was always concerned about "what the neighbors would think."

As an only child raised primarily around adults. I was encouraged to be independent and self-sufficient. In elementary school, I always carried extra supplies to offer to other classmates. I often felt like an outsider—because I had grown up in another country and was the new kid who spoke with a foreign accent—and so tried to make friends by offering these gifts of supplies to anyone who might need them. I quickly lost the British accent I had acquired living abroad as I wanted to conform to the dominant culture to be accepted. Being nice, helpful, and generous was the only way I could come up with to get along with everyone and have them like me. I also hid my homosexuality because I didn't have any role models to let me know that it was possible to be gay and still be liked and accepted. To that end, I even waited until I had moved out of my parents' house to come out to them, for fear of being rejected by them while I was still living there (and so still needed them).

The Main Type Two Defense Mechanism: Repression

When there is suffering, an anesthetic serves a purpose.[7] The Two's primary defense mechanism is *repression*, which operates like a kind of psychological anesthetic. Repression consigns specific perceptions or emotions to unconsciousness. It helps to insulate a person's psyche from a deeper source of pain so that the personality can keep the person functioning. Repression leaves the wound untouched, but the person is able to tolerate it—unfortunately, other feelings, not just pain and humiliation, get anesthetized in the process.

Twos habitually repress feelings that might impede achieving a connection with important others. For instance, Twos often repress their anger because they believe it may create a separation from—or, worse yet, prompt disapproval from—their loved ones.

Put another way, when a Two experiences an internal conflict between what they are feeling or thinking and what they believe they need to present to form a connection with an important person, they will repress their real thought or feeling to protect the relationship. They appear to "get rid of" the parts of themselves they believe someone won't like. This habit is why some people can experience Twos as fake or inauthentic, especially in charged situations.

Repression is the defense mechanism that automatically anesthetizes Twos from the pain of early needs not being met. It is also the mechanism for pushing unappealing emotions like sadness, anger, and envy out of sight in the hope that others will meet the needs and desires they are too proud to express. As what is repressed inevitably leaks out, however, Twos can often be experienced as "needy" by those who can observe this leakage in ways that Twos can't because their disowned needs have become a "blind spot" (or Shadow element) of their personality.

The Type Two Focus of Attention

It is important to note that Twos focus their attention on key people and relationships without really "deciding" to do so; rather, they tend to "read" people and pay attention to their needs and feelings automatically. Twos also habitually focus on managing their own presentation based on what they think other people will like. Twos are shape-shifters, and the shape they shift into depends on the data they collect from reading the people they want to attune to. For instance, if someone a Two wants to be closer to likes baseball, they will highlight the fact that they also like baseball, and they may even study up on what is going on in the world of baseball.

Since energy follows attention, Twos end up putting a lot of energy into meeting others' needs and suppressing their own. This outward focus on others draws Twos' attention away from their own internal experience (feelings, needs, desires) and their own "sense of self." Twos often lack a clear sense of their own emotions, needs, and preferences, but they can easily read and tune in to the emotions, needs, and preferences of others.

Even though they prioritize positive connections with important others, Twos can end up not being very present in their "closest" relationships. Their focus is on *doing for others* and *seducing the as-yet-unseduced*, not on being who they are and being present in their own experience of life and relationships. Thus, paradoxically, others can find these "Givers" preoccupied or unavailable for genuine personal contact in important moments. They focus much time and energy on achieving relationships, but Twos often feel they can't risk being present to enjoy them.

It would be a mistake to assume that all generosity and service Twos offer is strategic. Likewise, though, we can't overlook the amount of attention Twos consciously devote to winning friends and cultivating influence. Twos are good at finding ways to get what they want, often indirectly, through manipulation. Or prevarication. Or even creative orchestration. Twos can be quite bossy and powerful at times, especially when stressed, when operating behind the scenes, or when secure with those around them.

The Type Two Emotional Passion: Pride

Pride is the passion—the specific emotional motivation—of the Type Two. "Pride" in this sense does not mean the healthy, good feeling we have about ourselves as when we "take pride in" a job well done. Rather it is the false pride of self-inflation we know as one of the Seven Deadly Sins. Naranjo describes the passion of pride as "a passion for the aggrandizement of the self-image."[8] Pride as a "passion" is the unconscious need to puff yourself up so you can be exactly what other people want or need. Sandra Maitri observes, "our pride rests upon valuing ourselves and investing energy into how we would like to *see* ourselves—our idealized self-image—rather than perceiving ourselves directly, as we really are."[9]

If you are a Two, seeing pride in yourself can be tricky at first. It can be hard for Twos just learning their type to see that "the pride system" goes in two directions: inflation and deflation. Often, Twos are more conscious of feeling insecure and wanting approval (and never getting enough), than they are of inflating their self-image or taking on more than they can handle.

On the inflated side, Twos feel prideful when they believe they are able to meet everybody's needs. Consequently, Twos take on more and more responsibility for making others happy, even when they feel burdened or exhausted. They tend to think, "it's easier to do more than disappoint someone by saying 'no.'" Twos build up their own confidence by telling themselves that they can meet many needs—though not their own needs, which they ignore.

Over time, Twos may recognize the pride underlying the sense of power they feel from their imagined capacity to meet everyone's needs and the sense of superiority that goes along with not having conscious needs themselves. Pride manifests itself in Type Twos as a feeling of power in independence—a fantasy that they do not need to depend on the very people they have manipulated into depending on them.

When pridefully inflated, Twos see themselves as supercompetent, ready and able to handle anything. This pride-inspired vision of indispensability reflects the survival strategy of needing to be more than you are to compensate for the fear that you are really less than what others see in you.

The tendency for Twos to inflate their self-image with a fantasy of attractiveness or indispensability eventually runs into a reality that doesn't square with this puffed-up, false sense of self. Since "what goes up must come down," deflation results, and Twos adopt a diminished image of themselves as being excessively flawed and totally inadequate or unattractive in the eyes of others. When criticism, rejection, exposure, or failure punctures the Two's inflated prideful stance, Twos may feel embarrassed that they ever entertained a puffed-up or enhanced version of themselves.

In unconscious Twos, this regret helps repression submerge the pride underlying the pattern, resetting it for the next cycle of inflation.

The Type Two Cognitive Mistake:
"To Get You Must Give" or "People Only Like People Who are Relentlessly Likable"

In Chapter 1 we discussed the idea that, for each of us, personality manifests in all three of our centers of intelligence. We all get stuck in habitual ways of thinking that influence our beliefs, feelings, and actions, and this continues even after the mental models that create our overall perspective aren't accurate anymore. While the passion shapes the personality's emotional motivations, the "cognitive mistake" is the pattern preoccupying the personality's thought processes.[10]

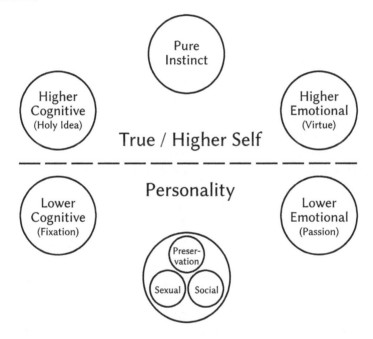

Type Twos' cognitive mistake centers on the underlying assumption that they have to seduce others into liking them. Conversely, they may think that it is "selfish" to focus on their own needs and desires. Long after they've left the early environment where their own needs weren't seen, in which they first learned to focus on others' needs, Type Twos retain the belief that responding to others' needs is good and expressing your own needs is bad.

These habitual ways of thinking form early in life and are difficult to change. They served a vital protective function for the developing self. But like the acorn shell inhibits the acorn's growth, Twos inhibit their own growth by staying within the confines of these habitual patterns of thought, even when the evidence suggests they should do otherwise.

Here are some key beliefs and assumptions characteristic of the Type Two personality. They reflect different aspects of the cognitive mistake that leads Twos to assume that they will not be lovable unless they work hard to earn value through supporting others:

- I am not lovable as I am.
- I can only get affection or care by seducing others into relationship through meeting their needs and being the person they want me to be.
- If I express my real feelings, desires, and needs (the core attributes of my real, unlovable self), I will be rejected or humiliated.
- I don't have as many needs as other people have.
- Not having many needs myself, it's easier to sacrifice my own needs in the service of meeting other people's needs (and making them happy) than to assert any needs or desires.
- Conflict produces bad feelings and disapproval and risks damaging relationships, so it should be avoided.
- I know how to make people like me. My ability to make people like me ensures my survival and well-being.
- Most people like happy people who flatter them and meet their needs.
- Most people don't like needy people who cause trouble or create conflict by expressing negativity, strong feelings, or opinions.
- When you give to others, they are obligated to give back to you.

These common Two beliefs and recurring thoughts support and perpetuate the manufacturing of a self-presentation that maximizes other people's positive feelings and minimize their negative opinions and reactions.

The Type Two Trap:
"I Make People Like Me By Being Less Like Me"

As it does distinctly for each type, the cognitive fixation for Type Two leads the personality in circles. It presents an inherent "trap" that the limitations of the personality cannot resolve.

For Type Twos, this trap can be summarized with the quandary "I make people like me by being less like me." Twos inevitably lose touch with who they really are by striving to "make others like them." By trying to become what they believe others will like, admire, and find attractive, they end up disowning their needs, feelings, and preferences—the substance of who they really are as unique and valuable individuals. Twos trap themselves by substituting the temporary lift of approval for the real love they desperately want. Through shifting into being the person they think others want them to be, they lose their own sense of self, and with it their ability to be present and to be nurtured in relationship.

Twos habitually manage their presentation so they can more easily create a positive rapport with specific individuals, but in doing this, they get confused about who they really are, how they really feel, and what they really want. In this way they get caught up in a vicious cycle of shape-shifting to attract others, then needing more support and validation from the outside to support a weakened sense of self. It's only by taking the risk to find out who they are—and letting go of the need to make everyone like them—that they find their way out of the trap.

The Key Type Two Traits

Strategic Helpfulness to Create Indispensability

Twos give of themselves selectively, with the (sometimes unconscious) expectation that they will receive something in return. This strategic "giving to get" represents a key unconscious habit of the Two.

One of the most ego-satisfying compliments Twos can receive is that they are indispensable. Twos feel most safe when needed by others, and so they may regularly create situations in which others need them.

Seductiveness

Twos experience difficulty in directly asking for what they need, so they seduce others as a way of getting what they need through the indirect routes of charm and apparent generosity. Seductiveness develops in Twos as a way to seek love or affirmation without asking for it directly. Naranjo speaks of seduction not only as eroticism, but also, and even more importantly in the case of Twos, as "seeming to have more to offer than is the case." They seduce through promising whatever they might need to promise to draw someone in, but may not be able to deliver on their commitments. So while it's true that Twos like to be wanted, they don't necessarily want to have to follow through on what they might offer. As Naranjo points out, Twos tend to live in the present, yet not in a way that represents a healthy "present-centeredness," but as a subterfuge, because "they don't want to think of the future consequences of their actions nor remember yesterday's commitment."[11]

Emotionality and Emotional Sensitivity

Twos are naturally emotionally sensitive, yet they struggle with emotionality—the outward manifestation of their feelings. At times a Two might avoid negative emotions through repression, only to be overwhelmed by them when they can no longer be repressed. Twos may become outwardly emotional when they would prefer not to be seen as emotional.

As Naranjo explains, "there is something excessive about the expression of emotion of E2 people, be it tender or aggressive. Their enthusiasm too ecstatic, their fits of anger too manipulative."[12] Twos can be impossibly cheerful as a way of overcompensating for an underlying sense of sorrow at not getting the love they need—or overly resentful when others don't give them what they need.

Whether an individual Two has this overt emotionality varies depending on the Two, but Twos all share a great capacity for feeling emotion. Twos may also suffer from anxiety, often out of a vague sense that it's not okay to be who or how they are (they need to be somehow different to be supported).

Twos can be particularly emotionally sensitive when it comes to criticism or perceived hurts or rejections. Any message, however small, that indicates someone dislikes them can feel crushing because their well-being is based on how others feel about them. Twos tend to take things personally, even when things aren't personal, which can make it hard for others to be candid with them. They can take others' negative opinions of them way too much to heart, feeling like they've failed in their task to achieve someone's positive regard.

Romanticism

Along with Type Fours, perhaps, Twos are the romantics of the Enneagram. Their deep need for love, together with their focus on relationships as a source of romantic satisfaction, gives them an affinity for all things romantic, whether it be a good love story, fantasies of fulfilling experiences with a romantic partner, or music or poetry that communicates romantic feeling.

Hedonism and Compensatory Overindulgence

As Naranjo himself asserts, Type Two personalities can be the most hedonistic of all the types of the Enneagram.[13] Like other Two traits, this hedonism derives from the unmet need for love and support the Two experienced early on in life. For Twos, hedonism consists of actively seeking pleasure and "taking in" what feels good. Twos seek pleasure in this way to satisfy their unconscious needs and compensate for a deeper sense of deprivation. Having a good time, engaging in pleasurable activities, and overindulging generally all reflect the Two's desire to feel good without having to do the work of figuring out what they truly need.

The Two's deeper need to be loved is displaced and repressed through this search for pleasurable experiences and sensory satisfaction.

The Type Two Shadow

Because Twos stake their well-being on managing their connections with others, they have a lot of blind spots when it comes to those relationships. Twos often don't recognize the need for the boundaries that are necessary to foster the balance between freedom and contact in a healthy relationship. For instance, Twos often don't realize that it can be good to say no to another's request and that sometimes it's best not to volunteer to help someone else.

Twos acting unconsciously are unaware of their deep unmet need for love and often compulsively give without limit, hoping this effort will earn others' affection. They cannot see that this approach often isn't the best path to a positive mutual connection. At its worst, Twos' over-giving can feel intrusive to others and burdensome for Twos even while they believe they are "just trying to help" or "maintain the relationship."

Especially because the Two pattern of "giving to get" can itself be a blind spot, eventually Twos exhaust themselves and become angry if others do not give back. This anger results directly from the fact that the Twos' real needs are in their Shadow and kept out of their consciousness through repression. This anger emerges periodically—sometimes passively, and sometimes actively—because the Two's unmet needs conflict with his or her unspoken, unconscious expectation of reciprocity. And because this anger itself is repressed in service to the Twos' desire to avoid conflict and the threat of separation, resentment can build under the surface until it explodes in what can seem to be highly irrational, surprising, or manipulative fits of aggression.

A big blind spot for Twos is their sense of self—who they really are. They often lose touch with themselves as they shape-shift to become what they think others want them to be. The effort the false self makes to forge connections with important others requires repressing so many needs, feelings, and opinions that others might find unattractive, the unaware Two will have a hard time knowing who they are and what they really feel, think, and need.

Another Two blind spot concerns their perception of self-worth. Focusing so much on what they think they need to be to please others often involves dwelling on the ways in which they believe they don't measure up. Like Ones in this respect, Twos may thus consign some of their positive attributes to their Shadow. Deeper down, Twos often believe they are unlovable, though this perception and the emotions related to it may also reside in Twos' Shadow.

Twos often have a blind spot concerning power and authority because their personality gives others much of the power to define their relationships. Twos' natural tendency is to support others in positions of power and require a lot of external validation from those they perceive as more powerful. So even though a Two might have the experience and qualities to be a good leader, he or she might not pursue this role, preferring to manage their image from a more comfortable subordinate position rather than being the one everyone is looking to for direction. (Though the Social Two is an exception to this.)

All of these blind spots in the Two Shadow trace back to the passion of pride and the mechanism of repression—a very powerful combination for pushing needs and feelings down to the deepest levels of the unconscious.

The Shadow of the Type Two Passion: *Pride* in Dante's Underworld

Dante's *Inferno* provides a vivid symbolic portrayal of the shadow side of the Type Two personality and its Passion of Pride. In Christian cosmology, Pride is the first and fundamental sin because it prompted Lucifer to elevate himself above his natural level and challenge the supremacy of God. (As Naranjo describes it, he dared "to say 'I' in the presence of the Only One."[14]) Pride caused Lucifer's rebellion against his maker and his subsequent expulsion from heaven.

The deep cone shaped cavity of Dante's hell was created by the prideful angel's (Lucifer's) fall. So in Dante's Inferno, Pride created the structure of Hell itself, and it is punished in its lowest region.

> The king of the vast kingdom of all grief stuck out with half his chest above the ice ... If once he was as fair as now he's foul and dared to raise his brows against his maker, it is fitting that all grief should spring from him.[15]

Although in the Enneagram map of personality, none of the passions is better or worse than any other, in the moral geography of Dante's underworld, pride is the worst of the sins. Lucifer himself is the symbol of pride, a three-faced monster trapped forever in a lake of ice at the very bottom of the pit. Surrounded by rebellious giants from the Bible and classical literature, each of the "arch-traitor's" mouths is chewing on a famous traitor from history. This literary image aptly depicts the far reaching harm that Pride can do and the depth of repression Type Two personalities may maintain to keep the Passion of Pride in the Shadow of the unconscious.

But why is pride so bad according to Dante? Pride causes the prideful to put their will above the will of nature (or God) and thus subverts the natural flow of the universal order—just as when Type Twos, motivated by the passion of pride, put their will above that of others or nature by trying to control who likes who and who's doing what.

The Three Kinds of Twos: The Type Two Subtypes

IN THE TWO PERSONALITY, pride manifests itself as a need to seduce others to strategically meet the needs Twos disown as part of their prideful stance. Each of the subtypes represents a specific effort to get needs met without having to ask, though the three Type Two subtypes each display different approaches to the driving need to seduce. In the subtypes, the passion of pride gets channeled into three different ways of trying to get needs met: indirectly, through others' protection and care (Self-Preservation); by gaining admiration and respect through one's knowledge and abilities (Social); or by creating an attractive image and adapting in order to woo specific individuals (Sexual).

The Self-Preservation Two is the most childlike Two; the Social Two is more of an adult "Power Two"; and the Sexual Two is like a force of nature, resembling the *femme fatale* archetype and its male equivalent. The Self-Preservation Two seduces by being charming, playful, and cute. The Social Two seduces groups through power and competence. The Sexual Two employs a more classic mode of seduction: wooing others through attractiveness and flattery, and seducing specific individuals into providing for all their needs and wants.

The Self-Preservation Two: "Privilege" (Countertype)
This "cute" Two expresses pride and a need for protection through youthful ways of gaining attention and affection. The unconscious strategy the Self-Preservation Two employs is to "seduce" like a child in the presence of grown-ups. This represents both an unconscious need to be taken care of and a sense that children are naturally lovable, inherently deserving of affection,

and usually more readily liked than adults. This Two has a childlike quality in presentation and emotional expression—no matter how old they are, this Two looks youthful or young. While the Sexual Two can seem overly adult, wild, and seductive in the usual sense of the term, the Self-Preservation Two unconsciously aims to attract love and attention through being cute and expressing a childlike sense of need.

As humans, we have a natural love of children, a biological imperative that ensures that we will care for children who are dependent on us for their survival. Children want and need to be loved not for what they do for others, but for who they are. This is a basic need of any child. So what is prominent in the Self-Preservation Two is this pure, young need for love. This Two "remains little" as a way of evoking care from others without having to ask for it, just as children shouldn't have to ask for love and care or aren't mature enough to articulate this kind of request directly.

Self-Preservation Twos thus unconsciously draw on the universal love of children by adopting the stance of a cute, youthful person. This presentation is a way of inviting people to like them and take care of them, just as a child's "cuteness" inspires people to love them. This is their way of expressing the idea that, deep down, they want to be loved not for being pleasing or giving to others, or because of qualifications, performance, or achievements, but just because of who they are; *they want to be loved for just existing*. This Self-Preservation Two pattern has this person taking the position of the child in the family because a child's needs naturally come first.

The name for the Self-Preservation Two, "Privilege," refers to the idea suggested by this personality: "I'm young, and therefore I'm the most important." This reflects this subtype's (unconscious) assertion of a kind of childlike priority, wanting others to place a special emphasis on meeting his or her needs. These Twos don't want to have to prove their importance to be important. Despite wanting to be the center of attention, they experience no accompanying feeling of having to do anything for it. They want to be seen without showing themselves.

Self-Preservation Twos need to feel unique and special—they have a compulsion about being the "cute" girl or boy who is liked by everybody. They charm or "give themselves" to others to remain the favorite. They excel at being the teacher's pet.

It's less easy to see pride in this type. The Self-Preservation Two is the countertype of the Twos; it's a Two that doesn't look like a Two. While the energetic direction of the flow of the Two personality (with its focus on seduction) is up and out toward others, the self-preservation instinct this Two has causes them to express more ambivalence about relationship. This Two moves toward others, but also has a "counter-move" away from others out of a need for self-protection. This Two is tender and sweet, but more guarded than the other Twos.

As might be expected from a more childlike character, the Self-Preservation Two is more fearful, less trusting, and more ambivalent about connections with others. Although these Twos may not be aware of how fearful they are—all Twos repress feelings—they may have a more pronounced need than other Twos to protect themselves in the presence of others, which might be perceived by some as an invisible "wall." The ambivalence about connection experienced by this type takes the form of mixed or conflicting feelings about establishing close connections with others, especially important or intimate others.

Like other Twos, Self-Preservation Twos focus on meeting others' needs as a way of gaining love, but they also feel a strong opposing pull to hide or withdraw in light of the threat of disapproval and rejection inherent in interacting with others. On the one hand, people and relationships feel compelling and important, but on the other hand, being close to people seems fraught with danger because it includes the possibilities of losing oneself or being judged, taken advantage of, humiliated, or rejected.

In this "youthful" Two, self-importance, irresponsibility, humor, playfulness, and charm are in the foreground. Until they engage in self-awareness work, this Two can be easily hurt and is hypersensitive to slights or anything that might sound like criticism or disapproval. They may have tantrums or sulk or withdraw when upset. Feeling hurt can result in pouting, angry recriminations, or childish accusations. They may manipulate through an expression of feeling instead of stepping up and saying what they want or what they dislike.

Dependency is prominent in this subtype, but mostly unconscious. These Twos, like other Twos, don't want to see themselves as needy or dependent on others, and yet they can engage in a pattern of remaining unconsciously dependent, wanting someone to take care of them, or engineering situations in which people end up taking care of them. Because of this childlike stance of (unconscious) dependency, the Self-Preservation Two has less freedom; a child, after all, is rarely, if ever, completely free. So these Twos often yearn to be free while at the same time yoking themselves to people in unhealthy or unconscious ways.

Although, like other Twos, Self-Preservation Twos can be very competent, on a deeper level they don't want to have to take responsibility for themselves. The thought of taking charge of themselves fills them with anxiety. They can wonder: "What am I to do with myself?" They have an underlying desire to be a child who will be excused for their ignorance, innocence, and the feelings they might express on a whim or "just because." In more mature Self-Preservation Twos, however, their need for structure can make them more methodical and more organized than other Twos.

Self-Preservation Twos can be self-indulgent and hedonistic. They are drawn to cultivate a sense of "euphoria" through parties, shopping, drinking, or indulging in food and fun—anything to distract themselves from having to contact themselves. They are sensation-seeking, and they look for pleasurable experiences to distract themselves from feelings of self-abandonment and inner deprivation.

This Two fantasizes a lot (about being loved or admired) and idealizes people, especially in the early stages of relationships. They unconsciously project their power onto others whom they see as all-good as a way of not having to be "good enough" or responsible themselves, which can make it hard for them to own their own power or have equal and truly contactful relationships.

The Self-Preservation Two can look like a Self-Preservation Six in that they are fearful and ambivalent about relationships, but in the Six the emphasis is on a more generalized fear, while this Two's fear mainly manifests in relationships. This Two can also resemble a Type Four in that they express more emotionality and a longing for love, but they repress their needs and feelings and focus on others more than Fours do.

Ben, a Self-Preservation Two, speaks:

Since I was young, I've always considered myself to be the central focus of interactions with others. Being good and cute, I expected other people to pay attention to me and felt I deserved their support. I often took recognition for granted. I avoided long-term decisions, commitments, and grown-up actions such as "settling down" or striving for healthy adult relationships. Thus, I unconsciously put off achieving independence by not truly dealing with the consequences and costs of things. Becoming an adult in an adult's world, facing life's challenges, taking full responsibility for myself on my own, and even having a more mature look appropriate to my age felt extremely difficult. For many years, the thought of doing all these things made me feel as if I would lose my biggest advantages in life: my charm and youthful likability.

The Social Two: "Ambition"

The Social Two is a seducer of environments—someone who is good in front of groups; a more adult, leader type. In contrast to the other Two subtypes, the Social Two appears as a powerful or intellectual person. This Two has a passion for power, and their pride is expressed through having influence and advantages and cultivating an image of being an influential person.

This Two is the most obviously proud subtype because they are ambitious, know the right people, do important things, occupy positions of leadership, and are usually admired for their accomplishments. In the Social Two, the passion of pride manifests itself as a sense of satisfaction in the conquest of an audience.

In contrast to the more childlike Self-Preservation Two and the more overtly seductive Sexual Two, the Social Two is a more adult "Power Two," the person who owns their own company, or works at a high level in an organization, or is a leader in their field.

The most intellectual of the Twos, the Social Two needs to be someone important to feed their pride—and to be important, you must use your mind more. Seduction operates in this case through the Social Two's ability to influence the larger group by being impressive, exceptional, and knowledgeable.

The Social Two's name, "Ambition," refers to this person's passion for being "on top," being "in the know," being close to people who are perceived as powerful, and for wielding power themselves. The Social Two has a passion for superiority—a passion to stand above. Because of their need for admiration, Social Twos are competitive and may at times be indifferent to, insensitive to, or in denial about the emotions of others. They tend to (unconsciously) believe that everyone wants to be like them, or that people are less able than they are, or that people are out to get them because they envy their superior skills.

Social Twos are skillful at working behind the scenes to extend their influence within the group and to help the larger entity move in directions that benefit them. They know how to orchestrate individuals within the group or community through the use of strategic giving as a way of gaining allegiance and respect. Although it often operates at a subconscious level, this Two has the strongest reliance on "giving to get" as a strategy in interacting with others. The Social Two almost always has a strategic angle when expressing generosity. They support others as a way of ensuring loyalty and reciprocal relationships. They think in terms of influencing the people around them through the offer or delivery of favors, and they make things happen through the promise of rewards or positive attention.

This Two can be a bit more introverted than the other Twos. They are more attuned to the effective cultivation of a public image that conveys power and authority; this makes them good performers in front of an audience, but it also necessitates a greater level of privacy or removal when they are offstage.

Social Twos can also be workaholics, with a tendency toward omnipotence. They may appear enthusiastic, confident or overconfident—and even manic at times. They tend to engage in power struggles, wanting to dominate and play the protector, and they may express a sense of territoriality at times. They usually have a highly positive sense of their work and their goals as well—they believe that they can accomplish anything.

People with this subtype tend to deny vulnerable emotions, such as shame, fear, despair, mistrust, jealousy, and envy. They may sincerely believe they are displaying vulnerability when they aren't, or they may use a show of vulnerability for effect with an audience. On the low side, when they are more unconscious and unhealthy, Social Twos may be indifferent toward or contemptuous of others. They may take a position of power and control over others in ways they don't see, and may even unconsciously exploit others, even while believing they are helping them.

The Social Two can resemble a Three or an Eight. Like Type Threes, Social Twos tend to be goal-oriented, competitive, and successful in their work. They typically get a lot done and have a reputation as powerful people who can lead the group. However, Twos usually have a softer presence and can show more vulnerability, warmth, or emotion on the way to achieving their goals, especially if such demonstrations support their larger aims, whereas Threes tend not to express vulnerable feelings as much. Like Type Eights, Social Twos can be powerful, influential, protective of others, and oriented to the big picture. Unlike Eights, however, Social Twos can display vulnerability more (or use a show of vulnerability to their advantage), and can more readily access their emotions in supporting others or establishing control.

Carol, a Social Two, speaks:

I was that kid in school that was friends with the teacher. I always got asked to take the lead on school events and student body activities. I was like the school diplomat. I was also involved in adult organizations, volunteering my time at non-profits or serving on a board of directors as the youngest member.

I go above and beyond in my jobs, working hard and diligently. I seek out influential leaders and get to know them. I don't do this consciously;

it just happens. On my first day of work at my current job, I sought out employee network groups and immediately joined two. After the first meeting of each group, I was asked to take a leading role, which I accepted gladly. I tend to overcommit and then get stressed out. But if I am not involved socially with groups I feel are important, I can get easily bored and even depressed. I need to be involved and making a difference.

After a lot of self-work and reflection, I realize my unconscious drive to lead and influence leaders reflects my underlying need for approval. Many times, it gets in the way of my taking care of myself or tuning into my own feelings. I am slowly getting better at having downtime where I can create, take a walk, or relax, but this still requires conscious effort.

The Sexual Two: "Aggressive/Seductive"

The Sexual Two is a seducer of particular individuals. Classical seduction is the main approach of this Two, who expresses a driving need to seduce other people as a way of getting their needs met. This seduction—a way of gaining allegiance or inflaming the desire of the other—occurs through the cultivation of an attractive presentation and the expression of feeling.

While the Self-Preservation Two is the countertype of Two, with conflicting impulses toward and away from people, and the Social Two is a more adult Two oriented to power and control, the Sexual Two is a generous, flexible, somewhat wild, action-oriented Two who is not afraid to woo others by using sexuality as a weapon of conquest. The Social Two tries to be important to feed their pride; the Sexual Two, in contrast, feeds their pride through having somebody's passionate attachment. Where intelligence or strategic skill helps the Social Two reach the goal of seducing the group, sexuality and charm is the stronghold of the Sexual Two in seducing specific people.

The Sexual Two displays the clearest tendencies toward seduction in the classic sense, using charm and sexuality as a way to lure in unsuspecting potential suppliers of love, favors, and other gifts. Sexual Twos transform their need for love into false needs, whims, and a sense of entitlement to do what they please when they please, not asking but taking. The purpose behind the Sexual Two's seduction is that it is a way to solve any problem or meet any need in life: this Two solves the dilemma of having needs but not wanting to express them by having a strong bond with somebody who will give them anything they want.

Sexual Twos have a need to be desired that fuels the need to seduce. Pride activates their impulse to inspire attraction in others so that they will give the Two whatever they want, though this Two's pride may not be so obvious if it is satisfied by "the loved one." Similar to the Sexual Four, the Sexual Two's strategy entails being very attractive and somewhat less ashamed of having needs. This pattern reflects a prideful sense that others will want to meet their needs because they are so appealing, charming, and generous.

This Two resembles the French expression of the *femme fatale* (or its male equivalent) archetype in that there is a kind of "dangerous irresistibility" to this personality. In a similar way, the "Aggressive/Seductive" title given to this subtype suggests an association with the archetype of a vampire. This Two is irresistible: somebody who is beautiful, but who possesses a dangerous kind of beauty. It's a beauty that needs to wield power over you and could end up consuming you. The name Aggressive/Seductive also suggests the forward momentum this subtype displays in moving toward others—an active, purposeful attitude that can include an element of aggression.

The Sexual Two can be direct and even dramatic in the execution of a classical seduction: the capturing of another person's affection and devotion involves an intense, targeted, and passionate effort on the part of the naturally sexy Sexual Two. And this Two aims to secure a relationship through this seduction in which they express devotion and generosity in exchange for whatever it is they want. Because the underlying motive of the aggressively seductive strategy is to get needs met—to basically get a blank check—it can be hard for these Twos to accept limits or to take "no" for an answer.

In this way, the Sexual Two's deeper need for love and need to seduce manifests in a character who uses beauty, charm, and promises of affection to attract a partner who will make them feel desirable and meet all their needs. This Two may need attention or money or pampering, but whatever it is, the strategy to obtain it centers around classical seduction designed to create a special connection through which the Two can have their needs and desires satisfied.

Sexual Twos justify their actions, words, madness, wildness, invasiveness, and selfishness in the name of love, as if love were the only emotion, the center of life, the experience that justifies everything. For people with this subtype, love may be conflated with liking or with being desired. For them, "love" is about enchanting, seducing, and attracting—about maneuvering themselves into a position in which they occupy a special place. Inspiring passion in someone else is their way to fix everything in life. In line with this, they may have a self-image of the "ideal lover."

Naranjo has suggested that in the "highly emotional and romantic [Two] character, 'help' translates as 'emotional support,' and on the whole, the personality is better evoked through 'lover' than 'helper.'"[16] We can see this especially in the Sexual Two: the personality might better be captured in the archetype of the "lover" than the names that are often ascribed to Twos: "helper" or "giver."

While the other Two subtypes can be look-alikes to other types, the Sexual Two may be the most recognizable as a Two and is in some ways the "classic" Two described in many Enneagram books. That said, the Sexual Two may be confused with the Sexual Four or the Sexual Three. For instance, Scarlett O'Hara, the heroine of *Gone With the Wind*, has sometimes been characterized as a Three or a Four, but Naranjo describes her as a good example of the Sexual Two personality. He points out that in the pursuit of her love object, Ashley, "exploitiveness and selfishness are scarcely hidden under the mask of false love"[17] and that she demonstrates this Two's sense that "desires are more important than principles."[18]

The energy of this Two can be seen as "double Two" in that this person moves toward others with the combined force of both the Two "up and out" energy and the Sexual, fusion-oriented, instinctual energy, which amplifies their momentum. In relationships, this Two may communicate both a sense of excitement and the intent of a hunter closing in on its prey. Passionate, seductive, and generous, Sexual Twos typically put a great deal of energy into making relationships happen, and can have a very difficult time letting go if a relationship doesn't work out.

Teri, a Sexual Two, speaks:

I always found it easy to flirt. I enjoyed meeting new people, but especially men! If I wasn't flirting for myself I would flirt for my girlfriends. They would be shocked at how easily I could go up to an attractive man and start a conversation. I used my smile and eyes and humor to grab their attention, and could tell when I had won someone's interest. It was my drug. I would get such a rush from that attention—but if it lasted for too long, I would either get scared or bored and want to be off to the next conquest. I also had this need to please the person I was talking with, so much so that I would not even stop to notice what I really believed, but would just naturally agree, wanting them to like me and to avoid any conflict. It took many years and an anxiety disorder for me to understand that need for attention, that need to be liked at all costs. At this point, I still love the connections I make with people, but they feel genuine now, not for show or to meet some dysfunctional need.

"The Work" for Type Two:
Charting a Personal Growth Path

ULTIMATELY, THE PATH OUT OF THE TWO TRAP of abandoning yourself to gain approval consists in having compassion for the part of you that needs to be loved, getting to know your "real self," and learning to love who you really are. When Twos learn to risk being themselves and open up to being loved for who they are (as opposed to the false images they create to get approval), they realize the freedom of being themselves unapologetically and not having to conform to the needs and preferences of others.

For all of us, waking up to habitual personality patterns involves ongoing, conscious efforts to observe ourselves, reflect on the meaning and sources of what we observe, and actively work to counter automatic tendencies. For Twos this process involves observing the ways in which they disown their needs, shape-shift to align with others, inflate their self-image to be all things to all people, and repress their real feelings to get the love they want. It is particularly important to explore the reasons behind extreme efforts to gain approval, surface and allow repressed feelings, and actively work to be conscious of your own needs and affirm the value of who you really are.

In this section I offer some ideas about what Twos can notice, explore, and aim for in their efforts to grow beyond the constraints of their personality and embody the higher possibilities associated with their type and subtype.

Self-Observation: Dis-Identifying from Your Personality by Watching It in Action

Self-observation is about creating enough internal space to really watch—with fresh eyes and adequate distance—what you are thinking, feeling, and doing in your everyday life. As Twos take note of their habitual patterns, they might look out for the following key patterns:

Denying needs and repressing feelings as a way to connect more easily with others

It can be hard to "observe" something that isn't there, but it is important for Twos to see how they avoid registering their own needs and feelings. This means noticing when you don't know what you are feeling or needing and keeping an eye out for what happens when repressed feelings and needs do arise. Rising anger or hurt feelings can be important clues that you have been repressing needs and unconsciously expecting others to meet them anyway.

Observe what happens when someone asks, "What do you need?" or "What are you feeling?" and ask this of yourself regularly. Often, Twos experience a sense of blankness or a void inside when faced with these questions. Pay attention to this kind of "void" or absence with the intention of discovering over time what you feel and need. Another good question to help "locate" your "self" is, "Where are you now?"[19]

Adapting, merging, helping, pleasing, and shape-shifting to engineer connections with specific individuals

Notice when you start to help or flatter people compulsively even though you don't want to or it exhausts you. Look out for ways you rationalize pleasing others even if it means doing something you'd rather not do. Observe the tendency to merge with or take on the feelings and preferences of others while downplaying or talking yourself out of your own experiences. Are you avoiding expressing a different opinion from someone you'd like to connect with? Does it bother you excessively if someone criticizes you or gets angry at you? Is it hard for you to stop thinking about your perceived mistakes in interactions with others?

Avoiding rejection and separation through maintaining an idealized (inflated) image of yourself, avoiding conflicts and boundaries, and managing your self-presentation (including lying and being inauthentic)

Observing these tendencies will include noticing when you say "yes" but want to say "no"; when you tell little white lies to maintain your image; and when you create a false impression of who you are to engender a connection. Look out for ways you rationalize making promises you'd rather not keep or presenting yourself to others in false ways designed to evoke their approval. If any of these things are happening, work to surface any underground assumptions you are making, such as the idea that creating an appropriate boundary will automatically lead to catastrophic rejection, separation, or disapproval.

Self-Inquiry and Self-Reflection: Gathering More Data to Expand your Self-Knowledge

As Twos observe these and other related patterns in themselves, the next step on the Enneagram growth path is to *understand* these patterns more. Why do they exist? Where do they come from? What purpose do they serve? How do they get you in trouble when they are intended to help you? Often, seeing the root causes of a habit—why it exists and what it is designed to do—is enough to allow you to break out of the pattern. In other cases, with more entrenched habits, knowing how and why they operate as defenses can be a first step to eventually being able to release them.

Here are some questions that Twos can ask themselves, and some possible answers they might explore to get more insight into the sources, operation, and consequences of these patterns.

How and why did these patterns develop? How do these habits help me cope?

Through understanding the sources of their defensive patterns, Twos have the opportunity to see how they deny, abandon, and limit their "real self" by presenting a false image to gain approval. If Twos can explore the reasons they may have needed to align with others and disown their needs to cope early on, they can have compassion for their young self who believed it had to conform to others to survive. Twos often had a history in which they had to take care of someone else so that that person would take care of them. By understanding how they coped with a world that didn't meet their needs by giving up their needs, Twos can take a step toward reclaiming their ability to accept and ask for what they need. When Twos can see how giving and helping and repressing feelings all operated as strategies for coping in an environment that didn't fulfill their emotional needs, they can begin to see more clearly how these strategies still operate in self-limiting ways.

What painful emotions are the Type Two patterns designed to protect me from?

Twos' reliance on seduction comes out of a strong love need coupled with a fear of rejection. Both feeling unlovable and being rejected can be extremely painful feelings for Twos. Repressing needs and feelings while seeking approval from others can help Twos avoid the sadness of not being seen and accepted for who they really are.

Twos' defensive patterns shield them from experiencing their fear of not being adequately loved and taken care of, and of being rejected for not being good enough. Image management in the service of relationship maintenance also helps Twos avoid their own pain and anger at not getting what they need from others. Repressing anger helps Twos feel safe, because it reassures them that they won't destroy or damage the connections with others that they need to sustain themselves.

If Twos can see how their (natural) need for love hasn't been fulfilled, and understand the ways in which their defensive (seductive) patterns constitute a strategy for seeking love through approval while avoiding the pain of rejection, they can begin to see how this coping strategy reflects deep unmet needs. If they can accept their needs and feelings they can start to find more direct and effective ways to find the love they want.

Why am I doing this? How do the Type Two patterns operate in me now?

Understanding why and how defensive patterns operate in the present moment is the most powerful way to begin to challenge and intercept them, and eventually let them go. By seeing that self-inflation is a way to maintain power and comfort in relationships, Twos can be more conscious about managing their tendency to merge with others and promise more than they want to deliver. By catching themselves in the act of saying "yes" when they want to say "no," or agreeing with others when they actually disagree, or offering help when they would rather not, Twos activate the awareness and self-confidence that will eventually allow them to say what they really think. Noticing why and how you are self-conscious and worried about what others think paves the way to becoming free of the self-denial entailed in altering to please others.

What are the blind spots of these patterns? What do Type Twos keep themselves from seeing?

Twos may avoid owning how fearful they are of close relationships—they may simultaneously seduce others to engineer a positive-feeling connection and distance themselves from those same others to protect themselves from rejection. Anger at needs not being met may be a blind spot for Twos until it gets so intense that it can't be contained by the desire to make a good impression. Inflation and self-aggrandizement in the service of having power over others may hide insecurity and low self-esteem. Shape-shifting to please and align with others leads to deep confusion for Twos about "who they really are" and a blind spot where their "true self" might be.

What are the effects or consequences of these patterns? How do they trap me?

Achieving deep connections and receiving real love is only possible when you are living from your "real self." This is an important contradiction that Twos avoid seeing when they are fixated in their Two patterns: seducing to get love ultimately doesn't work if you have to become someone you aren't to get it, because then you can't be "home" to receive it when it does come your way. Twos often satisfy themselves with approval when what they really want is love. And the more Twos seduce by seeming to have more to offer than is the case, they more they set themselves up for failure.

When Twos begin to self-reflect, they may find themselves in a difficult predicament: what they both want and fear most is love and relationship. Twos ultimately want to be seen and loved for who they are, yet they are afraid to be that person around others. They fear that if they allow themselves to need, ask for, and show up to get the love they want, they will be disappointed or rejected. But to have the chance to fulfill their deepest needs, they must take the risk to open themselves up to both satisfaction and the pain of rejection.

Self-Development:
Aiming for a Higher State of Consciousness

For all of us who seek to wake up, the next step in working with a type-based knowledge of the personality is to begin to inject more conscious effort into everything we do—to begin to actively think, feel, and act with more choice and awareness. In this section I provide some ideas for Twos about "what to do" after they've observed their key patterns and explored their sources, operation, and consequences.

This last section is divided into three parts, each corresponding to one of three distinct growth processes connected with the Enneagram system: 1) "what to do" to actively counter the automatic patterns described above in the "self-observation" section, 2) how to use the Enneagram's Inner Flow arrow lines as a map for growth, and 3) how you can study your passion (or "Vice") and consciously seek to embody its opposite, the antidote, the higher "Virtue" of the type.

The Three Main Type Two Personality Patterns:
"What to Do" to Address Them

Denying needs and repressing feelings as a way to connect more easily with others

Inquire frequently into the presence of needs and feelings. Twos benefit from asking themselves continually, "What do I really need?" and "How am I feeling?" Unaware Twos may believe that having their feelings will automatically mean alienating others, and they may also be afraid of feeling their painful emotions. It can be disconcerting to ask yourself what you need or what you are feeling and not have an answer. In light of this, Twos will need to start getting in touch with their needs and feelings through an intentional process; they will need to tolerate "not knowing" as a first step to developing on ongoing awareness of their needs and emotions.

Real feelings create and enhance, rather than thwart, connections. As a Two seeking to embark on self-work, it will help a lot if you have the support and understanding of others. When someone welcomes your anger, it can feel very liberating and healing. And working through emotional difficulties with others by sharing real feelings is what makes good relationships happen.

Learn to accept feelings and the emotional growth process. Recognize that all feelings are valid—and not "right" or "wrong"—as a way to help you open up to feeling more of your emotions. Create space to understand, learn about, and work with expressing your emotions. When you first start to feel your anger more often, you may express aggression in explosive, childish ways. Regardless of your experience, it's important for you to see that it's all a normal part of learning to own and manage your feelings and not make yourself "bad" for their (understandable) "messiness."

Adapting, merging, helping, pleasing, and shape-shifting to engineer connections with specific individuals

Liberate yourself through healthy separation. This pattern can be countered by a purposeful effort to locate and grow an ongoing awareness of a separate sense of your "self." This means actively making time to be alone. It's much easier for Twos to find themselves and develop their own center of gravity when they are alone. Make it a practice to focus your attention inside yourself when you are with other people. If your attention wanders over to them and you are energetically "sitting in their lap," bring your attention back to yourself. Notice when you are merged with someone or compulsively trying to achieve a connection, and consciously shift your attention two feet behind you so that you can energetically disconnect and locate your separate sense of "self" again.[20] Recognize that merging disguises a fear of intimacy.

Say "maybe" on the way from "yes" to "no." Try to stop saying "yes" when you want to say "no" by taking the intermediate step of saying "maybe"—it will buy you time to think of a way to say "no." Look for and dwell on your real experience of *not* wanting to help. Let that be okay, and notice if it feels like relief. Reassure yourself that others can do it without you.

Accept, but manage and contain, your emotions. Your emotions are important and valid. Value them as expressions of your true self. But also notice when you put pressure on others through expressions of emotion, and take the risk to call this what it is: emotional manipulation. Instead of making yourself "bad" for this, just recognize that it's a part of your coping strategy and try to work against it. Challenge yourself to own your needs and feelings, and find ways to soothe yourself when you are courageous enough to feel your pain.

Open up to receiving from others by living more from your real self. By noticing the underlying assumptions you have about reciprocal giving, you can both work against "giving to get," and learn to give without expectations and receive without feeling indebted. This frees you up to enjoy relationships for their inherent value as opposed to simply viewing them as a utilitarian route to survival.

Avoiding rejection and separation through maintaining an idealized (inflated) image of yourself, avoiding conflicts and boundaries, and managing your self-presentation (including lying and being inauthentic)

Focus on the freedom that boundaries provide. Spending time alone can help Twos realize that separation isn't so bad. Being alone doesn't have to lead to loneliness. Recognize that boundaries actually make us freer to express ourselves safely in relationships and allow for better and closer connections with others. Make a conscious effort to learn how to make and maintain good boundaries. Remember that "no" is a very good answer.

Find the sweet spot between inflation and deflation. Notice the tendency to inflate and deflate your sense of yourself and allow yourself to feel relief at just being who you are. Take note when you have fantasies of being the ideal partner or friend or when you want to be all things to all people, and stop to consider if this is really possible or desirable. Realize that it's okay (and actually liberating) to not be perfect or perfectly aligned with others.

Allow constructive conflict to enliven your relationships and strengthen your sense of self. Recognize that conflict can actually bring people closer together, and that when you express real opinions and preferences, you are honoring others by revealing your true self. Take the risk with trusted others to tell them what you really think, especially when you disagree or don't want to help. Notice if you lie to smooth out social interactions, and try to be more honest. Try not to promise more than you can deliver, and realize that this makes your relationships more authentic and deeper.

Face your pain in a conscious way so you can let it go. Allow yourself to feel the pain of neglect or rejection, and realize you can survive it. Learn to weather emotional injuries, and realize that growing a thicker skin doesn't mean your hurt doesn't matter. Learn to love and accept yourself as you are and risk opening up to receiving affection from others, knowing that if someone doesn't like you, it might be more about them than about you.

The Inner Flow for Type Two:
Using the Arrow Lines to Chart Your Growth Path

In Chapter 1, I introduced an Inner Flow model of the arrow lines that define one of the dimensions of dynamic movement within the Enneagram framework. The connections and flow between each core Type, its "growth-through-stress" point, and its "child-heart-security" point map one kind of growth path described by the symbol. As a reminder, the arrow lines suggest one kind of growth path for each type:

- The direction from the core point along the arrow is the path of higher development. The "growth-through-stress" or "growth–stress" point ahead represents specific challenges we can consciously navigate to break out of the limitations associated with our core point and grow in an important new direction.
- The direction against the arrow from the core point to the "child-heart" point indicates issues and themes that must be consciously acknowledged and owned from childhood so that we can move forward and not be held back by unfinished business from the past. This "child–heart" point represents qualities of security we unconsciously repressed, occasionally return to in times of stress, and can now consciously own as a way of furthering our forward progress.

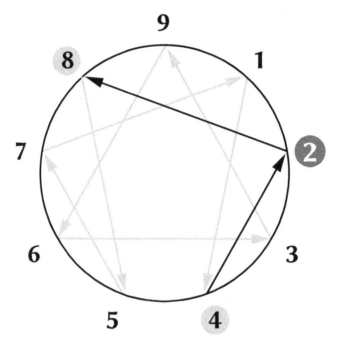

Type Two Moving Forward to Type Eight: Consciously Using the Eight "Growth–Stress" Point for Development and Expansion

Type Twos' Inner Flow growth path brings them into direct contact with the challenges embodied in Type Eight: owning their power and authority, allowing for more access to anger, and handling conflict and confrontation more consciously. Twos are typically more comfortable being the power behind the throne, but moving to Eight invites them to initiate more and to take the risk of leading and acting proactively rather than always reacting. Crucially for Twos, moving to Eight also means learning to be more direct and assertive as opposed to using indirect means to get needs met and sugarcoating messages to make them go down easier.

While it can be difficult at first for Twos (especially Self-Preservation Twos) to imagine themselves feeling comfortable with being authoritative, aggressive, and direct when appropriate, incorporating healthy Type Eight behaviors can provide a much-needed balance to Twos' habit of getting needs met covertly through seduction, charm, and strategic helpfulness. Eights' strength and self-confidence help Twos value themselves and be more bold in the things they do. Twos see their real power in helping and supporting others, and while this a legitimate strength, they can overdo the strategy of emotional support and underestimate the power of exercising authority in more direct ways. Focusing on embodying more of the Eight Point expands the range of ways Twos can make an impact on others, and it allows for more freedom in how they interact with others. Seeing conflict as a good thing—as a way of having positive contact through the exploration of legitimate differences—can also counter their tendency to merge emotionally with others.

Type Two Moving Back to Type Four: Consciously Using the "Child–Heart" Point to Work through Early Issues and Find Security in Support of Moving Forward

The path of growth for Twos calls for them to reclaim their needs and feelings as represented by the Four Point. Many Twos received the message early on that their needs and emotions were too much. In keeping with the coping strategy of adapting emotionally to others, Twos typically respond to this by repressing their emotions and disowning their needs as a way of maintaining connections. By consciously drawing on the strengths of Type Fours, Twos can expand their access to their authentic emotions, reclaim a healthy ability to self-reference (to balance out their disproportionate focus on others), and accept and express their needs with more confidence.

If Twos have been made to feel shame for their needs and feelings, as many have been, it can be important and healing for them to incorporate the Four stance that feelings are important and valuable expressions of your authentic self. By encouraging a shift of focus from others to self, the Two "move to Four" allows Twos to ground themselves in the legitimacy of their real feelings and needs, thereby strengthening their connection to their own inner knowing and their sense of self. Twos often experience an underlying sense of anxiety related to deep beliefs from childhood that their normal needs and feelings threaten their connections with the important people in their lives. The Two move to Four can help Twos relax in the knowledge that honoring their emotions and desires can support, rather than thwart or threaten, their ability to form positive relationships.

Navigated consciously, Twos can use the higher wisdom of the Four Point to establish a healthy balance between focusing on the self and focusing on others; between expressing sadness and hurt and a cultivating a sense of lightness; and between meeting others' needs and asking for what they need. They can consciously remind themselves that although it is often important to make room to empathize with others' emotions, all their own feelings are valid and valuable as well.

The Vice to Virtue Conversion:
Accessing Pride and Aiming for Humility

The developmental path from Vice to Virtue is one of the central contributions of the Enneagram map in highlighting a usable "vertical" path of growth to a higher state of awareness for each type. In the case of Type Two, the Vice (or passion) of the type is pride, and its opposite, the Virtue, is *humility*. The theory of growth communicated by this "Vice to Virtue conversion" is that the more we can be aware of how our passion functions within our personality and the more we consciously work toward the embodiment of its opposite, the more we can free ourselves from the unconscious habits and fixated patterns of our type and evolve toward our "higher" side.

The work of Type Two centers on becoming more and more conscious of how different forms of the passion of pride play a role in shaping the focus of attention and patterns of their personality. Twos can do this work by regularly asking if pride is playing a role in what they are thinking, feeling, and doing. As Twos become more familiar with their experience of pride, they can go even further by making conscious efforts to focus on enacting their Virtue, the "antidote" to the passion of pride. In the case of Type Two, the Virtue of humility represents a state of being that Twos can attain through consciously manifesting their higher potential.

Humility is a way of being that is free of the attachment to be better than you really are in order to know that you have value. Humility allows you to rest in the knowledge that you are "'good enough" as you are—that you don't need to be perfect or superior or recognized in a specific way to be worthy of love. Humility means learning to love and accept yourself for exactly who you are, no more and no less. When Twos can transcend the prideful need to see themselves as somehow better than they are—as indispensable, without needs, able to turn themselves into whatever others desire most—they can relax into the freedom that humility brings: to just be yourself, knowing that is good enough.

Internally, false pride can easily be confused with self-confidence. This can be problematic for Twos seeking to become aware of pride and at the same time allow for a real experience of their own goodness (as opposed to pride). After all, it's the early experience of "not being good enough" or "being too much" that initiates pride as a survival strategy in the first place. Twos' tendency toward self-aggrandizement and self-inflation motivates them to take on too much, thinking they have no needs or limits like other people. But this pattern inevitably leads to deflation, self-criticism, and a painful sense of lack when Twos don't deliver on their idealized view of themselves and can't be all things to all people.

To avoid the ups of self-inflation and the associated downs of self-criticism, it can be important for Twos to consciously cultivate a strong sense of humility—an ability to own their strengths, their good intentions, and the positive things they do, but also an awareness of how they can puff themselves up under times of stress or when trying to impress others. Aiming for humility as a growth path means observing the ups and downs, the inflation and deflation, and aiming for the middle, for the truth of who you are—developing your true strengths while also acknowledging your limitations.

The virtue of humility also plays an important role in the larger journey we all must take if we aspire to grow toward our true (or oak tree) Selves. Humility is required for us to be able to let go of our ego needs, suffer our fears and pains, and realize that the personality structure that makes us comfortable also limits our development. In this way, humility represents the quality we all must seek to embody to successfully dis-identify from the personality, such that we can see beyond the narrow view of the false self, that (mistakenly) believes itself to be all that we are and thus wants to stay in charge and in control.

Noticing pride and practicing humility teaches Twos to value who they are as a first step to becoming all that they can be, not through striving and helping and giving, but through relaxing into a confident sense that they are enough as they are.. Humility allows Twos to embrace a realistic assessment of themselves so they may realize their full potential and relate to others as their real self.

Specific Work for the Three Type Two Subtypes on the Path from Vice to Virtue

As Naranjo teaches, whatever type you are, the path from observing your passion to finding the antidote to the passion is not exactly the same for each of the subtypes. The path of conscious self-work has been characterized in terms of "grit, grind, and grace:" the "grit"[21] of our personality programming, the "grind" of our efforts to grow, and the "grace" that comes to us from doing our work in conscious and positive ways. Each subtype has to "grind against" something slightly different.

Self-Preservation Twos travel the path from pride to humility by making dependency needs more conscious, observing and working with fear and ambivalence in relationships, and noting how pride and mistrust keep defenses up and prevent real engagement and intimacy. Most of all, learning to be more resilient in the face of emotional hurts, as well as gently encouraging themselves to find ways to grow up and own their power, helps these Twos. Playing small doesn't work in adulthood, and you have just as much ability as anyone else to take charge of your life and be your own authority. Work to receive from others from a position of strength and competence as opposed to a pose of self-inflation or underlying need. Recognize that by holding on to your own value you invite others to give to you freely, based on an appreciation of your true worth, without manipulation or unconscious dependence. Remember: when you can support yourself from the inside rather than relying on others, you have the ability to both receive love from others and weather the occasional pain of rejection.

Social Twos travel the path from pride to humility by recognizing and owning how the need for power and admiration plays a role in the things they do; by becoming more aware of the strategic intent of their generosity; and by allowing for more real vulnerability and authenticity in relationships with others. These Twos benefit from seeing how their form of leadership may be unconsciously manipulative and working against a deeper need to see themselves as more competent than others. It is also important for Social Twos to make active efforts to receive as much as they give and to relax the manic tendency to work too hard. These Twos may experience a sense of omnipotence as a compensation for giving up their deeper needs for love and care. Slowing down and making sure their needs are getting met in direct ways can help them observe and work against their pride-fueled impulse to overwork. Remembering to focus on needs and vulnerable feelings serves to temper the important work these Twos do with a conscious sense of humility.

Sexual Twos can travel the path from pride to humility by actively developing aspects of their real selves; by finding varied ways to meet their needs; and by more consciously managing their energetic connections with others. By focusing on receiving and giving with presence and awareness, containing their seductive energy, and maintaining good boundaries, they can temper their pride with a more humble sense of their own intentions and impact on other people. These Twos can also aim for humility by being honest with themselves about their true intentions in relationships, noting when they manipulate or misrepresent themselves in the service of seduction, and taking the risk to be who they are as opposed to presenting themselves as the ideal love object. If you are a Sexual Two, be honest with yourself about whether or not you are basing your self-image on who you think you need to be to be loved or desired. Try to risk being yourself and allowing others to come to you.

Conclusion

THE TWO POINT REPRESENTS THE ENERGY of pride that fuels a need to seduce others into providing emotional support by being something "more." It also represents the ways in which we all inflate our sense of who we are to bolster our self-worth in a world that seems to reject us. The Two path of growth can show us how to transform false pride into the energy that will help us manifest our humble belief in the worthiness of who we really are without needing to help, please, or attract. In each of the Type Two subtypes we see a specific character who teaches us what is possible when we turn the survival strategy of self-aggrandizement into a peaceful acceptance of our inherent value and power through the alchemy of self-observation, self-development, and self-knowledge.

CHAPTER 11

The Point One Archetype:
The Type, Subtypes, and Growth Path

*Probably my worst quality is that I get very passionate about
what I think is right.*

—Hillary Clinton

*Freedom is not worth having if it does not include the
freedom to make mistakes.*

—Mahatma Gandhi

TYPE ONE REPRESENTS THE ARCHETYPE of the person who seeks to be good
and do "the right thing" to satisfy an urgent need to be virtuous and responsible and to avoid fault and blame. This drive provides a defensive protection in
a world that demands and rewards good behavior and punishes bad behavior.

This archetype also exists as the "superego," that part of the psyche that
stands in for the parental voice of authority. This internal force exercises its
power to tame the excesses born of raw impulses, animal instinct, and unre-
stricted forms of self-interested self-expression.

Type Ones are thus the prototype for that part in all of us that strives to
match high standards of good behavior as a way of proving ourselves worthy
and avoiding blame or fault. This archetypal stance prioritizes following the
rules as a way of bringing about a perceived higher good through invoking a
higher order.

This effort also necessarily involves stifling or "civilizing" natural impulses,
instincts, and feelings that would lead us to break the rules to our advantage.
Type Ones are vigilant not to let these forces get out of control. Ones tend to
inhibit their experience of the wisdom of the "animal within" and the natural
rhythms of spontaneity, instinctive expression, and play. Rigidity, criticism,

and continuous judgment are as characteristic of this archetypal character as their belief in justice, fairness, and good order.

Type One individuals are reliable, responsible, honest, well-intentioned, conscientious, and hardworking. They sincerely want to improve themselves and the world around them. Their specific "superpower" can be seen in their high integrity and the passion and dedication they bring to the fulfillment of their ideals and the pursuit of high standards. They have well-developed powers of criticism and an intuitive sense of the perfection of nature and the natural order of things. They are diligent, practical, and thrifty. They can be discerning and objective, meaning that they excel at analyzing situations and clarifying issues while separating out any emotions that may be involved.

As with all the archetypal personalities, however, Type Ones' gifts and strengths also represent their "fatal flaw" or "Achilles heel:" they get in their own way by overdoing their focus on virtue and thus undermine their own self-confidence, balance, and inner peace through over-control, self-repression, and excessive judgment. However, when they can learn to tame their sometimes harsh criticality and take things less seriously, they can call on their gifts of discernment, reliability, and idealism to make the world a better place.

The Type One Archetype in Homer's *Odyssey:*
The Phaeacians of Scheria

After encountering characters posing obstacles and threats along the way, Odysseus confronts the Phaeacians of Scheria, who are disciplined and proper, orderly, and conventional. They are courteous, concerned with etiquette, duty, and doing the right thing. Their king's castle is architecturally perfect, surrounded by bronze walls. They are expert sailors and are always careful to stay precisely on course.[1] Eventually they come to feel morally obligated to help Odysseus get back to Ithaca.

As virtuous as the Phaeacians are, even these "ideal" qualities have a downside. Anything taken to its extreme becomes a problem, including making moral judgments. Homer tells us that some find them to be "bloodless do-gooders," and that their perfectionism can be heavy and hectoring rather than graceful and helpful.[2]

The Phaeacians embody the Type One personality in striving to be paragons of virtue—but also as being rigid, self-righteous, and judgmental toward those who are not.

Trying to be perfect is not enough to protect the Phaeacians from the whims of fate, however. Poseidon resents their vessel's almost superhuman speed and the gifts they leave with Odysseus. He turns the Phaeacians' ship to stone just as it returns to the harbor and he prepares to raise a mountain around Scheria's port. The Phaeacians realize Poseidon's fury, and they rush desperately to begin a great sacrifice. We last see them in pious prayer and ritual, hoping only to appease the anger of a powerful god.

The Type One Personality Structure

LOCATED AT THE TOP-RIGHT CORNER of the Enneagram, Type One belongs to the "body-based" triad associated with the core emotion of *anger* and a focus of attention related to *order, structure, and control.*

Although Type One is a body type, the focus on judgment and standards can make Ones seem more head focused, energetically. This trait reflects the constant internal dynamic in which the mental function assesses, regulates, and often actively stops "wrong" impulses originating in the body.

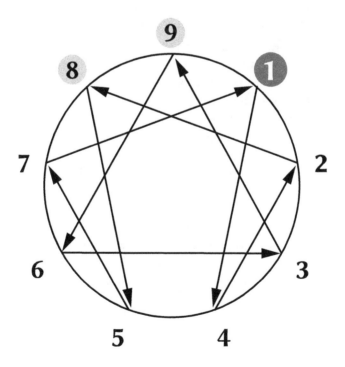

Naranjo notes that, fundamentally, the One is an over-civilized or over-controlled type. Typically, when Ones experience an impulse—to run, to express anger, to embrace someone—it moves up from the gut and through the body before being intercepted and judged by a well-developed critical function in the mind. If the impulse fails the inspection, the One's critical thinking function labels the impulse "wrong" and represses it.

Most often, this repression is routine. A frown may cross the One's face. A passing comment (maybe self-effacing) might deflect the moment. But if the impulse is "unacceptable" at a deeper moral level, it can trigger "reaction formation," a defense mechanism in which the One pushes the original impulse down hard into the unconscious through automatic generation and expression of the *opposite* impulse.

With each "wrong" impulse, the One's fixation with being correct and avoiding fault is in conflict with a natural and spontaneous impulse, instinct, or feeling. This conflict is frustrating, and the critical function that maintains it is relentless. This simmering anger then easily becomes resentment when confronted with "rule-breaking" or self-indulgent behavior. The One's perception that being a resentful person is itself "wrong" or "bad" encloses the personality in a cycle of judgment and anger, of reaction and often, regret.

The Early Coping Strategy: Type One

Type One personalities defend against criticism, real or threatened, and shame or punishment for being "wrong" or "bad." Ones often report that they experienced pressure early in life to do something well or correct at a time when they were too young to take on the burden of this responsibility. The experience of criticism from parental figures or others creates an anxious sense in the young One that there is a "right way" to do things. Doing the "right" thing and striving for faultless performance inspires supportive feedback and positive feelings.

Some Ones experienced this early responsibility because they lacked structural support (or psychological "holding") in their childhood environment. Chaos or uncertainty or anxiety in the family motivates the One child to take on the task of providing order and structure for himself and often others in the family. The coping strategy of adhering strongly to sound rules, routines, and standards of behavior provides the One with inner cohesion and security, as well as protection from criticism. If Ones can manage to put things in just the right order, they can actually relax somewhat and experience a sense of well-being.

On the other hand, criticism and anxiety coming from things *not* being in the right order quickly teaches the One child the dangers of following spontaneous impulses. The child learns that doing the "wrong" thing or not making a good enough effort is—and *should* be—something that invites negative feedback and painful feelings.

Naranjo explains that the Type One personality structure grows out of this early burden of responsibility coupled with little acknowledgment of the One child's essential goodness.[3] Natural frustration builds when a child has to exercise a high degree of self-control at too early an age. The One child denies this frustration through overcompensating in the other direction. She unconsciously turns away from the anger and frustration, displacing the energy of this emotion into efforts to be excessively good.

Ones also internalize a "parental" voice that functions thereafter as an internal critic or coach. This coping strategy of proactively criticizing oneself and trying to do things correctly prior to coming under parental scrutiny can avoid outside criticism and punishment. This guidance system keeps the One on track according to specific standards of ideal behavior in an ongoing way. But the internal critic that originally formed to protect the Type One becomes an ever-present voice or sense, detecting fault and imperfection in oneself and the outside world.

Derek, a Self-Preservation One, describes his childhood situation and the development of his coping strategy:

He was the oldest of three boys. His father was a military officer Type Eight who flew airplanes in Vietnam. His mother was a Type Nine "hippie." His parents divorced when he was young and the three boys went to live with their Dad. As the oldest of the three boys, Derek was "second in command." If something went wrong on his watch, there was hell to pay. At his mom's house, life was unconventional, and Derek felt responsible for trying to create stability—and avoid embarrassment. Derek's strong sense of responsibility at a very young age produced in him an anxiety and habitual attention focused on making sure things are "going right" and assessing how he and others are fulfilling their duties.

The Main Type One Defense Mechanism: Reaction Formation

Reaction formation is a psychological defense through which the human psyche turns something into its polar opposite to render it less threatening. So, in the face of "excessive demands and frustration" early in life, instead of feeling angry and rebelling, the One child takes on more responsibility, becoming a very good boy or girl.[4] The fundamental fixation to be good and do the right thing motivates the Ones' focus on "positive" feelings and their denial or repression of their "negative" feelings. Reaction formation serves to relieve the stress of this difficult internal conflict. Focusing on and expressing more acceptable "good" emotions allows the Type One to push "bad" feelings into the unconscious.

An example of reaction formation as an active defense might be the One's automatic tendency to be excessively nice to someone with whom they are actually angry or dissatisfied. Or reaction formation might turn a rising feeling of envy at another's success into an expression of admiration for them. Through reaction formation, any emotion can be denied (unconsciously) by bringing forward its "bright side" opposite. Reaction formation also functions to deny ambivalence: instead of feeling mixed feelings, like resenting someone you feel grateful for or hating someone you love, a One changes mental focus to allow themselves to feel only the positive end of this complex set of emotions.[5]

Reaction formation helps protect the One from outside criticism by ensuring that his or her expressions of emotion are controlled and appropriate. Reaction formation also defends the One against feeling the full force of internal judgment for feelings he or she feels it's "wrong" or "bad" to have (much less express) like "inappropriate" anger or selfish desire.

The Type One Focus of Attention

The focus of attention on trying to make things as right as possible makes Ones instinctively drawn to noticing "errors" or "imperfections" and then correcting them. The mental habit of judging against an inner ideal goes beyond just discerning right and wrong or good and bad. Through the inner critic, a Type One habitually assesses better or worse (and why) in everything they compare to this ideal. Whether the person instinctively directs this impulse more inward, toward society, or into personal relationships, the focus of attention remains on *striving for flawlessness* in order to avoid criticism and pain.

Ones develop a deep appreciation for what they view as "perfect," which comes from what they "feel" or "know" to be correct. The Type One focus is often frustrating, as the actual attainment of something perfect is an impossible standard. But Ones also describe feeling a wonderful sensation of peace and satisfaction when things do come together in the just right way. Their focus on achieving this feeling, however rare or temporary, motivates Ones to work hard and attend energetically to the details of everything they value in their quest for security and well-being that accompanies an optimal result.

It is important to note that Ones don't all focus their attention on fault-lessness in the same way, or apply it to every aspect of their lives. Some Ones may focus on order and cleanliness in their environment, while others may not mind having a messy office but rather focus intently on larger questions in the political or moral realm, like issues of right and wrong or social justice. Some of these differences in focus naturally occur at the instinctual level according to the emphasis on Self-Preservation, Social relationships, or Sexual bonding.

The Type One Emotional Passion: Anger

The passion is a specific emotional motivation at the core of the Personality. *Anger* is the emotional passion for Type Ones, but it operates in a particular way. What we commonly think of as overt aggression is more prominent in other types, such as Eights and the Sexual subtypes of Sixes and Fours. Type Ones experience and express anger more as resentment, frustration, self-righteousness, or irritation. Ones report that they most often feel resentment, a kind of low-level, background, tamped down anger that things aren't as they should be. Anger often manifests as irritation or frustration when it's controlled and rationalized, manifested by someone committed to being above reproach.

On the other hand, Ones can be fiercely angry when they feel righteous—and therefore "appropriate"—in expressing it.

Type One's anger has two main sources. First, it grows out of the frustrating experience of trying hard to achieve perfection; but also, Ones habitually recognize instances where others fail to meet—or even try to meet—the standards they inherently feel are "right" or "correct" or "appropriate." This perception adds angry resentment for the "bad" conduct of others to the One's frustration at how difficult it is to set things right in life.

The repressed or "sullen" form of anger is the side of the Type One personality that most people might not notice. Far from being a violent or disruptive personality, the One's underlying passion of anger actually ends up fueling an over-controlled or over-civilized character.[6] A One is more likely to appear to others as tense or critical or demanding or "committed," than they are to appear overtly mad or rude.

The Type One Cognitive Mistake:
"We All Can and Should Do Better"

In Chapter 1 we discussed the idea that for each of us our personality manifests in all three of our centers of intelligence. We all get stuck in habitual ways of thinking that influence our beliefs, feelings, and actions, and this continues even after the mental models that create our overall perspective aren't accurate anymore. Naranjo describes these fixed mental assumptions as the "cognitive mistake" or mental trance that underlies and shapes character. While the passion shapes the personality's emotional motivations, the "cognitive fixation" preoccupies the personality's thought processes.

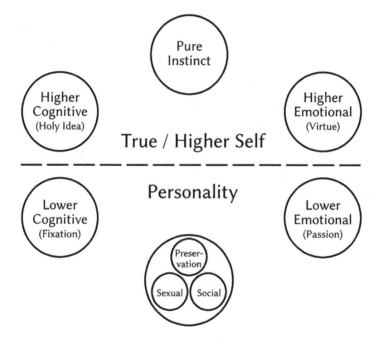

Type Ones typically believe that their object of attention is imperfect and that they must try to improve it, whether they are focused on themselves, their loved ones, or society at large. They also tend to think that it's bad to make mistakes and that bad behavior should be punished. These beliefs lead to behaviors like working hard and adhering to rules and codes of ethics. Emotionally, these beliefs and thoughts cause Ones to suffer the anxiety, frustration, and resentment we've discussed.

For example, a Type One person focused on her own imperfection may believe that she is unworthy and inadequate even when the evidence in how she lives her life shows that she is actually successful in many ways and more than adequate. Her cognitive mistake is that she can and should be doing better, even though objectively she always does her best to be ethical and diligent.

And yet these habitual ways of thinking are extremely hard to change. They formed early in life and served a vital protective function for the developing self. But like the acorn shell, we inhibit our growth by staying within the confines of these habitual patterns of thought.

Here are some key beliefs and assumptions characteristic of the Type One personality. The predominance and focus of these perspectives vary somewhat by subtype, as we'll see later in this chapter.

- I must strive to meet high standards of behavior and performance to avoid criticism and feelings of failure.
- I am flawed and far from perfect and therefore often bad.
- If I don't actively inhibit my emotions, impulses, and needs, I might say or do something inappropriate and bring shame on myself.
- I like to be someone people rely on to be fair and upright. If I'm going to be proud of anything, I guess I'm proud of that.
- If something goes wrong, but I did everything as correctly as I could have, then I can't be at fault.
- Pretty much everything in the world can be improved—and some parts definitely *should* be.
- Perfect is hard. It should be hard. It's rare, and it's hard. But it's worth it.
- If everyone did their part to follow what they *know* are the rules of decent society, everything would flow much more smoothly.

These kinds of core beliefs help Ones to make well-considered sense of the world. But the Type One's striving for perfection while focusing so much on flaws binds his or her understanding of "self" to this struggle to improve an endlessly imperfect world.

The Type One Trap:
"If Not 'Perfect,' What Does 'Good Enough' Mean?"

The patterns and habits that arise out of the coping strategy of proactively criticizing in light of specific standards of quality or perfection create a circular "trap" that Type Ones act out consciously and unconsciously. This "trap" reflects a basic conflict at the core of the One personality. Ones avoid criticism and punishment by holding themselves or others to a punishingly high standard. They then fuel this cycle with anger and resentment at failures to meet this standard. In this way their striving to free themselves or others from fault only reinforces Type Ones' habitual beliefs about being unworthy or unlovable. Thus, Ones' efforts to prove themselves acceptable and lovable ends up reinforcing their false belief in their imperfection and unlovableness. Clearly, when you only love what is perfect, it's hard to accept—to *relax* in the knowledge—that "just okay" really can be good enough for everyone.

The Key Type One Traits

Inner Critic
Most Ones will say that they have an inner critic that judges and otherwise comments upon almost everything they do. While some of the other personality types may experience this kind of internal critical dialogue some of the time, Ones report experiencing this voice as much as 90 to 100 percent of their waking hours. Other types who are also inwardly critical can decrease or even disregard this voice temporarily. But for a One, this critical function largely dominates their internal life.

A Type One's inner critic can sometimes develop to be more like an internal parent than simply a harsh inner judge. According to some Ones, the same impulse that criticizes the One for having done something poorly might be an encouraging impulse in the next moment, as if saying, "That was better, do that again next time."

Over-Control
Part of Type One's need to exercise control in their environment is so they can influence outcomes in a "good" or "right" direction, away from a "bad" or "wrong" one.

Ones can often be perceived by others as inflexible or rigid, which is a natural consequence of their tendency to over-control themselves and the things they say and do. They like the security of ritual, routine, and rules they know can be enforced, but it can be hard for them to see when control and adherence to rules becomes a problematic tendency to "over-control." Among other things, this often means that work has to come before play and they don't leave enough room for pleasure, fun, and relaxation.

Although Ones tend to be controlled in their expression of anger, they are not always conscious of how angry they really are. They try to inhibit their expression, but heightened anger, frustration, or resentment often "leaks out" in their nonverbal behavior. The One may be completely unaware that others can see this anger "leaking" through his or her control.

Virtuousness

Ones endeavor continually to be virtuous. Unlike other types, who have other kinds of primary motivations and may enjoy being "bad," Ones orient themselves toward being good citizens and doing the right thing. Generally, this is a well-intentioned, morally upright character. Ones truly want to be good and do the right thing as they see it for everyone's benefit.

In addition to a love of order, perfectionism may also be at work in obedience to authority and altruistic efforts to do good works. In all of these One tendencies, adherence to the guiding principles that rules and ideals supply can be seen to be both a strategy for gaining affection through virtuousness and a reaction formation defense against anger and frustration.

Perfectionism and Criticality

My Type One brother once made a comment that demonstrates the One's desire for perfection. I was cooking dinner at his house one night, and as I began to make the pasta sauce, he peered into the pot and remarked that the chopped onions I was sauteing were not all the same size. This kind of comment speaks to the concern with making things perfect or uniform. Ones can believe that if things are not made perfect, bad things will happen; in this case, perhaps my brother feared that imperfectly cut onions would result in a chewy marinara.

While perfectionism or "flawlessness" can be said to be the core focus or root strategy of the One, not all Ones relate to being perfectionists in the same way. As we will explore as we move into talking about the subtypes, a One's perfectionism and criticality varies with the subtype's instinctual focus toward self-preservation, social relationships, or sexual bonding.

The Type One Shadow

Generally, Ones have blind spots related to the Shadow side of their efforts to be good, do the right thing, and fulfill high ideals. Because they believe they are always right, they can be overly critical and punishing of themselves and others, but rationalize their harsh treatment as correct or justified. Ones can also be highly sensitive to criticism. It can be hard for them to hear sincere feedback from others because they are already beating up on themselves or fearing critical messages.

The Shadow side of believing in perfection is a tendency to fall into rigid, black-and-white thinking. Others can experience them as inflexible, or hyper-critical and see the standards they apply as unreasonable given that perfection is often not possible or desirable.

The attachment to the inner critic as a defense against the chaos of unre-stricted impulses can lead Ones to believe in unrelenting criticism as a nec-essary feature of their inner experience, rationalizing their judgments as a needed check on imperfections, even when it drives them into depression and anxiety. Ones thus have a blind spot about the downside of their tendency to criticize. In particular, they often fail to see and own their highly positive qualities. In this way, Ones demonstrate that "positive" attributes can also be shadow elements in the personality.

Ones may have a difficult time considering the validity of someone else's view of things if they perceive others as being unfair, biased, or morally lax. When taking what they see as a higher moral position in a conflict, it can be hard for them to let go of the perception that the other person "knows" he or she is doing something wrong and is doing it anyway. It can be difficult for Ones to accept that there are no moral absolutes. In these respects, their Shadow aspect is the ability to see beyond the black and white of their own inner sense of "right" and "wrong," or "better or worse."

Most of all, Ones have a blind spot related to their experience and expres-sion of anger. In some cases, Ones don't know (and can't admit) when they are angry. If there is too much pressure on a One to repress what may be irrepress-ible, something has to give. Leaking occurs when Ones try to deny, control, or hide their anger, but others see it in a clenched jaw, a curt or abrupt way of speaking, a strained tone of voice, or a tension-filled body.

Righteous outbursts can be one way that a One's anger may escape despite their intention to repress it. This happens when Ones channel their anger into a cause or an opinion about some sort of injustice that they feel a sense of righteous indignation about. Because this righteousness may be about what they see as an objectively unjust situation, or it may be on behalf of others, Ones can rationalize that they are actually being virtuous instead of angry. On rare occasions, Ones may also "act out" their Shadow in some form of "bad" behavior, when their efforts at virtue become too stressful, and their deeper impulses or needs (that normally stay hidden, even to themselves) escape their conscious control.

The Shadow of the Type One Passion:
Anger **in Dante's Underworld**

In Dante's *Inferno*, "the Wrathful" describes those that succumbed to the Passion of Anger in their lives. As punishment, the shades that went so deep into anger during their lives are now completely taken over by this emotion—muddy people, fighting each other, their faces scarred with rage—those that "anger overcame" are "covered" all over with mud, having a brutal, physical fight in the dingy swamp.

> *I, intent on looking as we passed, saw muddy people moving in that marsh, all naked, with their faces scarred by rage. They fought each other, not with hands alone, but struck with head and chest and feet as well with teeth they tore each other limb from limb.* [7]

Not all anger deserves this punishment, of course. The Pilgrim himself angrily shouts down one foul-tempered shade that accosts the boat: "May you weep and wail, stuck in this place forever, you damned soul, for, filthy as you are, I recognize you!"[8] Virgil praises the Pilgrim for being indignant because the shade's earthly life earned him that rebuke and more.

The extreme Anger punished in the underworld and shadowing the Type One personality is a mindset of hostility and resentment that habitually creates constant struggle. As we see in Dante's underworld, that kind of rage is always its own reward.[9] The Pilgrim last sees the shadow he recognized being attacked in the muck, so mad with anger that he turns to biting himself.

The Three Kinds of Ones:
The Type One Subtypes

IN EACH OF THE THREE TYPE ONE SUBTYPES, the passion of anger gets channeled through different drives related to trying to make things perfect. Ones either try to perfect themselves and the things they do (Self-Preservation), or they consider themselves to be perfect because they adhere to "the right way to be" (Social), or they try to perfect other people (Sexual).

The three Type One subtypes represent distinct characters as each of the three Ones manifests as a specific expression of anger. While they share the larger Type One themes in common, each subtype further specializes in or focuses on a different subset of the Type One concerns.

Naranjo, drawing on Ichazo, gives the three Type One subtypes descriptive titles as a way of suggesting each of their distinct patterns of attention. The Self-Preservation subtype has been named "Worry," the Social subtype is called "Non-Adaptability" or "Rigidity," and the Sexual subtype is "Zeal." Naranjo notes that the Self-Preservation Ones are the true "perfectionists"; the Social Ones are "perfect" in that they believe they know the right way to be; and the Sexual Ones focus on "perfecting others." While the larger category of Type Ones is sometimes referred to as "The Perfectionist," this mainly applies to the Self-Preservation Ones. Sexual Ones are more "reformers" than perfectionists.

The Self-Preservation One: "Worry"

For the Self-Preservation One, anger is most repressed. To render their own anger less threatening, the mechanism of reaction formation transforms the heat of anger into warmth. And this is a major shift—an angry person disconnecting from his anger to become a gentle, supportive person with good intentions. In this subtype, the anger of the One, together with defenses against that anger, manifest as good intentions, perfectionism, heroic efforts, obedience to rules, and an obsessive striving for perfection.

The outward result is an excessively gentle, decent, and kind person. In the quest to perfect themselves, Self-Preservation Ones believe it's bad to be angry and so make a virtue of being tolerant, forgiving, and sweet whenever possible. Underneath, these Ones are very angry, but they control it. Under pressure, however, this One's anger may leak out as irritation, resentment, frustration, or self-righteousness.

The Self-Preservation One worries a lot. This subtype has a need for foresight, a desire to plan everything out, and a compulsion to try to have everything under control. Self-Preservation Ones often had a chaotic family history where they had to provide the stability, even as young children. These Ones were usually the most responsible person in the family. Perhaps because their survival felt threatened by out-of-control elements in their early environment, this subtype has a lot of anxiety. They lack confidence that things will go as they should, so they display an excessive sense of responsibility that takes the form of worrying and fussing, even when things are going well.

This One has an ongoing sense that anything could go wrong at any minute unless they are on high alert to make sure that things happen as they should. This One also has a faulty sense of security with regard to survival and an implicit anxiety about things not going well and the consequences of failure. Self-Preservation Ones can sometimes let go of worrying if they become convinced there is nothing they can do about a situation, but it is difficult for them to stop being vigilant if there is something they can do to have an effect on the situation.

This tendency toward feeling anxious and constantly on guard can, in some cases, trigger obsessive-compulsive defenses; that is, Self-Preservation Ones can become obsessive in their thinking and compulsive or ritualistic in their behaviors as they attempt to reduce anxiety by thinking certain thoughts or engaging in certain behaviors. The Self-Preservation One does so to gain a sense of control over what is happening, and through gaining a sense of control, finally be able to relax. However, there are so many things to be done and worried about that this One is rarely able to relax.

This subtype is the epitome of a true perfectionist, as they are especially hard on themselves if they don't get things right. As Naranjo points out, Self-Preservation Ones have difficulty loosening their need for control and allowing for a flow to happen. Instead they feel compelled to insert themselves if necessary, to make sure every important detail gets scrutinized and perfected. The quest to do the right thing or to find the perfect solution is how the Self-Preservation One finds safety

The title of "worry" was given to this type as a descriptive label because they have a passion, or a strong emotional compulsion, to worry or fret. And more than having frequent worry as a character trait, the Self-Preservation One feels an insatiable drive to fret. Self-Preservation Ones typically experience three convergent aspects of this "worry/fret" drive. Constant fretting is used to 1) attain perfection, however small; or 2) avert misfortune, however large; or 3) free themselves from blame, however slight.

Anger lies beneath the fretting and constitutes this One's early response to having to worry in the first place. The young Self-Preservation One cannot allow himself to be conscious of his anger, as the experience of anger (or overwhelming frustration) itself represents a threat to the child who takes on too much too early. However, older Self-Preservation Ones are usually plenty angry and this anger shapes the personality in adulthood.

In relationships, Self-Preservation Ones demonstrate a sensitivity to being criticized and can become very angry when they feel blamed. In times of conflict, these Ones can be self-righteous, rigid, and unyielding. They tend to own up to their failings (sometimes too readily) and are forgiving when others admit guilt or apologize. Partners can feel criticized and held to impossibly high standards, but can also count of Self-Preservation Ones to be extremely reliable and trustworthy.

Self-Preservation Ones can get confused with Type Sixes, especially Social Sixes, who have characteristics that make them look One-ish, like black-and-white thinking and obedience to rules and authorities, or Self-Preservation Sixes, who also feel an underlying sense of anxiety and insecurity. What differentiates the Self-Preservation One from the fear-based Six, however, is the central, though mostly unconscious, role of the One's passion of anger. Sixes are motivated by fear and doubt as opposed to resentment. Self-Preservation Ones continually ask the question: "Why am I always the one working to improve reality, when it benefits all of us to try to make things right or better?" Sixes, by contrast, are preoccupied with coping with anxiety. Ones also have more confidence in the standards of perfection they apply, whereas Sixes continually doubt whether or not what they do is "right."

Eric, a Self-Preservation One, speaks:

My whole life I've been a worrier. I worried especially about getting in trouble or something going wrong because I didn't do my best at whatever it was I was supposed to do. As a young kid, I was pretty obsessive because it seemed to me that every time I didn't stay vigilant, something would go wrong and I would get punished. In reality, I was what parents call "a great kid." I always got good grades because I studied obsessively to get A's. I argued when I felt my mom or my dad was being really unfair, but I wouldn't have dreamed of getting into trouble on purpose. I was surprised to learn that not everyone has a "critical" voice going all the time, keeping them doing the right thing and away from doing the wrong things.

The Social One: "Non-Adaptability"

The Social One is less of a perfectionist and focuses more on being the perfect example for others of the right way to be. This One is not an internally anxious person striving to be perfectionistic, but rather a paragon of correct conduct. Social Ones have a need to represent the perfect model of the way to be or do things through their actions—to teach others by example. Ichazo labeled this type "Non-adaptability" and Naranjo calls this subtype "Rigidity," describing the Social One as having a kind of "school teacher" mentality. Non-adaptability or rigidity refers to the tendency of this character to rigidly adhere to particular ways of being and doing things, as a way of expressing exclusive ownership of the "right" way to be, think, and behave.

In this Social One subtype, anger is half-hidden. Where the heat of anger changes into warmth in the Self-Preservation One, in this personality there is a transformation of the heat of anger into cold. This character tends to be a cooler, more intellectual type, in which the main characteristic is control. However, the anger of the Social One is not completely repressed, because there is an equivalent of anger in their passion for being the owner of the truth. In this subtype, anger gets channeled into an overconfidence about being right or "perfect."

The Social One has a (usually unconscious) need to feel superior or to appear superior (because a conscious desire to be superior would constitute bad behavior). It is as if they are implicitly saying, "I'm right and you're wrong." They have an underlying need to make others wrong to have some power over them. If I'm right and you're wrong, then I have more right than you to control the situation. Like my Social One father always used to say: "I've never been wrong, except once, when I thought I was wrong, but I was mistaken."

Social Ones learn to repress emotions from a very early age; they were usually good kids who did not cause problems. They may have been young adults who acted "older" than they really were, who often forgot that they were children.

A person of this subtype may purposely not adjust to changing times or customs. A Social One tends to persist in a particular way of doing things that she thinks is right, despite others having evolved into doing it a different way. This One displays the general attitude, "This is how it is and I'm going to tell you how it should be."

Not surprisingly, Social Ones automatically take on the role of teacher. Social Ones have the sense that demonstrating and modeling what they are teaching is equally or more valuable than what that say. It's the idea that a good model goes a long way toward making the point being taught. They may also be unaware of the need to appear superior, but may receive feedback from others that they are acting like a "know-it-all."

This is the Type One who resembles Type Five in that this character can be more introverted and may seem a bit "above it all" and emotionally detached. They separate themselves from the crowd because they are perfect and therefore superior. They never feel completely comfortable in the groups they frequent; they tend to feel alienated. But while Fives focus primarily on conserving energy and resources, Ones focus more on making things perfect and their anger is closer to the surface.

In relationships, Social Ones can have high expectations. They tend to have more confidence in themselves than in others. They can seem remote at times, being self-sufficient to the point of not seeming to need others. It can also prove difficult for partners and friends to convince Social Ones that a perspective other than their own can be correct. They are great reasoners and will argue their point energetically. They dominate through making the other person wrong, and it can be hard to convince them of the validity of a competing point of view.

Francis, a Social One, speaks:

In my daily life, I tend to put a lot of energy into getting things right, and then get annoyed when others don't. For example, one thing I hate is when people park over the line of a parking space, because now the space beside it is too small for me to park my car. I therefore make a point of always parking right between the lines when I park my car (sometimes to my wife's utter exasperation: "I can't get out on my side!"), because that's the right way to behave and that's the way I would like everyone else to behave. So it's not so much being picky as it is about setting an example for everyone else.

In my profession as an orchestra conductor, my attention to detail in preparing for a rehearsal gives me great confidence when it's time to step in front of the orchestra at a performance. It's like when you know you've prepared well for a test. I know the music well, I've gone over every part, and I'm confident that I can set a good example to inspire the players to make good music.

The Sexual One: "Zeal" (Countertype)

While the Self-Preservation One is a perfectionist, and the Social One unconsciously takes on the pose of someone who is "perfect" in modeling to the right way to be, Sexual Ones focus on perfecting others. This One is more of a reformer than a perfectionist. They have a need to improve others, but don't focus on being perfect themselves.

This is the only One subtype that is explicitly angry and so is the countertype of the three One personalities. The Sexual One is impatient, can be invasive, goes for what he or she wants, and has a sense of entitlement. These Ones have an intensity of desire fueled by anger that motivates them to want to improve others. This can be expressed as a sense of excitement, passion, or idealism about the way things could be if people would reform their behavior, or if the reforms they envision were enacted by society. This makes them compelling and vehement.

This character feels entitled in the sense of possessing the mentality of a reformer or a zealot—one who knows how to live or do things better and so feels a right to assert their will over others. Like the mentality of a conqueror, this approach can be rationalized (and made virtuous) through the rhetoric of their adherence to a higher moral code or calling.

According to Naranjo, Ichazo gave this subtype the name, "Zeal," meaning "a special intensity of desire." Zeal suggests an intensity or excitement that fuels the desire to connect with others. It also means doing things with care, dedication, and fervor.

This One's anger infuses his desire with a special intensity or urgency and the person has the sense that "I have to have it," or "I have a right to it," or "I have to improve it (society or another person) to make it the way I know it should be."

In a collective sense, this can be seen in the idea of "manifest destiny," the ideology that justified the takeover of the western part of the United States from the Native Americans in the 1800s. Despite what our retrospective view of that period might be, this philosophy was a justification for the white man taking over land populated by "savages." Another example of this ideology can be seen in the minds of conquerors, as when the Spanish conquered South America. The rhetoric displayed there was, "I can take this because I'm noble and civilized."

In the Sexual One, this intensity of desire can support the impulse to reform or perfect specific others or to make the world a better place in the way this One believes it should be. Sometimes, this desire to perfect others grows out of a genuine belief in an enlightened vision of reform or idealism. However, it may at the same time be fueled by this instinctual subtype's need to make others more perfect. One woman I know with this subtype reported that she felt she would be justified in leaving her husband if he did not carry out her suggestions for his improvement. And she felt a need to help him become a better person so she could have a better partner.

In Western culture there can be an anti-sexual or anti-instinctual sentiment—the idea that it's not okay to act on one's desires. For instance, the sinfulness of sex is so pervasive that it can be hard sometimes not to feel improper or naughty if we allow ourselves to freely express our sexual desires. But the Sexual One has a different, more liberated, attitude with regard to sexual desire. There's a kind of "go for it" mentality that can then necessitate the finding of good reasons to support the rightness of whatever the Sexual One wants to do. Unlike the Self-Preservation Ones, these Ones don't question themselves as much. Instead they are concerned more with making others into the people they think they should be.

These Ones are avengers; they are not afraid of confrontation. They may be containing a murderous rage that they cannot see. Their anger can be like a volcano that erupts. They perceive themselves as strong. They have great strength and determination and can be very brave. They are also impulsive and do things quickly.

Sexual Ones have two sides: a more playful side oriented toward pleasure and an aggressive, angry side. Pain is the emotion they repress the most and the one they find most difficult to show. They may act out their unacknowledged pain by leading a double life as a way of breaking the rules. Some Sexual Ones display "trap-door" behavior, discharging their anger and pain through "bad" acts. An example of this is Eliot Spitzer. As the Attorney General of the State of New York, he crusaded against lawbreakers, going after Wall Street criminals and prostitutes in an effort to reform society. However, he later resigned as the Governor when he was caught having an ongoing relationship with a prostitute himself.

In light of this type of behavior, this One can look like a type Eight. Like Eights, they can be energetic, assertive, and strong. These Ones believe they have a right to impose their vision and get what they need, in the same way an Eight might overpower or dominate a situation to impose their own will. But Eights and Ones differ in that Ones are "over-social" and Eights are "under-social."

Sexual Ones bring intensity and energy to relationships. They can be forceful and insistent. They may attempt to reform their partners and friends, conveying the sense of being on a mission or drawing on a higher calling or authority in the things they do. They excel at pointing out what others might need to do to reform their behavior or meet specific standards, but focus less interest and attention in reforming their own behavior, seeing what they do as right.

Sally, a Sexual One, speaks:

I have a strong need for order in my relationships. This order is determined by my moral code of conduct, which holds my internal world together. When this is disrupted (which is quite often) I can be edgy, critical, demanding, and insensitive. I have often been unaware of how I wanted to (and tried to) fix or improve others. It just seems so right to bring order through clear communication and the sharing of insights.

I can be very jealous when others seem to enjoy closer connections than I do. And I am more than alert to my partner's placement of attention, especially on another woman! My intensity often surprises me! And I see now how challenging it can be for those around me.

"The Work" for Type One: Charting a Personal Growth Path

ULTIMATELY, AS ONES WORK ON THEMSELVES and become more self-aware, they learn to escape the trap of confirming their own unworthiness through excessive criticism by seeing and accepting imperfection, lightening up on themselves and others, and learning that they (and others) are lovable and acceptable as they are.

For all of us, waking up to habitual personality patterns involves making ongoing, conscious efforts to observe ourselves, reflect on the meaning and sources of what we observe, and actively work to counter automatic tendencies. For Ones this process can be tricky, however, because they already overdo self-improvement and "correct" behavior. In light of this, it may be particularly important for them to employ Enneagram-based growth strategies that take into account the ways they already overcompensate through a core life strategy based on "improvement."

In this section I offer some ideas about what Ones can notice, explore, and aim for in their efforts to grow beyond the constraints of their personality and embody the higher possibilities associated with their type and subtype.

Self-Observation: Dis-identifying from Your Personality by Watching It in Action

Self-Observation is about creating enough internal space to really watch—with fresh eyes and more distance—what you are thinking, feeling, and doing in your everyday life. As Ones take note of the things they think, feel, and do, they might look out for the following key patterns:

Measuring everything against an ideal standard and driving for perfection in yourself, others, and/or the external environment through the operation of an "inner critic"

This pattern includes continually criticizing yourself and being judgmental of others. While the main target of a One's critical tendency varies by subtype, Ones generally apply their standards of what is virtuous or correct internally and externally. This can lead to procrastination (delaying endpoints when trying to make things more perfect), "one right way" and "black and white" thinking, and self-punishing attitudes and behavior. In the extreme, Ones may believe that if something is not perfect, it's worthless. They may observe themselves devaluing and demoralizing themselves, leading to a cycle of efforts to improve, harsh criticism despite those efforts, and renewed efforts at improvement in light of that criticism.

Conscientiously following the rules as part of an overall effort to avoid making mistakes

Ones like structure and they find it in rules and routines. But being overly rule-bound can make Ones rigid and inflexible. Following rules can support the One tendency to believe they know the "one right way" to act. This habit may create an internal sense of safety or well-being—if you're following the rules, you can't be blamed!—but it can be hard to see when you're overdoing it to the point of making more anxiety and tension for yourself. (And this is another vicious cycle to watch out for.)

Repressing and over-controlling feelings, needs, and impulses

In a way that mirrors their experience of their early environment, Ones demand too much of themselves. As part of the "self-forgetting" triad of body-based Enneagram types, Ones neglect their deeper needs and vulnerable feelings in their total focus on doing the right thing and working hard to make things perfect. Ones benefit from noticing when they feel resentful and recognizing this as a clue to repressed needs and feelings. If you are a One you may notice that internal tension builds when you over-control natural impulses and feelings that you (automatically) judge as wrong or threatening.

Recognizing (and compassionately accepting) your deeper needs, impulses, and feelings can be an important first step in seeing and reversing the efforts you exert to work against the wisdom of your (healthy and appropriate) instincts and emotions.

Self-Inquiry and Self-Reflection: Gathering More Data to Expand Your Self-Knowledge

As Ones observe these and other related patterns in themselves, the next step on the Enneagram growth path is to *understand* these patterns more. Why do they exist? Where do they come from? What purpose do they serve? How do they get you in trouble when they are intended to help you? Often, seeing the root causes of a habit—why it exists and what it is designed to do—is enough to break out of the pattern. In other cases, with more entrenched habits, knowing how and why they operate as defenses can be a first step to being able to release them.

Here are some questions that Ones can ask themselves and some possible answers they can consider to get more insight into the sources, operation, and consequences of these patterns.

How and why did these patterns develop? How do these habits help you cope?

Through understanding the sources of their defensive patterns, Ones have the opportunity to unlock the fixed nature of the strict requirements ruling their lives. It helps Ones to explore how control and judgment may have been adopted by their young self as a defense against the pain of being criticized or punished. If Ones begin to feel more empathy for their younger self that was faced with impossible demands, they can practice extending more compassion to the present self that still lives under the mental burden of this defensive strategy.

Compassion for the predicament of the young self and observation of the "carrot and stick" dynamic of the inner critic reveals the One's survival strategy in an unfiltered way. These insights into how specific patterns unfold and operate defensively reveal the underlying reasons these patterns exist. Worrying, judging, and reforming are reasonable ways to try to exert control in an unpredictable world. Likewise, pushing "bad" or "ugly" or "dangerous" emotions firmly out of sight in favor of expressing the opposite makes the One acceptable to others and worthy of their support.

These patterns became ingrained because they provided real protection. And they still do, but Ones help themselves by recognizing that this coping strategy can only accommodate the self that would stay the "acorn" it was when this defensive shell formed.

What painful emotions are the Type One patterns designed to protect me from?

For all of us, the Personality operates to protect us from painful emotions, including what psychological theorist Karen Horney calls our "basic anxiety"— a preoccupation with the emotional stress of not getting basic needs fulfilled. Ones adopt a strategy of flawlessness as a way to provide themselves with a supportive structure that was missing or faulty. In this way, a One's virtue equates with "self-worth" and well-being, and mistakes and failures are experienced as painful personal flaws.

The One touching on this connection between virtuousness and self-worth might also be able to observe the underlying resentment or anger that comes from having to maintain this constant control. But anger fuels what many Ones readily see as "bad behavior," leading directly to guilt, worry, pain, and regret. Many Ones (and Self-Preservation Ones in particular) can best start by observing how afraid they might be to feel and express their anger fully. Self-reflection in this area usefully aims at exploring when and how Ones suppress their experience of "bad" or threatening emotions like anger, fear, or sadness. Recognizing reaction formation as the "real time" mechanism keeping the lid on these difficult emotions can give Ones valuable insights for making the protective patterns of personality conscious.

Why am I doing this? How do the Type One patterns operate in me now?

Through self-observation, any of the three Type One personalities can likely recognize how automatic the drive is to make things "right." For most, they can usefully trace this driving urge back to the pain they feel when they fail or get criticized. Ones may then see that the habit of blaming themselves and seeing themselves (or others) as imperfect is part of the negative cycle of judgment in the service of virtue that underlies many of their most ingrained habits.

When Ones study their exactitude more closely, in slow motion, they will likely see that the drive to be virtuous and "make things right" is enforced by a strong internalized authority or "superego." This inner authority or parental voice has one focus: ensuring the One's safety and well-being through adherence to standards, rules, and ideals. In practice, an individual One lives out this fixation in ways that vary according to his or her instinctual focus: either they expend a large amount of mental and emotional energy fretting and punishing themselves (Self-Preservation); they work to hold to and model a high standard (Social); or they try to make something or someone better (Sexual). Each of these patterns can be seen to proceed in cycles of anxiety and resentment as the One's world fails to measure up.

The other side of this pattern also reveals an important function of this drive to be virtuous: the inner critic affords the One relaxation from stress when he or she has made every effort to "do it right." Paradoxically, the demands of the superego that generate the One's resentment and anxiety also create a powerful motivation in the form of this mental relief.

What are the blind spots of these patterns? What do Type Ones keep themselves from seeing?

Type Ones show us that we can push positive attributes of our personalities into the Shadow as well as those we feel are negative. Ones tend to focus on what is wrong that they can correct and make better. As a result, they often fail to see and own what they are doing well. Ones can deepen their understanding of themselves by recognizing that they tend to disown, dismiss, or downplay their positive accomplishments and qualities. And when we can't increase our self-confidence and self-love by taking in our goodness, we tend to stay stuck in the defensive posture of our personality.

What are the effects or consequences of these patterns? How do they trap me?

As Ones watch their personality in action over time, they can usually recognize how their patterns of judging and exerting control perpetuate a never-ending cycle of effort and disappointment. Seeing all the way through these kinds of vicious circles in connection with specific patterns helps loosen their grip. Ones can be particularly open to and capable of change once they see how the habits they have relied on so steadfastly only deepen their sense of inadequacy and tension.

Self-Development:
Aiming for a Higher State of Consciousness

For all of us who seek to wake up, the next step in working with type-based knowledge of the personality is to begin to inject more conscious effort into everything we do—to begin to actively think, feel, and act with more choice and awareness. In this section I provide some ideas for Ones of "what to do" after they've observed their key patterns and done some investigation into their sources, operation, and consequences.

This last section is divided into three parts corresponding to three distinct growth processes connected with the Enneagram system: 1) "what to do" to actively counter the automatic patterns described above in the "self-observation" section, 2) how to use the Enneagram's Inner Flow arrow lines as a map of growth, and 3) how to study your passion (or "Vice") and consciously seek to embody its opposite, the antidote, the higher "Virtue" of the type.

The Three Main Type One Personality Patterns: "What to Do" to Address Them

Measuring everything against an ideal standard and driving for perfection in yourself, others, and/or the external environment through the operation of an "inner critic"

Observe the "Improvement Paradox." The first step for Ones is to try to stop being so hard on themselves. Their constant striving for improvement paradoxically keeps them fixated and resistant to real growth. They will often fight this, because self-correction is at the heart of their survival strategy, but having greater acceptance of and compassion for themselves is crucial to their development. Next steps include lightening up more in general, relaxing more, and making more time for fun and pleasure.

Accept "the perfection of imperfection." This can also liberate Ones from much of their energetic striving and overcompensation. But accepting imperfection—with respect to themselves or society—can be very difficult for Ones because their character is shaped so fundamentally around the rejection of the "imperfect." Ones can actively work to release themselves from the tyranny of internal standards by continually reminding themselves that *imperfection is okay, imperfection is inevitable* and natural and most of the time, and *"good enough" is good enough.*

Relax the inner critic. Ones can practice relaxing the requirements of the inner critic by questioning, challenging, and even joking with the inner judge. By actively countering the assumptions of the inner judge, Ones can learn to identify with a larger point of view than the narrow superego authority. This perspective supports Ones' conscious efforts to develop more compassion for themselves and others.

Conscientiously following the rules and laws of society as part of an overall effort to avoid making mistakes

Understand there are many "right" ways to do things. Ones can usefully focus on opening up to seeing things as gray, not just black and white. It helps Ones to realize that there are many good ways of doing things; usually, there is not just one perfect way. Sometimes rules can be misguided.

Don't be so hard on yourself. It can be good for others to reflect back to Ones how hard they are on themselves. The pressure to follow rules and "do it right" can be hard to bear, creating inner tension and stress. When Ones can see the level of control they exert within themselves more objectively, they can begin to find ways let up on themselves.

Develop more compassion for and acceptance of yourself. One of the really touching things about Ones is how hard they try. It is very important for Ones to develop more compassion for themselves as a first step to being more accepting and less tough on themselves and others. If you are a One and this seems difficult, start with giving yourself a lot of credit for how much effort you put into all the things you do. No one tries harder than Ones do to be good people—in fact, it is their tendency to be good to a fault that actually holds them back from living a more balanced, relaxed, and peaceful life. Remind yourself that the efforts you normally put into all you do are much more than enough. Ones can come to know that they don't have to achieve perfection to have integrity and value. They can relax their focus on what might still be wrong and choose to be untroubled by things being just as they are.

Repressing and over-controlling feelings, needs, and impulses

Prioritize pleasure and play. In addition to noticing when and how often they criticize themselves, Ones need to allow for more time for pleasure and play. Crucially important for a One's development is making an effort to lighten up, relax, and have fun. Ones benefit from taking themselves, other people, and things in general less seriously and carving out more time for pleasurable activities.

Incorporate more humor and relaxation. Ones usually have an excellent sense of humor. When they develop themselves, this humorousness can become even more pronounced. When Ones grow, they typically become more funny and more easygoing. For example, I believe comedian Jerry Seinfeld is a One. Consciously using humor to lighten up situations can be an excellent practice for Ones.

Own your positive attributes and value your feelings. Ones tend to look at themselves or others through a negative lens, focusing most on what is not right or not perfect. Therefore, it is important for them to make active efforts to focus on what they or others are doing well, what they excel at, and on what positive aspects of their talents and capacities are being demonstrated. In particular, it is important for Ones to make efforts to get in touch with, own, and express more of their feelings. If you are a One, regularly asking yourself, "What am I feeling?" can be a practice that helps you become more aware of the emotions you might be repressing.

The Inner Flow for Type One:
Using the Arrow Lines to Chart Your Growth Path

In Chapter 1, I introduced an Inner Flow model of the arrow lines that defines one dimension of the dynamic movement within the Enneagram framework. The connections and flow between each core Type, its "growth-(through)-stress" point, and its "child-heart-(security)" point map one kind of growth path described by the symbol. As a reminder, the arrow lines can be seen to suggest one kind of growth path for each type:

- The direction from the core point along the arrow line is the path of development. The "growth–stress" point ahead represents specific challenges perfectly suited to expanding the narrow focus of our core point personality.
- The direction against the arrow from the core point to the "child–heart" point indicates issues and themes that must be consciously acknowledged and owned from childhood so that we can move forward and not be held back by unfinished business from the past. This "child-heart-security" point represents qualities of security we unconsciously repressed, occasionally fall back into as a comfort in times of stress, and now must be reintegrated consciously.

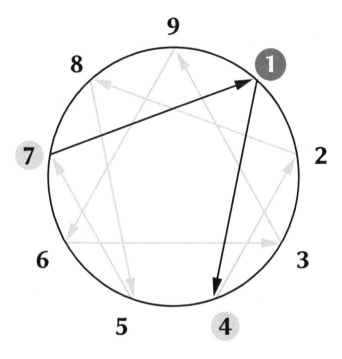

Type One Moving Forward Toward Type Four:
Consciously Using the Four "Growth–Stress" Point for
Development and Expansion

The Inner Flow growth path for Type Ones brings them into direct contact with the challenges embodied in Type Four: allowing for greater range and depth of feeling, more melancholy and longing, and greater creativity and self-expression (instead of just following the rules). Not surprisingly, Ones often report that they find being in contact with Four traits painful and uncomfortable. But exploring depth and expression of feeling with purpose and consciousness can give the One a sense of relief at finally releasing what they have spent considerable energy holding back. This shift may involve contact with the depressive or melancholic feelings, but exploring these feelings can provide the One with greater emotional freedom in all respects. The growth–stress point of Four shows the path of development the One can take to live more authentically by lessening the over-control of feeling.

The One working consciously in this way can make ready use of the tools healthy Type Fours use: artistic expression and emotional authenticity. The aesthetic sensibility characteristic of Type Four shows how art can be a liberating form of personal expression across the emotional spectrum. Also, as art is inherently creative and flexible, the artist's expression is ideally free of absolutes or preconditions. To get started, it is helpful for the One to select a medium that "feels right" and to give himself or herself time, space, and permission to express *without evaluating*. Over time, creating art in this way becomes less a focus of conscious design and more "in the flow" of the moment. This practice is naturally tailored to the One's path of exploring feeling and expression non-judgmentally.

Type One Moving Back to Type Seven: Consciously Using the "Child–Heart" Point to Work through Early Issues and Find Security in Support of Moving Forward

The path of growth for Type Ones calls for them to reclaim the playful and spontaneous impulses characteristic of Type Seven. Ones often had the experience in childhood that non-serious pursuits like free imagination and play were not okay. In a world that required them to be more adult and controlled (usually much too early), Ones commonly received messages discouraging their more creative, spontaneous qualities. These messages motivate the young One to repress these impulses habitually.

For this reason, "moving back to Seven" can be simply a soothing break in discipline for the over-controlled One. But Ones risk getting stuck in the back-and-forth between the seriousness and discipline of the One personality and the light rebellion and playfulness of the move to Seven. When pursued with little or no conscious self-awareness, the One is likely not reclaiming repressed spontaneity so much as temporarily escaping into bad behavior or stimulating activities. Self-recrimination and regret predictably follow.

Navigated consciously, a One can use "the move to Seven" developmentally to re-establish a healthy balance between responsibility and relaxation. Ones can focus on the qualities of this child-security point to recognize and understand their early need to repress the irrepressible Seven qualities. Ones can choose to consciously remind themselves that it's now okay now to have fun, lighten up, and choose pleasurable options. In this way, the "open possibility" perspective of Seven shows the One a way to consciously choose to shift attention away from the control and stress of trying to make things go right all the time. Learning the lesson of Type Seven—that making free time for play and fun is an *essential* element of life—can give a Type One a deeply rewarding foothold in the simple pleasures he or she was forced to leave behind in childhood.

The Vice to Virtue Conversion:
Accessing Anger and Aiming for Serenity

The developmental path from "Vice to Virtue" is one of the central contributions of the Enneagram map in highlighting a usable "vertical" path of growth to a higher state of awareness for each type. In the case of Type One, the "Vice" or the passion of the type is *anger* and its opposite, the Virtue, is *serenity*. The theory of growth communicated by this "Vice to Virtue conversion" is that the more we can be aware of how our passion functions within our personality and consciously work toward the embodiment of its opposite, the more we can free ourselves from the unconscious habits and fixated patterns of our type and evolve toward our "high side."

The work of Type One centers around becoming more and more conscious of how different forms of the passion of anger play a role in shaping the focus of attention and patterns of their personality. This is done through self-observation and continual inquiry into the presence of anger in their everyday experience. Ones do this work by regularly asking if anger is playing a role in what they are thinking, feeling, and doing.

After Ones become more familiar with their experience of anger and develop the ability to make it more conscious, they can take their work on themselves further by making efforts to focus on enacting their Virtue, the "antidote" to the passion of anger. In the case of Type One, the Virtue of serenity represents a state of being that Ones can attain through consciously manifesting their higher capacities.

Serenity is a way of being that is free of attachment to specific ways of doing things—to having to conform to the right way. Serenity is the patient, relaxed feeling that goes along with feeling a sense of completeness and wholeness, a feeling that everything is as it should be and that nothing needs to be changed or perfected. When Ones can start to transcend the energy and emotion of anger in all its forms, they can relax and go with the flow. They can harmonize with the natural rhythms of life without having to impose any evaluative judgments about what should be happening or how life should be conforming to specific standards.

To embody serenity as a One means you have examined and worked on being more aware of your anger and the psychological issues connected to it to the point where you can regularly rise above the compulsion to judge everything. Achieving a state of serenity means you can rest in a calm place inside yourself that is confident about your inherent goodness and beyond the heat of the anger of the conditioned personality. We all naturally go up and down along a vertical dimension of this Vice to Virtue continuum—as we work on ourselves we rise to higher levels of functioning, but because it's difficult to stay awake, we also slip back in times of stress. If you are a One, by focusing on serenity as a goal, and honestly observing the ways that anger, criticism, and the need to judge reassert themselves, you can consciously travel the path from being driven by the unconscious activity of your anger to having more frequent experiences of living from the Virtue of serenity that is your higher state of being.

Specific Work for the Three Type One Subtypes on the Path from Vice to Virtue

The path from observing your passion to finding its antidote is not exactly the same for each of the subtypes. The path of conscious self-work has been characterized in terms of "grit, grind, and grace:" the "grit" of our personality programming, the "grind" of our efforts to grow, and the "grace" that comes to us from doing our work in conscious and positive ways. Each subtype has to grind, or exert effort, against something slightly different. This insight is one of the great benefits of understanding the character of the three distinct subtypes of each of the nine types.

Self-Preservation Ones can travel the path from anger to serenity by slowing down and noticing where anxiety and worry come from, and when, how, and why these feelings arise. If you are a Self-Preservation One, unearth any and all beliefs you have in your "badness" or imperfection and challenge them: they aren't true! You are perfectly imperfect and you will handle the work part of life more easily and naturally if you can allow yourself to rest easier in the knowledge of your own extreme competence and good intentions. Most of all, make room for letting go of the need to control everything. Realize that the fear and worry over survival relates to an earlier part of your life that is over now. Own your essential goodness and watch how you criticize yourself in ways you don't need to, for things that don't matter, in ways that actually increase your burden. Notice that you are no longer in that same situation in which your survival seems threatened and punishment seems certain, but you may be acting like you are. Strive to relax more, make more room for pleasure, don't fix things that don't need fixing, and treat yourself with the same kindness and respect you show to others.

Social Ones can travel the path from the Vice of anger to the Virtue of serenity by reminding themselves that there is no ultimately right or perfect way in the world of the conditioned personality. Social Ones can relax into serenity

through learning that true power comes not from doing it right or being superior in your knowledge, but from the impulse beneath the fact that you want
so much to find the best way and share it with others. Your sincere desire to
find the best ways to do things and show others these paths to goodness and
improvement is clear proof that you are lovable as you are, and that you don't
need to prove your worth through what you can teach us. Remembering that
there are many right or good ways to the truth of things helps you embody
the humility and relaxation in the things you do that is the heart of serenity
for you.

Sexual Ones can travel the path from anger to serenity through being clearer
about the deeper motives behind the desire to perfect others. You are worthy
not because you help us learn how to reform and improve ourselves, but because you deeply value the higher goal of creating a better world. Explore your
impulses and feelings to the point where you gain a thorough understanding
of the sources of your zeal. Put your idealism and energy behind the task
of knowing yourself first, before you try to offer the gift of your love of the
right way to others. Your self-knowledge and humility will only deepen and
purify what you want to share with those around you. Your high ideals and
the energy you put behind their realization can truly change the world for
the better, but only after you make the unconscious fuel behind your passion
more conscious.

Conclusion

THE ONE POINT REPRESENTS THE ENERGY of anger in the service of virtue
and the ways in which we seek to control the "beast within" to cope with a
world that requires us to meet certain standards to be loved. Its path of growth
shows all of us how to transform our anger into the energy that can helps us
manifest our ideals. In each of the Type One subtypes we see a specific character who teaches us what is possible when we can turn righteous anger into
calm acceptance through the alchemy of self-observation, self-development,
and self-knowledge.

Appendix

Help with Identifying Your Enneagram Type:
Discerning the Difference Between Pairs of Types

THE PROCESS OF DISCOVERING your correct "core type" among the nine Enneagram types can be a tricky one. It can be difficult to find your personality type when you first encounter the Enneagram. We all have blind spots that can make it hard to recognize ourselves in the description of our personality type. Our inner experience of who we are often differs from how we might be viewed or described from the outside. We may naturally relate to more than one of the Enneagram's nine types because we do have experiences of several types, not just our core type. We may have overlapping characteristics with our "wing" types (on either side of our core type), the types we are connected to by the arrow lines, or the types of our parents. And we all hold a vision of who we would like to be—how we would like to see ourselves and how we would like to be seen by others—that may differ from how we actually are (in the present time). For all these reasons, it can be hard to see ourselves objectively and identify with a specific personality without some effort. Some people locate their type immediately; for others, the typing process takes a bit more time.

This appendix contains information designed to help you find your type. Often, if you can't be sure of which type you are right away, you can narrow it down to two or three types. The material below is intended to help you understand the similarities and differences between specific pairs of types so you can more easily discover your true (core) personality type.

Recognizing yourself in the patterns associated with one or the other of the nine types is the first step in finding your type, and exploring the three subtype versions of the types (in each of the type chapters) can be a useful and enlightening second step. One of the big advantages of Naranjo's subtype descriptions is that they provide even more specific and nuanced information through which you can find the best way to describe your particular habits and tendencies using the Enneagram map.

Ones and Twos

Ones and Twos can appear similar because both have sets of rules that they expect others to adhere to, and become upset and reactive when others do not follow those rules. However, on closer examination, Ones have a far more rules and expectations than do Twos, and their expectations cover a wider array of behaviors. For example, Ones often have rules governing work style, work product, how things should be organized, how people should behave in a variety of situations, dress codes that define what is appropriate and inappropriate attire in a variety of circumstances, and more. Twos' rules are far more focused on interpersonal relationships and how people should treat one another. Although Ones and Twos can both be self-critical and critical of others, most Ones are more consistently self-critical than Twos—and also more overtly judgmental of others. For example, the One's "inner critic" or judge is activated eighty to ninety percent of the time or more, whereas the Two's criticism of self and others is less frequent and more activated by highly distressing events like rejection and the perception of having failed others.

Some may confuse Ones and Twos because both are dutiful and want to perceive themselves (and have others view them) as "good" and "responsible." However, Ones and Twos have very different meanings for these words. Ones believe they are "good" and, therefore, valued, if they do everything right and make few mistakes, and "responsible" means they keep their commitments, do their work well, deliver it on time, and are punctual. Twos believe they are "good" and, therefore, valued, if they are thoughtful, considerate, and selfless, and "responsible" means they are always available when others are in need and they don't disappoint the people in their lives.

Ones and Twos are markedly different in many ways. For example, Ones speak definitively, offer opinions, judgments, and ideas, and use language that suggests they are evaluating people and situations—for example, Ones use words such as *should, ought, right, wrong,* and *appropriate* with great frequency. Twos, by contrast, speak in softer tones, ask questions of others to engage them and draw them into conversation, offer advice frequently, and focus on others in a way that makes people feel important. While Ones can be very warm, they are rarely as consistently warm and empathic as Twos.

A helpful way to understand the distinction between Ones and Twos is that while Ones look internally to determine whether or not they have done a good job or made a mistake, Twos are more highly affected by how others perceive them than by how they view themselves. In other words, Twos have a strong inclination to perceive themselves through the eyes of others rather than having a strong interior sense of how valuable they are and how well they did something. While they may not directly solicit the opinions of others regarding the merit of their work or behavior, Twos pay greater attention to the nonverbal cues and interpersonal behavior of others and are far more affected by their positive and negative reactions.

Ones and Threes

Ones and Threes have some strong similarities. Both are highly task-focused and have a deep desire to excel and to be perceived as highly competent individuals. However, Ones' drive to excel comes from an internal sense of satisfaction that they have accomplished a specific task to the very best of their ability. Threes, on the other hand, are driven by a need to feel they have succeeded in the eyes of others. In other words, Ones seek self-respect through their accomplishments by evaluating their own behaviors according to their own internal standards, and Threes seek the respect and admiration of other people, using external factors as their reference points. For example, Threes pay close attention to how important people respond to them, or their salaries, pay raises, and office trappings.

Both Ones and Threes emphasize tasks over relationships, and both styles focus on their objectives, then organize the work accordingly. However, for Threes, objectives are typically one more item on their "to-do" lists they can check off, while Ones like to organize their work at a refined level of detail; structuring work gives them pleasure and satisfaction. Threes, by contrast, focus far more on goals because goal accomplishment is precisely what makes them feel competent and successful, and they then organize the most efficient plan they can conceive to accomplish each goal. Their plans, while effective and efficient, are rarely as structured or systematic as those of Ones. Not viewing the end goal as the most important piece of the task process, Ones can tend to procrastinate for fear of making a mistake, where Threes, in contrast, tend to want to find the fastest, most efficient path to the goal and do not place as much attention on the possibility of making a mistake.

The difference between Ones and Threes is most obvious in the way each defines quality. While both would say they are quality oriented, Ones define quality as doing the best job they are capable of doing, with no errors or mistakes if humanly possible. Threes define quality as meeting customer expectations, then going slightly beyond that so that the customer is more than satisfied. However, from the Three point of view (with the exception of the Self-Preservation Three), doing every project and task as perfectly as possible is a poor use of time and resources and "good enough" is good enough. From the One perspective, if there are mistakes or they know it could have been better—even if the customer is not aware of this or concerned about it—quality has not been achieved. For Ones, "good enough" is rarely good enough.

Ones and Fours

Ones and Fours can appear similar in that they both take work tasks seriously and want to do the best job they can. But while Ones focus more on the structure and process and details of completing tasks, Fours focus more on relationships and people and their own creative expression. Both Ones and Fours are idealistic and appreciate quality, but while Ones attend most to making things as perfect as they can (according to the One's own internal standards), the Four values creativity, authenticity, and aesthetics above a specific ideal of perfection. Also, while both Ones and Fours base their judgments on their internal sense of what is ideal, Fours are much more conscious of how things look to other people.

Both Ones and Fours can be self-critical, but while the One's inner critic provides a running commentary about how things could have been done more perfectly, the Four experiences a deeper sense of something being fundamentally flawed within them. Ones take note of grammatical errors and things being out of alignment or less than ideal, often with little or no emotional reaction other than perhaps slight irritation, whereas Fours frequently notice what is missing in a given situation and in themselves in a larger sense, and may have deeper emotional reactions to what they see as absent or "not good enough."

Ones and Fours differ from one another in several ways. Fours attend to other people, paying a lot of attention to what interactions are like on an emotional level, and how much they feel connected or not to the people around them. Ones are more likely to focus on the structure of relationships or the work tasks they share in common.

Ones can tend to fall into seeing things in black and white, thinking there is one right way to approach a task, while Fours make a lot of room for creativity and self-expression and so are more likely to see many ways of approaching a project. While both styles will want to perform at a high level and may be perfectionistic in the things they do, the One's priorities are following the rules and the structure and making something as good as it can possibly be according to the One's standards, while the Four's focus is more on creative and authentic self-expression and on whether or not others perceived them as special and unique according to more artistic standards.

In terms of emotional tone, Ones and Fours can appear quite different to an outside observer. Ones can tend to seem reserved and at times may be annoyed or irritated with others when they don't follow the rules or perform up to their expectations. Fours on the other hand, tend to have more varied and prominent moods and can be very empathic with others' feelings, having a natural understanding that people have a range of emotions and moods, both in terms of their own experience and that of others. At times Fours can be dramatic and emotionally expressive in communicating with others, while Ones tend to be more controlled, straightforward, concise, and precise.

Ones and Fives

Ones and Fives can look a lot alike. Both Ones and Fives can be reserved, logical, and task-focused, and both styles can also appear serious and withdrawn at times. Both Ones and Fives value independence, self-reliance, and self-sufficiency, but Fives require more privacy than Ones. Both seek knowledge—Fives because they believe knowledge is power and Ones so that they can be more competent, informed, and correct in the things they do. Both appear intellectual and knowledgeable and excel at objective analysis. Ones strive for objectivity because they want to be responsible, they believe it is the correct thing to do, and it can prevent mistakes. Fives are naturally objective because they think deeply about things and detach from feelings when analyzing situations. Both understand boundaries and the need for them. Both Ones and Fives are diligent and practical. However, Ones are more rules-based and Fives are more appreciative of simplicity and the conservation of resources than reliant on a specific set of rules. Both types apply their own internal standards when judging their own or others' work.

While Ones and Fives share some characteristics in common, the two styles also have some fundamental differences. While Fives can be self-critical, Ones are much more self-critical than Fives. Ones have an internal critic that comments on almost everything they do and say. Ones also tend to be more judgmental of others than Fives; they can be openly angry or irritated when others do not follow the rules or do not do things the right way (according to the One's sense of "the right way"). Although neither style feels comfortable sharing emotions and both Ones and Fives tend to hold back their emotions, Ones' feelings tend to leak out more than Fives, who almost always maintain a calm, unruffled reserve, even in times of stress. Ones tend to experience some version of anger fairly regularly, and though they try to restrain feelings, at times their anger leaks out in the form of irritation, annoyance, or frustration, especially when people do not perform as the One thinks they should. Fives, on the other hand, are more likely to keep their thoughts, and especially their feelings, to themselves. Fives automatically detach from feelings and it is very rare for them to share their emotions with others, especially in the work setting.

Ones and Sixes

Ones and Sixes share several traits in common. Both Ones and Sixes excel at analytical thinking, and both worry about things going wrong. Ones tend to feel anxious about making mistakes, and Sixes tend to experience more general anxiety related to many different things potentially going wrong in life. In response to their worry, Ones try to be perfect and avoid making mistakes and Sixes catastrophize and imagine worst-case scenarios. Both Ones and Sixes are uncomfortable with success. Both styles create problems for themselves in completing tasks and moving toward success, Ones because they believe something is never perfect and so constantly criticize themselves, and Sixes because they continually doubt and question themselves and believe that becoming successful will make them a target. Both styles also tend to be activists in support of social causes they care about, Ones because they feel responsible for making the world a better place, and Sixes because they identify with underdog causes and are sensitive to people in authority positions exercising power over others in unjust ways.

Ones and Sixes also differ in specific ways. Ones worry about making mistakes and being wrong, according to their own standards, while Sixes worry about danger and external threats of all kinds. Ones are self-critical and tend to judge others, and Sixes doubt themselves and others. Related to self-criticism and self-doubt, Ones try,—and inevitably fail—to be perfect and Sixes either try and fail to find certainty, or find it in a specific source of authority.

One particularly stark contrast between Ones and Sixes is that Ones tend to obey authority, whereas Sixes tend to be suspicious of authority and may even rebel against it. Ones follow the rules, while most Sixes question them. (One exception to this is the Social Six, who adheres to an outside authority and may strictly follow the rules offered by that authority.) Both styles can procrastinate, but they do it for different reasons: Ones fear making a mistake and so always want more time to make what they do more perfect. Sixes continual doubting and questioning makes it hard for them to move forward.

In terms of relating to people, generally, Ones tend to trust people and give them the benefit of the doubt unless they break the rules or engage in some kind of bad behavior, whereas Sixes mistrust others initially until they have observed them enough to satisfy themselves that they are trustworthy. After a person has earned their trust, Sixes are very loyal and supportive.

Ones and Sevens

Ones and Sevens have similar styles in many ways. Both Ones and Sevens are quality oriented, with Ones displaying this in their attention to attaining high standards in their work and other things they do, and Sevens seeking to experience the best of everything, especially recreationally. Ones and Sevens are both idealistic and visionary. Ones want things to be perfect and work hard to make things fit an internally generated sense of the ideal. Sevens are supremely optimistic and positive as a way of denying negative feelings and realities, and they think a lot in terms of future possibilities. Both Ones and Sevens have a lot of energy. Ones apply themselves diligently to everything they do, and Sevens dedicate themselves fully to the many activities that interest them. While both styles can be perfectionistic, Ones are generally more consistently concerned with perfection than Sevens, who can let go of the effort to "do it right" if it becomes too onerous. Both intellectual and analytical, Ones and Sevens both like to problem-solve. Finally, both Ones and Sevens are sensitive to criticism, though the One is more likely to show it than the Seven.

One big difference between Ones and Sevens is that for Ones, work has to come before play, and for Sevens, planning for play and engaging in pleasurable activities is more primary. It's not that work isn't important to Sevens, as Sevens can be very dedicated to their work, but they may approach their job duties by making work into an enjoyable activity rather than a responsibility. Although Ones are idealistic, they can seem less than optimistic in that they look for ways to improve things, while Sevens are relentlessly optimistic. Ones like structure and can work within prescribed limits, while Sevens dislike limits and so may have a harder time with constraining elements of organizational structure. For instance, Sevens are not comfortable within a hierarchy and tend to equalize authority, while Ones work well within defined structure of authority. Further, Ones excel at managing the details of projects and tasks, while Sevens find this kind of work tedious. Because Ones naturally pay attention to errors that need correcting, they can seem to the Seven to focus too much on the negative—Sevens always want to focus on the positive aspects of things.

Interpersonally, Ones can at times be critical or inflexible, but they are strongly committed to self-improvement, and so will listen to others' feedback and dedicate themselves to working on relationships. Sevens bring a lot of positive energy and fun to relationships, but can feel challenged if difficulties need to be addressed and worked through with others.

Ones and Eights

Ones and Eights look similar in some respects. Both are high-energy and hardworking types, and both like to establish control and order. Both types tend to get angry, but they experience and express anger in distinct ways. Believing that showing anger is wrong, Ones tend to hold back their anger, but because it is hard for the One to completely shut it off, it tends to leak out as resentment, irritation, annoyance, or passive-aggressive behavior. Eights, on the other hand, feel and express anger more readily, and don't believe it is wrong to be angry. Ones usually get angry when people break the rules or engage in bad behavior, while Eights become angry for a wider range of reasons. Both Ones and Eights engage in "black and white," or "all or nothing," ways of thinking.

Both Ones and Eights like to be in control, but may assert control in different ways, with Ones relying on rules and structure and standards, and Eights exercising power in more direct ways. Ones and Eights are both concerned about justice and fairness and can work hard in support of a cause they believe in. And both styles can overwork and neglect their own needs.

There are also some key differences between Ones and Eights. Eights think in terms of the big picture, like high-level work, and dislike having to deal with details. Ones, on the other hand, excel at and may enjoy detail work. When engaged in a task, Ones focus a lot of attention on achieving perfection, taking pains to make something as good as it can possibly be, while Eights can be satisfied with "good enough." Eights tend to go with their impulses, can be excessive, and dislike being inhibited, while Ones tend to over-control their impulses and delay pleasurable activities, as they are typically more focused on correct behavior than indulging themselves. Eights are "under-social" in that they don't mind—or can like—going against convention, while Ones are "over-social" and almost always observe social conventions.

Internally, Ones are extremely self-critical, while Eights do not criticize themselves as much. On the contrary, Eights often move into action quickly, feeling much freer than Ones to exercise their power and their will, without overanalyzing things or entertaining critical thoughts about their intentions or behaviors. Ones will usually apologize if they believe they've made a mistake (and they value apologies), while Eights are much less likely to feel apologetic for the things they do. Ones typically observe and obey authority figures, while Eights don't like to be told what to do and may rebel against authority if they want or need to. When communicating with others, Ones tend to be polite and restrained, using words like "should" and "ought" and "must," while Eights can be direct, abrupt, intimidating, and even profane.

Ones and Nines

Ones and Nines have share several characteristics in common. In work settings, both appreciate structure and process. Both Ones and Nines make good mediators, Nines because they can easily see many sides of an issue and feel motivated to create harmony, and Ones because they have standards of fairness and can be objective and discerning judges. Both styles tend to have a difficult time noticing and asserting their own needs and wants, and both can be perfectionistic, though Ones are usually more perfectionistic than Nines. Both Ones and Nines can work well within and respect the existing authority structure, though Nines will sometimes rebel in subtle, passive ways if they feel controlled.

Many differences also exist between Ones and Nines. Ones tend to be fairly opinionated, often believing they know the one right way to do something, and Nines can have a hard time locating their own opinion as a natural consequence of being so attuned to other people's varied perspectives. Nines typically don't assert a position, while Ones often assume their position is the only correct point of view. Related to this, Ones tend to think in terms of black and white and believe there is "one right way," while Nines see many shades of gray. Although both styles want to avoid conflict, the Nine does so more than the One, who may not be able to stop from engaging in arguments when they feel strongly about something. Ones like to do things their way, and Nines adapt more easily to others, often preferring to follow along with someone else's agenda rather than having to assert their own. When accomplishing a task, Ones make a lot of effort to make things perfect, relying on their own internal standards of the ideal, whereas Nines are more oriented to what other people think and want. Ones usually have a clear vision of the correct way to do things, while Nines seek consensus, wanting to hear from others when making decisions about what the standards should be. Ones are more observant of rules and will confront those who do not follow the rules, while Nines are more easy-going and much less likely to confront people who don't obey guidelines.

Twos and Threes

Twos and Threes can look very much alike. Both manage their image and presentation to please or attract others, and both are competent doers with active energy. While both styles pay a lot of attention to creating an impression that matches what others value, Twos focus on meeting others' needs and being friendly, likable, and accommodating, while Threes focus on achieving goals and attaining success to win the admiration and respect of others. Although both Twos and Threes feel driven to accomplish many things, Twos are more relationship-oriented and Threes more task-oriented. Though both Twos and Threes want to have the approval of others, Threes are motivated by the good feeling they get when they reach a goal and the satisfaction that comes with appearing successful, while Twos are motivated by earning others' affection and being considered indispensable. Both Twos and Threes can be confused about who they really are—with so much energy going into the maintenance of an image designed to impress others, it can be hard for people of both styles to have a clear sense of self. Related to this, both Twos and Threes tend to avoid their emotions, Threes because feeling can get in the way of doing, and Twos because feeling can get in the way of forging positive connections with other people.

Despite their many shared characteristics, Twos and Threes also differ in significant ways. While both styles repress or go numb to their feelings, Twos do this less completely and tend to feel and express more emotions more often than Threes do. While Threes can be very competitive and see winning as important, Twos are less oriented to competition, seeing aligning with others as more important than coming out on top. Although both Twos and Threes can become angry at times, Twos tend to express anger when their unacknowledged needs are not met and Threes when someone puts an obstacle between them and their goal.

When it comes to work, Threes can prioritize work so much that they become workaholics. Twos can also be very hardworking, but they also prioritize relationships and pleasure. Threes pay a great deal of attention to goals and performance and so can be highly focused on efficiency and what it takes to get to the goal. In contrast, Twos prioritize what others need from them, and so they adapt their agendas more to the goals of others or the goals of the larger group. When Threes are focused on a goal, they may have a hard time being present to listen to other people, whereas Twos' primary focus is on tuning into other people, and so they tend to be very empathic and present for friends, colleagues, and important others, even at the expense of their connection to themselves. In contrast to Threes, who can focus like a laser on a goal, Twos may abandon their own goals in favor of meeting others' needs or supporting others' efforts. Finally, Twos and Threes differ in terms of what they avoid most: Twos work hard, sometimes behind the scenes, at achieving positive connections with others to avoid experiencing rejection. Threes structure their work and other goal-directed activities to avoid failure. Because of this, Twos can be less direct and assertive than Threes, and Threes can be more driven to win and reframe failures as learning experiences.

Twos and Fours

Twos and Fours share some characteristics in common. Both styles have an awareness of image and pay attention to how others perceive them, but Twos want to be seen as likable and friendly and Fours prefer to be viewed as special and unique. Their sensitivity to how others see them and feel about them also contributes to both styles being self-critical, as both Twos and Fours can judge themselves for not being good enough to earn other people's love. Both Twos and Fours can feel their emotions fairly readily, though Twos can sometimes repress feelings and may at times be out of touch with their inner experience, while Fours can overdo or overidentify feelings or dwell in some feelings in an extreme way to avoid other feelings. Interpersonally, both Twos and Fours pay a great deal of attention to relationships and make achieving connections with others a priority. And people of both styles have a great capacity for empathy, and so are typically skilled at creating relationships based on their ability to understand other people's thoughts and feelings.

Twos and Fours also differ in many respects. When working on a project with others, Twos tend to be optimistic, upbeat, and supportive, while Fours often focus on what is missing. Twos want to be helpful through meeting others' needs and so neglect their own needs because their attention is so focused on others. Fours have more access to their own needs and wants and make their own desires more of a priority. Twos are more other-focused, meaning they pay more attention to what others feel and need than their own feelings and needs; Fours are more self-referencing, focusing their attention more primarily on themselves and their own inner experience. When interacting with others, Twos place a high value on being liked and so often adapt their presentation to be more of what they think others want them to be, while Fours value authenticity and so do not alter as much to please others. Twos tend to be averse to conflict, as they fear conflict can destroy valued connections with others, while Fours are more able to engage in conflict when necessary, finding it more important to express truthful feelings and needs than accommodate others and avoid anger. Overall, Twos are usually upbeat and highly positive in their mood and emotional presentation, while Fours can dwell more in melancholy and sadness.

Twos and Fives

While Twos and Fives are in some ways opposites, they do share some traits in common. Both Twos and Fives can withdraw when feeling vulnerable, though Fives rely on this strategy more often and in more situations than Twos, and the Self-Preservation Two withdraws more frequently than the other Two subtypes. People of both styles can need time alone, though for Fives this is a more regular experience than for Twos. Twos usually need to develop an ability to be alone more as part of their self-work, whereas Fives usually need to develop an ability to be with others more. Twos most often feel the need for alone time after having been around people a lot, or after they have done some development work and realize they neglect their own experience in favor of focusing a great deal of attention on others. Both Twos and Fives also place a high value on independence, though for Fives this is more of a way of life, and for Twos independence may be a value they hold as an unconscious defense against feeling too dependent on others (as they depend on others' approval to support their self-esteem).

In many ways, Twos and Fives are quite different. Twos feel their emotions fairly frequently, and Fives have the habit of detaching from emotion. Because of this, Fives can seem very reserved and unemotional and analytical, while Twos tend to appear much more emotional and to react to things with more feeling. In line with this, Fives have a more objective, intellectual way of approaching tasks and discussions in contrast to Twos' more intuitive, feelings-based approach.

Twos like to be around people and actively seek out close relationships with others, while Fives highly value their privacy, personal space, and alone time, and are generally less relationship-oriented. Related to this, Twos focus their attention on other people's feelings and needs to a large extent, while Fives often purposely avoid becoming too involved with other people—especially with the emotions and emotional needs of others. Fives hold the belief that they can easily be drained of energy and resources if they interact a great deal with others, while Twos can feel energized and affirmed by contact with other people, especially close friends and individuals who are important to them. Twos tend to give very generously to others, and can even give too much, whereas Fives are usually more withholding, having a regular concern that people will take too much of their resources, like time and energy, that they need for themselves. Additionally, Twos can have a difficult time making appropriate boundaries between themselves and others, while Fives tend to be very mindful of establishing firm boundaries with others. For example, Twos can have a hard time saying "no" to people, even when they want to, while Fives can relatively easily say "no" if they don't want to meet another person's need. Similarly, Twos usually consider themselves to be high-energy people who can readily devote a good deal of their time and energy to others, while Fives have the sense they have limited energy and so pay attention to conserving their energy for their own needs.

Twos and Sixes

Twos and Sixes can look very similar to one another. Both Twos and Sixes can worry and be fearful, but their fears have different sources. Sixes worry about overall safety, bad things happening, and problems occurring, while Twos worry more about whether or not people will perceive them in a positive light, the possibility of being rejected, and the safety of specific individuals who are important to them. Both Twos and Sixes are good at reading people, but they do so with different aims. When applying their attention to others, Sixes look for hidden agendas and ulterior motives, whether someone is trustworthy or not, and potential threats, whereas Twos try to ascertain other people's moods and needs as a way to connect with them and create rapport. When relating to people generally, Twos tend to be aware of managing their image to please or align with others, while Sixes do not consider their image and how others might be perceiving them as much. In addition, Twos want to be seen and appreciated by other people, while Sixes would often rather hide because being noticed can make them feel vulnerable.

Both Twos and Sixes can worry about what will go wrong and work hard to make things go well—Sixes because they are good troubleshooters and want to anticipate problems before they happen, and Twos because they want to please others and appear competent and attractive. When it comes to making decisions, both Twos and Sixes can have a difficult time deciding. Twos have a hard time making choices because they often don't know what they need or want. They focus so much attention on other people, that they can be unfamiliar with their own preferences. In contrast, decisions can be challenging for Sixes because they continually doubt themselves and question their potential choices. They may also fear choosing the wrong thing and imagine the negative consequences that might result.

Twos and Sixes also differ in significant ways. Sixes usually feel suspicious of or rebellious toward authority figures, while Twos tend to want to form good relationships with authorities. Twos often want authority figures and other important people to like them, so rather than being mistrustful, they will usually lead with behaviors designed to achieve a positive relationship with authorities if they can. Also, Sixes catastrophize and engage in worst-case scenario thinking much more than Twos do. Twos are usually optimistic, and while they might sometimes imagine that people don't like them, they usually don't think in terms of the worst case. Another contrast between Twos and Sixes exists in the way each deals with conflict. Twos would like to avoid conflict most of the time if they can, while Sixes, and especially counterphobic Sixes, can sometimes move toward conflict, especially if they feel motivated to challenge an authority figure who they believe is abusing their power.

Specific commonalities exist between Twos and the Self-Preservation Sixes. Both Twos and Self-Preservation Sixes are warm and focus considerable energy on creating friendships; they try to avoid showing aggression (though they both may do so when reactive). Twos try to attract friends out of a desire to be liked and affirmed, as this provides them with a sense of well-being. In a slightly different way, Self-Preservation Sixes want to create relationships that will serve as alliances to keep themselves safe amid friendly others who can band together against outside threats. Twos are motivated to form friendships by the need to be liked and seen as indispensable, and also so that they will have friends to meet their needs in the same way they meet others' needs. The Six has a strong need for safety against attack or other kinds of dangers.

Twos and Sevens

Twos and Sevens can look alike. They both tend to be upbeat, energetic, and fun-loving. Both Twos and Sevens tend to be positive and optimistic, Twos because they want people to like them (and they know people like happy people), and Sevens because they like to be happy and not sad, as they can experience "negative" emotions as threatening and anxiety provoking. Both Twos and Sevens have hedonistic tendencies; both like to have a good time and experience pleasure. However, the aims behind their pleasure-seeking differ. Twos want to have positive experiences with others to build and enjoy relationships and also as a way to indulge (or overindulge) themselves in response to deeper feelings of need deprivation. Sevens have the habit of seeking pleasure as a defensive way of avoiding less positive experiences, including feelings of discomfort, pain, or anxiety. People of both styles enjoy relating to other people and may idealize individuals they like, Twos because they want others' to affirm their likability and Sevens because they like the stimulation that comes with engaging with interesting individuals.

There are also significant differences between Twos and Sevens. Twos pay a great deal of attention to other people, focusing on the moods and needs of others as a way of aligning with them to create positive connections, while Sevens focus more on their own needs and wishes, seeking fulfillment of their own desires as a way of averting or distracting themselves from more negative experiences. In addition, Twos will often adapt themselves to others and abandon their own needs in an attempt to strengthen their bonds with others, while Sevens do what they want to do and do not often give up what they need to please someone else (though the Social Seven is an exception to this). In relating to others, Twos also actively manage their image as a way of attracting others by being what they think they want them to be, while Sevens do not focus as much on interpersonal interactions in terms of how people perceive their image. On a fundamental level, Twos are motivated by pleasing others; Sevens are motivated by pleasing themselves.

Twos tend to be more feeling-oriented, having regular contact with their emotions, while Sevens are more mental and more oriented to thinking. When completing a task, Sevens can have a difficult time focusing, especially if the task is tedious or boring, while Twos have an easier time focusing on completing a task, especially if what they are doing is in some ways being seen and evaluated by others. Sevens like to have many options, and they can feel limited if they don't, while Twos don't necessarily need or want more options, as having many choices can make it more difficult for Twos to make a decision (because they often don't know what they need).

Social Sevens can look more like Twos than the other two Seven subtypes because Social Sevens are more oriented to being of service to others. Social Sevens may be confused with Twos because in addition to the commonality of being people-oriented, Social Sevens will sacrifice their own needs, in a way similar to Twos' style, to support the needs of the group. This habit of being conscious of the group and what others might need can make the Social Sevens seem a lot like the friendly, outgoing, generous Twos. However, despite the Social Sevens' tendency to give more or sacrifice their own self-interest more than the other Sevens, the Social Sevens can still be distinguished from Twos by their knowledge of their own needs and wants and their tendency to avoid difficult feelings.

Twos and Eights

Although they are very different, Twos and Eights do have some commonalities and can appear similar. In particular, Social Twos can look like Eights and (especially female) Social Eights can look like Twos. Twos and Eights both tend to be protective of others, especially important others in the case of Twos, and weaker or more vulnerable others in the case of Eights. Both Twos and Eights can be impulsive, self-indulgent, and hedonistic, Twos because they may overcompensate for not knowing what they need (and thus may often feel deprived), and Eights because they move quickly into action, often without thinking, and don't like to have inhibitions put on their desires. People of both styles can be excessive in the things they do, like eating, working, and giving, Eights because they have big energy and appetites and don't like to feel limited, and Twos because they often don't know exactly what they need and so can overdo it at times. Also, Twos tend to abandon themselves when they focus on others' needs at the expense of their own, and Eights tend to forget their own needs and limits when they, for instance, habitually take on more and more and work without being able to recognize their limitations. Both Twos and Eights like to be in control, Eights because they see the big picture and want to make order and move things forward and meet their needs, and Twos because they want to appear competent and do things in a specific way that they think will impress others.

There are also several contrasts between Twos and Eights. Twos focus a great deal of attention on their image and on how people are perceiving them, while Eights may express an attitude of "not caring what others think of them." Most Eights can relatively easily feel and express anger and confront conflictual situations, even if they don't "like" conflict. While Twos can occasionally confront people and engage in conflict, most often Twos repress their anger and avoid conflict because they fear it may alienate people they want to maintain a connection with. Eights' attention typically focuses on power and control and who has it and how they use it. Twos may sense this at times, but they primarily pay attention to what people need and how they feel, not how much power they have. Although they do not always have to be the boss or the leader, Eights can easily step into a leadership role, especially if there is void in that area. Although Twos can be good leaders, they usually feel more comfortable being in a secondary support position: the leader's right-hand or the power behind the throne. And while Eights can dominate and impose their will rather easily, Twos tend to read a situation in terms of what is required of them and then alter their behavior to be what others need them to be, rather than asserting their own will all the time (though sometimes they do so in a prideful "I know best" kind of way). Finally, Eights tend to avoid expressing vulnerability and usually even deny any sense of vulnerability at all. Twos, on the other hand, can more easily express vulnerability, as they often feel vulnerable feelings, such as hurt or sadness, and may even use their vulnerability in unconscious ways to manipulate others.

Twos and Nines

Twos and Nines are two types that share a lot of traits in common. They both tend to focus on others, and so they often forget or neglect their own needs and wants in favor of allowing others' needs and desires to be in the foreground. Both styles overadjust to others, with Twos altering their behavior to be what they think other people want them to be so they will like them and Nines blending with others' agendas to create harmony and reduce tension and separation. Twos and Nines can both make good mediators because they easily see and understand others' perspectives and opinions—in fact, they can both usually see others' points of view more clearly than their own.

To outside observers, Twos and Nines both appear likable, friendly, and caring. People of both types have little or no contact with their anger, though some Twos do feel anger occasionally when their unexpressed needs are not met. Uncomfortable with anger and oriented to maintaining positive connections with others, both Twos and Nines regularly avoid conflict, though again, some Twos can be more open to conflict at times when their more emotional nature drives them there. Both Twos and Nines can engage in passive-aggressive behavior as it may be hard for them to assert themselves and express anger in more direct ways out of a fear that they will break important connections with other people.

While Twos and Nines can look very similar, they do have some contrasting traits. While both types focus their attention primarily on others instead of themselves, Twos tend to focus more on feelings and tend to feel their emotions more readily, while Nines focus more on maintaining an energetic harmony with others. Twos tend to feel a wider range of stronger emotions more frequently than Nines, who tend to be more emotionally steady and even. Twos move more actively toward others, proactively reading their needs and preferences to aid in their effort to align with them emotionally, while Nines do not seek out connections with others as actively and do not read people's needs as much. In addition, Twos are more selective when it comes to the individuals they seek to establish relationships with. Twos tend to be more attracted to some people than others, while Nines are more democratic and do not make purposeful efforts to pursue connections with particular people in the ways that Twos typically do. Twos tend to have a more active, higher energy level and a faster pace than Nines, who usually appear more relaxed and easy going. While both styles can abandon themselves in favor of paying attention to others, Twos tend to repress needs and feelings, while Nines "forget" or avoid paying attention to their desires and agendas. Nines tend to tune out to their own agenda, while Twos often have a clear agenda (especially with respect to achieving interpersonal connections), even while they may not pay attention to what they need.

Threes and Fours

Threes and Fours can look similar as they have some characteristics in common. Both Threes and Fours focus their attention on how others perceive them. While Threes pay a great deal of attention to creating an image of success and achievement according to external standards in specific contexts, Fours focus on communicating an image based on their own unique sense of what they think is important to express. In addition to focusing on image, both of these styles also belong to the heart triad and so are oriented at a fundamental level to feelings and emotional connection. But although both Threes and Fours are feelings-based styles, Threes tend to avoid emotion to more easily accomplish tasks and get things done, and Fours tend to feel their emotions more regularly and can even at times overidentify with their own feelings. People of both styles can prioritize relationships and often place importance on approval and recognition. Finally, both Threes and Fours can be intense, creative, hardworking, and competitive.

Significant differences also exist between Threes and Fours. Threes tend to focus their attention on tasks, goals, and work, while Fours place more importance on feelings, self-expression, and emotional connections with others. When Threes focus on tasks, they usually look for the shortest, more efficient, and fastest path to their goal, while Fours favor a more nonlinear, creative, organic approach to self-expression. Threes numb out their feelings to get things done while Fours believe that all feelings should be felt and authentically expressed. Threes pursue goals to achieve success as defined by the context or group, while Fours seek to manifest ideals related to love and emotional depth through creativity, relational connection, and authentic expression as a way of feeling special and unique.

Threes orient themselves to what others define as successful, placing a high degree of value on attaining the material signs of success like nice clothes and nice cars, while Fours put more attention and emphasis on their own internal sense of how they feel and what they value. Threes focus on specific goals and how to reach them. In contrast, Fours focus their attention on what is missing and needed in a given situation. When presenting themselves to others, Threes strive to match the image of whatever other people will think is most attractive or admirable, even if it means conforming to appear as something they're not (and thus losing sight of who they actually are), while Fours value authentic self-expression. In doing this, Threes identify with an image of success (and an idealized self-image), often appearing genuinely confident and competent. Fours identify with a deficient self-image and usually have the sense that they are flawed in some way. Threes pay attention to competing, winning, and avoiding failure, while Fours focus most on authentic connection, self-expression, and aesthetics. (Although the Sexual Four may be as competitive as a Three, they compete more out of a more emotional sense of trying to prove themselves worthy or superior, which is often motivated by anger or unconscious envy.)

Threes and Fives

Threes and Fives have some similar characteristics. Both types value emotional control and tend to avoid paying attention to their emotions. Threes numb out their feelings to prevent emotions from interfering with accomplishing tasks, achieving goals, and maintaining their image, while Fives habitually detach from their emotions and focus more on thinking and analyzing. Fives find more comfort and safety in the mental realm, and Threes find comfort in doing and performing.

From the point of view of others who might want to forge a close relationship with them, both Threes and Fives can at times seem unavailable and hard to connect with. Threes can seem inaccessible because they overidentify with their image and so may not be able to connect to and live from their real self, and Fives because they tend to withdraw from others as a way to reduce uncomfortable and potentially taxing emotional entanglements. Related to this, both Threes and Fives value independence and self-sufficiency.

Significant differences also exist between Threes and Fives. Threes tend to be dependent on others for approval and admiration, while Fives pride themselves on their independence and objectivity and don't evaluate themselves based on others' perception of them. Threes pay a great deal of attention to creating an image of success that others will admire as a way of feeling valued and worthwhile, while Fives do not focus on their image in this way. In work situations, Threes are primarily oriented toward doing tasks and working toward goals, while Fives prioritize observing, thinking, analyzing, and developing knowledge. Threes expend a lot of energy on work—they spend whatever large amounts of time it takes to achieve their chosen goals, even if it means working overtime—while Fives focus on conserving energy and avoiding tasks and relationships that will drain them of their energy. Fives have the sense that they have a limited amount of energy to expend and so engage in continual efforts to be economical when it comes to resources like time, energy, and effort. Threes, on the other hand, can be workaholics, often work without limit, and can even bring work on vacations. Threes can also be highly competitive in the different areas of their lives, and can put a great deal of energy toward winning at all costs. Fives, who can at times seem aloof or above it all, can easily disengage from an effort if they conclude that it is not worth the expenditure of their energy and other resources.

Threes and Sixes

Threes and Sixes have some traits in common. Threes and some Sixes, and especially counterphobic Sixes, can be very hardworking, assertive, and forward-moving. Both Threes and Sixes specialize in reading people, though they do this for different reasons. Threes scan their audience to determine what others value to create an image of themselves that others will see as successful and admirable. Sixes read people to answer an inner sense of threat and protect themselves by looking for hidden agendas and ulterior motives. Both styles can be personable and friendly, with Threes looking for approval from others and Sixes wanting to create safety through knowing who their allies are. And both can also be practical and solution-focused, though Threes focus on goals and finding the most efficient path to get to the end-result, and Sixes prioritize anticipating problems and dangers so they can prepare and find fixes proactively.

Threes and Sixes also differ in specific ways. Threes focus on moving quickly and efficiently toward their goals, while Sixes can procrastinate for fear of doing it wrong or because they are looking for problems. Threes are skillful at matching an image of success and tend to appear confident in whatever they do, while Sixes can waver through doubting and questioning. Sixes can also become stuck in fear or paralyzed by overanalysis and imagining the worst-case scenario. When engaging in work tasks and in their lives in general, Threes pay attention to doing whatever it takes to achieve success and like to be recognized for their achievements. Sixes usually fear success and so may tend to sabotage themselves (sometimes in an effort to avoid attracting the attention of others). Related to this, while Threes are action-oriented and success-oriented, Sixes often avoid taking action that might lead to success because they fear that success leads to exposure and exposure may lead to being attacked. Being very goal-oriented, Threes work toward goals without slowing down long enough to think about what might go wrong, while Sixes almost always think of what could go wrong, which makes them skilled troubleshooters—they naturally think about potential obstacles in the process of accomplishing a particular task so they can prepare and account for them. Finally, Threes can usually work well with authorities, as long as they don't interfere with Threes' progress toward their goals, whereas Sixes tend to be suspicious of or rebellious toward authority figures, fearing they will use their power against them in unfair ways.

Threes and Sevens

Threes and Sevens can be look-alike types, sharing many characteristics. Threes and Sevens both have a lot of energy and they both work hard, especially on projects that they are interested in and invested in. Threes and Sevens can both be charming, engaging, and attractive. Threes employ these qualities to gain people's approval, admiration, and cooperation, and Sevens use charm as a first line of defense, to diffuse negativity, and to create an upbeat, positive mood when interacting with others. Both Threes and Sevens are optimistic and confident about reaching goals, Threes because they want to create an image for others of achievement and success, and Sevens because they habitually view things in a positive light, and believe in endless possibilities and opportunities as a way of avoiding difficult feelings. Related to this, both styles avoid negative feelings that might slow them down, Threes because difficult emotions interfere with doing and looking good, and Sevens because they fear becoming stuck in uncomfortable experiences, like anxiety or sadness.

There are also some traits that distinguish Threes from Sevens. Threes excel at focusing on and completing tasks, while Sevens can find it more difficult to maintain their focus and finish tasks because they tend to get distracted. Threes expend a lot of effort on cultivating their image and managing others' perceptions of them, while Sevens don't pay as much attention to gaining others' approval through achieving a particular image. Furthermore, Threes tend to be other-oriented in that they rely on others' approval and admiration to affirm their sense of themselves, while Sevens are self-referencing, meaning that they focus more on their own internal experience, their own needs and desires, than on whether or not others approve of them.

Threes prioritize work, even bringing work on vacation at times. In contrast, Sevens prioritize pleasure, fun, and recreational experiences over work. Threes usually work well within authority structures and workplace limitations, as long as they support their forward progress toward their goals, whereas Sevens dislike hierarchical structures and so equalize authority to avoid acknowledging any limitations that might be put on them. Finally, Sevens often focus on planning for the future instead of paying attention to the present, while Threes tend to focus more on the present and what needs to be done today with regard to the immediate tasks in front of them.

Threes and Eights

Threes and Eights can look very similar to each other, having several characteristics in common. Both Threes and Eights are hardworking and have a great deal of energy for work tasks. Both can also overwork, with Threes being driven to finish tasks and reach goals no matter how much effort and time it takes, and Eights wanting to accomplish big things and being prone to forgetting their physical needs and limits. People of both types can feel and express anger when necessary, but they usually get angry for different reasons. Threes often express anger and impatience when others create obstacles between them and their goals, while Eights tend to express anger more frequently and about a wider array of issues, including when someone hurts someone they feel protective toward, when someone impedes their forward progress generally, when someone tells them what to do, when someone is unfair or unjust, and when others injure them. Both Threes and Eights can be direct and assertive in the interest of moving tasks and projects forward, and both can be goal- or results-oriented.

Both types can enjoy being in positions of leadership, with Threes liking to have a say over how things go and appreciating the image-enhancing effects of achieving a high status position within an authority structure, and Eights wanting to be in control and have the power to set the agenda and move work forward. Both Threes and Eights can also have a difficult time expressing vulnerable emotions. Threes habitually avoid their feelings because they can interfere with doing and making progress toward a goal, and Eights deny vulnerable feelings as a way of maintaining a sense of strength, power, and control. People of both types may also see the expression of vulnerable feelings as a sign of weakness.

Threes and Eights also differ in particular ways. Threes focus attention on cultivating an image of success to gain the admiration of others, while Eights do not pay much attention to their own image and how people perceive them. In terms of motivation, Threes work for the achievement of goals and tasks in the service of achieving success and looking good to others, whereas Eights are motivated by a desire for power and control and the satisfaction of their physical needs. When it comes to the achievement of goals, Threes excel at finding the most efficient way to reach their goals, while Eights can have difficulty knowing how much force to apply in a given situation in order to move closer to their goal. Related to this, Threes are skilled at ascertaining how they will impact others, while Eights have a blind spot with respect to how they impact others.

Threes can work within existing organizational structures, as long as those do not impede their progress toward goals, whereas Eights can be rebellious toward authorities and tend to want to break the rules if it suits their purposes. Eights value the truth, but can have a hard time distinguishing the difference between their truth and the objective truth. Threes are good at designing their "truth" according to an image they want to create to match the values of a specific audience. In other words, for Eights, truth is what they say it is, and for Threes, whose fixation is "deceit" or "self-deceit," truth is relative and can be adapted to suit the circumstances. Finally, Eights usually know who they are—especially in terms of a general sense of their identity and their power and strength—but Threes can be confused about their identity. Threes can believe they are their image and not realize that who they really are—their true self—is different from the image they create.

Threes and Nines

Threes and Nines share some characteristics. Both Threes and Nines tend to be optimistic, upbeat, and likable. People of both types can be hardworking and practical, though Threes more regularly focus on working excessively hard. Threes and Nines also both depend on external support for a sense of identity and direction. Threes read other people to see what they view as successful and then design their own image to match that picture of success to gain the approval and admiration of others. Disliking conflict and lacking a clear sense of their own inner agenda, Nines reference others and then go along with the wishes and wills of others as a way of finding direction and creating harmony. In addition, both Threes and Nines can be hard to contact at times. Threes focus a great deal of attention on their lists of things-to-do and identify strongly with their image. This can make it hard for them to be present and interpersonally aware from a real, solid sense of who they are. Similarly, Nines tend to forget themselves and merge with what others want to do as a way of being in harmony with other people and avoiding conflict. Some of the time, however, Nines realize later that they didn't really want to go along with that plan, but they didn't know it, because they tend not know what they really want in the moment.

There are also some key differences between Threes and Nines. On a basic level, Threes focus on accomplishing tasks and reaching goals; conversely, Nines focus more on maintaining comfort and harmony. Threes are fast-paced, decisive, and forward moving. Nines move at a slower pace and have a tendency to sit on the fence. Threes are very work-oriented, and can often be workaholics. And while some Nines can be very hardworking (especially Social Nines), many Nines can have a harder time accomplishing things, as they can become caught up inertia, paralyzed by indecision, or distracted by less essential tasks. Threes usually focus very keenly on their goals until they achieve them; in contrast, Nines tend to become easily distracted from their own priorities, as their attention tends to get pulled away from their goals and toward supporting others' goals and agendas. Threes can engage in conflict if necessary, especially if it means removing an obstacle to their forward momentum, while Nines usually take great pains to avoid conflict. Nines like to stay comfortable, and they tend to avoid moving out of their comfort zone to accomplish tasks they might view as disturbing their peace, like expressing strong opinions in public or confronting someone about something they did incorrectly. In contrast, Threes will more readily endure discomfort if it serves their progress toward their goal. Finally, Nines have a strong dislike for being the center of attention, while most Threes enjoy being in the spotlight and may even actively seek out situations in which others notice them.

Fours and Fives

There are some clear similarities between Fours and Fives. Both types can be introverted and can tend to withdraw from others. Fives regularly make boundaries and move away from interpersonal contact out of a need to conserve energy and internal resources and a fear that interacting with others will drain them or invade their private space. Fours also tend to need distance from others periodically to engage more deeply with their own internal experience. Although Fours have much more regular contact with their emotions than Fives do, both Fours and Fives can intellectualize, meaning they can focus on thinking as a way of disconnecting from feelings. Both styles are self-referencing, which means that they both focus more attention on their own internal experience than on the experience of other people. Related to this, both Fours and Fives can be introspective, paying a large amount of attention to what is going on inside themselves.

Significant differences also exist between Fours and Fives. Fours represent one of the most emotional types; they have contact with their feelings on a deep level much of the time. Fives, on the other hand, are among the least emotional, habitually detaching from their feelings. When it comes to relating to others, Fives tend to avoid deep connections, as they feel more comfortable limiting their emotional entanglements, whereas Fours typically seek out deep emotional connections with others. Fives usually keep their feelings to themselves and value self-sufficiency, and Fours tend to share their feelings with others and value emotionally authentic relationships.

When evaluating a situation or task, Fives communicate a detached, objective point of view. In contrast, Fours' particular strength is their emotional intuition, and they tend to see things more in terms of the emotional or emotionally creative aspects. Fives enjoy being alone and having a large amount of private time, and while Fours can also appreciate time alone, they are also sensitive to abandonment and loss, and they appreciate maintaining strong emotional connections. Fives tend to be reserved and withholding, and they can be sensitive to intrusion when in a relationship. Fours are more dramatic, romantic, and passionate in their relationships. In addition, Fives can easily feel drained by the needs of others, while Fours are usually very sensitive and empathic in the face of others' needs. Finally, Fives tend to minimize their needs and desires, while Fours often dwell in an experience of desiring and longing for their needs to be met. Thus, when Fours lack what they need they feel the pain acutely, while Fives detach from pain and focus on hoarding, economizing, and conserving as a way to cope with not having enough of what they need.

Fours and Sixes

Fours and Sixes can have very similar outward styles. Both Fours and Sixes are intuitive and skilled at reading others—Sixes because they protect themselves from threats by looking to see what other people's intentions are, and Fours because they are emotionally intuitive and empathic—and these traits help them form supportive relationships. People of both types can be good troubleshooters, Fours because they naturally see what's missing in a specific situation, and Sixes because they automatically think about what might go wrong so that they can prepare for it. Both Fours and Sixes can challenge authorities and the established way of doing tasks and projects. Fours can be nonconformist because they have original perspectives and they are oriented to depth and the authentic expression of feelings. And Sixes can rebel because they think in contrarian ways and feel unsafe with and suspicious of those who have power over them. Both Fours and Sixes tend to have negative feelings about themselves. Fours usually feel that they are defective or missing something in some way, and Sixes tend to doubt, question, and blame themselves. Both Fours and Sixes can get stuck in life and have a hard time moving forward, Fours because they can be overly self-critical and overly attached to specific emotions, believing things are hopeless, and Sixes because they can overthink issues and events, experience "analysis paralysis," doubt their abilities, and fear success.

There are also clear distinctions between Fours and Sixes. Fours are sensitive to how they might be perceived by others and want to be seen as unique and original. Sixes, on the other hand, do not focus on the image others have of them as much. Fours want to stand out and be viewed as special in the eyes of others, and Sixes identify more with the underdog and the "everyman/everywoman" archetype. Fours live primarily from and in their emotions, while Sixes dwell more in their heads and are predominantly mental and analytical. Sixes' most regular emotional experiences involve fear, doubt, and worry, while Fours more often feel emotions related to sadness and melancholy. Sixes search for certainty and inevitably don't find it or adhere to something specific out of a need for certainty. Fours mainly focus on what they don't have that others have—often an unattainable love relationship—thinking that they can at last be happy if they can attain it. Finally, Fours' chief aim is to feel loved and appreciated for who they are, while Sixes focus more on feeling safe in the world.

Fours and Sevens

Fours and Sevens share some traits in common that can make them look alike. Both types are very idealistic, with Fours focusing on ideals of love and connection, and Sevens focusing more on envisioning the ideal in a wider array of imaginative realms. Most notably, Fours and Sevens both appreciate and seek out intense and stimulating experiences. Fours do this because they live from their feelings, they appreciate the rich experience of deeply felt emotion and passionate connections with other people, and they dislike mundane experience. Sevens pursue intensity and stimulation because they want to keep their mood up and their experiences fun and positive as a way of moving away from less positive, less intense, potentially empty, boring, or unpleasant alternatives. In this, both types have an aversion to the everyday, the mundane, and the ordinary, finding this realm of experience potentially empty and thus boring or even anxiety producing. Both Fours and Sevens value creativity and self-expression, Fours because they want to be seen and understood as special and unique and because they appreciate aesthetics and artistry, and Sevens because they are natural visionaries who imagine varied future possibilities, have many interests and ideas, and appreciate the stimulating and exciting aspects of creative expression.

In relating to others, both Fours and Sevens are self-referencing; that is, they both focus their attention more on their own experience as opposed to focusing primarily on others. When Fours pay attention to their own experience, they usually do so in an emotional way, focusing on their feelings and moods. When Sevens focus attention on themselves, however, they most often focus on their thoughts, future plans, and desires for amusement and pleasurable experiences, and they look to the outside world for entertainment opportunities. Both Fours and Sevens can also be sensitive to criticism, with Fours feeling criticism as an extra blow to their already diminished sense of themselves as not good enough, and Sevens experiencing it as a hurtful interruption of their youthful desire to focus on what's positive.

Fours and Sevens also differ in specific ways. Although both styles are idealistic, Sevens tend to be relentlessly optimistic and Fours can be somewhat pessimistic, especially to the outside observer, as Fours tend to draw attention to what is missing. Also, Fours and Sevens have very different profiles when it comes to their experience of feelings. Sevens tend to focus on and dwell in positive feelings, naturally having very upbeat, happy temperaments. Connected to this, Sevens can have a difficult time staying with more difficult emotions, such as sadness or discomfort. Fours, on the other hand, are more comfortable with a wide range of emotions and tend to feel darker feelings like disappointment or melancholy more regularly and more comfortably. Similarly, Sevens often reframe negatives into positives, while Fours can feel irritated when people tell them to "look on the bright side." Fours have a tendency to focus on what is missing or unavailable that they would like to have or be, and this leads them to be more aware of the negative side of situations, issues, and relationships.

Fours comfort with feelings makes them good supporters of others who are experiencing difficulties, while Sevens have a harder time being with and empathizing with others who are in pain. Sevens feel challenged by dealing with suffering, feeling much more comfort and ease focusing on positive feelings. Conversely, Fours can find richness in suffering and see it as a real and valuable part of human experience. Furthermore, Fours seek deep connections with others based on the sharing of authentic feelings, whereas Sevens can feel hesitant about making commitments and exploring relationships on a deep emotional level because they dislike feeling limited and so tend to move away from engaging too deeply with others at times. Lastly, Fours value authenticity and depth, while Sevens prioritize charm and a positive, fun-loving presentation (which Fours can find superficial or insincere).

Fours and Eights
Fours and Eights can appear similar. People of both types are willing to engage in conflict and can confront people if necessary, though Eights tend to do this more regularly than Fours. Fours and Eights can both feel and express big emotions, though Eights tend to express anger more frequently than other emotions, and Fours can more readily feel a range of emotions,

tending especially to experience melancholy more regularly than people of other types. Both Eights and Fours are drawn to intensity, and both types also feel things passionately, though Fours are much more likely than Eights to feel their vulnerable feelings. Both Fours and Eights can be impulsive, and both can feel justified in breaking the rules—Eights because they are bigger than the rules, and Fours because they prioritize their internal experience and their own needs and wants over the rules. In the work setting, both Fours and Eights can work hard and be deeply involved in their work, with Fours viewing work as an opportunity for self-expression and collaborative artistry and Eights wanting to make a big impact, achieve and maintain power, and mentor and protect the people they work with.

Significant differences also exist between Fours and Eights. Fours typically experience a wider range of emotions than Eights, with Eights feeling more anger and impatience than Fours and Fours feeling more melancholy and sadness than Eights. Importantly, Eights dislike being vulnerable and expressing any vulnerable feelings—and regularly deny the existence of such feelings. In contrast, Fours feel vulnerable emotions on a regular basis and can even feel some degree of comfort in a true and deep experience of their vulnerability. Eights have a difficult time recognizing their own physical limits, dependency needs, and softer emotions, while (with the possible exception of some Sexual Fours) Fours are much more familiar with their limitations, their sense of dependency, and their softer emotions. In addition, Fours usually put much more effort than Eights into getting their own physical and emotional needs met. And when in relationships, Eights typically express love through protection and power, while Fours express love through an expression of feelings and their desire for connection.

While people of both types may challenge established authorities, Eights are usually more regularly rebellious than Fours. Generally, Eights focus their attention on the big picture and strategize about how to move things forward, while Fours pay more attention to the creative process and on attracting attention and being appreciated for their unique contributions. When working with others, both Fours and Eights can have big energy. Eights tend to be very assertive and can even be aggressive and dominating, while Fours are more oriented to achieving emotional connections with others (though Sexual Fours may also be assertive or aggressive). Related to this, Eights tend to misperceive the impact they have on others, while Fours are emotionally intuitive and can be highly sensitive to how they affect the people around them. In communicating, Eights tend to be direct and straightforward, while Fours express themselves more descriptively in terms of how they are experiencing something emotionally. Eights do not pay very much attention to their internal processes, while Fours can be very introspective.

Fours and Nines

Fours and Nines have some characteristics in common. They can look alike in that they both place a great deal of importance on the cultivation of relationships and the achievement of connections with other people. In addition to this, both types can lose themselves by merging with loved ones, though Nines do this more regularly than Fours, who can more easily sense their independent needs and desires. Both Fours and Nines can relatively easily understand other people in a deep way, Fours because they are emotionally intuitive and sensitive to the moods and feelings of others, and Nines because they can often see others' perspectives more clearly than their own and they align with other people to create harmony. On the downside, Fours and Nines can both feel overlooked and unimportant to others, and they may both regularly have the feeling they are misunderstood by others. For Fours, however, they most often experience emotions related to being misunderstood or "not good enough." For Nines, their experience is more one of being overlooked and not heard, usually because Nines themselves have a hard time taking a strong position or expressing a clear opinion. Another key similarity is that both types have fears about not belonging. Fours tend to feel like misfits, while Nines often have a deep underlying concern about whether or not they belong to the group.

Fours and Nines also differ in significant ways. Fundamentally, Nines are other-referencing and Fours are self-referencing, meaning that Nines primarily pay attention to other people's opinions, agendas, and moods, while Fours prioritize their own internal experience, focusing more on their own needs, feelings, and desires. Fours also feel a wider range of emotions more deeply than Nines do; Nines tend to be more steady and even emotionally. Nines can easily have their attention drawn away from their own priorities and toward less essential substitutes and others' agendas, whereas Fours are more aware of and focused on satisfying their own needs and wants. Nines are oriented to creating harmony among people, while this is much less of a priority for the Four, who may even create or contribute to discord if necessary as a way to push for authentic communication of feelings. Nines avoid conflict much of the time, while Fours can engage in conflict if necessary or may even create conflict.

Nines usually do not state their preferences, often because they don't know what they want, but sometimes because they believe that others' opinions are more important than their own or they don't want to create a conflict. In contrast, Fours tend to believe that their opinions are of value and that it is important to say what they think. And Fours do not always adapt to others, regularly feeling moved to express their own disagreement or unique perspective, whereas Nines have the tendency to overadjust to others, often thinking that if they do not adapt to others, the connection between them will be broken. Because of this tendency to adapt to others' Nines also have a difficult time saying "no," making boundaries, and asserting themselves. Fours, on the other hand, can more often and more easily make boundaries with others and assert their own agendas.

Fives and Sixes

Fives and Sixes are alike in many ways. Both Fives and Sixes can be reserved and withdrawn. More phobic Sixes, in particular, resemble Fives, as both types tend to be introverted and to seek a sense of security by moving away from other people. Fives maintain a distance between themselves and others because they want to guard against being depleted, while Sixes are wary of others and withdraw out of a fear that other people might represent some kind of danger or threat. Both types are slow to trust others when forming relationships. This is because Fives and Sixes both have safety and security concerns, though phobic Sixes tend to feel more actively fearful and anxious about outside threats, while Fives excel at avoiding fearful situations well before they occur. Fives and Sixes can be vigilant when it comes to interacting with others and protecting their boundaries, and both can become angry when their boundaries are challenged. Fives have a need for clear boundaries because the want to prevent intrusions and other potentially energy-draining interactions with others, while Sixes have a regular fear of being attacked or shamed in some way. Both Fives and Sixes are analytical, thinking types who intellectualize on a regular basis, meaning they rely on their thinking function a great deal as a way of avoiding feelings—they may think about feelings, but have a hard time actually feeling them.

Fives and Sixes also differ in some of their traits. Counterphobic (Sexual) Sixes can look very different from Fives, being much more extroverted than the more introverted Five. Sixes have more apparent issues with authorities than Fives do. Sixes can be suspicious of and even openly rebellious toward authority figures, while Fives can follow authorities if they choose to (and if they don't, they may go against the established authority in a more quiet, less noticeable way). Sixes focus their attention on questioning and doubting in the quest for certainty, while Fives pay more attention to the accumulation of knowledge, the reduction of needs, and the economical use of resources like time and energy. Fives value emotional control, while Sixes do not prioritize the control of emotions in the same way.

When analyzing a situation, Fives can be very objective in their analysis, as they habitually detach from emotions. Sixes, on the other hand, can have a hard time distinguishing their intuitions from their projections—they may confuse the reality of what they are perceiving with what they fear is true. Interpersonally, Fives withdraw from others to avoid feeling pressed to meet their emotional needs, while Sixes do not fear meeting others' needs and can be very generous with their time and energy with people they trust.

Fives and Sevens

Fives and Sevens have several characteristics in common. Both Fives and Sevens are mental types, "living" most of the time in their heads (or their thinking function), though they do it in different ways. Believing knowledge is power, Fives tend to think in terms of gathering and compartmentalizing information, and Sevens tend to think in terms of planning and interrelating and interconnecting ideas. Sevens have a nonlinear way of thinking that gives them a talent for finding connections and parallels between dissimilar things, while Fives prioritize collecting and compartmentalizing information, especially about topics they have a strong interest in. Furthermore, both Sevens and Fives have active imaginations and sincerely enjoy learning new things and pursuing intellectual interests. Fives and Sevens both guard against becoming too committed in social interactions, Fives because they fear being drained by others' needs and Sevens because they like to have many options and dislike feeling limited. In addition, people of both styles intellectualize; that is, they both avoid feelings by going into thinking and analysis and detaching from emotions.

There are also clear differences between Fives and Sevens. Sevens live in the future much of the time, in fantasies and plans about pleasurable activities yet to happen, while Fives don't live in the future or think in terms of planning and play in this same way. Sevens are relentlessly positive, habitually and automatically reframing negatives into positives, while Fives tend to be more removed and objective in their analysis of situations and events. Sevens focus attention on having multiple options and limitless opportunities, while Fives focus on how to conserve energy and do what they have to do in the most economical way, given their perception that their resources are limited and they feel at risk of being depleted. In fact, Sevens have a hard time making commitments because having others depend on them makes them feel constrained and limited and uncomfortable. Fives are more able to make commitments, precisely because they are so good at protecting their private space and making boundaries. While Sevens are often very socially active and gregarious, Fives tend to make social promises much more carefully and to a very small number of people in their lives.

When it comes to feelings, Sevens actively seek out excitement and stimulation as a way of avoiding feelings like frustration, discomfort, and sadness, whereas Fives merely detach from feelings, automatically letting them go and focusing instead on thoughts and ideas. Sevens unconsciously deal with their fear and anxiety by charming and disarming others, while Fives detach and withdraw from others to avoid interactions that might feel intrusive or inspire difficult feelings.

Fives and Eights

Some clear similarities exist between Fives and Eights. Fives and Eights can both feel and express anger if someone challenges their boundaries, but while this is one of the only situations in which Fives will openly express anger, Eights tend to become angry more frequently over a wider range of issues. Both Fives and Eights have a great deal of difficulty experiencing (and, especially, expressing) vulnerable emotions. Fives detach from emotions and withdraw from situations that might inspire vulnerable feelings, while Eights deny their vulnerability and overcompensate by focusing on and finding ways to communicate their strength and power.

Fives differ from Eights in many respects. Socially, Eights tend to be extroverted and have a great deal of "big" energy, while Fives are usually more introverted and withdrawn, with a much more reserved and low-key energetic presence. While both Eights and Fives like to be in control, Eights will take control in a more overt, active, aggressive way, while Fives tend to control things more quietly and less obviously, with less expenditure of energy. Eights tend to be excessive in the things they do, while Fives are minimalistic, conservationist, and economical.

When analyzing a situation, Eights can have trouble distinguishing between the objective truth and their own version of the truth, and Fives have the particular talent of being able to be objective analysts. Eights are impulsive; Fives are more thoughtful. For example, Eights tend to move into action before they think things through, while Fives tend to think a great deal about a particular move before going into action. Fives suffer more from the possibility that they will think too much and not take action. When in relationships, Eights usually make it clear where they stand, while Fives can be difficult to read and may withhold information about what they are thinking and feeling, even with close others. Lastly, Eights rebel against any inhibition of their large capacity for pleasure or power, whereas Fives tend to minimize and inhibit their own needs and desires and can feel depleted by life and relationships. Fives may even forgo the possible pleasure that a relationship may bring because the cost seems too high in terms of time, space, or emotional energy. In contrast, most Eights feel energized by relationships and especially physical intimacy (or the promise of it).

Fives and Nines

Fives and Nines share some traits in common, especially from the point of view of an outside observer. Energetically, Fives and Nines can both appear reserved and withdrawn, though Nines do not so much withdraw from others as they forget themselves and neglect their own agendas and preferences in favor of creating harmony and alignment. Both can be good mediators, as Nines can easily see all points of view and Fives are objective analysts. Both Fives and Nines dislike conflict and can be passive-aggressive, though Nines may do this out of an inability to feel their anger directly, and Fives may engage in this behavior because they do not want to express their emotions openly or get involved in an emotional situation that could be costly energetically. People of both styles have a way of distancing themselves from their own internal experience—Fives by detaching from emotion, and Nines from forgetting about their own preferences and opinions. When it comes to working with others, both Fives and Nines like structure and regularity, both want to be consulted about what they think and may need time to reflect on that, and both have a sensitivity to and a dislike of being controlled by others.

There are also some significant differences between Fives and Nines. In relating to others, at the most basic level, Nines tend to merge with others, as they find comfort in being in harmony with people, while Fives tend to withdraw from others, as they fear being depleted by the needs and demands of other people. Nines are other-referencing, tending to pay attention primarily to other people, while Fives are self-referencing, focusing more on their own internal experience and boundaries. Related to this, Nines are overly adaptive to others, while Fives are under-adaptive to others. Frequently not knowing what they want, Nines tend to avoid stating their preferences and then may later feel resentful that they went along with others and their wishes were not heard. Fives, on the other hand, almost always know what they want, and are adept at preventing others from interfering with what they want to do. Nines are often perceived as friendly and affable and easygoing, while Fives tend to be perceived as more aloof and reserved.

Wanting to be close to others in a harmonious way, Nines often don't perceive their need for boundaries, and as a result they don't make boundaries with others, while Fives prioritize making and maintaining their boundaries. Similarly, Nines have a hard time saying no and expressing their own preferences in the face of other people's wishes, while Fives can much more easily say no. Sometimes, Nines will say yes and mean no, while Fives will say no when they want to say no. Because of their boundary issues, Nines may also have a hard time separating from others, while Fives separate from others very easily, sometimes to a fault, as withdrawal constitutes one of their primary forms of self-protection. For Nines, paying attention to others' agendas gets in the way of knowing their own; for Fives, paying attention to their own agenda makes it hard to let in and make room for the agendas (and feelings) of others.

Sixes and Sevens

Sixes and Sevens have some traits in common. Both are mental types and so both are primarily thinking-oriented, though they do think in different ways about different topics. Sevens focus on planning future activities, new and interesting ideas, and interrelating and synthesizing information. Sixes think about what might go wrong to proactively prepare for it, and they also think in contrarian terms, questioning ideas and opinions they hear from others in an effort to find what's true or solve problems. Sixes and Sevens are both quick thinkers, however, with good imaginations, though Sixes tend to imagine worst-case scenarios, while Sevens imagine highly positive scenarios. Both types are "fear types," though they both may or may not be actively aware of their fear. In particular, Sevens and counterphobic Sixes can look very much alike, as both move toward threats in the environment to face dangers—the Seven with charm and an engaging presentation and the counterphobic Six with strength and the willingness to intimidate. People of both types can get caught up in thinking too much and not move into action, with Sixes becoming caught up in doubt and Sevens being distracted by new ideas and multiple options or not wanting to commit to (or be limited by) a specific course of action.

Sixes and Sevens also differ in specific ways. Sevens tend to be very optimistic, while Sixes, who usually describe themselves as realistic, may look more pessimistic to outside observers when they draw attention to problems or threatening or negative possibilities. Sevens have a sunny outlook and reframe situations in positive terms, while Sixes tend to focus on what might go wrong so they can prepare for potential problems occurring. Sevens and Sixes have different styles when it comes to managing fears or concerns. Sevens move toward the source of fear with charm and pleasantries to disarm the fearful threat with soft power, while Sixes tend to be vigilant and watchful to see the threat coming ahead of time so they can prepare to meet it. Counterphobic Sixes tend to move toward threatening situations with strength, while phobic Sixes withdraw from them, and Social Sixes obey one kind of authority or another as a way of coping with anxiety.

Sevens focus their attention on positive possibilities and interesting and fun things to do—they want to maintain good feelings and avoid pain and discomfort. Sixes can hardly avoid feeling pain and discomfort, as they focus their attention on self-doubting, questioning ideas and seeming realities, and detecting potential dangers. Sixes look for certainty and rarely, if ever, find it, or find it and hang on to it. Sevens are playful and adventurous, while Sixes are careful and strategic. Sevens plan for fun, while Sixes prepare for dealing with problems. Sevens see endless possibilities for interesting activities in an unconscious effort to keep a safe distance from anxiety and discomfort, while Sixes actually seek out problems to solve as a way of feeling safe. Sixes tend to have problems with authorities—they can be questioning and suspicious of authority and also rebellious and challenging of authority—while Sevens equalize authority and simply deny hierarchical power relationships, seeing themselves as being on the same level with and friendly with both superiors and subordinates. Sevens expect success and have a confident presentation, while Sixes expect things to go wrong and may a worried, even paranoid presentation. Sevens have difficulty with commitments, as they fear limits, while Sixes are very loyal and dedicated and committed once they trust someone or something.

Sixes and Eights

While Sixes and Eights are alike in some general ways, phobic Sixes can look quite different from Eights and counterphobic Sixes can look a lot like Eights. Both Eights and counterphobic Sixes can appear strong and intimidating to others, and both styles tend to move toward threatening or difficult situations "fearlessly," to deal with the problem head-on. However, Eights truly have little or no fear, while counterphobic Sixes act against threats to quell a deeper and ongoing sense of fear that is not always experienced consciously in the moment (but represents the "fight" part of "fight or flight"). Eights and all Sixes tend to rebel against authority. And Sixes and Eights can both be protective of others they care about. Eights tend to protect the weak and vulnerable, and Sixes are frequently drawn to supporting underdogs or underdog causes. In addition, Sixes and Eights can both be very hardworking and practical, though Eights are more prone to over-working, wanting to move big things forward quickly, and Sixes can be more cautious and careful and can get slowed down by overanalysis and endless questioning of what they are doing.

Eights also differ from Sixes in some clear ways, with Eights' style contrasting even more obviously with the style of phobic Sixes. Eights feels relatively little fear and vulnerability, as the Eights' approach to life is based on a denial of vulnerability and an overcompensatory confidence in their power and strength. Phobic Sixes on the other hand, feel fearful and thus vulnerable much of the time, and so they anxiously stay vigilant for threats and other dangers. Eights do not engage in self-doubt very often, while Sixes continually doubt themselves. Sixes tend to overthink and can become paralyzed by overanalysis and thus fail to act. Eights tend to act quickly without thinking. Because Eights like to move things forward quickly, they get impatient if others slow their forward progress, while Sixes tend to procrastinate and slow themselves down based on fears that there will be some sort of bad outcome or another. Sixes are slow to trust others and they inspect people carefully to look for hidden agendas and ulterior motives, while Eights generally trust people who appear competent until their trust is broken. Eights can directly confront a conflictual situation, as can counterphobic Sixes, while the phobic Six would rather avoid conflict, but can engage in it if necessary or provoked.

Sixes and Nines

Sixes and Nines can look similar. Both Sixes and Nines can be loyal, caring, and supportive of others. Sixes and Nines both procrastinate. Sixes procrastinate because they fear things will go wrong and they fear success, while Nines put off work and other tasks when they have a hard time accessing and staying with their own agendas. Also, at times, Nines can passively resist forward movement as a way to resist going along with what others want them to do (without saying so and risking potential conflict). Sixes can resist their own forward progress because they become caught up in questioning, overanalyzing, and doubting. In addition, phobic Sixes and Nines both want to avoid conflict, though Nines are more extreme in this regard. And people of both types tend to be self-effacing and humble. They both dislike being in the spotlight, but for different reasons. Sixes fear even positive attention can make them open to attack, and Nines are very uncomfortable being the center of attention, as they do not even place themselves at the center of their own attention.

Sixes and Nines also have distinct characteristics that reveal the differences between their styles. Nines tend to merge with others and trust others easily, while Sixes tend to stand apart and be suspicious, especially at first, until they gather enough information to ascertain whether or not someone is trustworthy. Nines tend to go along to get along and to overadjust to others preferences—they tend to comply with the wishes of others as a way of avoiding discomfort and potential separation. In contrast, Sixes are by nature mistrustful of others, and may question or test people before going along. In light of this tendency to go along with other people's preferences, Nines are easily distracted from their own agenda, while Sixes tend to remain alert in their focus of attention on potential threats.

Nines can see many different points of view, and usually take on a mediating role when parties in a group differ in opinion. In contrast, Sixes think in contrarian terms: they can see one side, and then they can see the opposing side, and they tend to see things not in terms of many equally plausible points of view, but in terms of questioning and countering whatever view is put forward. Nines dislike conflict and do not usually have contact with their own anger (which might lead them into a conflict), and in this they differ greatly from the counterphobic Six, who may get angry and move toward conflict in certain situations as a way of dealing with a potential threat. Sixes tend to be somewhat (or very) anti-authoritarian, while Nines, wanting to avoid conflicts and create harmony, will usually go along with and cooperate with authority, at least on the outside.

Sevens and Eights

Sevens and Eights can look alike. Both types tend to be visionary thinkers, able to see the big picture and future possibilities. Both can engage in conflict if necessary, though some Sevens feel more comfortable with confrontation than others. Sevens and Eights can both be uninhibited, self-indulgent, and excessive when it comes to seeking pleasure. And both styles appreciate intense and stimulating experiences. In interpersonal interactions, both Sevens and Eights dislike being limited or controlled by other people. Individuals of both styles can be rebellious, though Eights will rebel more openly in a straightforward fashion, and Sevens prefer a charm-based, diplomatic approach. Eights believe the best defense is a good offense, and Sevens opt for expressing opposition to potential limitation through soft power and the maintenance of multiple options, with charm as a first line of defense.

Both Sevens and Eights will break the rules if it suits their purposes, and both types can take on a great deal of work and overbook themselves. For Sevens, overbooking represents a difficulty with saying no to exciting possibilities and interesting activities, and for Eights, overworking can reflect a tendency to want to do everything and forget their physical needs and vulnerability. Both Eights and Sevens avoid or deny softer, more vulnerable emotions, with Eights regularly denying their vulnerability and Sevens avoiding pain and discomfort.

Significant differences also exist between Sevens and Eights. While Eights can be rebellious when someone has authority over them, they can also work with a good authority they respect and even enjoy being the leader at times. In contrast, Sevens equalize authority, making friends with bosses and subordinates as a way of denying a vertical power structure that might constrain them. In terms of where their attention goes, Eights focus on power and control, while Sevens focus on planning and play. And while both types have access to their anger, Eights are more likely than Sevens to express anger. Eights are direct and like to move things forward in a strong and forceful way, while Sevens can have a difficult time focusing on work tasks and get distracted, especially when the work is tedious or routine. Eights like to make order and push projects forward quickly and effectively to their conclusion, while Sevens prefer the idea stage to the implementation stage and can have problems with following through. Sevens intellectualize to escape from feeling into thinking, finding difficult feelings uncomfortable to be with, while Eights move into action without thinking things through. Eights also deny softer feelings or project them onto those they perceive as weaker and then seek to protect. And finally, when analyzing or evaluating a situation, Sevens reframe negatives into positives, while Eights aren't afraid of seeing and dealing with the "negatives" and tend to see issues in terms of "all or nothing" or "black and white" polarities.

Sevens and Nines

Sevens and Nines can look alike in that they share some common traits. Both have friendly, optimistic dispositions. When interacting with others, both have personable, affable styles and like to be around people. Wanting to be liked, both Sevens and Nines tend to act in ways that make it easy for other people to like them. Both like to keep things positive and avoid conflict if possible, though many Sevens can do conflict if necessary and most Nines would prefer not to. When performing tasks, both Sevens and Nines can have a hard time maintaining a clear focus on the job at hand, with Sevens typically being distracted by more interesting things to do and think about, and Nines being frequently distracted by others' agendas, environmental claims, and inessential tasks.

Sevens and Nines also differ in several respects. While both styles are primarily, if unconsciously, concerned with avoiding uncomfortable feelings, Sevens pursue excitement, self-indulgent activities, and fun things to do as a way of avoiding discomfort, whereas Nines neglect themselves and forget their opinions and desires to avoid experiencing anger and discomfort. Sevens are fast-paced, high-energy characters, while Nines operate at a more relaxed pace, often experiencing inertia and indecision related to decisions and tasks. When interacting with others, Sevens are self-referencing, focusing their attention mainly on their own agenda; in contrast, Nines are other-referencing, paying attention primarily to others and not having a clear or direct experience of their own desires. Nines merge with others and go along with other people's agendas, while Sevens have their own clear agenda that usually takes priority over other people's agendas when there is any kind of conflict between them. It's usually easy for Sevens to know what they want, while it's difficult for Nines to know what they want. For a Nine, it's easier to know what they don't want than what they do want. Nines typically don't state their preferences—which they often don't know—and then can become resentful of others whose agenda they passively follow along with when they deferred their own, even though they didn't really want to. Sevens have their own agendas and don't let other people deter them from the things they really want to do.

Eights and Nines

Eights and Nines have some similar characteristics. Both dislike being controlled by others, but they differ in how they respond to attempts at control from the outside. Eights openly rebel, fight against, and potentially actively overpower the other person. Nines take a much more passive approach to asserting control, often seeming to agree or go along, while passively resisting—saying "yes," but acting out "no." Both styles are part of the "self-forgetting" triad of types, and so both can forget their own needs and wants. Eights do this through excess and overwork, denying their physical vulnerabilities and taking on too many responsibilities. Nines do this through focusing on others and losing conscious contact with their own emotions and priorities. And both Eights and Nines can readily enjoy and seek out worldly comforts and pleasures.

Eights and Nines also differ in key ways. Eights' primary focus of attention is on power and control, while Nines' attention goes first to creating harmony and avoiding conflict. Disliking conflict and interpersonal tension, Nines often unconsciously avoid any internal sense of their own anger that might cause them to be at odds with someone else, while Eights have easier access to their anger, and may feel angry frequently and have a much easier time engaging in conflict. Eights are highly opinionated and are direct and straightforward in asserting their opinions, while Nines often do not know their position because they pay so much attention to understanding others' perspectives. For Nines, having an opinion means risking conflict, so they are motivated to avoid their own positions, desires, and strong feelings.

Nines can see easily everyone's point of view and are open to seeing many sides of an issue, while Eights see their own view most clearly and tend to see issues in terms of black and white. Indentifying with multiple perspectives makes Nines excellent mediators in that they can see all sides of an issue and are motivated to help create harmony and consensus. In contrast, Eights tend to want to assert their own opinions and have their own way. Nines have a difficult time making boundaries and saying no, while Eights have an easy time asserting their will and rejecting requests. Interpersonally, Eights are often perceived by others as being intimidating, while most people see Nines as likable, approachable, and friendly. Eights tend to have a big impact on others, while Nines can have a difficult time making an impact and can also be harder to contact interpersonally. Eights like to break the rules, make their own rules, and frequently rebel against authority, while Nines like structure and can more easily work with authority figures. And while people of both styles avoid a certain realm of internal experience—Eights deny their vulnerable, softer emotions, and Nines avoid or forget their anger and preferences—Eights are much more open about expressing themselves in the world and acting in forceful ways to get what they need and want.

Notes

Introduction: Self-Awareness and the Enneagram

1. Jung, Collected Works 8, p. 137, quoted in Hopcke, 1989, p. 13

2. Tarnas, 1991, pp. 3-4

3. Myss, 2013, p. xiii

Chapter 1: The Enneagram as a Framework

1. Hopcke, 1989, p. 81

2. Naranjo, 1995

3. Naranjo (1994), quoted in Maitri, 2005, p. 54

4. Naranjo, 1994, p. 199

5. Maitri, 2005, p. 190

6. The subtype descriptions throughout this book are based on Claudio Naranjo's articulation of the Enneagram's 27 subtype personalities. While specific citations are given throughout the text, material has generally been drawn from Naranjo's books (1994, 1997, and 2012) as well as 2004, 2008, and 2012 workshops taught by him. Gonzalo Moran also contributed to my subtype characterizations. I am very grateful to him for generously sharing his knowledge and his interpretations with me and for translating portions of Naranjo's 2012 book on the subtypes.

7. Naranjo, workshops, 2004, 2008

8. In defining this new (as far as I know) interpretation of the conscious use of the Enneagram's arrow lines for growth, I draw on the work of Sandra Maitri (2000, p. 249), A. H. Almaas (as cited in Maitri, 2000, p. 249), and David Burke (as cited in Stevens, 2010, p. 134-135).

9. Bourgeault, 2003, p. 63

Chapter 2: The Enneagram as a Universal Symbol

1. Smith, 1992, p. vii

2. Huxley, 1944, p. vii

3. Bourgeault, 2003, pp. 64-65. Bourgeault cites Maurice Nicoll as the original author of this parable and notes it was popularized by philosopher Jacob

Needleman. Nicoll was one of G. I. Gurdjieff's students and has written extensively on Gurdjieff's teachings. Needleman has also written many articles and books about the Gurdjieff work. Gurdjieff is one of the main sources of information about the symbolic meaning of the enneagram.

4. Helen Palmer also taught a version of this interpretation of the inner triangle of the Enneagram in the Enneagram Professional Training Program courses I took in 1996 and 1997.

5. Schneider, 1994, p. xx

6. Schneider, 1994, p. xxiii

7. Skinner, 2006

8. Ouspensky, 1949, (In Search of the Miraculous), p. 294

9. Ouspensky, 1949, (In Search of the Miraculous) p. 280

10. Lawlor, 1982, p. 21

11. Schneider, 1994, p. 3-4

12. David Burke discussed this idea in his presentation at the annual conference of the International Enneagram Association in 2010.

13. Schneider, 1994, p. 42

14. Schneider, 1994, p. 43

15. Schneider, 1994, p. 40

16. These three "centers of intelligence" in the enneagram also have correlates in our physical brains: 1) the brain stem, or reptilian brain, 2) the limbic system, or emotional brain, and 3) the cerebral cortex, the seat of higher thinking. (See Killen, 2009; Lewis, Amini, and Lannon, 2000)

17. Stevens, 2010

18. Stevens, 2010

19. Stevens 2010; Bertrand Russell, 1945

20. Blake, 1997, p. 27

21. Addison, 1998; Smoley & Kinney, 1999

22. Bennett, 1974, p. 2

23. Needleman, 1992, p. 360

24. Webb, 1980, p. 5

25. Ouspensky, 1949 (ISM), p. 19; (See also Ouspensky, 1950)

26. Ouspensky, 1949 (ISM), p. 226

27. Ouspensky, 1949 (ISM), p. 226

28. Arica web site (www.arica.org)

29. Interviews with Oscar Ichazo, p. 91

30. Arica web site (www.arica.org/articles/effross.cfm)

31. Arica web site (www.arica.org/articles/effross.cfm)

32. Claudio Naranjo, keynote address at the 2003 annual conference of the International Enneagram Association.

Chapter 3: The Point Nine Archetype

1. Goldberg, 2005, p. 17

2. Goldberg, 2005, p. 18

3. Homer/Lattimore, 1965, p. 139

4. Naranjo, 1994, p. 258

5. Naranjo, 1994, p. 259

6. Maitri, 2005, p. 34

7. Naranjo, 1994, p. 246 and Evagrius/Sinkewicz, 2003

8. Naranjo, 1994, p. 246

9. Naranjo, 1994, p. 255

10. Naranjo, 1994, p. 255

11. Wagner, 2010, p. 497

12. Wagner 2010, p. 510

13. Naranjo 1994, p. 256

14. Naranjo, 1994, p. 256

15. *Inferno*, Canto VII, p. 129, Dante/Musa, 1971

16. Naranjo, 2008 subtype workshop

17. Naranjo, 1994, p. 260

18. David Burke, personal communication.

Chapter 4: The Point Eight Archetype

1. Horney, 1950

2. Jung ("The Concept of Libido" CW 5, par. 194), quoted in Goldberg, 2005, p. 32

3. Kahn, 2002, p. 26

4. Kahn, 2002, p. 26

5. Naranjo, 1997, p. 389

6. Naranjo, 1997, p. 389; Kahn, 2002, p. 26

7. Naranjo, 1995

8. Maitri, 2005, p. 53

9. Naranjo, 1995, p. 164

10. Homer/Fagles, 1996, 9:119-128

11. Goldberg, 2005, p. 28

12. Homer/Fagles, 1996, 9:306-312

13. Naranjo 1994, p. 147-148

14. Naranjo, 1997, p. 388

15. Karen Horney (1945) as quoted in Naranjo, 1994, p. 133

16. McWilliams, 1994, p. 101

17. Naranjo 1994, p. 127

18. Naranjo, 1997, p. 389

19. Maitri 2005, p. 54

20. Naranjo, 1994, p. 140

21. Drawing on Ichazo, Naranjo calls these fixed mental assumptions the "cognitive mistake" that underlies and shapes character. Drawing on his expertise in NLP (Neuro-linguistic programming), Enneagram author and teacher Tom Condon refers to the mental fixation of a given personality as the "trance" of the type.

22. Naranjo, 1994, p. 142

23. Naranjo 1994, p. 142

24. Naranjo, 1994, p. 142

25. Naranjo, 1994, p. 142

26. Ichazo's early name for Type Eight was "Ego-Venge:" Lilly & Hart, 1994, p. 223

27. Naranjo, 1994, p. 141

28. Naranjo, 1994, p. 145

29. Palmer, 1988, p. 319

30. *Inferno* V:39, p. 125, Dante/Musa, 1971

31. *Inferno* V: 30-36, Dante/Musa, 1971

32. Gonzalo Moran, personal communication

33. Naranjo, 1990, p. 127; 1997, p. 391

34. Naranjo, 1997, p. 389

35. Maitri, 2005, p. 53

36. Maitri, 2005, p. 53

37. Maitri 2000, p. 259

38. Maitri, 2005, p. 68-69

39. Maitri, 2005, p. 68

40. David Burke, personal communication

Chapter 5: The Point Seven Archetype

1. Hopcke, 1989, p. 107-108

2. Hopcke, 1989, p. 108

3. Maitri, 2005, p. 172

4. Homer/Lattimore, 1965, p. 152

5. Homer/Fagles, 1996, 10:39-47

6. Naranjo, 1994, p. 170

7. Naranjo, 1994, p. 171

8. Naranjo, 1994, p. 171

9. Naranjo, 1997, p. 349

10. Naranjo, 1994, p. 161

11. Naranjo, 1994, p. 167

12. Maitri, 2005, p. 174

13. Naranjo, 1994, p. 161

14. Maitri, 2005, p. 175

15. Maitri, 2005, p. 176

16. Wagner, 2010; Tolk, 2004

17. Maitri, 2005, p. 176

18. Naranjo, 1994, p. 161

19. Naranjo, 1994

20. Naranjo, 1994, p. 162

21. Naranjo, 1994, p. 162

22. Naranjo, 1997, p. 353

23. Naranjo, 1994

24. Naranjo, 1997, p. 353

25. Naranjo, 1997, p. 353

26. Naranjo: 1994, p. 162

27. Naranjo, 1994, p. 162

28. Naranjo, 1994, p. 162

29. Naranjo, 1997, p. 353

30. *Inferno* VI:34-38, 46-48, Musa, 1971

31. *Inferno*, p. 125, Musa, 1971

32. Goldberg, 2005

33. Eliot, 1943, pp. 13-20

34. Maitri, 2000

35. Maitri, 2005, p. 185

36. Maitri, 2005, p. 186

37. Naranjo, 1994, p. 161

38. David Burke, personal communication

Chapter 6: The Point Six Archetype

1. Maitri, 2005, p. 155

2. Maitri, 2005, p. 153

3. Erickson, 1959

4. In his writings about the Enneagram types, Naranjo highlights the fact that, when speaking about Type Six, it is difficult to talk about one single character. (1997, p. 297)

5. Naranjo, 1995, p. 151

6. Naranjo, 1995, p. 151

7. Homer/Fagles, 1996, p, 234

8. Goldberg, 2005, pp. 56-57

9. Naranjo, 1995, p. 144

10. McWilliams 1994, p. 107

11. McWilliams: 1994, p. 108

12. McWilliams, 1994, p. 113

13. American Psychiatric Glossary, 1994

14. American Psychiatric Glossary, 1994

15. Naranjo 1994, p. 231

16. Drawing on Ichazo, Naranjo calls these fixed mental assumptions the "cognitive mistake" that underlies and shapes character.

17. Naranjo 1994, p. 233

18. Naranjo, 1994, p. 235

19. Naranjo, 1994, p. 238

20. Naranjo, 1994, p. 236-237

21. *Inferno* III:52-57, 64-66, Dante/Musa, 1971.

22. Naranjo, 1997, p. 297

23. Naranjo, 1994, p. 240

24. Naranjo, 1997, p. 299

25. Naranjo, 1997, p. 299

26. Naranjo, 1994

27. Naranjo, 1997, p. 303

28. Naranjo, 1994, p. 299

29. Naranjo, 1995, p. 152

30. Maitri, 2000, p. 255

31. Maitri, 2005, p. 167

32. C. S. Lewis, quoted in Connolly, 1944.

33. David Burke, personal communication.

Chapter 7: The Point Five Archetype

1. Singer, 1972, pp. 187-188

2. Singer, 1972, p. 188

3. Singer, 1972, p. 188

4. Naranjo, 1994, p. 71

5. Almaas, 1998; Maitri, 2005

6. Naranjo, 1994, p. 72

7. Horney, 1950, p. 260

8. Goldberg, 2005

9. Goldberg, 2005, p. 68

10. Homer/Fagles 362-365, 1996, p. 240

11. Naranjo, 1997

12. Naranjo, 1994, p. 94

13. McWilliams, 1994, p. 122

14. Naranjo, 1997, p. 244

15. Naranjo, 1994, p. 66

16. Naranjo, 1995, p. 73

17. Drawing on Ichazo, Naranjo calls these fixed mental assumptions the "cognitive mistake" that underlies and shapes character.

18. Wagner, 2010; Tolk, 2004

19. Wagner, 2010; Tolk, 2004

20 Naranjo, 1994, p. 86

21. Naranjo, 1994, p. 86

22. Naranjo, 1994, p. 85

23. Naranjo, 1994, p. 84

24. Naranjo, 1994

25. Naranjo, 1994, p. 89

26. Naranjo, 1995, p. 123

27. Naranjo, 1995, pp. 123-124

28. *Inferno* VII:25-31, 58-60, Dante/Musa, 1971

29. *Inferno* VII:25-31, Dante/Musa, 1971

30. *Inferno* VII:73-96, Dante/Musa, 1971

31. Naranjo, workshops, 2008 and 2012

32. Naranjo, workshops, 2004, 2008, 2012

33. Naranjo, 1997, p. 244

34. Naranjo, 1997, p. 245

35. Naranjo, 1997, p. 253

36. Maitri, 2005, p. 195

37. David Burke, personal communication

Chapter 8: The Point Four Archetype

1. Jung, 1961, p. 398

2. Homer/Lattimore, 1965, p. 170-171

3. Goldberg, 2005, p. 80

4. Goldberg, 2005

5. Goldberg, 2005, pp. 84-85

6. Naranjo, 1994, p. 97

7. Naranjo, 1994, p. 97

8. Naranjo, 1997, p. 192

9. McWilliams, 1994, p. 108

10. Naranjo 1994, pp. 96-97

11. Naranjo, 1994, pp. 97

12. Naranjo calls these fixed mental assumptions the "cognitive mistake" (or "crazy ideas") that underlies and shapes character.

13. Naranjo, 1997, p. 192

14. Naranjo, 1997, p. 193

15. Naranjo, 1990, p. 67

16. Naranjo, 1994, p. 111

17. *Inferno*, XIII: 101-102, Dante/Musa, 1971

18. *Inferno* XIII:64-72, 76-78, Dante/Musa, 1971

19. *Inferno* XIII:70, Dante/Musa, 1971

20. Naranjo, 1995, p. 126

21. Maitri, 2005, p. 147

22. Goldstein and Kornfield, 1987, p. 75

23. David Burke, personal communication

Chapter 9: The Point Three Archetype

1. Jung, 1961, p. 397

2. Hopcke, 1989, p. 86

3. Naranjo, 1995

4. Homer/Fagles, 1996, line 348, p. 281

5. David Daniels often says this in his workshops and trainings.

6. McWilliams, 1994, p. 135

7. Naranjo, 1994, p. 215

8. Naranjo, 1994, p. 199

9. Naranjo, 1994, p. 199

10. Naranjo, 1997, p. 134

11. Naranjo, 1997, 136

12. Naranjo, 1997, 135

13. Naranjo, 1997, p. 135

14. Sinkewicz (Evagrius), 2003, p. 64

15. Naranjo describes these fixed mental assumptions as the "cognitive mistake" or "crazy ideas" that underlie and shape character.

16. Naranjo, workshops, 2004, 2008, 2012

17. Moran, 2013

18. Naranjo, 1994, p. 215

19. Naranjo, 1994

20. Bourgeault, 2003, p. 60

21. Almaas, 1998, p. 268

22. *Paradise*, Dante/Musa, 1984, p. 297

23. Almaas, 1998, p. 268

24. Naranjo, 1997, p. 135

25. David Burke, personal communication

Chapter 10: The Point Two Archetype

1. Jung, CW 9, Section 422, quoted in Goldberg, 2005, p. 100

2. Singer, 1972, p. 232

3. Naranjo, 1997

4. Homer/Lattimore, 1965, pp. 90-94

5. Goldberg, 2005

6. Palmer, 1988

7. Singer, 1953 p. 83

8. Naranjo, 1994, p. 176

9. Maitri, 2005, p. 112

10. Naranjo coined the phrase describing these fixed mental assumptions as the "cognitive mistake" that underlies and shapes character. He also referred to these fixations as "crazy ideas" because we stick with them even when they are obviously outmoded, false, or even destructive.

11. Naranjo, 1997, p. 93, 96

12. Naranjo, 1997, p. 94

13. While many people might think that the pleasure-loving Type Seven is the most hedonistic type in the Enneagram system, Naranjo says that "E7 is almost as hedonistic as E2." (1997, p. 100)

14. Naranjo, 1994, p. 174

15. *Inferno* XXXIV: 28-30, 34-36, Dante/Musa, 1971

16. Naranjo, 1997, p. 93

17. Naranjo, 1997, p. 93

18. Naranjo also notes that Scarlett's "never-too-scrupulous sense of honor allows her to read the letters that the man she is interested in writes to his wife, to whom she is the hidden rival." (1997, p. 96) He also cites Cleopatra, Carmen, and Elizabeth Taylor as good exemplars of the Sexual Two personality. (1997, pp. 96-98)

19. Helen Palmer used to ask this question repeatedly in her guided meditations in her Enneagram Professional Training Program workshops and I found it to be particularly helpful.

20. Helen Palmer suggested this once in one of her Enneagram Professional Training Program workshops and I found it to be a particularly helpful suggestion.

21. David Burke, personal communication.

Chapter 11: The Point One Archetype:

1. Goldberg, 2005, p. 113

2. Goldberg, 2005

3. Naranjo, 1994

4. Naranjo, 1994

5. McWilliams, 1994

6. Naranjo, 1994, p. 41

7. *Inferno* VII: 109-114, Dante/Musa, 1971

8. *Inferno* VIII: 37-39, Dante/Musa, 1971

9. *Inferno* VIII: 61-63, Dante/Musa, 1971

References

Addison, Howard A. *The Enneagram and the Kabbalah: Reading Your Soul.* Woodstock, Vermont: Jewish Lights Publishing, 1998.

Almaas, A. H. *Facets of Unity: The Enneagram of Holy Ideas.* Berkeley, CA: Diamond Books, 1998.

Bartlett, Carolyn. *The Enneagram Field Guide: Notes on Using the Enneagram in Counseling, Therapy, and Personal Growth.* Portland, Oregon: The Enneagram Consortium, 2003.

Bennett, J. G. *The Enneagram.* Sherbourne: Coombe Springs Press, 1974.

Blake, A. G. E. *The Intelligent Enneagram.* Boston: Shambhala Publications, Inc., 1996.

Bourgeault, Cynthia. *The Wisdom Way of Knowing: Reclaiming an Ancient Tradition to Awaken the Heart.* San Francisco: Jossey-Bass, 2003.

Connolly, Cyril. *The Unquiet Grave: A Word Cycle.* New York: Curwen Press, 1944.

Dante Alighieri. *The Divine Comedy: Volume I, Inferno.* Translated by Mark Musa. New York: Penguin Books, 1971.

Dante Alighieri. *The Divine Comedy: Volume II, Purgatory.* Translated by Mark Musa. New York: Penguin Books, 1981.

Dante Alighieri. *The Divine Comedy: Volume 3, Paradise.* Translated by Mark Musa. New York: Penguin Books, 1984.

Eliot, T. S. *Four Quartets.* New York: Harcourt Brace Jovanovich, 1943.

Erickson, Erik. *Identity and the Life Cycle.* New York: W. W. Norton & Company, 1959.

Evagrius Ponticus. *The Praktikos Chapters on Prayer.* Translated with an introduction and notes by John Eudes Bamberger. Trappist, Kentucky: Cistercian Publications, 1972.

Goldberg, Michael J. *Travels With Odysseus: Uncommon Wisdom from Homer's Odyssey.* Tempe, AZ: Circe's Island Press, 2005.

Goldstein, Joseph and Jack Kornfield. *Seeking the Heart of Wisdom: The Path of Insight Meditation.* Boston: Shambhala, 1987.

Homer. *The Odyssey*. Translated by Robert Fagles. New York: Penguin Press, 1996.

Homer. *The Odyssey of Homer: Translated and with an Introduction by Richmond Lattimore*. Translated by Richmond Lattimore. New York: Harper Perennial, 1965.

Hopcke, Robert H. *A Guided Tour of the Collected Works of C. G. Jung*. Boston: Shambhala Publications, Inc., 1989.

Horney, Karen. *Neurosis and Human Growth: The Struggle Toward Self-Realization*. New York: W. W. Norton & Company, 1950

Horney, Karen. *Our Inner Conflicts: A Constructive Theory of Neurosis*. New York: W. W. Norton and Company, 1945.

Huxley, Aldous. *The Perennial Philosophy*. New York: Harper & Row, 1944.

Interviews with Oscar Ichazo: New York: Arica Institute Press, (1982).

Jung, C. G. *The Collected Works of C. G. Jung*. Edited by W. McGuire. Vol. 8, *The Structure and Dynamics of the Psyche*. New York: Bollingen Foundation, 1960.

Jung, C. G. *The Collected Works of C. G. Jung*. Edited by W. McGuire. Vol. 9, part 1, *The Archetypes and the Collective Unconscious*. New York: Princeton Univerity Press, 1959.

Jung, C. G. *Memories, Dreams, Reflections*. Recorded and edited by Aniela Jaffe. New York: Vintage Books, 1961.

Kahn, Michael. *Basic Freud: Psychoanalytic Thought for the 21st Century*. New York: Basic Books, 2002.

Killen, Jack. "Toward the Neurobiology of the Enneagram," *The Enneagram Journal*, 2:1 (July 2009): 40-61.

Lao Tzu. *Tao Te Ching*. Translated and interpreted by David Burke. Salisbury, Australia: Boolarong Press, 2007.

Lawlor, Robert. *Sacred Geometry: Philosophy and Practice*. London: Thames & Hudson, 1982.

Lewis, Thomas, Fari Amini, and Richard Lannon. *A General Theory of Love*. New York: Vintage Books, 2000.

Lilly, John C. and Joseph E. Hart. "The Arica Enneagram of the Personality," in *Who Am I? Personality Types for Self-Discovery*, ed. Robert Frager (New York: Jeremy P. Tarcher, 1994), 221.

Maitri, Sandra. *The Enneagram of Passions and Virtues: Finding the Way Home*. New York: Jeremy P. Tarcher/Penguin, 2005.

Maitri, Sandra. *The Spiritual Dimension of the Enneagram: Nine Faces of the Soul*. New York: Jeremy P. Tarcher/Putnam, 2000.

McWilliams, Nancy. *Psychoanalytic Diagnosis: Understanding Personality Structure in the Clinical Process.* New York: The Guilford Press, 1994.

Moran, Gonzalo, "How the Passion of Vanity Manifests in the Sexual Three," *Nine Points Magazine*, 2013 (online at ninepointsmagazine.org).

Mouravieff, Boris. *Gnosis: Study and Commentaries on the Esoteric Tradition of Eastern Orthodoxy, Book One, Exoteric Cycle.* Robertsbridge, East Sussex: Agora Books, 1989.

Myss, Carolyn. *Archetypes: Who Are You?* Carlsbad, CA: Hay House, 2013.

Naranjo, Claudio. *Character and Neurosis: An Integrative View.* Nevada City, CA: Gateways/IDHHB Inc., 1994.

Naranjo, Claudio. *The Enneagram of Society: Healing the Soul to Heal the World.* Nevada City, CA: Gateways Books and Tapes, 1995.

Naranjo, Claudio. *Ennea-type Structures: Self-Analysis for the Seeker.* Nevada City, CA: Gateways/IDHHB, Inc., 1990.

Naranjo, Claudio. *Transformation Through Insight: Enneatypes in Life, Literature, and Clinical Practice.* Prescott, AZ: Hohm Press, 1997.

Naranjo, Claudio. *27 Personajes en Busca del Ser: Experiencias de Transformacion a La Luz del Eneagrama* (2nd ed.). Barcelona: Editorial la Llave, 2012.

Needleman, Jacob. "G. I. Gurdjieff and His School," in *Modern Esoteric Spirituality*, ed. Antoine Faivre and Jacob Needleman (New York: Crossroad, 1992), 360.

Ouspensky, P. D. *In Search of the Miraculous: Fragments of an Unknown Teaching.* New York: Harcourt Brace Jovanovich, Inc., 1949.

Ouspensky, P. D. *The Psychology of Man's Possible Evolution.* New York: Vintage Books, 1950.

Palmer, Helen. *The Enneagram: Understanding Yourself and the Others in your Life.* San Francisco: Harper San Francisco, 1988.

Russell, Bertrand. *The History of Western Philosophy.* New York: Simon and Schuster, 1945.

Schneider, Michael S. *A Beginner's Guide to Constructing the Universe: The Mathematical Archetypes of Nature, Art, and Science.* New York: Harper, 1994.

Shirley, John. *Gurdjieff: An Introduction to His Life and Ideas.* New York: Jeremy P. Tarcher/Penguin, 2004.

Singer, June. *Boundaries of the Soul: The Practice of Jung's Psychology.* New York: Doubleday, 1953.

Sinkewicz, Robert E. *Evagrius of Pontus: The Greek Ascetic Corpus.* Oxford: Oxford University Press, 2003.

Skinner, Stephen. *Sacred Geometry: Deciphering the Code.* New York: Sterling, 2006.

Smith, Huston. *Forgotten Truth: The Common Vision of the World's Religions.* New York: Harper One, 1976.

Smoley, Richard, and Jay Kinney. *Hidden Wisdom: A Guide to the Western Inner Traditions.* New York: Penguin/Arkana, 1999.

Stevens, Katrina. "The Enneagram: Fundamental Hieroglyph of a Universal Language," *The Enneagram Journal*, 3:1 (July 2010): 119-145.

Tarnas, Richard. *The Passion of the Western Mind: Understanding the Ideas that Have Shaped our World View.* New York: Ballantine Books, 1991.

Tolk, Lauren. "Integrating The Enneagram and Schema Therapy: Bringing the Soul Into Psychotherapy." Ph.D. diss., Wright Institute, 2004.

Wagner, Jerome. *Nine Lenses on the World: The Enneagram Perspective.* Evanston, IL: NineLens Press, 2010.

Waterfield, Robin (translator). *The Theology of Arithmetic.* (Attributed to Iamblichus). Grand Rapids, Michigan: Phanes Press, 1988.

Watts, Alan. *The Wisdom of Insecurity: A Message for an Age of Anxiety.* New York: Vintage Books, 1951.

Webb, James. *The Harmonious Circle: The Lives and Work of G. I. Gurdjieff, P. D. Ouspensky, and their Followers.* Boston: Shambhala, 1980.

Acknowledgments

F IRST AND FOREMOST, I want to thank Claudio Naranjo for his lifetime
of work in the articulation of the human personality and the process of
psycho-spiritual transformation. His brilliant synthesis of different streams
of thought has been the chief and most direct inspiration for this book. I
also want to pay tribute to Oscar Ichazo for his seminal work in developing
the Enneagram framework as part of his larger multidimensional model for
human growth.

I am grateful to my dear friend and college English-major-buddy, Jeff
Koppelmaa, for his enthusiastic support of this project and his thoughtful editing of much of the material in this book. This book may not have come into
existence at all if it weren't for the expert help and guidance of Brooke Warner,
who as my coach, editor, and publisher, enabled me to make my vision a reality. I want to thank Krissa Lagos for her excellent work editing what turned
out to be a very long book, Carissa Bluestone for serving as a thorough and
dedicated proofreader, and Dianna Jacobsen for her timely design help. And I
appreciate the efforts of everyone on Brooke's staff at She Writes Press for all
their hard work in the production of this book.

I am deeply grateful to Randall Alifano for helping me to become the
person who could write this book and to my incredibly wise and supportive
psychotherapy colleagues, friends, and fellow travelers in this work: Kyle Cor-
siglia, Elizabeth Cotton, Debra Miller, and Delia Shargel.

Ginger Lapid-Bogda offered early, enthusiastic, and strong support of
my Enneagram work, and I am very grateful for her generous mentorship
and particularly for encouraging me to develop and communicate Claudio
Naranjo's subtype descriptions. Matt Ahrens supported me in large and small
ways as a friend and co-teacher and I am thankful to him for being an insightful thought-partner in the evolution of my understandings of the types
and subtypes. I am extremely grateful to Gonzalo Moran, who helped me to
recognize and articulate the subtypes at a deeper and more refined level. I feel
incredibly lucky to have met Dirk Cloete and thank him for his timely support during key moments in this process and also for being such a welcome
"kindred spirit" in my life. I also want to appreciate Lucille Greeff for her

work with Dirk in developing practical applications of the Enneagram that capture the true spirit of the system and that are also technically sophisticated and cutting-edge.

I am very appreciative of the generous and unwavering support of my parents, Paul and Marijane Chestnut. My cousin, Chris Fasano, helped me to understand the significance of the Enneagram in my early days as a student of the system and I am deeply grateful to him for sharing his wisdom and insights with me. I am thankful for the love and support of my brother, Patrick Chestnut, and my beautiful sister-in-law, Stephanie Ott, and my *great*-aunt, Sister Therese Perry, as well as my longtime friends Val and Neil Cronin, Rick Canvel, Denise Daniels, Marianne Chowning Dray, Maddy Dray, Todd Dray, Jennifer Joss, Jan and Jon Kellogg, Teri Klein, Felix Ott, Anne Stern, Robert Preston, Mahoko Kuramasu, Stacy and Mark Price, and Ed and Susan Setton. In addition to making my life more fun and meaningful, they all stepped forward in different ways to assist me throughout the process of writing this book. I want to communicate a special thank you to Marianne Chowning Dray for her friendship, her objectivity, her humor, and her wise counsel.

This book has been greatly enriched by the testimonials provided by my friends and colleagues, who generously shared their personal stories for the subtype and "early coping strategy" examples that appear in the text. I promised to keep their identities anonymous, so I won't mention them by name, but they know who they are, and I am so very grateful for their significant contributions. I want to thank my psychotherapy clients, past and present, who have inspired me through the courage they have shown in doing their personal growth work. It has been a great honor to be able to accompany them on their journeys.

I am also grateful for the companionship and support of the friends and teachers I have come to know in the Enneagram community: Valerie Atkin, Georgia Bailey, David Burke and the gang in Brisbane, Jutka Freiman, (Lisa) Byungbok Han, Sandy Hatmaker, Karl Hebenstreit, Liz Holdship, Dr. Kim, Joni Minault, Peter O'Hanrahan, Debbie Ooten, Dale Rhodes, Pamela Roussos, Terry Saracino, Samantha Schoenfeld, Jane Tight, JoAnne Tybinka Blasko, Marsha Underhill, Jerry Wagner, Barbara Whiteside, and Beverly and Alan Wise. I'm also very thankful to Tom Condon, Russ Hudson, Jerry Wagner, and the late Don Riso for their crucial and high-quality work in helping so many people all around the world to gain access to the Enneagram of personality and the larger project of personal development through enhanced self-awareness.

Finally, I want to thank my principle and earliest Enneagram teachers,

Helen Palmer and David N. Daniels. Helen has been a long-term and steadfast supporter of me and my work and a huge source of learning, spiritual
guidance, and intellectual inspiration. Dr. David Daniels has been like a
second father to me—I am grateful to him for motivating me to follow in
his footsteps and to (join the family business and) study psychology. His deep
dedication to the Enneagram work, and his genius in moderating panels of
self-observers to bring out the essence of this amazing and life-changing
teaching, first showed me the power of the Enneagram map to help bring
about human growth and healing.

About the Author

B EATRICE CHESTNUT is a practicing psychotherapist, coach, and business consultant based in San Francisco. She holds graduate degrees in communication studies and psychology and has been working with the Enneagam for over twenty-three years. An experienced teacher and group facilitator, she has taught at Northwestern University and trained students in interpersonal learning groups at Stanford University and the University of San Francisco's Law School. She was the president of the International Enneagram Association (2006–2007) and founding co-editor of the IEA's *Enneagram Journal* (2008–2009).